All about the ECERS-R

Environment Rating Scales

ECERS–R

Early Childhood
Environment Rating Scale
Revised edition

ITERS–R

Infant-Toddler
Environment Rating Scale
Revised edition

FDCRS

Family Day Care Rating Scale

SACERS

School-Age Care
Environment Rating Scale

FPG Child Development Institute
The University of North Carolina at Chapel Hill

All about the ECERS-R

A detailed guide in words and pictures to be used with the ECERS-R

Debby Cryer | Thelma Harms | Cathy Riley
FPG Child Development Institute

Cover design by Thelma Harms and Sarah Bradley
Production manager: Pat Conte
Book design by Michael Brady
Printed in China

Contents

Acknowledgements / vii
About this book / ix

Space and Furnishings / 1

1 Indoor space / 3
2 Furniture for care, play and learning / 9
3 Furnishings for relaxation and comfort / 15
4 Room arrangement for play / 25
5 Space for privacy / 35
6 Child-related display / 45
7 Space for gross motor play / 57
8 Gross motor equipment / 69

Personal Care Routines / 77

9 Greeting/departing / 79
10 Meals/snacks / 89
11 Nap/rest / 103
12 Toileting/diapering / 111
13 Health Practices / 123
14 Safety practices / 135

Language-Reasoning / 145

15 Books and pictures / 147
16 Encouraging children to communicate / 159
17 Using language to develop reasoning skills / 169
18 Informal use of language / 177

Activities / 187

19 Fine motor / 189
20 Art / 199
21 Music/movement / 211
22 Blocks / 219
23 Sand/water / 231
24 Dramatic play / 237
25 Nature/science / 253
26 Math/number / 267
27 Use of TV, video, and/or computer / 279
28 Promoting acceptance of diversity / 287

Interaction / 297

29 Supervision of gross motor activities / 299
30 General supervision of children (other than gross motor) / 307
31 Discipline / 317
32 Staff-child interactions / 329
33 Interactions among children / 341

Program Structure / 351

34 Schedule / 353
35 Free Play / 367
36 Group time / 379
37 Provisions for children with disabilities / 389

Parents and Staff / 399

38 Provisions for parents / 401
39 Provisions for personal needs of staff / 409
40 Provisions for professional needs of staff / 415
41 Staff interaction and cooperation / 421
42 Supervision and evaluation of staff / 429
43 Opportunities for professional growth / 435

Acknowledgements

There are many ECERS-R users who ask us seemingly unlimited questions about what ECERS-R terms mean, and how to make sure they are scoring correctly under certain classroom conditions. If all these people had not cared enough to ask, we would not have known what was needed in this book. We owe much thanks to all the ECERS-R users who have helped us by asking for our help. These include the many groups to whom we have provided training on the scale since its publication, but also those who communicate their questions to us by internet, telephone, and even the (old-fashioned) mail. We are sorry that the book will not answer all questions; we know new questions will arise and enjoy hearing from all of you!

We would like to show our appreciation to the early childhood staff members, who allowed us to photograph in their settings, showing both strengths and weaknesses, and who even allowed us to sometimes "set up" examples that did not show "best" practices. It takes a lot of courage to show what you do when it is good, but even more so when it is not perfect. Also, we thank the parents of children in the classrooms for trusting us in photographing their children; and especially the children, for being what they so naturally are—completely amazing, enthusiastic, and wonderful, each and every one of them.

The authors of this book were greatly supported by our colleagues, who helped with the many tasks required to put together this work. We would like to thank specifically:

Adele Richardson Ray, who cooperated with us in much of the initial work that set the framework for the development that followed, and later reviewed and commented on drafts of the various sections. Adele has been one of our greatest supporters over the years, making possible much of our work, as a team member on various projects, co-authoring books with us, and being our everlasting friend.

This work would not have been possible if we had not had the benefit of our dedicated team at the Frank Porter Graham Child Development Institute at the University of North Carolina at Chapel Hill. All of our team members work closely together on many projects, and this book represents only one of them. While some of us have been working on this book, others have been taking responsibility for the other things all of us must do, ensuring that everything is completed.

It is difficult to specify any one team member as being responsible for any one part of this book. There has been lots of sharing of tasks, but we especially want to recognize the contributions of the following people:

Kristina Spence Lee, who took the lead in ensuring that we had the photographs to illustrate the necessary points. Not only did Kris provide us with many of the photographs, but she also worked behind the scenes to ensure that situations were set up to capture the essence of the text, necessary permission was obtained, and coordinated our work with child care programs. Her organizational skills became especially valuable as we had to create easy-to-access data files from our slide archives, and add to them as needed.

Acknowledgements

Megan Porter, who also took significant responsibility for ensuring we acquired many of the photographs we needed. We were very lucky that Kris and Megan turned out to be fine photographers, combined with their understanding of what we were looking for. Megan also helped with preliminary drafts of the text for some of the items. These first attempts at the sections were helpful in speeding up the work of the authors when it came to writing the actual sections.

Lisa Waller, who provided help with reviewing and editing the text, and also helped with acquiring photographs. Over the past few years, Lisa has provided input into the interpretations of the ECERS-R that are given in this book. In many ways Lisa has kept the rest of our projects on course as we devoted time to this book development.

Left to right: Kim Winton, Tracy Link, Kris Lee, Thelma Harms, Debby Cryer, Lisa Waller, Cathy Riley, Vanessa Loiselle

Tracy Link, who provided help with reviewing and editing the text, and also helped with photographs. Tracy, a newer member of our team, was valuable in reading the text to ensure that less experienced scale users would understand the ideas we have tried to express in words and pictures.

Also, we thank additional members of our team. They too helped with this book, and our work would have been far more difficult and time consuming without their support: Kim Winton, Rebecca Decker, Elisa Allen, Sarah Rapalus, and Vanessa Loiselle.

Our book designer, Michael Brady, also of the Frank Porter Graham Child Development Institute at the University of North Carolina at Chapel Hill, has worked closely with us on the format of the book, contributed ideas that make the book user-friendly and pleasant to read, and completed all the work under an impossible timeline.

Some of the material contained in this book was piloted in a course given over the past year by the authors. This course was under the direction of Dr. Roanne Moreno, Palm Beach Community College, FL. Portions of the materials were also piloted as part of the Quality Care for Children Initiative, Barbara Kamara, Head, District of Columbia, Department of Early Childhood Development, and the Santa Barbara County Office of Early Care and Education Quality Improvement Training, Sharol Vicker, Program Quality Improvement Specialist.

We especially wish to thank the Winston-Salem Foundation (provided by the Leon and Renee Kaplan Fund) that partially supported this work.

Finally, we want to acknowledge the cooperation and support provided by our publisher, the PACT group of the Kaplan Early Learning Company. Hal Kaplan has been enthusiastic and a fine partner in this effort. His staff, especially Jana Brown-Smith, Lee French, Sarah Bradley, and Pat Conte, have worked closely and patiently with us to ensure that the book is everything we wanted it to be.

We are fortunate to have many friends in our work, those who work directly with us on a daily basis, and those who help us in many other ways. We could not have done this alone, so we are glad to have all of you!

DEBBY CRYER
THELMA HARMS
CATHY RILEY
Frank Porter Graham Child Development Institute
University of North Carolina at Chapel Hill

July, 2003

About this book

This book is to be used as a resource guide to the ***Early Childhood Environment Rating Scale–Revised Edition*** (ECERS-R), by Thelma Harms, Richard M. Clifford, and Debby Cryer, published by Teacher's College Press, Columbia University, New York.

When using this book, have a copy of the ECERS-R accessible so the resource guide and the scale can be used side-by-side. The information in this book is not particularly useful without the ECERS-R book because it applies only to the requirements within that scale. This resource guide defines what the requirements in the scale mean, in terms of assigning scores to any classroom. Definitions of words used in the scale are provided, with descriptions of what to look for and the rules that are used to score.

Before using the ECERS-R scale and this resource guide, it is recommended that basic introductory training be completed, using the ECERS-R video training package. The package consists of an interactive video, a *Video Guide and Training Workbook* for use with the video, and an instructor's guide.

About the photographs in this book

Information in this guide is provided as text, with photographs to support meanings. The photographs in this book have been taken over many years, in many early childhood programs. Almost all represent real situations that we have been allowed to document and use as we explain quality practices. There are many positive examples of practices shown.

In showing examples of less positive practices, we have sometimes used situations that were arranged for us to photograph. *Therefore, the photographs used in this book do not always represent the actual practices used in the classrooms where we have been allowed to photograph.*

It is important to remember that there is a lot of flexibility in how the requirements of the ECERS-R can be met. Things can be done very differently in different classrooms, and the same requirement may still be met in each. This is why all classrooms that score high do not look the same. For example, cozy areas can differ substantially from one classroom to another but they still might meet the ECERS-R requirements as long as they provide a substantial amount of softness, are accessible to the children, and so on. Or teachers with different personalities and styles might both meet the requirements for positive interactions with children even though they may be quite different in their personalities.

In some cases we have used the same photograph several times in this book to show that different aspects of quality can be observed while looking at the same scene. The same photograph, therefore, might be shown as an example for several different items. For example, one photograph is used to show something about interactions and also about the toys that can be used for sand play. This is because as observers collect information in a classroom, one single instance might give information for several aspects of early childhood care and education. Observers should be able to apply the complex information collected in a classroom to the appropriate requirements of the scale. Sometimes information observed will be simple, and apply to only one requirement, but in many other cases, one observed instance will give information that should be considered in scoring several items. It should be remembered, however, that it would be unusual for one instance to carry the power to determine a score, but that scores are usually based on many pieces of information collected during the entire observation period.

We are not able to represent all the possibilities for how requirements can be met through the photographs we have included in this book. There will be many other options. However, the photographs we have included should be used to help the reader understand certain important aspects of evaluating whether the requirement is met.

Who should use this book?

People in many different early childhood professions use the ECERS-R to see how well a program is meeting children's needs—to see whether children receive the protection, learning opportunities, and positive relationships they need for successful development. For example, practitioners (teachers, administrators) who provide programs for young children frequently use the ECERS-R to ensure the quality of the program they are creating. Program monitors use the ECERS-R when evaluating programs for licensing or other quality assurance systems (accreditation, credentialing). Researchers use the scale to collect data on the quality of early childhood programs.

For ECERS-R scores to be meaningful and truly representative of the quality of an early childhood program, the scale must be completed accurately, with a clear understanding of what each indicator requires. Although the ECERS-R words appear to be clear upon reading, there is actually great variation in interpretation across scale users. This creates problems if the user's interpretations are either too demanding or too accepting. Observers who are too demanding give very low scores even though a classroom might be meeting the requirements properly. Observers who are not demanding enough—who give credit for the slightest evidence of any indicator, provide scores that are too high. Neither makes appropriate use of the scale.

For scale scores to be useful, they must be accurate enough to maintain the proven relationship between ECERS-R program quality and children's positive development. This relationship is not supported if scale scores are systematically too high, too low, or inconsistent across classrooms.

This book will be helpful to everyone who wants to use the ECERS-R accurately, towards the end result of clearly understanding early childhood programs, so improvements can be implemented. It will be helpful to the practitioner who is using the ECERS-R in self-assessment, and needs to know what to do to meet a requirement. It will be useful also to those who provide technical assistance in program quality enhancement efforts, so that the guidance provided is based on accurate interpretations. It will be especially useful to those who evaluate program quality for monitoring or research, by increasing reliability among observers.

Using the book will not necessarily create an observer who is considered "reliable," which means that this person would score items very similarly to another reliable observer. This is because reliability must be developed within any group of observers who want to be "reliable." They must go out and observe together and correct differences in scoring until they score similarly enough to meet the standards of the group in question.

However, *consistent use of the information in the book will encourage the development of the skills needed for a group of observers to become reliable* with one another. In addition, the reliability of the group will be more consistent with that of the ECERS-R authors.

How this book is organized

Subscales, items and indicators

This guide follows the organization of the ECERS-R, with subscales that contain a number of items. Each item consists of numbered indicators at four quality levels. The subscales and the items within each one are listed on page 7 of the ECERS-R.

The ***subscales*** are organized primarily to help the observer collect information that is likely to be found under similar circumstances. They provide a practical, and conceptual, organization for the items, which makes the scale easier to use. For example, items in the first subscale require that the observer look at the space and furnishings for the children. Many of the requirements in these items are relatively easy to see at the beginning of an observation, so they are placed together at the beginning of the scale. Also, the items represent issues that are often thought of at the same time, for example, when setting up or making plans to change a classroom.

There are 43 ***items***, organized into 7 ***subscales*** in the ECERS-R. Each of the numbered ***items*** represents a dimension found in any early childhood program.

Most of the items (1–37) allow the observer to examine the quality of what children actually experience in a program. These items are considered most directly related to how children develop. In research, a relationship has been shown between higher scores on the scale and better child development outcomes in a wide range of areas. The outcomes include those that are usually thought to be important for later success in school and in our society—namely, cognitive development, language, and social/emotional skills.

The items in the last subscale (items 38–43) look at the quality of provisions for the adults involved in the program—the parents and staff. The items about staff and parents are supportive of the other items. They deal with providing a comfortable and convenient work environment for staff, as well as professional development opportunities to encourage staff competence. Communication with parents is also considered to help balance the child's life in the two settings of home and the early childhood program.

All items are presented as a 7-point scale with descriptions of what is required under 1 (inadequate), 3 (minimal), 5 (good), and 7 (excellent). Each description is made up of one or more numbered ***indicators*** that must be scored when completing an observation and evaluation of a classroom. An ***indicator*** is a specific requirement that must be scored "Yes," "No," or (where indicated) "NA."

This book provides a "General Information" section about each item in the ECERS-R. This general information is followed by a section called "A Closer Look at Each Indicator," which gives specific information about each requirement. This will help you understand what each indicator means, what to look for in deciding whether or not it is true, and how to score it.

Understanding the meaning of ECERS-R scores

Many things will affect the care and education that teachers provide for the children in early childhood programs. The cultural preferences or other beliefs of the adults involved, the curriculum approach used, the physical conditions of a building, finances, or staffing issues are some examples of variables that affect what a program is able to provide in terms of scores on *the Early Childhood Environment Rating Scale–Revised Edition*. Because of these variables, it is unlikely that programs will do well on *all* the requirements of the scale. Instead, programs will have both strengths and weaknesses in their scores, which give program staff an opportunity to consider where change is needed, and to determine how to create desired improvement.

The important thing to remember, when considering ECERS-R scores, is that the individual requirements of the scales are far less important than the average total score for any classroom. *It is the average total score that is related to positive child development, but not any of the single requirements by themselves.*

The scales are weighted, through repetition of important requirements, to ensure that key aspects for positive development are more heavily represented than single details. This provides some flexibility with regard to how and when requirements are met while ensuring that the larger concepts within the scales, of protection, learning, and positive relationships, are adequately measured.

Flexibility is possible to some extent in how a program wishes to provide high quality. As long as the classroom's average total score meets enough of the requirements of the scale, a center can consider which indicators they will provide to improve chances for better child development, while recognizing that they are not providing others. Having a few relative weaknesses in a program will not harm children's development substantially, *unless too many requirements are not met*, causing the average total score to be too low.

Here are some examples of how this works.

- The staff in a program decide that art materials should not be accessible to preschoolers without intense supervision. They believe there would be too much mess and waste of art materials. So art materials are only used with the whole group, under close teacher supervision. Art materials are not accessible at any other times, limiting children's opportunities. This decision would cause the classroom to score low on the ECERS-R Art item.

  The score on this one item, in itself, would not be likely to affect the children's overall development significantly. However, if the children were denied access to using many other materials as well, this would create a lower average total score, because many item scores would be low. Since access to a variety of materials that children can learn from is important to children's development, this requirement is weighted in the scale through repetition in various items.

- Teachers in a room think that manners are very important for 2-year-olds during meals and snacks. They believe that the children should wait until food is served to everyone before eating anything from the plate that is placed in front of them. They enforce the no-eating rule with no flexibility and punish children for eating ahead of time by taking their food from them.

  This action by the teachers would cause low scores on several items (e.g., Meals/snacks, Discipline, Staff-child interactions), decreasing the chances for a high average total score. If this type of practice, which has been shown to be associated with negative child development, is continued through the day, then other items would also be affected, making the chance for a high average total score impossible.

- The teachers are concerned because the building has some limitations that will cause the program to get several low scores. For example, the facility is not handicapped accessible, the playground is far from the building, or space in the rooms is limited. When the staff members first read the scale, they became discouraged because they feel that these things are not under their control and they will be penalized even though they are providing a good program.

  However, by doing the best they can to improve many items that are under their control (such as the 4 language items, the 6 personal care routine items, the 10 activities items, the 5 interaction items, and the 4 program structure items, and several of the space and furnishing items) they can maximize higher scores, while minimizing the effects of the lower scores they will receive because of the things they can not control at the time. Then, the resulting average classroom score should be relatively high and meet children's developmental needs.

A higher average score will reflect the high quality of the program, which provides lots of stimulating activities and warm staff interactions with children and parents. Classrooms can get a high average score even if there are some limitations in the facility that cannot be changed, if the program is providing high quality experiences in other areas.

It is important for program staff to understand what they are choosing to do or not to do, and to balance these choices in terms of what is possible. The ECERS-R assists program staff to make *well-informed* choices as to which areas the staff might emphasize in program improvement. It is not required that all things be perfect for a high average total score on the scales. But early childhood staff who wish to provide children with what they need for present well-being and future success need to be well informed about the choices they are making and to minimize low scores whenever possible.

How to use this book

This guide is to be used whenever an ECERS-R user wants to know:

- Why an item or indicator is important, because the rationale for each item is presented
- What the words or terms in an item or indicator mean, according to the authors of the scale
- How much and what kind of evidence must be found to give credit for any indicator
- How to look for, and document, the evidence needed to score

Since the guide is organized by subscale, then items within the subscale, and then indicators within the item, the user only needs to go to the item of interest, read the general information, and then the specifics about the indicators.

For example, if two observers were having a disagreement about what sanitary conditions are required at meal/snack times, they would only have to turn to Item 10, Meals/snacks, and look at the indicators related to this issue (1.3 and 3.3). Or if a teacher wanted to improve her block area, but did not know how to tell if she provided "enough blocks for two children" (Indicator 3.1) or "enough for three or more children" (Indicator 5.1), she would find Item 22, Blocks, then read the General Information section, and then read the information provided in the two indicators of interest.

The whole book can be used as a comprehensive introduction to the scale. People who want to improve their scoring accuracy can study the ECERS-R by using this book, so that their understanding of what is required is vastly improved. But it is more likely that the book will be used as a reference, like a dictionary or encyclopedia, to look up information on an "as needed" basis.

Observing classrooms with the ECERS-R

To use the ECERS-R ***accurately***, an ***observation period*** of at least 2½ to 3 hours must be completed in the classroom being evaluated, followed by an interview with the classroom's teacher (20–30 minutes). As indicated in the scale, the observation must be done during the time of day when children are most active and when most children are present, and it must include both play/learning times and routines, such as a meal, toileting, and preparation for nap.

The scale should be used to assess one classroom at a time. Multiple observations should not be completed in different classrooms during the same observation time period. Too much valuable information is lost while the observer is in the other room, such as the types of materials children are allowed to use, the kinds of interactions that occur, or whether certain routines are carried out so that they meet requirements.

The specific period of the observation (2½ to 3 hours) is required, to allow the observer to sample enough of what is needed to score all observable items accurately. (Additional time of 20–30 minutes will be needed to ask classroom teachers questions about indicators that were not observed.) A shorter time cannot be used to observe in the classroom, because many important aspects of care and learning will be missed and the observer will not be given sufficient opportunity to discover the scope and variation in practices used. For example:

- In some items, the observer must actually observe one or more instances of a behavior during the observation. When the observation is shortened, there is less chance that the behavior will be seen, and the score will not be a fair representation of what actually occurs.
- Classrooms change dramatically over time, with periods of greater stress occurring at different times. The observer must be present to see what happens during both the more relaxed and the more stressful times in order to give balanced scores.
- Indoor and outdoor times vary greatly, and both should be observed sufficiently.
- Changes in staffing and the children in the group can occur throughout the day. A good sample of who is usually present and how that affects scores is needed. As children enter or leave the classroom, changes in practice may occur. As teaching staff come and go, a reasonable sample of the impact of these changes must be considered in scoring.

Often we are told that a director of a program knows her classrooms so well, that she can complete the scale on classrooms in the center without actually doing a formal observation, but rather by sitting in the office, and scoring from memory. This leads to unreliable scores that are usually inflated. This is because the scores are based on assumptions, rather than on a systematic continuous observation of the required length.

We are also told that some observers can complete scoring the items without actually having the scale present during the observation. This also leads to inaccurate scores because the observer does not have the scale to read, to be sure that each of the large number of indicators is properly considered.

Completing the scale accurately requires that the observer is in the classroom, constantly referring to the scale, while searching for the evidence needed to score the indicators. All items should be completed and scored before leaving the facility in which the classroom is located, so that if any information is forgotten or was not collected, the observer can still access the classroom.

Being a good ECERS-R observer

When completing the ECERS-R, it is necessary for observers to ***minimize*** their impact on the classroom environment. Therefore, an accurate ECERS-R requires that the observer ***not participate or interfere*** in classroom activities at all under usual circumstances.

If the observers talk to the children, this takes away the chance to see how the teacher would interact with them (or not) at that time, under those conditions. If observers talk to the teacher, the teacher will not be able to do what she would normally be doing at that time. If observers help with tasks then they cannot see how these tasks are handled without their help. If they make suggestions to the staff about how to improve what they are doing, this changes things as well.

Observers must arrange for the visit before arriving at any program. Permission is needed to observe, teachers must be notified, and a clear explanation of what to expect should be provided. The age-range of children in the program's classrooms must be known so that the classroom observed with the ECERS-R will be one with preschool- or kindergarten-aged children. The observation must be scheduled to take place on a regular day, for example with no fieldtrip planned, or other activity that would prevent observation of the typical operation of the classroom. A time will have to be set when a classroom staff member is free of care giving responsibilities and can answer questions about things that were not observed. Usually these are all arranged with program administrative staff before the visit.

Observer guidelines have been established to help observers minimize their effect on a classroom. These guidelines should be followed throughout the observation:

- Upon arrival at the facility, have everything you need to complete the observation—an ECERS-R book, score sheet, any materials that should have been put into the scale (such as Playground Safety Guidelines, Meal Requirements, Additional Notes), pencils, and other materials such as a tape measure. However, do not bring extra materials into the room, such as purses, back packs, tote bags, because these are often put down and forgotten resulting in things being lost or misused by others. They can also contain things that are dangerous to young children.

- Be sure to introduce yourself to the person in charge of the facility. Unless arrangements for the observation have been made ahead of time, do not go into a classroom until you are shown where to go by a responsible staff member.

- Observe only in the classroom that you are evaluating. Use all your observation time with this group of children, rather than looking at other places or classrooms in the building.

- Upon entering the classroom, introduce yourself to the classroom staff, briefly telling about what you will be doing. Be sure to explain that you cannot participate in the classroom in any way—that you will be working the whole time to see what children's experiences are during the observation. However, you will need to ask about the information required to complete the top of the score sheet—about numbers of children and staff, ages of children, and any disabilities among the children in the group. Do this with as little disruption as possible.

- Stay with the children in the class, as they go from one place to another. If they are indoors, you should be observing indoors also. If they move to another place in the building or go outside, you should follow along.

- Do not interfere with classroom activities in any way. Station yourself around the perimeter of the classroom as unobtrusively as possible. You may move around the perimeter to get a better vantage point during the observation and move into areas for a closer look when it is obvious that children will not be needing to access those areas.

- Move, if you are in the way of teachers or children. Remain sensitive to what is happening around you in the classroom.

- If it does not interfere with the ongoing program, sit in a chair or on the floor so that children are not intimidated by your height. Do not sit on other furniture, such as shelves, tables, the children's chairs near an activity table, or on play equipment.
- If you are observing with someone else, refrain from talking with the other person while you are in the classroom.
- Take notes on a pad and/or on your score sheet to help in scoring and forming questions that you may need to ask.
- Never leave your materials. Keep them with you throughout the observation.
- Try to keep a neutral facial expression so that children and/or staff are neither drawn to you nor concerned about your response to them.
- Teachers will be involved with the children during your visit and should not be asked to talk with you or answer questions.
- Acknowledge children if they approach you. If they ask, you can tell them that you are watching them play today or that you have to finish your work. Do not otherwise take part in classroom activity or encourage children to interact with you in any way.
- Look at materials that are in plain view on open shelves, if you can do so without disturbing the group. However, a close inspection of these materials is best done when the class is out of the room.
- Do not look through drawers, in cabinets, or in other closed spaces without the permission of the classroom staff. When the class is out of the room and you have gotten the teacher's permission, you may take a few minutes to look in storage spaces.
- Score as much as possible before the end of the observation, so that all items will be scored after interviewing the classroom staff.
- Upon completion of the observation, be sure to thank classroom staff (and say good-bye to both children and adults).

Improving accuracy in scoring

Specific strategies can be used to improve efficiency in collecting information and ensuring accurate scoring. The strategies provided here can be used in collecting information for many items in the ECERS-R.

Observing the right things at the right times

When completing the ECERS-R, some things that need to be observed happen only at certain times of the day, while others can be observed at almost any time. When observers are aware of the *special* things to look for at certain times, they can focus attention on these when they happen and collect all other information at the other times.

Examples of items containing indicators that must be observed at special times include:

Item 2, Furniture for routine care, play and learning:
Whether tables and chairs are "child-sized" must be observed while most children are sitting at tables, for example at lunchtime.

Item 7, Space for gross motor play, and item 8, Gross motor equipment:
Should be observed while children use the gross motor areas.

Item 9, Greeting/departing:
Must be observed as children/parents enter the classroom or depart.

Item 10, Meals/snacks:
Must be observed as soon as the set-up begins to see whether appropriate procedures, such as disinfecting tables and proper hand washing, are carried out; observation must continue until the end of the meal/snack.

Item 11, Nap/rest:
Set-up of nap area must be observed, as well as a sample of the supervision that occurs during this time.

Item 12, Toileting/diapering:
Must be observed as it occurs, with a sample of instances that indicate the general practice.

Item 13, Health practices:
Certain circumstances require observation. For example, whether noses are wiped and hands washed as needed.

Detailed explanations of what to look for and when to look are provided in this book for each item. The experienced and accurate observer knows when to pay attention as needed.

Keeping track of handwashing, greeting and other daily events:

To accurately score some ECERS-R items, it is necessary to observe a sample of practice and count to see whether certain requirements have been sufficiently met. Simple charts help to keep a fairly accurate count of certain ongoing events, such as greeting or handwashing. Several examples of informal charts you can keep on your notepad or on the score sheet are shown below. Examples of such charts are provided for each item in the more detailed sections of this book. Here are some examples of these charts that accurate observers find useful.

To keep track of whether parents and children were greeted

	Child	Parent
(1)	✓	X
(2)	✓	✓
(3)	✓	✓
(4)	X	X

Key: The numbers refer to the children and parents who arrived. Under the column "Child," a check means "greeted." Under "Parent," a check means parent greeted. Other notes can also be added using a letter or symbol, e.g., "warmly" might be a "w"; individual greeting might be "ind."

To keep track of whether hands were adequately washed, for example at toileting or before meals/snacks

	Hand-washing	Comment
(1)	✓	water only
(2)	✓	teacher supervised
(3)	X	no soap
(4)	X	didn't rinse

Note: You will have to keep track of children to see if they wash their hands, thoroughly or not, whether teachers supervise, etc.

Calculating the "substantial portion of the day"

The term ***substantial portion of the day*** is used in many of the items in the ECERS-R to ensure that children have sufficient access to the play and learning materials and experiences that are most likely to optimize their development.

Substantial portion of the day is defined in the "Explanation of Terms Used throughout the Scale," found on page 6 of the ECERS-R. Determining whether access is provided in any classroom for the substantial portion of the day requires a specific strategy. This strategy is discussed in each item where the term is used. However, a general explanation for calculating whether the requirement is met is provided here.

1. Be sure to consult the table on the next page for calculating the "substantial portion of the day." This table should be pasted onto the back page of the scale for easy reference. This table may be photocopied to attach to the scale.

2. Ask the director or teacher when the center opens and closes daily, in order to get the total number of operating hours.

3. Ask for a copy of the schedule used in the classroom being observed, or copy the schedule if it is posted. This schedule can serve only as a starting point in calculating "substantial portion of the day," since schedules are highly individual in nature. Some teachers start their schedules when they arrive, not when the children arrive. The teacher may arrive at 8:30 AM, but the center may open at 6:30 AM and some children start their day then. Several questions must be asked to get additional information about what materials children have access to at various times:

    - Do you generally follow this schedule?

    - Which centers may the children use at each time listed in the schedule? What materials may the children play with? (These questions help you find out what is meant by entries on the schedule such as "table toys," "free choice," "centers," "teacher-directed activities"). The important thing to find out is what the children have access to at each time.

4. You will be in the classroom for a relatively long period of time, at least 2½ to 3 hours. Judge what goes on during different segments of the schedule based on what you

you observe. Take notes to create your own **observed *schedule*** that represents what has happened during the observation.

5. Based on what you have observed, determine whether the classroom follows the posted schedule or whether you will have to create a schedule that represents what usually happens in the classroom.
    - If the posted schedule is a reasonably accurate representation of what was observed, you can make assumptions about what is accessible to children the rest of the day.
    - If the schedule does not represent what was observed, you will have to construct a complete schedule of the day, based on what you observed, and what the classroom staff report to you when you ask questions about what usually happens during the times you were unable to observe.
    - If the children in the classroom being observed are in another room or area before the teacher arrives and/or after she leaves, find out what they have access to in these areas. If possible, look at the other area used to see what materials are available. Use this information in the calculation of the substantial portion of the day.
6. Use a work sheet to calculate how much time children had access to the required materials in each item where the term "substantial portion of the day" is used.

Some people find it helpful to cut out the chart below and paste it into their ECERS-R.

Calculating "substantial portion of the day"

Number of hours of operation	Substantial portion (1/3) of these hours
4	1 hour, 20 minutes
4.5	1 hour, 30 minutes
5	1 hour, 40 minutes
5.5	1 hour, 50 minutes
6	2 hours
6.5	2 hours, 10 minutes
7	2 hours, 20 minutes
7.5	2 hours, 30 minutes
8	2 hours, 40 minutes
8.5	2 hours, 50 minutes
9	3 hours
9.5	3 hours, 10 minutes
10	3 hours, 20 minutes
10.5	3 hours, 30 minutes
11	3 hours, 40 minutes
11.5	3 hours, 50 minutes
12	4 hours

Space and Furnishings

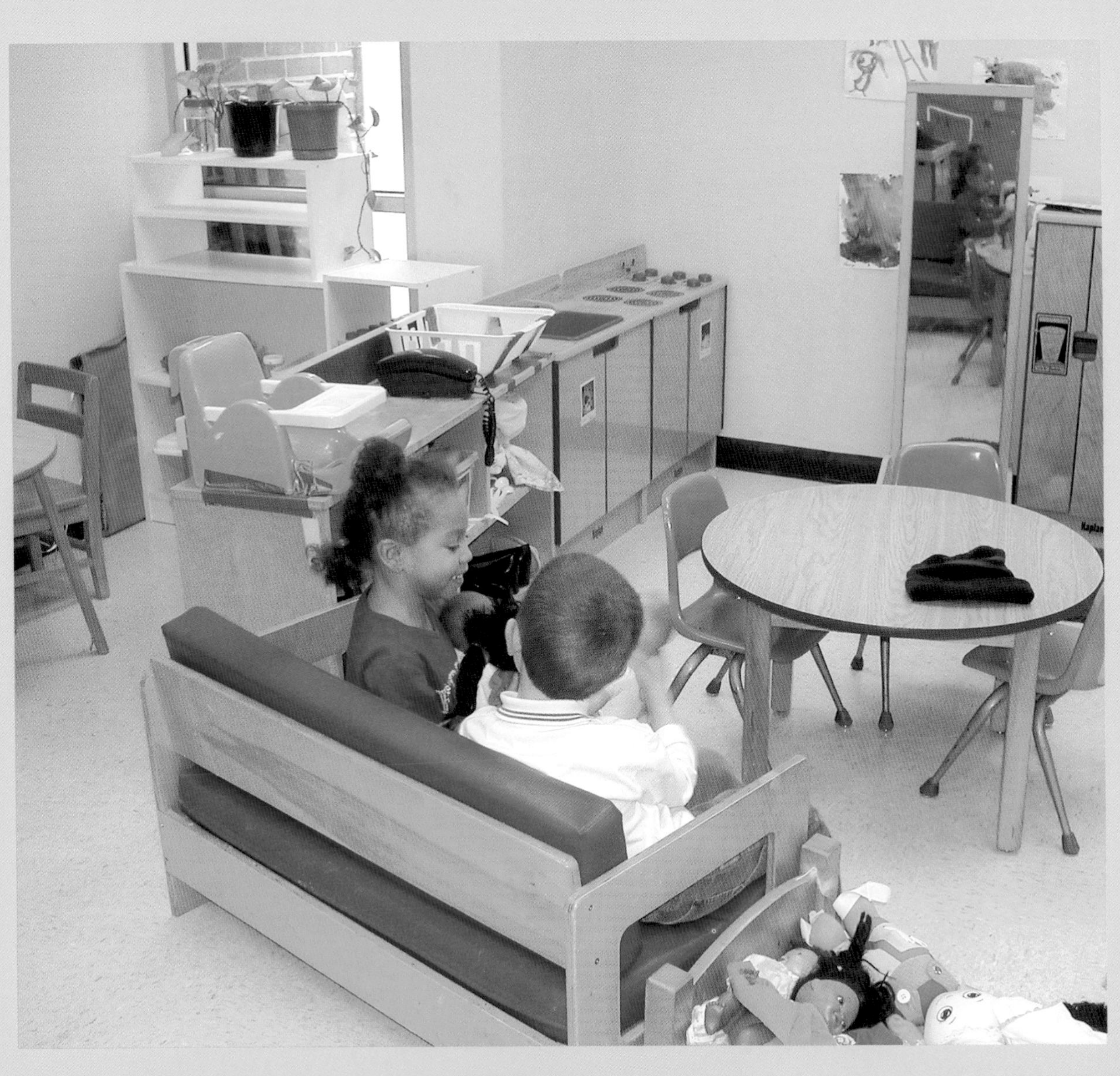

1 Indoor space

General information about this item

When we score this item, Indoor space, we consider only the space in the room used by the group most of the day. Additional spaces used by the children in the group, such as a hallway, a separate lunch room, another room where they spend early morning or late afternoon hours, or indoor gross motor space, are considered in other items.

The amount of space in the room where the children are most of the day is important because it influences the number and types of activities children can effectively engage in at the same time. Insufficient space can lead to conflicts among children due to crowding. It can also cause limitations in the program because materials easily become disorganized or must be minimized if the space in which they are used is cramped.

In order to decide whether there is sufficient or enough space, scoring should be based on observation of how the space functions when in use, not on the square footage. Look at the areas in the room used for routines such as meals/snacks as well as those used for play activities such as dramatic play, blocks, art, and books.

Scores should be based on the observer's judgment of how the space would work if the largest number of children allowed in the group at one time were attending, even if the observation takes place on a day when fewer children are there.

The condition of the space is also important because it affects both the comfort and self-image of the children who are playing in the room and the adults who work there. Space that is in poor repair or poorly maintained encourages rough and neglectful behavior towards the surroundings and materials, and can be depressing or dangerous.

1.1.1 a

1.1.1 b

1.1.1 a–b When most of the space in the classroom is crowded, as shown in these two examples, there is insufficient space.

A closer look at each indicator

1.1 ***Insufficient space*** means not enough space for the children, adults, and furnishings in the room used by the children most of the day. During meals and snacks there may not be enough room for the staff to walk between the tables while children are seated. Activity areas, such as blocks and dramatic play, may be so small that most of the space is used for the materials and furnishings, and there is not enough space for children to play. Score 1.1 "Yes" only if the room is extremely crowded. (See photos 1.1.1 a–b.)

Indicator

1.2 This indicator assesses the basic amenities needed for children and adults to use the space comfortably.

Lacks adequate lighting means much of the room is too dark to use materials that require reading or working with small objects comfortably. The room may seem gloomy or dim.

Lacks adequate ventilation means that the room is stuffy, has a persistent unpleasant odor, or has a heavy scent of cleaning or deodorizing agents. Adequate ventilation requires good air circulation. This can be provided by windows that open, exhaust fans, or an effective air circulation system.

Lacks adequate temperature control means that the space is too cold or too warm for the adults and children in the group, and nothing is done to correct this problem during the observation. It must be obvious that many of the children and/or staff are uncomfortable. Observers should not judge the adequacy of temperature control based on their own comfort, but should look and listen for signs that staff and children are uncomfortable.

Lacks adequate sound-absorbing materials means that the noise level is so high that staff and children have to raise their voices to be heard. A room that lacks sound-absorbing materials (e.g., rugs or ceiling tiles) reflects and magnifies the unavoidable sounds of conversation and use of materials. Noise pollution may hinder good language development. It also creates tension and over-excitement, which are distracting and prevent children from sustained involvement in constructive play and learning.

Since a reasonable amount of noise is expected in a program where children are active and verbal, this indicator is marked "Yes" only when the noise level becomes detrimental to the program.

Noise that travels from another classroom is counted if it adversely affects the observed classroom.

1.1.4 a Immediate attention should be given to cleaning up spills.

1.3 ***Poor repair*** means that there are major repair problems that present health and safety risks. For example, there is substantial damage to the walls, ceiling, floors, floor covering, or other aspects of the space. Common problems are missing or detached ceiling tiles, torn rugs, holes or dents in walls, damaged or missing floor tiles, or peeling paint on walls. Such repairs usually require facility maintenance skills that go beyond what staff can do in daily clean-up.

Rooms that are in ***poor repair*** can cause health problems (e.g., exposed asbestos) or pose safety hazards (e.g., tripping, splinters). If this is true, score 1.3 "Yes." Repair problems that can cause accidents can also be counted under Item 14, Safety practices.

1.1.4 b Neither adults nor children can use an overflowing trash can for ongoing cleanup.

1.4 ***Poorly maintained*** means that there is evidence that the room is not cleaned or kept up routinely. Tables may not be washed thoroughly after eating or messy play; chairs have ingrained dirt; trash cans are over flowing even in early morning; sinks are dirty; or evidence of previous art activities, such as paint drips or glued bits of paper, is dried on the tables or easels. (See photos 1.1.4 a–b.)

A ***poorly maintained*** room adversely affects the health of the children as well as the sense of organization and peacefulness in the space.

Indicator

1.3.1 a This room has sufficient space and might also meet higher quality requirements for this item.

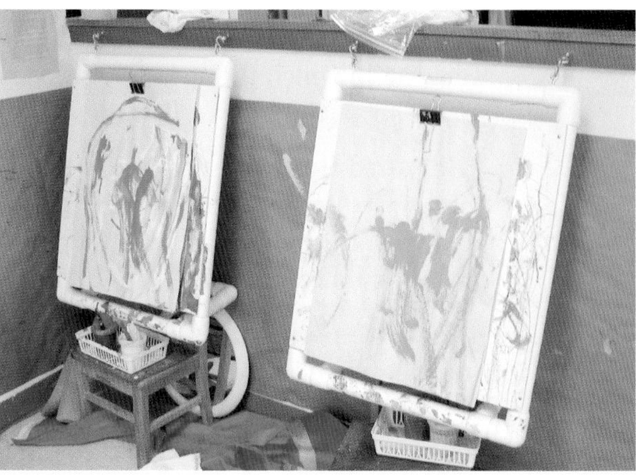

1.3.1 b These easels are installed side by side against the wall and take up little space.

3.1 ***Sufficient space*** means enough space to accommodate children, adults, and furniture needed to run the classroom. A space that is uncrowded due to a lack of basic furnishings and materials cannot be considered to have sufficient space if the addition of the needed furnishings and materials would result in crowding. Remember this indicator is at the minimal level, so "enough" space means only that the classroom can function adequately. (See photo 1.3.1a.)

In some cases one space might meet the requirements of this indicator, while another that is the same size, or even larger, will not. This is because one space might be used more efficiently than the other. For example, it is possible to make a relatively small space function adequately by using proportionally smaller furniture rather than larger furniture that serves the same purpose. A single two-sided easel permits two children to paint as well as a side-by-side double easel that takes up much more room. In a small room, the size of the routine care furniture, such as the tables, chairs, and open shelves used for accessible toy storage, can make the difference between crowded and enough space.

Space can also be "stretched" by leaving just enough materials out in a center for use in play and storing excess materials elsewhere. For example, in the dramatic play area, if there is an over abundance of dress-up clothes that are rarely used because they are stuffed into a drawer or heaped in a dress-up box, the dress-up clothes could be sorted using the categories in Item 24, Dramatic play, as guidance. The dress-up clothes that are kept in the dramatic play area could be hung on pegs to save space, and the rest stored and later rotated into the area.

The fact that a smaller space might sometimes be used more efficiently than a larger space means that it is not

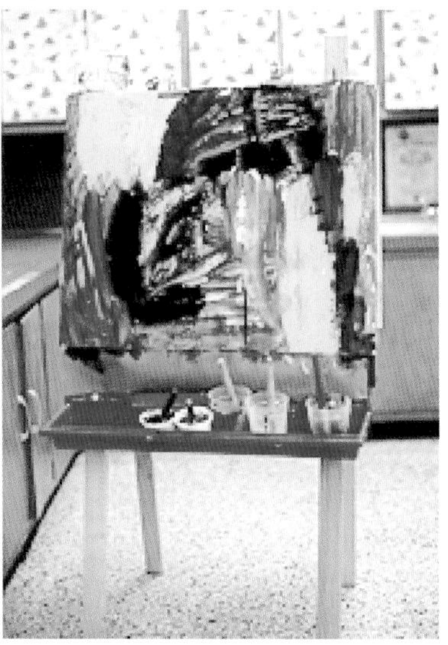

1.3.1 c This easel permits two children to paint at the same time, is easy to move, and takes relatively little space.

1.3.1 d This easel allows four children to paint at one time but takes up a large amount of space. Often only one or two children use it at a time.

Indicator

only the size of the classroom that impacts the scoring decision for this indicator. The way in which the space is used has an effect as well. (See photos 1.3.1 b–d, preceding page.)

3.2 ***Adequate lighting*** means that there is enough light, either natural light from windows or skylights, or artificial light from lamps or lighting fixtures, so that staff and children can read and use toys that have small pieces without eyestrain. The room should have enough light overall so that it looks bright and cheerful.

Adequate ventilation means that there is enough air circulation so that there are no unpleasant or strong odors in the room for any length of time. Odors from the bathroom or from cleaning products should either not be present at all or disappear very quickly.

Adequate temperature control means that the room is kept at a comfortable temperature. If needed, a source of cooling in summer and heat in winter is present so that children and adults seem comfortable. Since sensitivity to room temperature varies greatly, judge the adequacy of the room temperature based on how the children and adults are reacting. If they are flushed and perspiring, or, at the other extreme, the staff are dressed very warmly and are urging the children to put on sweaters or jackets indoors, then there is inadequate temperature control, even though the observer may not be uncomfortable.

Adequate sound-absorbing materials means that the sound in the room is at a level where people can hear one another speak without raising voices or shouting. The usual sounds of play, such as the wheels of play cars running on the floor and block structures being built or the voices of excited children, are not magnified to an uncomfortable level where they become disruptive noise. The classroom has sufficient ***sound-absorbing materials,*** such as ceiling tiles, carpets and soft furnishings, and there is a sound-absorbing barrier between classrooms. A reasonable level of sound is maintained that permits children and adults to hear and be heard without constantly raising their voices.

3.3 ***Space in good repair*** means that there are no major repair problems, such as hanging or missing ceiling tiles, holes in doors and walls, broken window panes, and gauged, splintery floors, and relatively few minor ones, such as frayed spots on the rug that can cause tripping accidents, a little peeling paint, or unpainted areas on walls.

3.4 ***Space is reasonably clean and well maintained*** means that when messy activities are included in the program, the space and furniture used to conduct the activities are cleaned thoroughly after the activities are completed.

Observe to see if the room looks as if it is being cared for regularly. For example, daily maintenance is done, such as emptying wastepaper baskets, sweeping floors, vacuuming the rugs, and cleaning dry paint off the easels. Larger jobs, such as cleaning carpets or bleaching sinks, are done often enough so that the room is basically clean, and the predictable messes resulting from recent activities, such as an art project or serving snack, are cleaned up relatively easily. (See photo 1.3.4.)

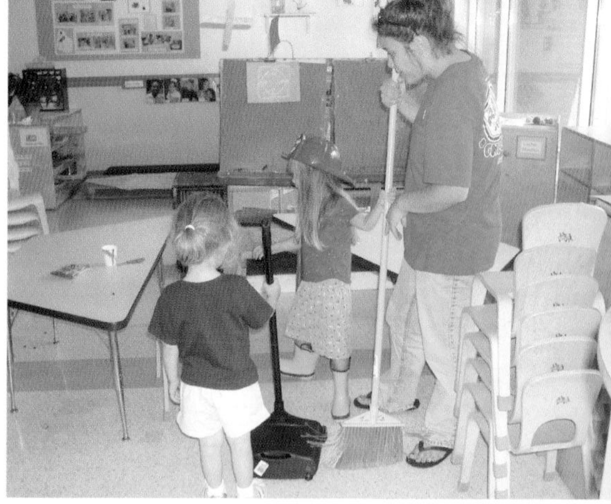

1.3.4 Children can participate to ensure that the room is kept clean.

Indicator

3.5 This indicator requires that the space is accessible to all children and adults ***currently using*** the classroom. A score of "NA" (not applicable) is permitted if there are no children or adults currently using the classroom that have physical disabilities requiring adaptations to the environment in order to provide access.

To meet the requirements for accessibility, the classroom and the bathroom (including toilet stalls) must be accessible to individuals with disabilities, including those using wheelchairs. All doorways regularly used by people in the class (both children and adults) to enter toileting areas, gross motor areas, the building, etc. must be at least 32" wide. The door handles must be operable with limited use of hands, which is not possible with round doorknobs. The entrance door threshold should be ½" high or less and, if over ¼", must be beveled to make it easier to roll over. If there are two or more bathrooms regularly used by the children in the classroom, only one of them must be accessible. (See photos 1.3.5 a–c.)

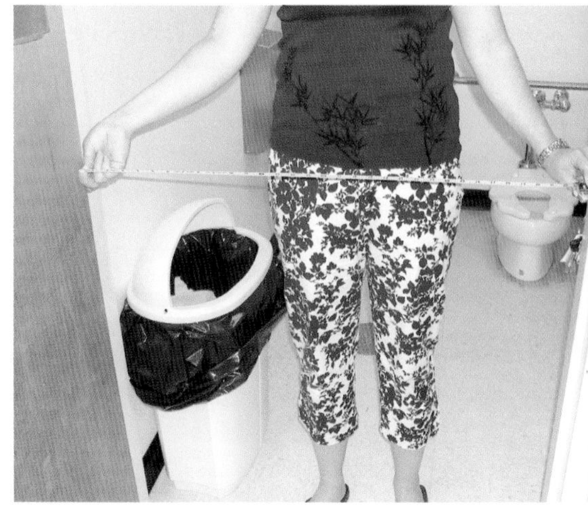

1.3.5 a This doorway is wide enough to be handicapped-accessible. Do not consider easily movable objects, such as the trash can, as impediments.

A child with a disability should be able to use the same bathroom as his/her classmates. Therefore, even if there is an accessible bathroom in another part of the facility, it cannot be counted if it is not usually used by the rest of the group. A staff member or other adult with physical disabilities who is responsible for supervising children will also need access to the children's facilities to help them.

1.3.5 b This door handle can be operated with limited use of hands.

Access to the children's restroom is considered in this item, under Indicators 3.5 and 5.3. Accessibility to the building itself, and to the floor where the classroom is located, is considered under this indicator and also in Indicator 5.3.

Score 3.5 "NA" if no child or adult currently using the classroom needs handicapped-accessible space. Please note that access to the various play areas in the room is considered under Item 4, Room arrangement, and not in this item. Adaptations to toilets (e.g., bars to help with stability) are considered in Item 2, Furniture for routine care, play, and learning, Indicators 3.3 and 5.3. Access to adult restrooms is considered in Item 39, Indicator 3.5, Provisions for personal needs of staff.

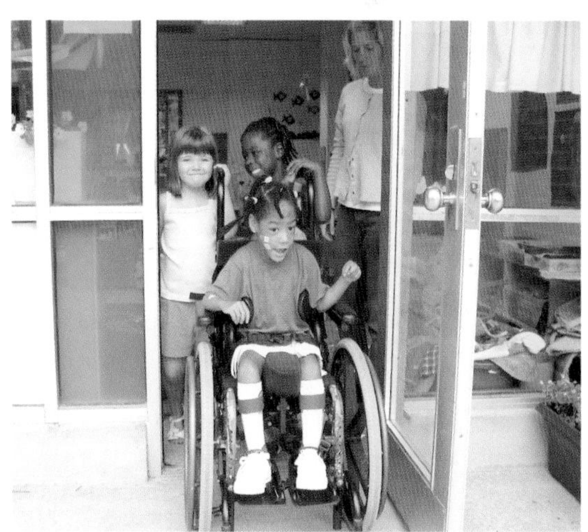

1.3.5 c This doorway meets the width and threshold requirements for accessibility but the round door knobs cannot be operated with limited use of the hands.

5.1 ***Ample indoor space*** means that there is a lot of space in the room for different types of activities. Consider both the areas used for routines such as meals/snacks and nap/rest, as well as the areas used for activities with various materials, including books, puzzles, small building toys and fine motor toys, blocks, and dramatic play props.

Look at the space as it is being used to assure that there is plenty of space for children to use the materials as well as for the materials and furniture needed in almost all of the activity areas. If two or more activity areas are crowded, do not give credit for this indicator.

Indicator

1.5.1 a–b In these classrooms, there is ample space for everything needed in a high quality environment.

Staff should be able to move around freely and assist the children during meals and snacks while the children are seated at the table. If a child with physical disabilities is enrolled in the program, there should be enough space to comfortably accommodate any special equipment needed by the child without crowding other children or limiting activities. (See photos 1.5.1 a–b.)

5.2 ***Good ventilation*** means that the room has good air circulation resulting in a fresh, pleasant odor throughout the observation. Odors from air fresheners, cleaning agents, or bathroom use are apparent only very briefly or not at all.

5.3 To meet the requirements of this indicator, the space must be handicapped-accessible for all children and adults with disabilities, regardless of whether anyone with a disability uses the room or is currently enrolled in the program. Accessibility is legally required in all public facilities so that everyone can have equal access, and is therefore required at the good level for all centers. For the definition of accessible see Indicator 3.5. (See photo 1.5.3.)

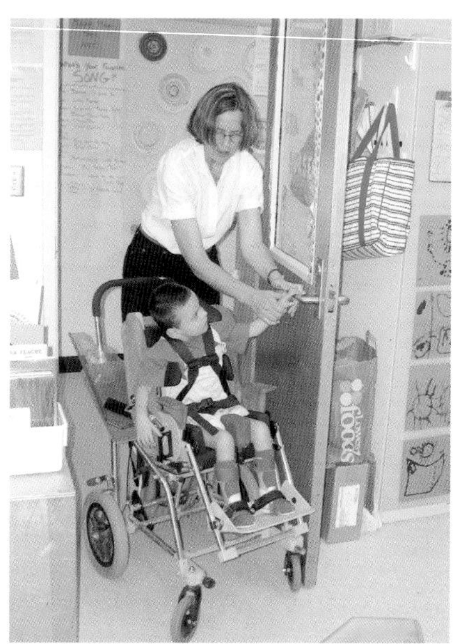

1.5.3 This large doorway and lever door handle make this classroom accessible for children and adults with disabilities.

7.1 Staff should be able to control the natural light coming in from windows, skylights, or doors. Natural light can be too bright at certain times, causing glare that can interfere with classroom activities. Adjustable blinds, curtains, or other provisions should be present and adequate to prevent any problems with natural lighting.

7.2 ***Ventilation can be controlled*** means that the staff in the room have control over the ventilation. If a door or a window needs to be opened for ventilation, it must have safeguards such as screens or a locking gate, so that children's health and safety are protected. If a ventilating fan is used, ask the teacher if she can control it herself.

2 Furniture for care, play and learning

General information about this item

This item looks at the furniture used by the children for routine care, play, and learning activities. Basic furniture for routine care considered in this item includes tables and chairs for meals and snacks, cots/mats for rest or nap, and cubbies for storage of children's personal items and creative work. Basic furniture for play and learning includes tables and chairs where children can use materials and open shelves for materials, which children can access independently. Additional furniture to facilitate specific types of play, such as an easel for art activities, a woodwork bench, sand/water table, or furniture for dramatic play, are also considered in this item. Gross motor equipment is not considered in this item, even if it is located in the classroom or other spaces used indoors.

Furniture in the classroom should support the children's independence in meeting their routine care needs and in conducting their play and learning activities. There are two important reasons for encouraging children's independent use of furnishings. First, being able to handle their surroundings helps children feel competent and secure. Second, staff working with groups of children need to make the best use of their time and energy. Therefore, staff should not have to spend time helping children to use furniture, for example, lifting them onto chairs or putting their things away for them because their cubbies are not within reach.

Furniture should also be safe, appropriately sized, and available in sufficient quantity for the total number of children enrolled in the group. Low, open shelves help in the organization of learning materials offered to children and give children opportunities to make independent choices about the materials they want to use. Low tables and chairs in activity centers are useful for working with puzzles and other table top toys, as well as for serving meals and snacks.

2.1.1 Materials are crowded because there is only one storage shelf in this classroom.

A closer look at each indicator

1.1 ***Insufficient basic furniture for routine care*** means that there are not enough tables and chairs, cubbies, or cots/mats to meet each child's routine care needs. For example, each child does not have his own personal space for belongings, or if a program has meals and snacks as a whole group, there are not enough tables and chairs for the highest number of children attending at any time to be seated. For programs operating more than 4 hours, where a nap is required, ***insufficient basic furniture*** also means that each child does not have a cot or mat for sleeping or resting.

Insufficient furniture for play and learning means that there are not enough low, open shelves available to make materials accessible to the children, or enough tables and chairs to use for activities. (See photo 2.1.1.)

2 Furniture for care and play

Indicator

Large toy boxes and crates are not acceptable substitutes as furniture to store play and learning materials in place of low open shelves, because many materials are impossible to organize for independent use in such boxes. For example, if blocks are stored in a box, children have to empty the blocks out in order to see the different sizes and shapes that have been heaped randomly on top of one another in the box. In contrast, when blocks are sorted and stored on open shelves, children can easily see the different sizes and shapes and thus make informed choices as they build without first taking all the blocks out.

On the other hand, smaller boxes and other containers can be used to store materials separately, such as interlocking blocks and other manipulatives in the fine motor area, small vehicles or small block people in the block area. Boxes or other containers can be put on open shelves to offer materials to children. However, the containers are not considered storage furniture while the open shelves are. If there are a sizable number of open shelves for storage of materials and only a few boxes, do not give a score of "Yes" on 1.1. However, if most of the toys are stored in crates or toy boxes and there are very few open shelves, a score of "Yes" is appropriate.

2.1.2 If there are several serious problems, such as broken table legs, then 1.2 is true.

1.2 ***Poor repair*** means that the furniture used is unsafe and needs repair. Examples include chair seats with protruding nails, tables with broken legs, or sleeping mats that are torn, with exposed padding. (See photo 2.1.2.) The observer should look at all furniture used by the children to determine the general overall condition, and document any safety concerns. However, score 1.2 "Yes" only if the furniture that is used by the children has several serious problems that can could cause injury. Do not count furniture that children do not use, such as a desk and chair meant only for the teacher, or chairs that have been put into storage.

3.1 ***Sufficient furniture for routine care, play, and learning*** means that there is enough furniture for nap, meals/snacks, and storing children's possessions, as well as enough furniture to meet the learning needs of each child enrolled (see photo 2.3.1a). This indicator looks at the quantity, and not the size or other property, of the furniture. Consider whether there are enough tables and chairs, cots/mats, and cubbies to store personal belongings for the maximum number of children attending at one time. Also consider whether there are enough open shelves for materials (see photos 2.3.1 b–c, next page) and places for children to sit at tables while working with materials.

2.3.1 a This classroom has sufficient furniture for care, play, and learning, including chairs and tables, cubbies, cots or mats, and low, open shelves.

3.2 ***Most furniture*** means that almost all of the furniture used by the children is in ***good repair,*** and there are *no* serious concerns for any child's safety when basic furniture is used. If there are any repairs needed that may cause serious harm to the children, then score this indicator "No." However, if there are one or two minor repairs needed, and they do not pose a safety threat to children, then score this indicator "Yes." For example, in a classroom where only the cabinet handles on the child-sized stove are missing, but all other furniture is in good repair, score this indicator "Yes."

Indicator

2.3.1 b Since there are few storage shelves, materials are heaped on the shelves making it difficult for children to use materials independently. Credit cannot be given for Indicator 3.1.

2.3.1 c Having a sufficient number of open shelves makes it possible to organize materials for independent use.

Sturdy means that the furniture will not break, fall over, or collapse when used. If furniture falls over, look to see why that happened. For example, if a toy storage shelf is placed where it is easily knocked over or put on an uneven surface and it falls during the observation, this may not be due to the sturdiness of the furniture itself, but rather to its placement. In contrast, an open storage unit is not sturdy if the shelves collapse when children place toys on them. If the furniture itself is not sturdy, then score the indicator "No." However, do not consider safety concerns due to the placement of the furniture in this indicator. Such issues should be addressed in Item 14, Safety practices.

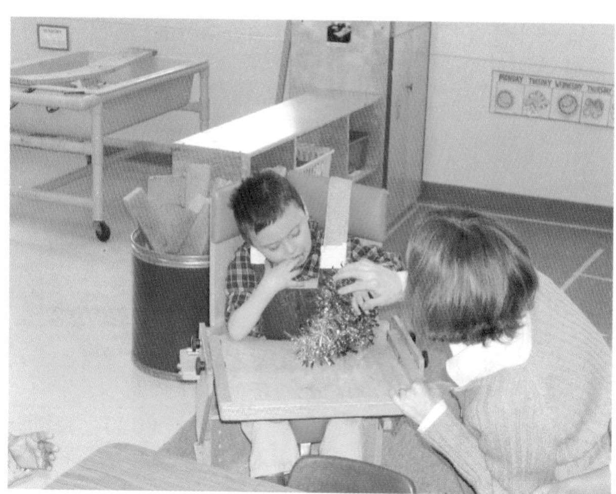

2.3.3 This child has the adaptive furniture he needs to do activities.

3.3 This indicator should be scored "NA" (not applicable) if there are no children with diagnosed disabilities requiring ***adaptive furniture*** enrolled in the group. If there are ***children with disabilities*** enrolled in the group, who require adaptations to furniture or special equipment, then adaptive furniture should, at a minimum, allow some participation in activities. For example, a seat equipped with a tray makes it possible for a child to have meals while attending the program. This adaptation meets the requirement at the minimal level of quality because it helps the child gain independence (see photo 2.3.3). However, this indicator does not require that the adaptation provide the child the opportunity to sit at a table with his peers during meal times, which is required in Indicator 5.3 of this item.

The allocation of space for adaptive equipment is not considered in this indicator, but in Item 4, Room arrangement, Indicator 3.4.

2 Furniture for care and play

Indicator

5.1 ***Child-sized*** means that children's feet are able to touch the floor, but not necessarily rest flat on the floor, while they are seated, and that tables are an appropriate height so that children can rest their elbows on the top of the table, while their legs fit comfortably underneath the table. (See photos 2.5.1 a–c.) Children should not have to perch on the edge of the chair to touch the floor because this can cause the chair to slip out from under them, increasing the possibility of injuries from falls. Consider not only if tables and chairs are too large, but also if they are too small.

This indicator only addresses the size of tables and chairs for children. If cubbies or other furnishings present a problem due to size, consider this under indicator 7.1.

Most furniture means that 75% of the children observed have *child-sized* chairs and tables. To help determine if tables and chairs are child-sized, observers should check at those times in the schedule when all children are sitting at the tables, for example, during lunch or snack. It also helps to use a recording system to determine if the 75% requirement is met. Such a chart should include all children present in the group during the observation. Below is an example of a simple chart for scoring whether chairs and tables are child-sized.

Child	Child-sized?
1	yes
2	no (chair too high)
3	yes
4	yes
5	yes
6	no (chair OK, table too high)

2.5.1 a These chairs and tables are child-sized, permitting the children's feet to touch the floor and their elbows to rest on the table. A child who needs adaptive furniture is also comfortably seated with her peers. In addition, all furniture is in good repair.

2.5.1 b These children are sitting on chairs that are too high, so their feet dangle and do not touch the floor.

5.2 To meet the requirements of this indicator the observer should check to see that ***all furniture is sturdy and in good repair.*** At the (3) minimal level, the requirement for good repair and sturdiness applies to ***most*** of the furniture, but at the (5) good level, the requirement increases to ***all*** furniture. However, if there is only one very minor problem, such as a slightly wobbly chair or a couch covering that is worn, then do not count off for these small things, unless there are many small problems, and the overall impression is one of poor repair.

5.3 This indicator can be scored "NA" when there are no children with diagnosed disabilities requiring ***adaptive furniture*** enrolled in the group. If there is a child with particular disabilities requiring adaptive equipment enrolled in the group, then the adaptive equipment must ***permit*** the child to be included in activities with the other children in the room (see photo 2.5.1a). For example, the table used by children in the group may need to be adjusted so that a wheelchair will fit underneath the table, thus making it possible for the child to join other children at meal times and for table top

2.5.1 c Although these children's feet rest on the floor, their elbows can't reach the table because the table is too high. Therefore, the furniture is not child-sized.

Indicator

2.7.1 a These cubbies are located in the room so that they are convenient for the children to use independently.

2.7.1 b This provision for storing children's coats and materials is not convenient because it is outside the room and requires adult supervision when children wish to access their things.

activities. Bolsters or other supports may be needed so that children with mobility impairments can participate in activities on the floor with other children.

The allocation of space for adaptive equipment is not considered in this indicator but is addressed in Item 4, Room arrangement, Indicator 3.4.

7.1 ***Convenient*** means that routine care furniture is located within the room and is easily accessible. Children's cubbies should be located in the room so that children have easy access to space for their personal belongings and work. If the cubbies are within reach of the children, the children are more likely to use their cubbies independently with little help from the staff. Cubbies located outside the classroom may cause problems with supervision and therefore cannot be considered ***convenient to use.*** (See photos 2.7.1 a–b.)

2.7.1 c The cots used for nap are conveniently stored inside the classroom for easy access.

Mats/cots should be stored in the room for easy access by staff. If mats are located in the classroom, it is easier to prepare for nap and to provide a smooth transition (see photo 2.7.1 c). Preparation for nap is a busy time because children are usually toileting and washing hands. Therefore, having the mats/cots easily accessible in the classroom will help the staff to quickly prepare for nap. Having mats/cots easily accessible in the room also allows the children to take part in helping staff prepare for nap.

7.2 Making use of different types of more specialized furniture in the learning environment is important because it provides children with varied opportunities to learn, explore, and discover. At the highest level of quality, some additional furniture for specific play and learning activities is required in addition to basic tables, chairs, cubbies, and open shelves. (See photos 2.7.2 a–c, next page.) A ***woodwork bench, sand and water table, or easel*** is required to offer enriching activities to children. Since the word ***or*** appears, only one of the three pieces of

Indicator

2.7.2 a

2.7.2 b

2.7.2 a–c A woodwork bench, easel and/or sand/water table extends children's play experiences.

furniture needs to be used. The furniture does not have to be used during the observation; however, it must be obvious that at least one of these is used on a regular basis for the appropriate activity and not placed in storage. If additional furniture is present, but obviously not regularly used for its intended purpose, then do not give credit for 7.2. For example, if only a sand/water table is present in the room, but filled with extra books or other toys or is used as a place to store materials, do not give credit (score 7.2 "No").

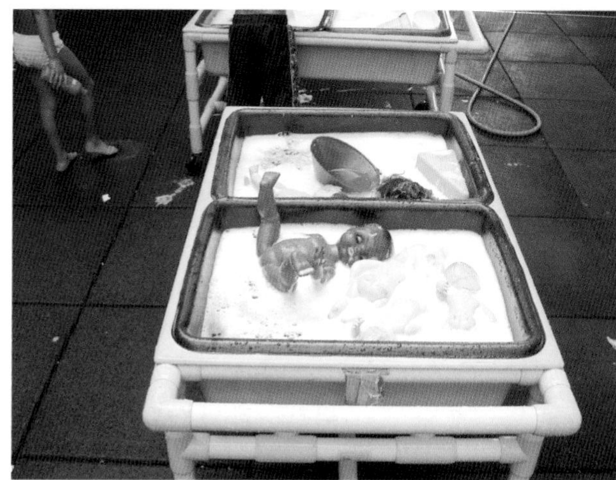

2.7.2 c

Indicator

3 Furnishings for relaxation and comfort

General information about this item

Children need softness in their physical surroundings. It helps them relax and feel comfortable. Softness is provided through furnishings, such as wall-to-wall carpeting, rug areas, cushions, or padded chairs and couches. Including soft toys, such as cloth puppets, soft dolls, or stuffed animals of various sizes, also provides softness.

Not only does this item look at the amount of softness the children have access to during play, but also the condition of the soft furnishings and toys. Since germs can live for a relatively long period of time on rugs, exposed padding from tears in mats or furniture, and the cloth covering of toys, it is important that soft furnishings and toys are kept clean and in good repair.

This item considers only the softness accessible to children during play. Softness provided during personal care routines, such as blankets, mats, or cots for nap or rest, are not given credit in this item.

A closer look at each indicator

1.1 In order to score this indicator "Yes," there can be ***no soft furnishings*** in the indoor environment for the children to use while they play. (See photo 3.1.1.) Examples of ***soft furnishings*** include wall-to-wall carpeting, rugs, mats, soft couches or chairs (both upholstered furniture and beanbag chairs), mattresses, futons, or cushions.

3.1.1 In this classroom, there are no soft furnishings such as rugs, pillows, or upholstered furniture accessible to children.

3.3.1 A large rug, which children can sit on, and several cushions have been added to provide some softness in the book area.

3.5.1 a The addition of several soft pieces of furniture makes this book corner a cozy area.

3 Furnishings for relaxation

Indicator

Accessible to children means that the ***soft furnishings*** must be within children's reach and that they are allowed to use the soft furnishings to sit, work, play, or lounge on. Soft furnishings provided during personal care routines, such as blankets and mats for rest, are not given credit in this item. Even if there is only one soft furnishing accessible to children, this indicator is scored "No."

1.2 In order to score this indicator "Yes," there can be ***no soft toys accessible to children.*** Examples of soft toys include cloth puppets (even if they have hard heads or hands), dolls that are completely soft or that have soft bodies, and soft toy animals of all sizes, from those that can be held in one hand to large animals children can sit or lie on. Only accessible soft toys that children can reach and are allowed to play with are given credit. If soft toys are used to decorate the room and are not accessible for children to use, they are not given credit in this item. Even if there is only one soft toy accessible to children, this indicator must be scored "No."

3.1 ***Some soft furnishings*** means that there are at least two soft furnishings in the room being observed that the children may use in play. This can include any of the floor coverings or furniture given as examples in Indicator 1.1, or something else that provides similar softness for the children. (See photo 3.3.1, page 15.)

In order to give credit for being a rug, the rug piece must be large enough to permit at least one child to stretch out and lounge comfortably on the rug, with several toys to play with. Therefore, one carpet square (1 ft. x 1 ft.), of the type that is sometimes used for each child in a group to sit on in circle time, is too small to give credit as a rug to play on.

In order to give credit for being a ***soft*** floor covering, there is no requirement for minimum thickness or softness, because the floor covering will be softer than a concrete, wood, or linoleum floor surface. Any type of large carpet (covering wall-to-wall or a large area) or rug that is put on top of a hard floor (such as concrete, tile, wood, or linoleum), even indoor-outdoor carpeting, is considered a soft floor covering because it is softer and usually warmer than the uncovered floor. To be given credit as ***some*** soft furniture at this minimal level, the furniture must be large enough for at least one child to use, for example, two cushions whose combined size is equal to a bed pillow, a child-sized padded chair, or a padded backrest cushion.

If *either* some soft floor covering *or* soft furniture is accessible to children, score Indicator 3.1 "Yes."

3.2 ***Some soft toys accessible*** means at least three soft toys are accessible to children. ***Accessible*** means the toys are within children's reach and that children are allowed to play with them. (See photos 3.3.2 a–b, next page.) Examples of soft toys are included in Indicator 1.2. Score this indicator "Yes" if the number of toys required is accessible.

5.1 A ***cozy area*** means a substantial amount of softness is provided in one place for the children. The soft furnishings in the cozy area must allow a child to completely escape the hardness of the typical early childhood classroom. (See photo 3.5.1 a, page 15.) One *small* soft thing, in itself, does not create a *cozy area*. Thus, a small padded chair, a small child-sized beanbag chair, a few small stuffed pillows, or a carpeted corner by itself is not enough. However, credit can be given for a combination of such small furnishings that are gathered together in an area.

Indicator

Large furnishings, such as a mattress, adult-sized couch, or adult-sized beanbag chair, might be given credit if they provide the required substantial amount of softness, by allowing the child to completely escape the hardness of the floor and/or wall. Judgment of whether a soft area can be given credit as a ***cozy area*** should be based on the amount of softness provided, not on whether the area is aesthetically appealing. (See photos 3.5.1 b–l, on pages 18–19.)

Accessible means that the children are permitted to use the cozy area for lounging, reading, and other quiet activities. A cozy area must be accessible to children ***for a substantial portion of the day*** (1/3 of the time the facility is open). In order to calculate the amount of time the children have access to a ***cozy area,*** the provisions in all rooms where the children spend time may be included. For example, if the children are in rooms other than the main classroom from 6:30–8:30 AM and after 4:00 PM, the observer should go into these rooms to see if there is a ***cozy area*** that children are free to use and whether it meets the criteria in 5.2. Also, the teacher should be asked whether the children have access to the cozy area while they are in those rooms. Based on these answers, credit can be given towards the substantial portion of the day for other rooms in addition to the main classroom used by the group. (See pages 22–24 for examples of calculating substantial portion of the day for this item.)

If there are two or more ***cozy areas*** in the room being observed (the main classroom), each area does not have to meet all the requirements of Indicators 5.1 and 5.2. However, there must always be one area providing a substantial amount of softness, where children can depend on being able to relax, which is *not* used for active physical play. It must be obvious that a child, who wants to use a cozy area, is not constantly interrupted by active play. If children start to use the cozy area for active physical play, the staff must be observed redirecting the active play to another area.

A combination of accessibility to all cozy areas can be used to judge whether a cozy area is accessible for a substantial portion of the day, to score this indicator "Yes."

3.3.2 a A minimum of three soft toys is required to give credit for 3.2. The child is holding one, and two others are next to her, allowing credit at the minimal level.

3.3.2 b Since only two soft toys are seen in the cozy area, the observer must look for additional accessible soft toys before scoring 3.2.

5.2 The ***cozy area*** may be used for short periods as a group space (e.g., for dancing or circle time), but it should be protected from active play for most of the day. (See photos 3.5.2 a–b on page 20.) A cozy area should be away from active play equipment and have protection from active children through its placement in the room or by a barrier. It should not be located where there is a lot of traffic. Staff should be diligent to ensure that children engaged in active play do not interfere with a child in the ***cozy area*** by jumping on or running into the child who is relaxing. If active physical play occurs in the ***cozy area,*** staff must be observed stopping such play.

Activities suitable for the cozy area are quiet ones such as reading, daydreaming, relaxing, and listening to soft music. If no active physical activities are allowed in the ***cozy area,*** score this indicator "Yes."

Continued on page 20.

3 Furnishings for relaxation

Indicator

3.5.1 b–l Cozy areas come in many sizes and shapes. A cozy area must provide a substantial amount of softness, which allows children to completely escape the hardness of the typical early childhood classroom.

3.5.1 b

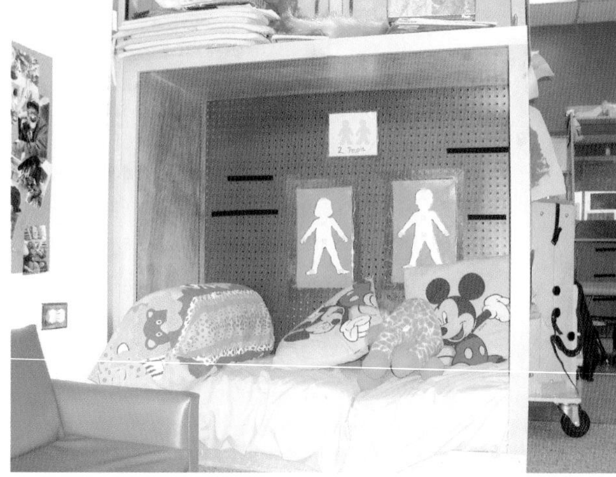

3.5.1 c

3.5.1 d

3.5.1 e

3.5.1 f

3.5.1 g

Indicator

3.5.1 h

3.5.1i

3.5.1j

3.5.1k

3.5.1l

3 Furnishings for relaxation

Indicator

3.5.2 a The cozy area can be used for short periods as a group space.

3.5.2 b This cozy are cannot be given credit for 5.2 because it is used for active play, and the staff does not stop such use.

Continued from page 17.

5.3 In order to judge whether the *soft furnishings* are ***clean,*** consider the appearance and the odor of the furnishings, such as carpeting, rugs, chairs, couches, and cushions. If most of them smell and look clean, then give credit.

In good repair means that most of the soft furnishings are not torn or frayed. Look especially to see that there are no tears in the covers of beanbag chairs, cushions, and couches that expose the padding or stuffing. Germs can collect in the foam rubber or other padding on children's upholstered couches or chairs. Deflated beanbags cannot be given credit for soft furnishings in good repair because they no longer provide adequate softness due to their poor condition. ***Most soft furnishings*** means almost all with only one or two minor exceptions, for example, covering that is worn but not torn, and no stuffing is exposed.

7.1 Look around the room to see if there are soft furnishings in other areas of the room ***in addition to the cozy area.*** (See photo 3.7.1.) Wall-to-wall carpeting, several rug areas, and cushions or padded furniture in other areas can be given credit. Give credit only for additional soft furnishings that can be used during play. If there is a carpet under tables that cannot be used to sit or play on, it cannot be given credit for soft furnishings. However, indoor/outdoor carpeting that is accessible for play can be given credit, even though it is not very thick, since it is softer than the bare floor. Additional soft furnishings may include cushions or padded furniture in the housekeeping area, a rug or cushions in the library area, or rugs in the block or fine motor areas. At least two additional soft furnishings must be observed in order to score this indicator "Yes."

7.2 ***Many*** means enough ***soft toys*** to ensure that children do not have to compete over them. (See photo 3.7.2.) The actual number may vary with the age of the children and the size of the group. For example, 2's and 3's may be more interested in soft toys than older 4's or kindergartners.

For younger children, there should be at least two soft, cuddly toys for each child in the group. For older 4's and kindergartners, at least 10 toys or enough for half of the group must be accessible when there are more than 20 children attending

Indicator

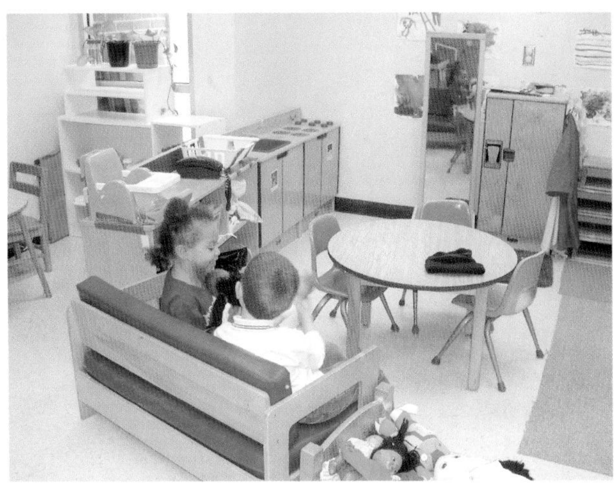

3.7.1 In addition to the softness in the cozy area, a child-sized couch is accessible in the dramatic play play area.

3.7.2 Many soft toys are freely accessible to children.

at one time. See Indicator 1.2 for examples of soft toys. As in the other indicators, ***accessible*** means that the children have easy access to the toys and are allowed to use them. The observer should count only those soft toys that are ***clean*** (see Indicator 5.3 for definition of clean) and accessible to the children. To score "Yes," both the number and condition of the toys are considered.

Indicator

Calculating "Substantial Portion of the Day"

Example 1

This schedule is based on an observation period of 4.5 hours (from 8AM – 12:30PM) and information collected during the teacher interview about how unobserved time during the day is used and what is accessible to the children.

Time	Scheduled activity	Time to use cozy area
6:30 – 7:45	Breakfast in cafeteria and TV time for those who are finished with breakfast	
8:00 – 8:30	Children go to regular classrooms and play with table and rug toys (puzzles; legos; duplos with cars, people, and trucks; stringing beads and cards; pegboards)	
8:30 – 8:45	Prepare for breakfast/children wash hands	
8:45 – 9:15	Breakfast	
9:15 – 9:45	Circle (teacher reading time)	
9:45 – 10:45	Centers (housekeeping, art, sand and water, nature/science, writing table, blocks, music, computer and cozy book area)	**1 hour**
10:45 – 11:15	Outdoor Play (gross motor activities only)	
11:15 – 12:15	Prepare for and eat lunch	
12:15 – 12:30	Story, put out cots, prepare for nap	
12:30 – 2:45	Nap	
2:45 – 3:00	Wake up from nap; bathroom	
3:00 – 3:25	Snack and story	
3:25 – 4:25	Centers (housekeeping, nature/science, writing table, computer, fine motor area and cozy book area)	**1 hour**
4:25 – 5:25	Outdoors or indoor gross motor	
5:30 – 6:30	Table and rug toys (puzzles; legos; duplos with cars, people, and trucks; stringing beads and cards; pegboards) Prepare for departure	

1. Figure the total number of hours that children are allowed to attend.

   (6:30AM to 6:30 PM = 12 hours)

2. Calculate 1/3 of the operating hours to determine "Substantial Portion of the Day."

   (12 hours ÷ 3 = 4 hours)

3. Add up all times that children may have access to the cozy area.

   (see shaded times on schedule = 2 hours)

4. Compare the amount of time children may have access to the cozy area to the time requirement for substantial portion of the day. If the amount of time children may have access to the cozy area is the same or greater, then score "Yes." If the amount of time is less than the time requirement for substantial portion of the day, then score "No." For example, the schedule above indicates:

   2 hours (opportunity to use cozy area) **is less than 4 hours** (time requirement for substantial portion of day), and therefore the time requirement for a substantial portion of the day is not met.

Calculating "Substantial Portion of the Day"

Example 2

This schedule is based on an observation period of 4 hours (from 9AM – 1PM) and information collected during the teacher interview about how unobserved time during the day is used and what is accessible to the children.

Time	Scheduled activity	Time to use cozy area
9:00 – 9:30	Arrival/quiet centers open (cozy book area, computer, writing table, math, science and fine motor)	**30 minutes**
9:30 – 9:45	Snack	
9:45 – 10:00	Clean up snack/bathroom/wash hands	
10:00 – 11:00	Outside (gross motor activities only)	
11:00 – 11:45	Free Choice of Centers (fine motor, art, blocks, dramatic play, nature/science, math, sensory table, computer, writing table and cozy book area)	**45 minutes**
11:45 – 12:15	Large group activity (M,W,F is music/movement and T,Th is art activity)	
12:15 – 12:45	Prepare for and Eat Lunch	
12:45 – 1:00	Clean up/bathroom/prepare for quiet time	
1:00 – 1:45	Quiet time/quiet centers available (cozy book area, fine motor, math, and science)	**45 minutes**
1:45 – 2:00	Clean up all centers and prepare for departure	

1. Figure the total number of hours that children are allowed to attend.

   (9 AM to 2 PM = 5 hours)

2. Calculate 1/3 of the Operating Hours to determine "Substantial Portion of the Day."

   (5 hours ÷ 3 = 1 hour and 40 minutes)

3. Add up all times that children may have access to the cozy area.

   (see shaded times on schedule = 2 hours)

4. Compare the amount of time children may have access to the cozy area to the time requirement for substantial portion of the day. If the amount of time children may have access to the cozy area is the same or greater, then score "Yes." If the amount of time is less than the time requirement for substantial portion of the day, then score "No." For example, the schedule above indicates:

   2 hours (opportunity to use cozy area) **is greater than 1 hour and 40 minutes** (time requirement for substantial portion of day), and therefore the time requirement for substantial portion of the day is met.

Calculating "Substantial Portion of the Day"

Example 3

This schedule is based on an observation period of 3.5 hours (from 9AM –12:30 PM) and information collected during the teacher interview about whether what was observed represents the typical daily practice.

Time	Scheduled activity	Time to use cozy area
9:00 – 9:20	Arrival/group time to discuss activities for the day	
9:20 – 9:45	Whole group art activity	
9:45 – 10:00	Whole group reading time (teacher directed)	
10:00 – 10:45	Outside time (gross motor activities only)	
10:45 – 11:30	Free choice of centers (fine motor, art, blocks, dramatic play, nature/science, math, sensory table, computer, writing table and cozy book area)	**45 minutes**
11:30 – 11:45	Clean up/bathroom/prepare for lunch time	
11:45 – 12:15	Prepare for and eat lunch	
12:15 – 12:30	Clean up/bathroom/prepare for departure	

1. Figure the total number of hours that children are allowed to attend.

   (9 AM to 12:30 PM = 3 hours and 30 minutes)

2. Calculate 1/3 of the Operating Hours to determine "Substantial Portion of the Day."

   (3 hours and 30 minutes ÷ 3 = 1 hour and 10 minutes)

3. Add up all times that children may have access to the cozy area.

   (see shaded times on schedule = 45 minutes)

4. Compare the amount of time children may have access to the cozy area to the time requirement for substantial portion of the day. If the amount of time children may have access to the cozy area is the same or greater, then score "Yes." If the amount of time is less than the time requirement for substantial portion of the day, then score "No." For example, the schedule above indicates:

   45 minutes (opportunity to use cozy area) **is less than 1 hour and 10 minutes** (time requirement for substantial portion of day), and therefore the time requirement for substantial portion of the day is not met.

4 Room arrangement for play

General information about this item

The arrangement of the spaces used by children in a classroom affects how well the staff can supervise the children to protect their health and safety, as well as to enhance their learning. If furnishings, such as high toy shelves or hanging decorative fabric, are placed so that they obstruct the view of staff, thus creating "blind spots," effective supervision becomes very difficult.

The arrangement of furniture and materials in a room also organizes the play space for children. If materials are placed in a random, helter-skelter way without a functional organization, children find it difficult to become involved in meaningful, sustained play. They waste a lot of time looking for things that go together, and often cannot find a suitable protected place in which to use them. In order to support productive play, the organization in the room should clearly convey to children, where certain materials are accessible, where they may be used, and where they should be returned.

Classrooms that offer many hands-on activities are usually organized in a number of *interest centers*. In each interest center, children will find all the materials they need for a particular kind of play and an appropriate play place in which to use the materials. Thus, the art center would have various art materials in usable condition, each type stored separately on open shelves, with a table nearby on which to use them and a convenient place for work to dry. An easel for painting might be included in this area, with paint in various colors, soft brushes, paper held firmly in place, and easy access to drying space. (See photos 4.7.1 a–h on pages 30–31 showing how to evaluate interest centers.)

In programs where use of individual workspace is encouraged, for example, in the Montessori method, the same basic principles of organization are present. The children know where the materials are kept on open shelves in a particular area, where they may play with them, and where to return them. The interest centers may look different, but the principles are the same.

Well-arranged space offers:

- Many different types of interest centers for a variety of learning and play opportunities;
- Play spaces that are protected from unnecessary interruptions so children can engage in activities with more concentration;
- Clarity of organization that promotes independence and care for the environment;
- Places to play and learn in smaller groups, with a friend, or individually.

Indicator

A closer look at each indicator

1.1 If ***no interest centers are defined,*** it is not possible to tell where materials that go together are kept or where they can be used. The simple presence of a sign naming an area as the "book corner," "block area," or "art center" does not necessarily mean that the labeled space meets the requirements of a *defined interest center.*

The observer should look around the room to see if any interest center can be identified. Where are art materials accessible and where are they supposed to be used? Do blocks, dramatic play, fine motor, books, nature/science, or music have a pre-arranged space? If the observer cannot identify any interest centers, the children will not be able to do so either. Therefore, 1.1 would be scored "Yes." (See photo 4.1.1.)

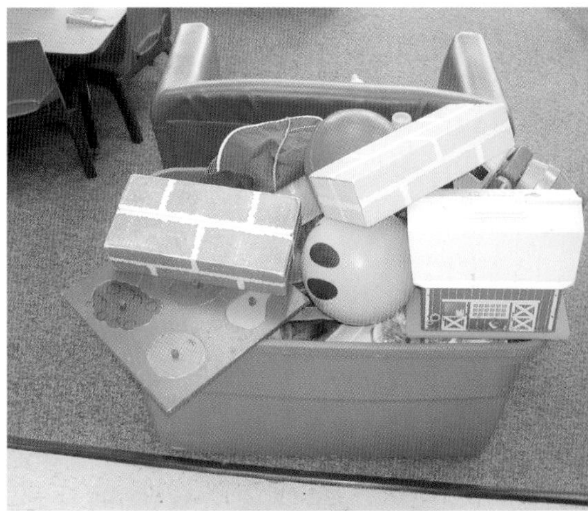

4.1.1 Play materials are randomly placed into an open storage container, with no indication of appropriate play spaces in which to use them.

However, if there is at least one area in the room where a specific type of activity takes place, all materials used for that type of play are placed together and there is appropriate space to use them, then 1.1 is scored "No."

A ***clearly defined interest center*** should contain:

- Materials that stimulate and support a specific type of play, such as blocks and accessories, including people and vehicles, for building; books, flannel boards, puppets, and other language and literary materials; fine motor materials, such as interlocking blocks and manipulatives; art materials for drawing, painting, collage, clay or play dough; music and movement materials, such as instruments, dance props, and a CD or tape player
- Accessible storage for the materials offered in the interest center, including low, open storage shelves, containers to keep materials that go together separated from other materials
- Uncluttered shelves or use of picture-word labeling on the shelves and containers that children can understand, so that selection of materials and participation in clean-up become more independent
- Suitable space to use the materials, such as a table or easel for art materials, a flat rug area for block building, a table or rug area for puzzles and other fine motor materials, an open area for music-making and movement activities, a cozy area for quiet reading, or an area near water on an easy-to-clean floor for messy play, such as finger painting, sand play, or a discovery table
- A drying arrangement, where needed, for products that are produced in activity areas, such as a place to dry three-dimensional clay, play dough, or glued wood constructions, or a clothesline or rack for drying paintings or collages

1.2 ***Visual supervision*** means that staff can see and monitor all children as they play in the indoor space. Being able to see the entire play area helps to avoid safety problems and prevent conflicts among children.

It also keeps the staff in touch with the children's play so that they can take full advantage of "teachable moments." For example, if several children are building a fire station in the block area using blocks and various emergency vehicles, a staff member could bring over a book to provide additional information. Such timely

Indicator

extensions of learning cannot happen if the staff cannot see what children are doing.

The age and ability of the children should be taken into consideration when deciding whether the visual supervision is difficult enough to score 1.2 "Yes." Generally, younger children, children who have difficulty interacting with others or who need more help, require closer supervision. However, regardless of the age and ability of the children, play areas that have hidden spaces, for example spaces behind hanging fabric, tall shelves, partial walls, and under or in some lofts, may be so difficult to supervise that a score of "Yes" should be given on this indicator. (See photos 4.1.2 a–b.)

The number of staff present, and where they place themselves, should be taken into consideration. In cases where there are always two or more staff members with a group, and it is observed that one person is usually watching the area that is difficult to supervise, this indicator may be scored "No." However, remember that if one adult is ever alone in the room supervising children (for example, early morning or late afternoon), the difficulties of supervising during these times must be considered when scoring.

4.1.2 a High shelves obstruct staff view of many play spaces, making visual supervision of play difficult.

4.1.2 b In this room, a high lattice for plants obscures the view of the loft area and the activity areas on the other side of the block shelves.

3.1 Look to see whether there are at least two areas, each of which clearly meets the basic definition of an ***interest center.*** Look for areas where a particular type of play is featured, and where both materials and suitable play space are available. Several typical centers are listed under Indicator 1.1. At this minimal level, the interest centers need only to be easy for children to recognize and play in (e.g., materials placed together with space to use them).

3.2 In order to decide whether the play space is ***not difficult to supervise visually,*** take into consideration the age and ability of the children, the number of staff present, and how diligent they are in watching the children, as well as how difficult the space is to supervise. Base the score on what is observed. (See photos 4.3.2 a–b.)

4.3.2 a

4.3.2 b

4.3.2 a–b Low shelves and the absence of other obstructions make the visual supervision of play in these rooms not difficult for staff.

4 Room arrangement for play

Indicator

3.3 ***Sufficient space*** means enough space for ***several activities*** to go on at the same time without children being extremely crowded. It is important to be able to provide a variety of activities simultaneously so that children can have choices. This indicator is at the minimal level so it is not required that each type of activity should have its own center. Look to see that there is space enough for at least three different types of activities to go on at the same time for some period of the day. (See photo 4.3.3.) If a space is used *only* for routines such as meals, it cannot be counted to meet this indicator. However, if it is used for both routines and play, it may be given credit.

4.3.3 There is enough space for at least three activities to go on at one time so children can have choices.

3.4 If there are no children with disabilities enrolled in the group, this indicator should be scored "NA." However, if a child with any type of disability is enrolled in the group, observe to see whether ***most*** spaces have been made accessible, if needed by the child. For example, a child who is visually impaired may need modifications such as a rope mounted on the wall to lead him to particular areas, and clear pathways to get there. A child using a walker needs pathways that are wide enough to accommodate the equipment. Note that at this quality level, it is not required that all spaces are accessible, but ***most*** need to be accessible, with only a few exceptions, if there is a child enrolled who needs such accommodations. (See photo 4.3.4.)

4.3.4 The room has been arranged for this child to access most activity areas.

5.1 This indicator requires at least ***three different interest centers*** that are not only defined, but ***conveniently equipped.*** Conveniently equipped means that play and clean-up can go smoothly because the necessities for the type of play are where they need to be. For example, an art center, where messy activities are often used, requires placement on an easy-to-clean floor, near a sink, with enough space to store and use materials without crowding. A block area would need to have a floor surface that reduces problems with noise and is level for building, with space and shelves to store, as well as to use, the blocks and accessories.

5.2 ***Quiet centers*** are those where children usually play with materials that require them to sit and concentrate. These include materials such as books, manipulatives, art, puzzles, the computer, small table toys, and listening stations with earphones. ***Active centers*** include materials that require more movement or generate more noise, such as music and movement, dramatic play, and block building. Look around the room to see whether there is sufficient space between active and quiet centers so that quiet centers and the more active centers do not interfere with one another. Since a barrier such as a toy shelf does not cut down on noise, separation in physical space is needed. (See photos 4.5.2 a–c, next page.) To give credit, *all* ***quiet areas*** must be sufficiently separated from noisy areas.

5.3 ***Most activities are not interrupted*** means that the room is arranged so that traffic paths move around rather than through most activities. (See photos 4.5.3 a–c, next page.) This can be accomplished by using the open storage shelves to partially surround areas and divert traffic around them. Commonly used traffic paths, such as the entry door(s) to the room, the door or path to the toileting or

Continued on page 30.

Indicator

4.5.2 a Barriers such as the book case and open toy shelves do not sufficiently cut down on the noise from the more active dramatic play, block, and gross motor areas adjacent to the book and cozy area. Actual distance between quiet and active or noisy areas is needed.

4.5.2 b A basket of musical instruments, which invites children to be active and noisy, is accessible in the library center, which is a quiet area.

4.5.2 c The listening center, in which children independently use books on tape without earphones, should not be located in the quiet book and cozy area.

4.5.3 a Open storage shelves, used to provide materials for various activities, are placed to divert traffic around, rather that through, the activities.

4.5.3 b Play with blocks and manipulatives is often interrupted because the rug area where these materials are used is directly in the path to the door.

4.5.3 c Several interest centers, including dramatic play, manipulatives and blocks are set up in the pathway to the door, so that children walk through the interest centers, not around them.

Indicator

4.7.1 a–h Evaluating Interest centers

4.7.1 a This block area, located in the corner of a classroom (meeting requirements for 5.3), is well defined (meeting requirements for 3.1 and 5.1) and conveniently equipped with plenty of storage for blocks, a good surface, lots of space for block-building, and labeled shelves (meeting requirements for 7.2).

4.7.1 b The music materials in this classroom are located in a cabinet within a large, clear space. When the cabinet is opened, and children can access the materials, the area becomes the music center, meeting requirements for 3.1 and 5.1. However, if the cabinet is usually closed, this cannot count as a defined interest center (does not meet requirements for 3.1, 5.1).

4.7.1 c The space for this dramatic play area is clearly defined by furnishings, and well equipped with storage for the dress-ups and props preschoolers use to pretend family roles (meeting requirements for 5.1).

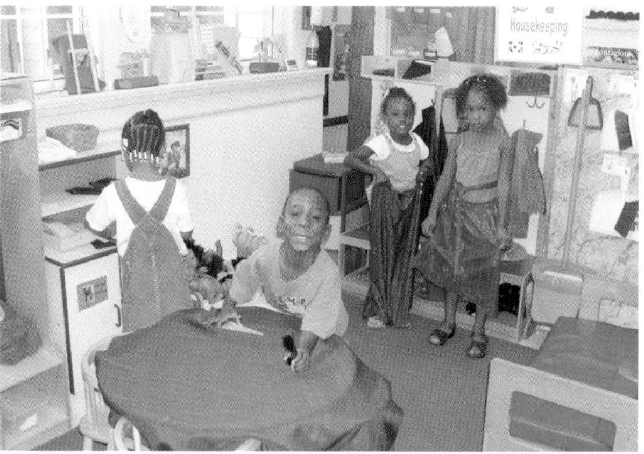

4.7.1 d This dramatic play area is clearly defined (meeting requirements for 5.1) and has a convenient play space (meeting requirements for 7.2). The dolls, clothing, cleaning tools, cooking and eating utensils are organized for independent use.

Continued from page 28.
handwashing areas, and the children's cubbies, should be kept clear of activities. Minimizing interruption of activities avoids conflicts and supports more sustained play. To give credit, only a few minor problems causing interruptions can exist, and no major problems that make play very difficult or frustrating for children.

7.1 ***At least five different*** interest centers are required in this indicator, in order to provide a ***variety of learning experiences.*** Materials, and the activities that children engage in while using them, differ in many ways. Some materials, such as manipulatives and small building toys, enhance fine muscle development. Others,

Indicator

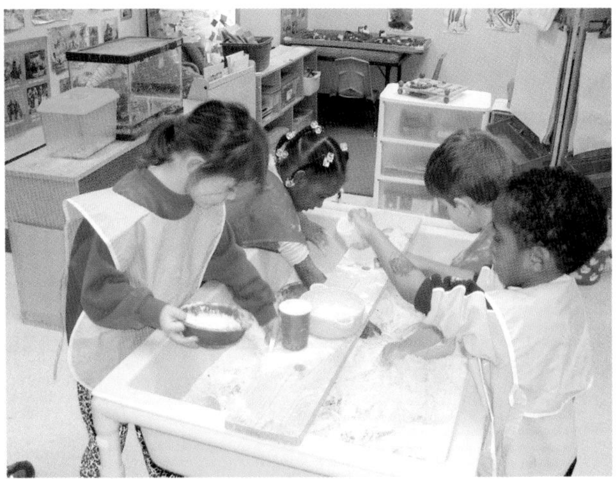

4.7.1 e Extra toys for this sand center are stored near the sand table, and a board is provided to keep the sand from being cluttered with toys, making the center "conveniently equipped" (meeting requirements for 5.1).

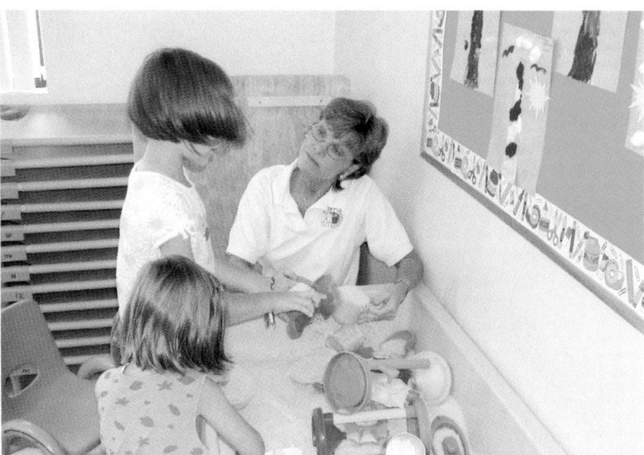

4.7.1 f This sand center is defined (meeting requirements for 3.1), but there is no convenient storage place for all the toys (not meeting requirements for 5.1).

4.7.1 g This puzzle area is well defined (meeting requirements for 3.1) and has a convenient floor space to play with the puzzles (meeting requirements for 5.1), but the shelves are too crowded for easy independent use (not meeting requirements for 7.2).

4.7.1 h The computer center in the class is away from active play areas, has a well-defined place for each computer user, with storage for the computers out of children's reach, meeting the requirements for an interest center for 5.1.

such as dramatic play, art, and books, encourage imagination and language. Science and math materials help to introduce concepts of number, sequence, classification, and cause and effect. In order to introduce children to varied approaches to learning, a high quality program offers open-ended play experiences such as sand and water or art, as well as opportunities to find the right answer with puzzles and math games, and ways to explore social roles through dramatic play. To give credit, the *five interest centers* must each be *clearly defined,* as discussed in the General Information section of this item and in Indicator 1.1 (see photos 4.7.1 a–h).

Indicator

4.7.2 a Children know exactly where dress-ups should be stored because of the clearly labeled shelves.

4.7.2 b Photographs with words are used to label these shelves in the block center.

4.7.2 c Pictures with words are used to label the shelves in this fine motor area. Sets of materials are in see-through containers for easy choice and access.

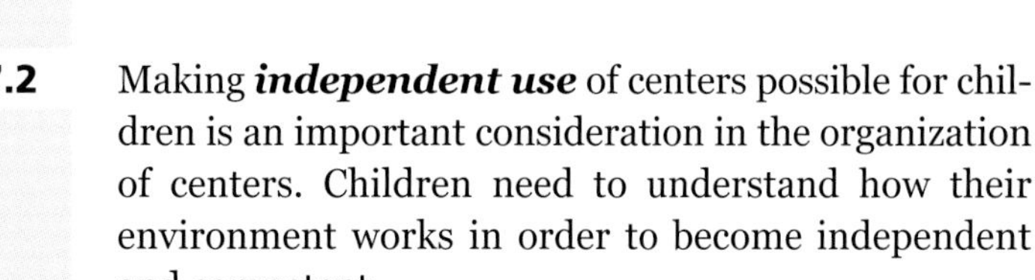

7.2 Making ***independent use*** of centers possible for children is an important consideration in the organization of centers. Children need to understand how their environment works in order to become independent and competent.

In order to make materials easy for children to access from and to return to interest centers, materials should be:

- Stored on low, open, uncrowded shelves
- Stored in containers, if needed, that clearly identify what is inside, such as see-through containers or containers labeled with pictures of what is inside
- If stored in containers, they should be those without lids or with lids that are easy to open and close
- Put on shelves that have child-friendly labels telling where materials belong, such as outlines of blocks of different sizes and shapes and picture-word labels for block accessories (vehicles, farm animals, wild animals, etc.); labels for various fine motor toys; dramatic play clothes hung up and props on labeled shelves or in labeled containers sorted by type; books stored with the front covers showing so children can tell what they are about; and art materials stored in labeled containers and/or on labeled shelves

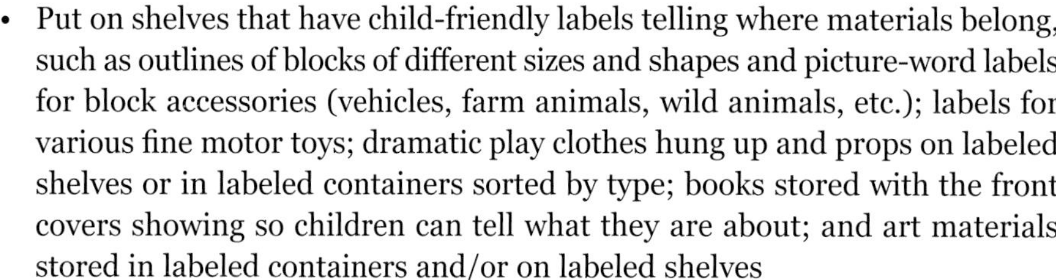

(See photos 4.7.2 a–c for examples.)

In order to make productive use of materials, play space in interest centers should be:

- Close to where the children access stored materials
- Suitable for using the particular materials, for example, a level, relatively large open area covered with a rug for block play; tables and/or an easel, preferably near a source of water, for art materials; tables and/or a rug area for using puzzles, small building toys, and manipulatives; a soft, comfortable place to

Indicator

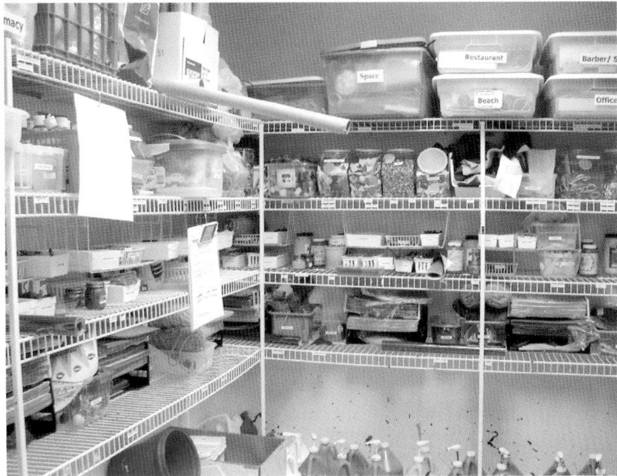

4.7.3 a Storage of extra materials for use by all classrooms allows teachers in this center to add new experiences to children's play.

4.7.3 b Extra materials for preschool classrooms are stored in a shared hallway.

4.7.3 c

4.7.3 d

4.7.3 c–d Extra materials can be stored in the classroom, on open shelves that are out of children's reach or in closed cabinets.

read books; tables and/or a rug for using math and nature/science materials; and a separate space large enough for dramatic play furniture and props

- Large enough to accommodate the number of children permitted to use the area at the same time without crowding; for example, if only two children are allowed to use the relatively small writing center at one time, only two chairs are available at the writing table; four children might be allowed at once at the larger art table or in the housekeeping area

It does not matter exactly how the support for independent use is given as long as the system works. If almost all ***centers are organized*** so that children can use them independently, give 7.2 a score of "Yes."

7.3 Since children are excited by new experiences and materials, ***additional materials*** need to be ***available*** to add to or substitute for similar materials. ***Available*** means that staff have relatively easy access in the facility to additional materials in storage that they can make accessible to the children when they feel that a change

Indicator

in materials is needed. Additional materials of various types should be available. (See photos 4.7.3 a–d, preceding page.)

It is necessary to ask the staff about whether they have additional materials, and if so, what materials they have. If possible, the observer should ask the staff to show the additional materials. It is also necessary to ask how often different materials are rotated into the centers. Materials should be changed in most centers at least monthly.

The requirement for additional materials to rotate into a center occurs in a number of other items including Item 15, Books and pictures (7.1); Item 19, Fine motor (7.1); Item 24, Dramatic play (7.1); Item 25, Nature/science (7.2); and Item 26, Math/number (7.2). It is wise to get information to score all these items at the same time and keep a record of which centers have additional materials for rotation.

In order to give this indicator a score of "Yes," there should be materials to rotate into almost all centers, with no more than one exception, for example, in an interest center that has many materials already accessible. The amount of materials available for rotation may vary by interest center and the amount of materials currently accessible in each center.

5 Space for privacy

General information about this item

The constant pressure of sharing toys, space, and adult attention in a group setting is stressful for children. Being able to relax and feel protected from intrusion or competition, as children play alone or with a friend, helps them regain their inner peacefulness. In contrast to the adult notion of privacy, which includes being in a place where it is not possible to be seen or heard by others, children can easily forget about the people and activity around them if no one bothers them or interrupts their play. Thus, a single child or a pair of children can experience a sense of privacy in a space that is in view and can be easily supervised by an adult, as long as the other children and the adults do not interrupt them.

An example of the ability children have to maintain a sense of privacy in the midst of activity is the Montessori practice of having a child use a small throw rug to create a private work space for himself. Once the child has rolled out his throw rug, the space on this rug is his own work space, and no one is allowed to interrupt him. This rule is understood by the other children and reinforced, when needed, by the staff. Thus, no physical barriers or relatively isolated placement in the room is necessary to reinforce the child's privacy to work independently.

Please note that isolation used as punishment (e.g., time out) is not considered under this item. Only space for privacy chosen by children to meet their own needs for a private space is given credit in this item.

Space for privacy can be found or created spontaneously by children, either indoors or outdoors, but it also should be planned by the staff. Since the need for privacy in a group setting is basic, planning for private spaces is essential in a high quality program. Planned private spaces can be created by using protective physical barriers such as toy storage shelves to create a small separate area or by limiting participation in an activity or area to one or two children at a time.

Commonly observed areas for privacy that are limited to one or two participants are the computer, writing table, single easel, or a small table with two chairs reserved for quiet activities such as puzzles or drawing. Even an activity using the sand/water table can be space for privacy if use is limited to one or two children at a time, and the rule is adhered to consistently by staff.

No matter how the need for privacy is met, private spaces must be easy for staff to supervise in order to protect children's health and safety.

A closer look at each indicator

1.1 This indicator describes a situation that ignores children's need for privacy. The children may be required to join in group play for much of the day or may lack staff

Indicator

protection from constant interruptions and competition from others. Observe to see if staff protect children from constantly being interrupted or having their toys taken away by others, or if that occurs repeatedly without the staff taking action to help the children who are seeking privacy. If one or two children succeed in finding a private place to play, away from the group, observe to see whether staff call them back to the group without finding another protected place for them to play. Rooms that are very crowded with furniture and materials or include too many children may also lack space for privacy.

Score "Yes" only if children are not allowed at all to have space for privacy.

3.1 At the minimal level, observe to see whether children are ***allowed to find or create privacy*** for themselves, even if the space they find is not safe or easy to supervise. Often children seek privacy outdoors by crawling under platforms or hiding in secluded places. Indoors they may take toys to play with behind room dividers or furniture, or ask to have a tent made by draping a sheet over a table. Large hollow block constructions can be used to make a space for privacy, if the number of occupants is limited. Score 3.1 "Yes" if children find or create spaces for privacy, either indoors or outdoors, and staff do not stop them. (See photos 5.3.1 a–c.)

3.2 This indicator addresses the requirement that all spaces used for privacy be ***easily supervised by staff.*** Look from various angles in the room and outdoors at the spaces used by children for privacy as well as those planned by staff to provide private space. Score "Yes" only if it is possible for staff to easily see children in private spaces, as staff move around the room engaged in usual caregiving activities. If staff cannot see children except by looking through a small opening or at an unusual angle, then the private space is not *easily* supervised by staff, and 3.2 must be scored "No." (See photos 5.3.2 a–e, next page.)

Continued on page 38.

5.3.1a–c Each of these children has created a private space by using furnishings in the classroom meant for other purposes. Watch to see if children are allowed to use their self-created spaces for privacy.

5.3.1 a

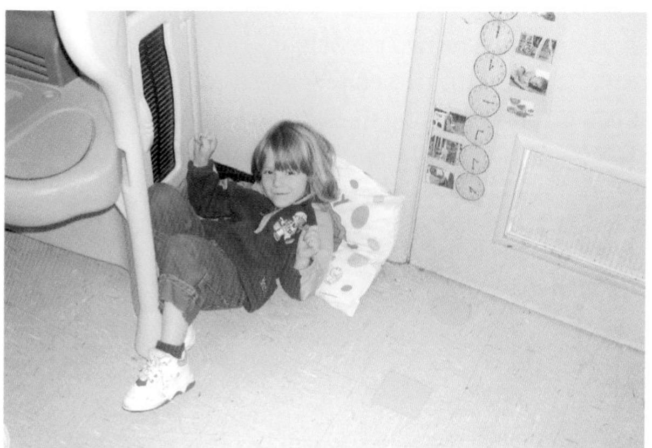

5.3.1 b

5.3.1c At this minimal level, the space for privacy found by this child can be given credit in this indicator, even though it may not be easy to supervise.

Indicator

5.3.2a Note how the space for privacy is hidden by tall shelves and a cover over the top, which makes it very difficult to supervise.

5.3.2b From this angle, the observer can see that staff cannot supervise this space for privacy as they engage in usual caregiving activities.

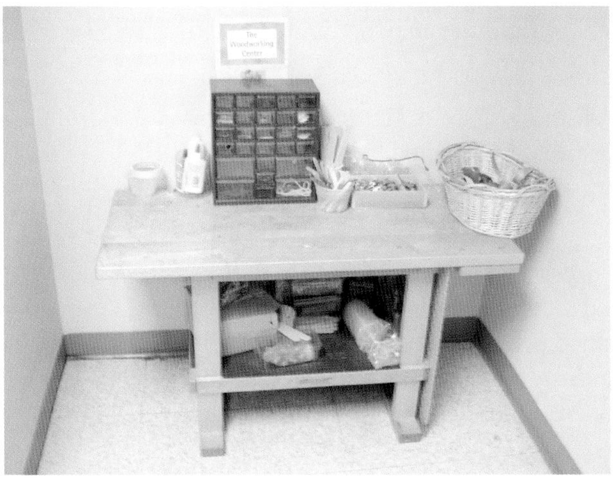

5.3.2c This carpentry table for one or two children is placed in a closet from which the door has been removed. Unfortunately, it does not meet Indicator 3.2 because it is not easy to supervise.

5.3.2d This tent-like space for privacy has very small openings, making it difficult to supervise the children playing inside.

5.3.2e With the entry flap closed, it is almost impossible to see what the children are doing.

5 Space for privacy

Indicator

Continued from page 36.

5.1 ***Space set aside*** means that the staff have planned space for privacy. This might include a computer where only one or two children may play at one time, a small table with only two chairs where only two children may write or use manipulatives, or a small space with a soft chair or cushions and a few books separate from the larger book center. In order to give credit for this indicator, the staff must not only set aside private space, but must also assure that it is ***protected from intrusion*** by other children.

In order to judge whether the private space is ***protected from intrusion,*** observe whether staff redirect other children who also want to play in the private space to other spaces, or whether they allow them to wait, watch, or pull up another chair to participate. Unless the private space is kept private, that is, limited to one or two children without the pressure of onlookers, it is no longer a private space. To give credit, the privacy rule must be enforced by staff during the observation, if it is needed to protect the privacy of a child. If the child's privacy is not threatened by another, and the rule seems to work without teacher intervention, credit can be given.

Private space may have time limitations, and staff may keep a list with children's names waiting for turns. For example, use of the computer may be limited to 20 minutes for one or, at most, two children sharing a turn.

Score this indicator "Yes" if it is clear that at least one space is set aside for use by one or two children and the child in the space is usually protected from intrusion by others. (See photos 5.5.1 a–j, pages 39–40.)

5.2 Since children are subjected to group pressures throughout the major part of the day, the space that is set aside for privacy must be accessible to them for a long period. ***Accessible*** means that the children are allowed to use the space that is set aside for privacy, not only that it exists. At least one planned private space must be accessible to children for a ***substantial portion of the day,*** that is, 1/3 of the total time the program is open for the children to attend. (See examples of calculating substantial portion of the day, pages 42–44.)

As in all indicators requiring substantial portion of the day, the observer must find out what other rooms children in this group use at other times, see whether there is planned private space accessible to the children, and find out how long it is accessible to them while they are in that room. All space that is set aside and accessible to the group being observed may be counted towards calculating substantial portion of the day.

Score this indicator "Yes" if a space for privacy is accessible for the required amount of time.

7.1 In a high quality program ***more than one space*** for privacy is required in the room where the children spend the major part of their day. Having more than one space set aside makes it easier for children to experience privacy when they want it. Having two or more spaces for private play cuts down on competition and permits children to engage in uninterrupted, calm play. Private spaces need to be clearly designated for one or two children to use. See the General Information section of this item for a further explanation of what constitutes a private space.

Score this indicator "Yes" if, during the observation, it is clear that there are at least two private spaces in the main classroom used by the group. Even if there is more than one computer, computer space can only count as one private space.

Continued on page 40.

Indicator

5.5.1 a–j Various activities can be offered in spaces set aside for privacy.

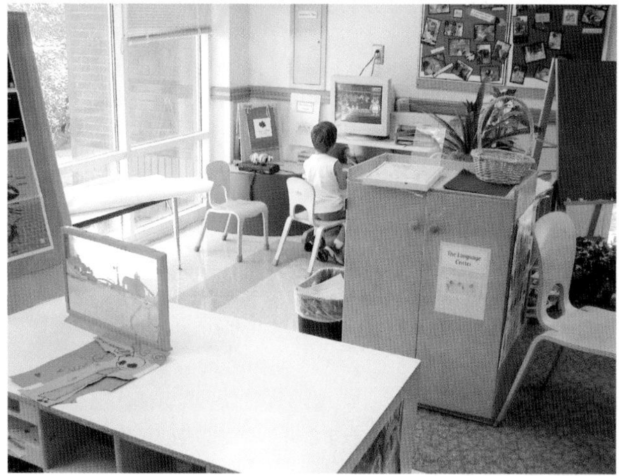

5.5.1 a

5.5.1 b

5.5.1 c

5.5.1a–c Computer use limited to one or two children at a time.

5.5.1 d Carpentry table limited to two children at a time. Note the label on wall limiting number of participants.

5.5.1 e Sand/water table for one or two.

5.5.1 f A light-table activity for one child.

Indicator

5.5.1 g Planned space for privacy outdoors that can be easily supervised.

5.5.1 h A small writing or drawing table for one.

5.5.1 i Just enough space for one or two children to draw.

5.5.1 j A listening center for one or two.

Continued from page 38.

7.2 This indicator requires that classroom staff ***set up activities*** in private spaces ***away from general group activities.*** This takes the planning process a step further by encouraging staff to pay attention to the private spaces in the room and make them more attractive by selecting different types of activities.

Examples of activities that can be set up in private spaces for one or two children to use include:

- A computer with programs that are appropriate for children and encourage active participation and creativity. If two computers are used side by side, use should be limited to one child per computer to count as private space. If a single compter is in an area, one or two children can use it together.
- A writing table, with one or two chairs, and dark pencils, thin felt pens, blank, unlined paper, and stencils with shapes, letters, numbers, and objects.
- A small cozy area for one or two children to use books, flannel board stories, or puppets.

- A drawing table, with one or two chairs, containing felt pens of different colors and thicknesses, crayons, blank, unlined paper of different colors, sizes, and shapes, some stapled into "books" with a few pages.
- A dramatic play table or small nook with appropriately sized dramatic play props, rotated so that they are seen as special by the children, such as a barn with animals, a gas station with vehicles, fire house with small emergency vehicles, play house with furniture and a play family.
- A small art table where an art material or activity previously offered as an activity for a larger group is repeated for one or two children to use independently, such as water colors and paper, wood glue sculptures, clay or salt-flour dough to make sculptures that will be fired or baked so that they are preserved, stringing buttons or decorative large beads on wire or shoelaces to make jewelry that can be taken home.

In cases where specialists come into the room specifically to work with one or two children who have special needs, credit is not given for this indicator because it is not done by the regular staff for all the children as part of the ongoing program. Only private space activities equally accessible to any child in the group are given credit in this indicator.

Score this indicator "Yes" if there is at least one activity set up in a private space accessible to children.

5 Space for privacy

Indicator

Calculating "Substantial Portion of the Day"

Example 1

This schedule is based on an observation period of 4.5 hours (from 8:00 AM – 12:30 PM) and information collected during the teacher interview about how unobserved time during the day is used and what is accessible to the children.

Time	Scheduled activity	Time to use space for privacy
6:30 –8:00	Breakfast in cafeteria and TV time for those who are finished with breakfast	
8:00 – 8:30	Children go to regular classrooms and play with table and rug toys (puzzles; legos; duplos with cars, people, and trucks; stringing beads and cards; pegboards)	
8:30 – 8:45	Prepare for breakfast/children wash hands	
8:45 – 9:15	Breakfast	
9:15 – 9:45	Circle (teacher reading time)	
9:45 – 10:45	Centers (housekeeping, art, sand and water, nature/science, writing table, blocks, music, computer and cozy book area)	**1 hour**
10:45 – 11:15	Outdoor play (gross motor activities only)	
11:15 – 12:15	Prepare for and eat lunch	
12:15 – 12:30	Story, put out cots, prepare for nap	
12:30 – 2:45	Nap	
2:45 – 3:00	Wake up from nap; bathroom	
3:00 – 3:25	Snack and story	
3:25 – 4:25	Centers (housekeeping, nature/science, writing table, computer, fine motor area and cozy book area)	**1 hour**
4:25 – 5:30	Outdoors or indoor gross motor	
5:30 – 6:30	Table and rug toys (puzzles; legos; duplos with cars, people, and trucks; stringing beads and cards; pegboards) Prepare for departure	

1. Figure the total number of hours that children are allowed to attend.

   (6:30AM to 6:30 PM = 12 hours)

2. Calculate 1/3 of the operating hours to determine "Substantial Portion of the Day."

   (12 hours ÷ 3 = 4 hours)

3. Add up all times that children have access to space for privacy.

   (see shaded times on schedule = 2 hours)

4. Compare the amount of time children have access to space for privacy to the time requirement for substantial portion of the day. If the amount of time children have access to space for privacy is the same, or greater, then score "Yes." If the amount of time is less than the time requirement for substantial portion of the day, then score "No." For example, the schedule above indicates:

   2 hours (opportunity to use space for privacy) **is less than 4 hours** (time requirement for substantial portion of day), and therefore the time requirement for substantial portion of the day is not met.

Indicator

Calculating "Substantial Portion of the Day"

Example 2

This schedule is based on an observation period of 4 hours (from 9AM – 1PM) and information collected during the teacher interview about how other time during the day is used and what is accessible to the children.

Time	Scheduled activity	Time to use space for privacy
9:00 – 9:30	Arrival/quiet centers open (cozy book area, computer, writing table, math, science and fine motor)	**30 minutes**
9:30 – 9:45	Snack	
9:45 – 10:00	Clean up snack/bathroom/wash hands	
10:00 – 11:00	Outside (gross motor activities only)	
11:00 – 11:45	Free choice of centers (fine motor, art, blocks, dramatic play, nature/science, math, sensory table, computer, writing table and cozy book area)	**45 minutes**
11:45 – 12:15	Large group activity (M,W,F is music/movement and T,Th is art activity)	
12:15 – 12:45	Prepare for and eat lunch	
12:45 – 1:00	Clean up/bathroom/prepare for quiet time	
1:00 – 1:45	Quiet time/quiet centers available (cozy book area, writing table, fine motor, math, and science)	**45 minutes**
1:45 – 2:00	Clean up all centers and prepare for departure	

1. Figure the total number of hours that children are allowed to attend.

   (9 AM to 2 PM = 5 hours)

2. Calculate 1/3 of the operating hours to determine "Substantial Portion of the Day."

   (5 hours ÷ 3 = 1 hour and 40 minutes)

3. Add up all times that children have access to space for privacy.

   (see shaded times on schedule = 2 hours)

4. Compare the amount of time children may have access to space for privacy to the time requirement for substantial portion of the day. If the amount of time children may have access to space for privacy is the same or greater, then score "Yes." If the amount of time is less than the time requirement for substantial portion of the day, then score "No." For example, the schedule below indicates:

   2 hours (opportunity to use space for privacy) **is greater than 1 hour and 40 minutes** (time requirement for substantial portion of day), and therefore the time requirement for substantial portion of the day is met.

Indicator

Calculating "Substantial Portion of the Day"

Example 3

This schedule is based on an observation period of 3.5 hours (from 9AM –12:30 PM) and information collected during the teacher interview about whether what was observed represents the typical daily practice.

Time	Scheduled activity	Time to use space for privacy
9:00 – 9:20	Arrival/group time to discuss activities for the day	
9:20 – 9:45	Whole group art activity	
9:45 – 10:00	Whole group reading time (teacher directed)	
10:00 – 10:45	Outside time (gross motor activities only)	
10:45 – 11:30	Free choice of centers (fine motor, art, blocks, dramatic play, nature/science, math, sensory table, computer, writing table and books)	**45 minutes**
11:30 – 11:45	Clean up/bathroom/prepare for lunch time	
11:45 – 12:15	Prepare for and eat lunch	
12:15 – 12:30	Clean up/bathroom/prepare for departure	

1. Figure the total number of hours that children are allowed to attend.

   (9:00 AM to 12:30 PM = 3 hours and 30 minutes)

2. Calculate 1/3 of the operating hours to determine "Substantial Portion of the Day."

   (3 hours and 30 minutes ÷ 3 = 1 hour and 10 minutes)

3. Add up all times that children have access to space for privacy.

   (see shaded times on schedule = 45 minutes)

4. Compare the amount of time children have access to space for privacy to the time requirement for substantial portion of the day. If the amount of time children have access to space for privacy is the same, or greater, then score "Yes." If the amount of time is less than the time requirement for substantial portion of the day, then score "No." For example, the schedule above indicates:

   45 minutes (opportunity to use space for privacy) **is less than 1 hour and 10 minutes** (time requirement for substantial portion of day), and therefore the time requirement for substantial portion of the day is not met.

6 Child-related display

General information about this item

The main purposes for displaying materials in a classroom are to extend the children's learning experiences and to nurture their pride in achievement. Materials that are displayed where children can easily see them can reinforce and recall past experiences and also stimulate interest in upcoming events. When children see their own work displayed they realize that their work is valued and respected by others.

Two-dimensional or flat work such as paintings, collages, photographs, charts, and posters can be displayed on bulletin boards, walls, doors, and on the backs and sides of the low, open shelves where accessible materials are stored. Three-dimensional objects that have height, width, and depth such as sculptures made of clay or play dough and constructions made by nailing or gluing wood, styrofoam and/or paper boxes together, may be displayed on the tops of shelves or hung from the ceiling.

There are many places in a classroom to display materials of interest to the children. This item considers only the display contained in the classroom where the children in the group spend the majority of the day. Although many programs also use the hallways for display, this does not count in scoring the item because the children are usually in the halls only to go from one place to another. They barely have time to see what is displayed there, much less to discuss and benefit from the experience.

It is always important for the display in a classroom to be meaningful to the children, so they can enjoy and learn from it. In some cases, fire prevention rules will limit the location and amount of display allowed in a classroom. For example, to slow the progress of a fire, no objects can be hanging from the ceiling, or only a percentage of the wall space can be used for display. Under these conditions, it is especially important that those items selected for display are carefully chosen to be meaningful to the children. A well placed and carefully selected display is likely to meet the requirements of this item, even if the display space is limited.

The display in the classroom needs to be changed frequently, at least monthly, in order to keep up with the topics of current interest and the vast amount of children's artwork created in a productive classroom. Parents become tuned into display that is changed frequently because their enthusiastic children point out their own work and talk about items relating to current interests. If the display is rarely changed it becomes the familiar, expected background that is taken for granted and is no longer noticed.

The content of the display is also considered in this item.

Indicator

Two-dimensional display might include:

- Art work done by the children, including painting, drawing, collage, finger paint, and printing with objects and stamps.
- Photographs of the children engaged in various classroom activities, of their families, of pets, and of trips the children have taken.
- Posters showing children and adults of various races, ethnic and cultural groups, ages, and differing levels of abilities.
- Charts, lists, and narratives written by the staff as they take down what children tell them during free play or circle time; for example, a list of each child's favorite breakfast which was discussed at circle time, the explanation several children gave about a block structure they had created (which also might contain a photo of the building, or a chart comparing the heights of the children in the group).
- Seasonal displays related to the changes in the weather or holidays that are celebrated during the various seasons, including those commonly celebrated in the United States as well as cultural holidays associated with various racial and ethnic groups.
- Photos, pictures or charts related to what is being studied at the time in various curriculum areas, such as pictures of sea creatures when the class is preparing to visit or has just returned from the aquarium.

Three-dimensional display might include:

- Sculptures done by the children in a material that is easy to mold with the hands and holds its shape, such as clay or play dough.
- Carpentry creations using wood, styrofoam, bottle caps, and other materials that have been nailed together.
- Object sculpture made by gluing pieces of wood, paper boxes, styrofoam, and other objects into a three-dimensional form (not to be confused with collage which is a two-dimensional medium).
- Other three-dimensional objects not made by the children, such as artifacts of another country (e.g., African musical instruments to look at when the class is studying Africa, Mexican sculptures or a large Mexican hat, Swiss cow bells).

What is displayed can provide information useful in scoring several other items as well, including Item 16, Encouraging children to communicate; Item 20, Art; Item 25, Nature/science; Item 26, Math/number; and Item 28, Promoting acceptance of diversity.

A closer look at each indicator

1.1 ***No materials displayed*** for children means that there are neither two- nor three-dimensional things displayed in the children's classroom for children to look at. Count only display in the classroom where children spend most of the day. Do not give credit for materials meant for staff or parents, such as the daily schedule for staff or a parent bulletin board. Score "Yes" only if there are no materials at all

Indicator

displayed for the children to look at. See the General Information section for examples of materials that might be displayed.

In some cases, there are no materials displayed, but staff put up something during the observation. If displaying materials for the children is obviously not a regular practice, do not count the item that has been put up during the observation. (See photo 6.1.1.)

1.2 Displayed materials are considered ***inappropriate for the predominant age group*** if over 50% of the materials are not meaningful for over 50% of the children in the group. For example, in a group of older 2's and young 3's, if all of the displayed materials consist of letter and number cards placed around the room, the alphabet posted up high near the ceiling, and one poster of a teddy bear, the displayed materials would be considered inappropriate because most of the children would not know what the number and letter symbols meant. Although the picture of the teddy bear was appropriate, it made up less than 50% of the display. However, 4- and 5-year-olds would find such materials meaningful because they often know something about letters and numbers. (See photos 6.1.2 a–c.)

6.1.1 This room looks barren because it has no materials displayed for children to look at and think about.

6.1.2 a

6.1.2 b

6.1.2 a–c The display in this room is considered inappropriate for younger preschoolers (2 ½ to 3 ½ years old) because it portrays concepts in a way that is not meaningful to these children (seasons, months of birthdays). However, this display is considered appropriate for older 3's, 4's, and 5's.

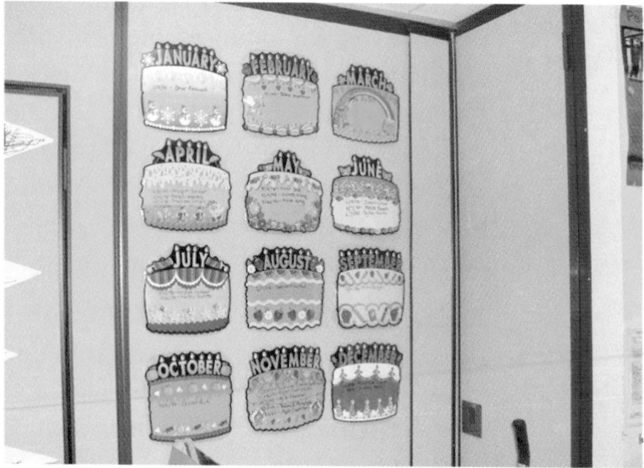

6.1.2 c

6 Child-related display

Indicator

Materials that show violence, give negative messages about any racial or cultural group, or are frightening to children are considered inappropriate for *all* preschool- or kindergarten-aged children.

Score 1.2 "Yes" only if more than 50% of the display is inappropriate for more than 50% of the group or if *any* of the materials show violence or prejudice.

3.1 ***Appropriate materials*** means that 75% of the display is meaningful to the children because it is age-appropriate and developmentally suitable, and none of the display is violent or frightening or gives negative messages about any racial or ethnic group. For examples of appropriate display see the General Information section for this item. Score 3.1 "Yes" if almost all materials are appropriate and none are violent or prejudicial.

3.2 In this indicator, ***some*** means that two or more pieces of work done by the children are displayed. The nature of the work does not matter as long as the displayed work is done by the children in the group. The children's work may include drawing, coloring or other art projects, or letter or number practice. The work may be two- or three-dimensional. The quality of creativity or individuality of the work is not assessed in this indicator, only the fact that a small amount of children's work is displayed in the classroom. Score 3.2 "Yes" if at least two pieces of children's work are displayed and can be easily seen by the children. (See photos 6.3.2 a–c.)

5.1 The purpose of this indicator is to judge whether the display in the room is currently relevant for this particular group of children. ***Much*** of the display means about 30% of the materials displayed. It is not important to count the objects since they may be of different sizes, but rather judgment should be based on the overall impression of how much of the display relates closely to *both* current activities and this particular group of children.

Relates closely to current activities means that a portion of the display obviously is related to some major theme or interest the group has been focusing on during the past month. For example, if the group is talking about the season of the year or preparing for an upcoming fieldtrip to the zoo, these topics should be clearly represented in the display. The intent here is for the staff to use the display as a teaching tool that changes as topics of interest or themes change. Artwork done by the children does not count for this indicator unless it is related to a current theme or topic being explored in other areas of the curriculum during the past month.

Relates closely to the children in the group means that the children can see representations in the display of themselves, such as things they have said or activities they have completed. Such representations may include photos of the children

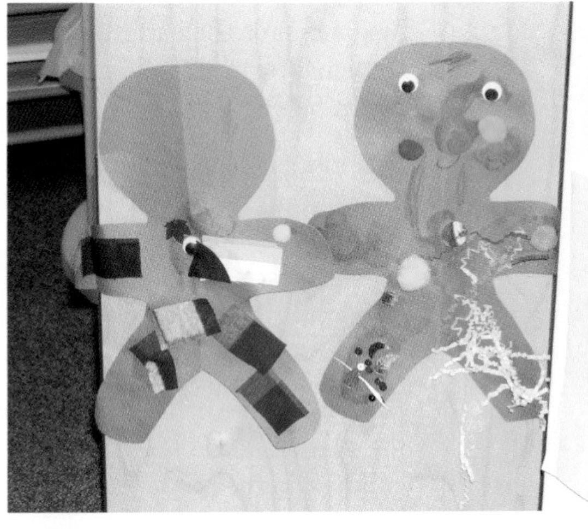

6.3.2 a

6.3.2 b

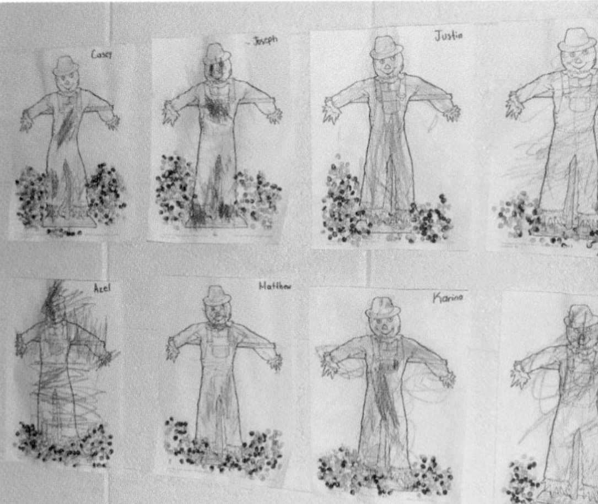

6.3.2 c

6.3.2 a–c Since children made collages using the pre-cut forms in photos a and b, and scribbled on the stencils of the scarecrows in photo c, we can give credit for some children's work displayed.

engaged in various activities, their families and pets, self-portraits recently drawn by them, a height chart with their names on it, stories dictated by the children, or charts resulting from a group discussion with input from the children.

It will be necessary to find out which themes or topics were focal points during the past month. This information may be available from a monthly planning form posted in the room. If such a form is not posted, ask the staff to share their planning form, if they have one, or else ask what topics of interest or themes they have focused on in the past month. Common themes include major holidays, seasons, families, community helpers, trips taken by the group, or major activities such as planting a garden. (See photos 6.5.1 a–j.)

Continued on page 51.

6.5.1 a–j Display related to current activities and the children in the group

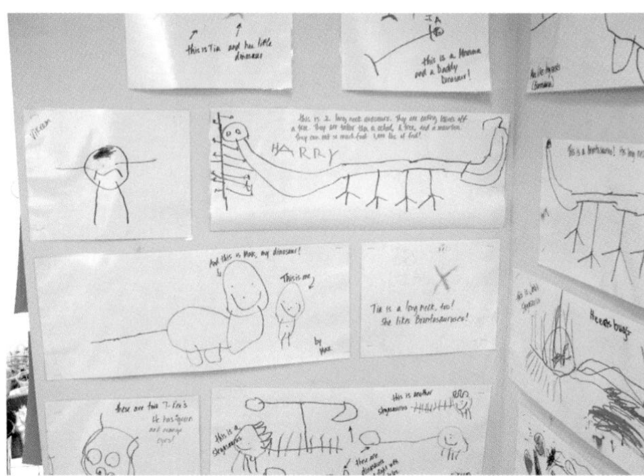

6.5.1 a This display of dinosaur drawings was done while the theme of the month was studying dinosaurs. As part of the theme, the group read factual books, visited a local museum, and played with the many realistic plastic dinosaurs in the block area. (This display is also a good example of Indicator 7.1.)

6.5.1 b In preparation for celebrating Halloween, this group took a fieldtrip to select some pumpkins to carve. Photos were taken that were later displayed in the classroom.

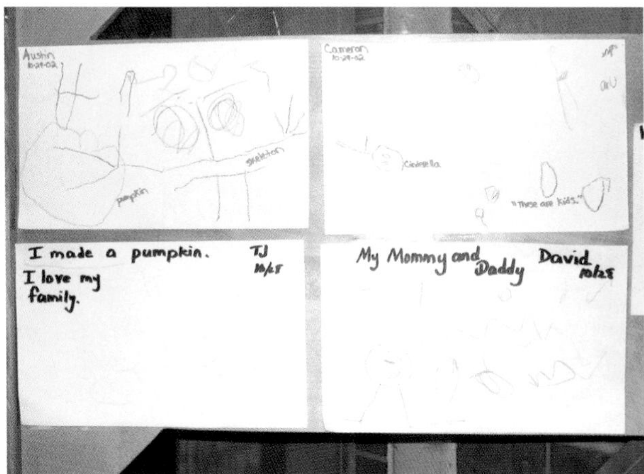

6.5.1 c

6.5.1 d

6.5.1 c–d As they were discussing Halloween, each child in this group was encouraged to draw a picture of something they experienced on Halloween evening. (These drawings are also good examples of Indicator 7.1.)

Indicator

6.5.1 e–g [below] This chart about favorite breakfast foods was part of a discussion of nutrition, and was displayed for the week to help children remember the discussion. It relates to both parts of 5.1, current activities and children in the group.

6.5.1 e

6.5.1 f

6.5.1 g

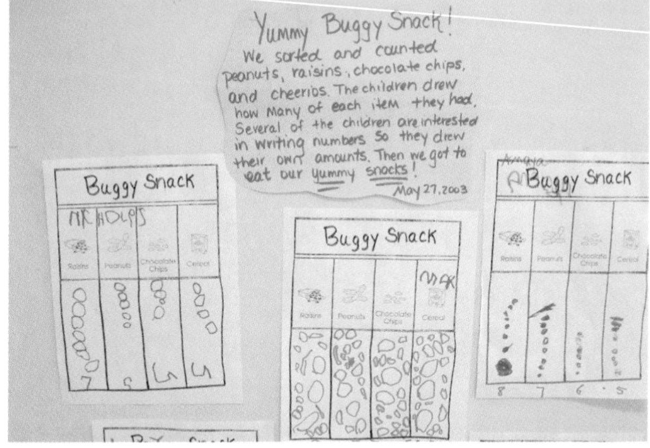

6.5.1 h This display shows an activity that relates to both nutrition and math.

6.5.1 i The display in the science area relates to the current activity, sprouting sunflower seeds. In addition to the poster showing a sunflower with its root system, many drawings made by the children about their seeds are displayed.

6.5.1 j In order to give credit for display relating closely to current activities, check to see whether the trip to the fire station occurred within the last month. If the children in the photos are those currently in the class, credit can be given for display being related to the children in the group even if the trip was taken several months ago.

Indicator

Continued from page 49.
In some cases, differing themes or topics are not used in a classroom because the same information is presented to children every day. For example, a classroom may emphasize learning the alphabet, numbers, shapes, and colors the whole year, and focus on no other topics. The program may display materials on these topics, which are rarely changed. In this case, the materials do not count to meet the requirement of the indicator because they do not relate to some major theme or interest the group has been focusing on during the past month. They relate to an unchanging topic instead.

Relating the display to current activities and to the particular children in the group ensures that the materials displayed will be of great interest because they will be current and personally relevant to the children. Score 5.1 "Yes" if at least 30% of the display in the classroom is closely related to current activities *and* the children.

5.2 ***Most*** of the display means that 50% or more of the display is work done by the children. Again the quality of the work is not being judged in this indicator. Any work done by the children, including projects that show little individuality, can count. However, if the children's work is hard to see because of where it is placed, credit cannot be given. (See photo 6.5.2.)

Sometimes observers find it difficult to decide whether 50% of the display is work done by the children, even if there is a great deal of children's work displayed. Especially in a room with a lot of display, including photos, numbers and letters, and science pictures, as well as many pictures and objects created by children, the decision may seem overwhelming. The observer does not need to actually count the materials to find out if half are by the children. Instead, the observer should rely on the overall impression that the display gives. If the split between children's work and the other items displayed is 50/50 or too close to tell, give credit for this indicator by scoring "Yes."

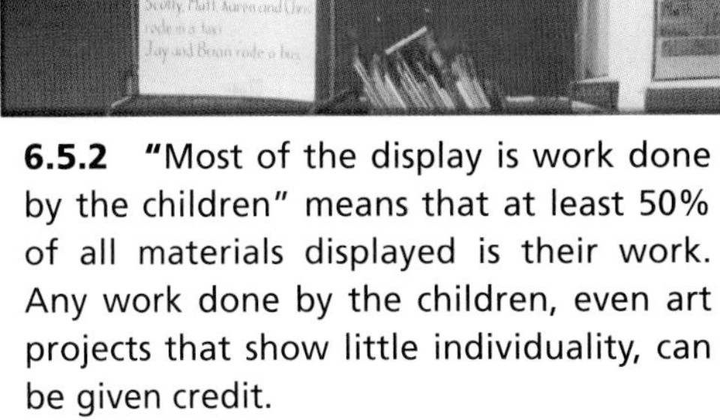

6.5.2 "Most of the display is work done by the children" means that at least 50% of all materials displayed is their work. Any work done by the children, even art projects that show little individuality, can be given credit.

5.3 ***Displayed on the child's eye level*** means at the level where the children can easily see the displayed materials. The height of the children will make a difference. All preschool/kindergarten children, even older 2's and 3's, will be able to see things displayed on the backs of low shelves or on the lower portion of the walls. However, older 4's and 5's may also be able to see things posted a little higher on the walls. Children cannot be expected to look up to the top of the wall near the ceiling to see displayed material. Display should be easily visible to children in order to be given credit. (See photos 6.5.3 a–d, next page.)

Many items means that most of the lower portion of the room is used for display of some sort. The display does not have to be of children's work; any appropriate display is counted. Both two- and three-dimensional materials can be counted. To score 5.3 "Yes," consider both the quantity and placement of displayed materials.

7.1 ***Individualized children's work*** means artwork that the children have carried out in their own way. To be considered individualized work, children have to have exercised choice, that is, they decided to create the work and were not told exactly what to do or shown a pattern to follow. However, a general subject may be sug-

Indicator

6.5.3 a

6.5.3 b

6.5.3 c

6.5.3 a–c These photos are displayed on the child's eye level, where it is easy for children to see them, and where they stimulate discussion.

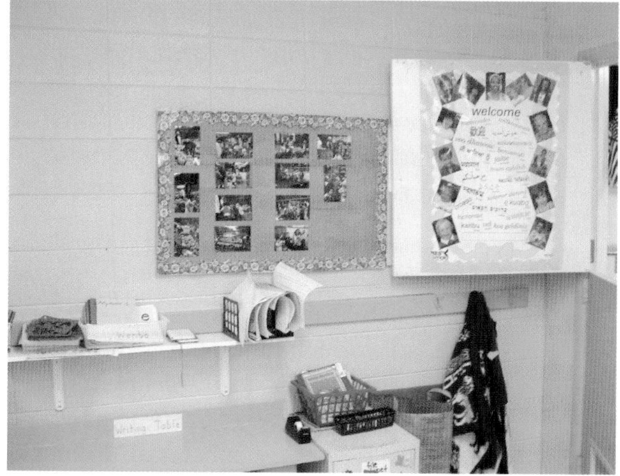

6.5.3 d These photos of the children are not displayed at the child's eye level. They are too small and displayed too high for the children to see them.

gested by staff, as long as each child can interpret it in his own way. Thus, if the subject is winter, if white, black, and blue paints are put out, and if each child can paint his own winter picture, credit can be given for individualized work.

Predominates means that *most* of the displayed children's artwork is varied in the medium used (e.g., drawing, painting, collage, clay) *and/or* subject matter (e.g., scribbling, faces, people, blotches of paint colors). Some media, such as printing and spatter painting, tend to produce work that looks very similar. As long as all the work in such media does not look exactly alike, credit can be given for individuality.

Also take into consideration that the work of older 2's and young 3's will generally tend to look more similar to one another than the work of 4's and 5's. Since older children have more control over the medium they are using and have more content to express, their work shows greater individual differences. Score 5.1 "Yes" if more than 50% of the children's displayed artwork is individualized. (See photos 6.7.1 a–f, next page.)

Continued on page 54.

Indicator

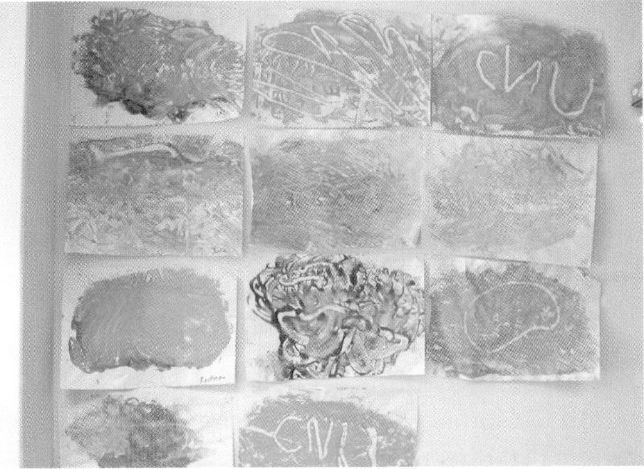

6.7.1 a Individualized children's work shows a lot of individual variation, even if many of the children use the same medium or interpret a common theme. These fingerpaintings were done by younger children, yet each one is unique.

6.7.1 b Here play dough was used to mold anything the children wanted to make with their hands, which resulted in different objects. When children use cookie cutters with play dough, the result does not show individual variation and cannot be given credit for individualized work.

6.7.1 c

6.7.1 d

6.7.1 e

6.7.1 c–e These works show different media as well as great individual variation in the way children represent their ideas about a theme.

6.7.1 f This sign limiting an area to two children, uses individualized children's work.

Indicator

Continued from page 52.

7.2 ***Three-dimensional artwork*** means work that has height, width, and depth. In contrast, two-dimensional work has only height and width and is flat like a painting or collage. Three-dimensional work is sculpture in form. Clay or play dough can be used in either a two-dimensional or three-dimensional way. When it is rolled out and forms are cut out with cookie cutters the result is a flat or two-dimensional form. When it is used as a sculptural material to build up and out with the hands, it is a three-dimensional experience.

Other three-dimensional activities commonly used are carpentry and wood scrap or paper box sculpture, that is, gluing wood scraps or paper boxes into a form that has height, width, and depth. However, gluing things to a flat surface, such as styrofoam "peanuts" or small pieces of wood to cardboard, is a two-dimensional medium.

Similarly, when pieces of paper are decorated and then stapled into a cylindrical shape, credit is not given for three-dimensional work, because the basic art experience is two-dimensional. See the General Information section for additional information about two- and three-dimensional media. (See photos 6.7.2 a–e.)

Give credit for 7.2 only if three-dimensional work is displayed.

Indicator

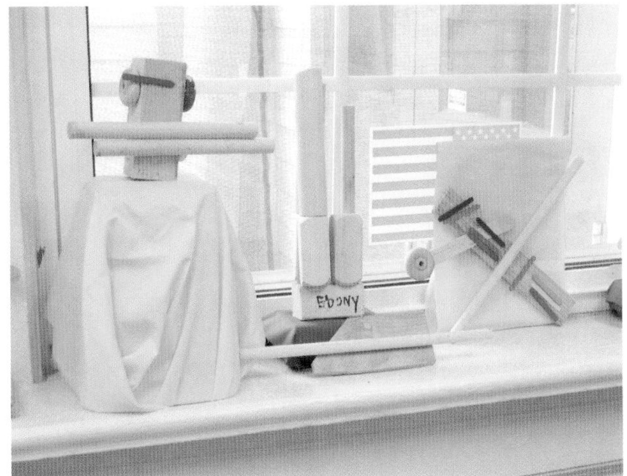

6.7.2 a

6.7.2 b

6.7.2 c

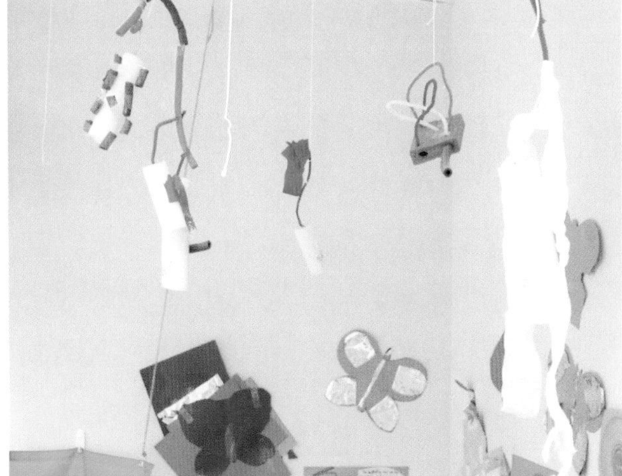

6.7.2 d

6.7.2 a–e Three-dimensional work, which has height, width, and depth, can be displayed on the tops of toy shelves, on display tables, or hung from the ceiling.

6.7.2 e

7 Space for gross motor play

General information about this item

The development of large muscle coordination is one of the major tasks for pre-school-aged children. Since children need to develop large muscle coordination through *active* movement, plenty of safe space must be provided that allows this. Both indoor and outdoor spaces are acceptable for gross motor play, but outdoor space usually allows more freedom of movement and provides the fresh air that is absent in indoor spaces.

In this item, the amount of space that can be used by the children is considered, although no specific amount is required (for example, square feet or meters per child). Base decisions about the amount of space on how well it can be used by the children for gross motor activity.

Because the majority of serious accidents in early childhood programs occur during gross motor play, this item considers the safety of the space in the requirements at the lower quality levels. Safety should be evaluated in terms of general hazards of the space, including the adequacy of fall zones around and between gross motor equipment.

7 A Outdoor spaces are used for gross motor activities.

Note that safety of the gross motor equipment, as opposed to safety of the space, is considered in Item 8, Gross motor equipment. In addition to being considered here, safety issues that are related to gross motor play space are also considered in Item 14, Safety practices.

At the higher levels of quality, the convenience and organization of the space are emphasized.

All spaces regularly used for gross motor activities should be considered in scoring this item. Outdoor space is defined as space that exposes children to fresh air during gross motor play. Indoor gross motor space is enclosed, as inside a building, even if windows are present. Obviously, there will be some spaces that are "in between" such as screened porches, semi-shelters, or covered patios. The observer must determine whether these are considered indoor or outdoor spaces, taking into account the amount of fresh air and exposure to the natural world that are provided. (See photos 7A–B.)

7 B Indoor spaces can also be used for gross motor activities.

To be considered in this item, the space must actually be used for gross motor play. For example, an outdoor porch or garden that is used for some play activities, but

Indicator

not for gross motor play, would not be counted. On the other hand, a block area used for dancing every afternoon would be evaluated as an indoor gross motor space.

Even if gross motor areas are not used during the observation, the spaces must be examined before the item is scored (e.g., if the weather is bad or no one is using the space). To supplement observed information, questions can be asked of staff to get more information about how the area is used, what types of activities are done in the space, and how the space is arranged. Another option for observing the outdoor space in use is to return to the program on another day, when the weather permits outdoor play.

A closer look at each indicator

1.1 ***Gross motor play*** requires a certain amount of large muscle (legs, arms, trunk) movement, even if the movement is somewhat restricted as in exercising or dancing, as compared to running. Thus, to count as gross motor space, such movement must be possible for a reasonable number of the children in the group. In other words, the space cannot be so small that children are unable to carry out gross motor activities or that only very few children can use the space at one time.

If *any* ***outdoor*** *or* ***indoor space*** is regularly used by the children (on a daily basis or almost daily) for gross motor play, score 1.1 "No."

1.2 The safety of all spaces regularly used for gross motor activities should be considered in scoring this indicator. A ***very dangerous*** space is one where serious safety hazards exist.

Although an original "Note for Clarification" for Indicator 3.2, printed in the ECERS-R, implies that safety of gross motor equipment is included in this item, safety of such equipment is covered in Item 8, Gross motor equipment. Only issues related to safety of the space (not the gross motor equipment) are considered in this item. Fall zones, with required cushioning surfaces, are considered part of the space (not equipment), and thus considered here.

Anything other than gross motor equipment that is in the space, such as fences, storage sheds, air conditioning units, dramatic play structures, benches, picnic tables, or water areas, must also be assessed for safety in this item.

Characteristics of "safe"

The Consumer Product Safety Commission (CPSC) provides guidelines for determining whether outdoor anchored equipment is safe for children in the publication, "Handbook for Public Playground Safety." The complete handbook is available at no cost when downloaded from the Internet website, http://www.cpsc.gov.

As part of the CPSC requirements, there are guidelines for safe fall zones, with requirements for adequate cushioning surfaces to minimize injury from falls. In addition, organization of areas on the playground, location issues, appropriate surfaces, and general safety suggestions are discussed. The major points covered in the Handbook are summarized in the Playground Information Sheet located at the end of this item.

7.1.2 a It is helpful to use a measuring device to determine if the cushioning under gross motor equipment meets the Consumer Product Safety Commission (CPSC) requirements.

Indicator

It should be noted that CPSC only provides fall zone guidelines for outdoor anchored equipment. However, in using the ECERS-R, similar standards should be applied in determining whether other gross motor equipment is safe for the children who use it. For example, a high unanchored indoor climber will require an appropriate fall zone with adequate cushioning surface, just as an outdoor anchored structure would, because children might be injured from falling off either one.

The requirements for verifying the resilience of fall zone cushioning surfaces not covered in the chart on the Playground Information Sheet (such as poured or installed foam or rubber surfaces) are as follows: the materials must meet the ASTM F1292 requirements for the material used under equipment. This is best verified with a written statement from the manufacturer.

Anything permitted by the staff to be used for stimulating gross motor activity must have an adequate fall zone if there is the potential for children to be injured from a fall. Height and velocity should be considered when determining whether a fall zone with cushioning surface is needed. Although the CPSC Guidelines apply only to anchored equipment, for purposes of scoring, similar standards should be applied to all surfaces onto which serious falls can occur.

Although falls from significant heights are often emphasized in determining the safety of a gross motor space, other issues should also be considered to determine safety. Everything in the space used by the children should be considered. Often there are structures or other types of equipment present that are considered hazards. For example, long bolts on fences are considered protrusions; exposed links or wooden points on top of fences can be catch points for clothing; spaces between stairs or between railings of stairs used by children might cause entrapment; or certain types of natural objects, such as plants, insects, water areas, or rocks might be considered safety hazards. The location and characteristics of the space and the hazards associated with accessing or using it must be considered in determining the safety of the gross motor space. For example, having to cross a busy street or being near traffic with inadequate barriers, might be safety issues.

To score 1.2, the observer must determine whether the space, indoors and/or outdoors, is very dangerous. ***Very dangerous*** means that there are either major safety hazards observed, or that there are many minor safety hazards of any type. All spaces used must be inspected—cushioning surfaces and fall zones must be measured to determine adequacy. The observer should bring a tape measure and something to dig or probe with (see photo 7.1.2 a, previous page), and the whole space accessible to children must be carefully examined.

Major safety hazards are those that are likely to cause serious injury requiring hospitalization or medical care, such as broken

7.1.2 b

7.1.2 c

7.1.2 d

7.1.2 b–d All spaces shown are unsafe due to inadequate cushioning and fall zones. Problems with equipment and safety issues would also be considered in several other items within the scale.

Indicator

7.1.2 e

7.1.2 f

7.1.2 e–f These are very dangerous areas for children to use because there is insufficient cushioning under the climbing equipment.

bones, major bleeding, drowning, or strangulation. (See examples in 7.1.2 b–f.) *Minor hazards* are those that are only likely to cause mild injury, such as small cuts, bumps and bruises, and splinters. (See examples in photos 7.1.2 g–h.)

Score 1.2 "Yes" if the gross motor space (all spaces used regularly for gross motor) is judged very dangerous—there are major safety hazards, many minor hazards, or a combination of both. The observer must make this judgment by weighing such factors as the severity of the hazard, the likelihood of its occurrence, and the amount of time children use the space or equipment that is associated with the hazard.

It is best to list all hazards observed (except those associated with gross motor equipment, which are considered in Item 8, Gross motor equipment) to make the scoring decision. If the list is very long or contains an obvious and very serious hazard (such as inadequate fall zones under high equipment or cars driving through the space while being used), then 1.2 would be true (score "Yes").

Do not score "Yes" if there are hazards that have little likelihood of actually causing serious injury, or if there are only a few minor hazards, such as tree roots, that do not seem to cause problems.

3.1 ***Some space*** means that indoor and/or outdoor space is used for gross motor play by the children in the group for at least 1 hour each day in a program operating 4 or more hours per day (give or take a few minutes). In programs operating less than 4 hours per day, at least ½ hour is required.

The hour does not need to be provided all at one time but can be made up of a combination of shorter periods.

7.1.2 g Plant stems and branches that are located in outdoor play areas may cause small cuts and scratches. These are considered minor safety hazards associated with mild injuries.

7.1.2 h Large, exposed tree roots are considered minor safety hazards.

Indicator

All children do not have to be able to use the space at the same time, but the space should be accessible to all children for at least an hour per day.

There is no specific amount of space required (in terms of square feet or meters). However, the space must accommodate the type of movement required of the gross motor skills being practiced by the children. In other words, it must be large enough to accommodate some running and other large muscle movements that preschool-aged children naturally want to do.

If the only space available is outdoors, and there are long periods (a week or more) in which the space cannot be used, due to bad weather, then credit cannot be given for 3.1, unless some space is used indoors during those times. Any indoor space that allows gross motor activity of any kind (for example, marching, dancing, balancing, or exercising) can be counted if it is used.

3.2 See Indicator 1.2 for a discussion on determining whether the gross motor space is dangerous or ***generally safe.***

The note indicated with a dagger † on page 15 in the ECERS-R text should read:

> "Although no gross motor area that challenges children can ever be completely safe, the intent of this indicator is that major causes of serious injury are minimized, such as injury from falls onto inadequate cushioning surfaces or entrapment, pinching of body parts, and protrusions from *non-gross motor* equipment that is in the space."

This clarification means that the safety of gross motor equipment is considered in Item 8, Gross motor equipment, while all other safety considerations associated with spaces used for gross motor are considered in this item.

A space can be considered generally safe even if it cannot be easily supervised. The ability to supervise space is not considered in this item, but is considered in Item 29, Supervision of gross motor activities.

To determine whether the space is ***generally safe,*** the observer must weigh such factors as the severity of any hazards present, the likelihood of accidents due to the hazards, and the frequency of use of the space that is associated with the hazard. Consider carefully the requirements concerning gross motor space listed on the ***Playground Information Sheet*** (on pages 62–63).

Score 3.2 "Yes" if the gross motor space (all spaces used regularly for gross motor) has no major safety hazards that are very likely to cause serious injury, and if there are no (or only a few) minor hazards.

It is best to list all hazards observed to make the scoring decision. If the list is very long or contains an obvious and very serious hazard (such as inadequate fall zones under high equipment or cars driving through the space while being used), then 3.2 would not be true (score "No").

5.1 Be sure to read the note for this indicator in the ECERS-R text (marked with the double dagger ‡ on page 15).

Adequate space outdoors requires that there is room for children to freely use gross motor skills, such as running, climbing, riding tricycles, and playing ball. They should be able to do this without being restricted by the size of the space or by crowded or cluttered conditions. Not all children in the group need to use the

Continued on page 64.

Playground Information to Use with the Environment Rating Scales

Based on information from the U.S. Consumer Product Safety Commission,* Handbook for Public Playground Safety, *Pub. No. 325. These guidelines are a basic overview of areas to review when scoring playground and safety items in the ECERS-R, ITERS-R, FDCRS, or SACERS. This list is not to be used as a comprehensive guide for playground assessment.

Catch Points and Protruding Hardware – There should be no dangerous pieces of hardware, such as protruding bolt ends and narrow gaps in metal connections or open "S" hooks at the top and bottom of swings. Exposed hardware can cut children, puncture skin, or catch clothing drawstrings, which could strangle a child. The top of fences less than 4 feet in height also should be checked for protrusions.

Entrapment – Children can get trapped and strangle in openings where they can fit their bodies but not their heads through the space. Therefore openings in guardrails, spaces between platforms, between ladder rungs, and uprights in protective barriers, should measure less than 3.5 inches or more than 9 inches. However, if the ground is the bottom edge of a space between 3.5 inches and 9 inches, it is not considered an entrapment hazard because the child will not be in danger of choking.

Pinch, Crush, Shearing, and Sharp Hazards – Equipment should not have sharp points or edges that could cut skin. Moving pieces of equipment, such as suspension bridges, track rides, merry-go-rounds, or seesaws, should not have accessible moving parts that might crush or pinch a child's finger or other body part.

Protective Barriers – A protective barrier is an enclosing device around an elevated platform that is intended to prevent both inadvertent falls from the platform and deliberate attempts to pass through the barrier. In other words, children should not be able to jump over it or move through it.

For preschoolers, full protective barriers are preferred because they provide more protection from falls. Protective barriers are required for platforms that are over 30 inches above the ground. The top surface of the barrier should be at least 29 inches above the platform. No child should be able to climb over, under or through the barrier. For equipment used *only* by school-aged children, including 5-year-olds, any platform more than 48 inches above the ground requires protective barriers. The top surface of the protective barrier must be at least 38 inches high.

Guardrails – A guardrail is an enclosing device around an elevated platform that is intended to prevent inadvertent falls from the platform. A child might be able to climb over, under or through the guardrail.

For preschoolers through 4 years of age, guardrails prevent falls from elevated platforms that are higher than 20 inches, and up to 30 inches, above the ground. For preschoolers through 4 years of age, the top surface of the guardrails should be at least 29 inches above the platform, and the lower edge should be no more than 23 inches above the platform. For equipment used *only* by school-aged children, including 5-year-olds, any platform more than 30 inches above the ground (but not over 48 inches above the ground) will need guardrails at least 38 inches above the platform, with the lower edge no more than 28 inches above the platform.

When mixed age groups of preschool- and school-aged children use the same equipment (e.g., 4- and 5-year-olds) the most stringent requirements are applied to ensure safety for all. For example, platforms used by the group will require protective barriers, rather than guardrails if they reach the height listed for preschoolers. Guardrails and barriers must be of the height required for school-aged children, which is higher than required for preschoolers.

Platforms that are layered on equipment, (e.g., one platform leading up to another in a step-like manner), so that it would be impossible for preschoolers to fall more than 20 inches from one level to another (or school-aged children to fall 30 inches to another platform) do not require barriers or guardrails if they would interfere with the intended use of the equipment (e.g., stepping up to the next level).

Tripping Hazards – There should be no exposed concrete footings, abrupt changes in surface elevations, tree roots, tree stumps, and rocks, which can trip children or adults.

Protective Surfacing – The surfaces under and around play equipment should be soft enough to cushion falls, which are the most frequent causes of injuries on playgrounds. For specifics on depth of material, see the chart below. When the surfacing in much used areas becomes displaced (e.g., under swings, slides) it should be raked back or replaced to maintain correct depth.

Fall Zones – Resilient surfacing shall extend beyond the external limits of stationary equipment for a minimum of 6 feet. Swings shall have resilient surfacing that extends 2 times the length of the pivot point to the surface below. The surfacing shall be to the front and rear of the swing. Tot swings shall have resilient surfacing that extends 2 times the length of the pivot point to the bottom of the swing seat, both in the front and rear of the swing. Tot swings are defined as swings with enclosed seats. Tire swings shall have resilient surfacing that extends a distance of 6 feet plus the measurement from the pivot point to the swing seat and 6 feet to the side of the support structure.

Equipment Spacing – Play structures should be spaced at least 12 feet apart to allow children space to circulate around or fall without striking another structure. Moving pieces of equipment should be located in an area away from other play structures so children have adequate room to pass from one play area to another without being struck by a moving swing or by another child exiting from a slide.

Critical Heights of Playground Equipment for Various Types and Depths of Resilient Surfaces

Based on Information from the U.S. CONSUMER PRODUCT SAFETY COMMISSION (CPSC Publication No. 325),* Handbook for Public Playground Safety. *When no requirement is provided for a specific height of equipment, we have used the requirement for the next higher height, so requirements are conservative, erring on the side of safety.

	Wood Chips	Double Shredded Bark	Uniform Wood Chips	Fine Sand	Coarse Sand	Fine Gravel
Equipment Height	**Uncompressed Depths of Materials In Fall Zone					
Five feet or less	6 inches	6 inches	6 inches	6 inches	6 inches	6 inches
Six feet	6 inches	6 inches	6 inches	12 inches	12 inches	6 inches
Seven feet	6 inches	9 inches	9 inches	12 inches	12 inches	9 inches
Eight feet	9 inches	9 inches	12 inches	12 inches	12 inches	12 inches
Nine Feet	9 inches	9 inches	12 inches	12 inches	N/A	12 inches
Ten Feet	9 inches	9 inches	12 inches	N/A	N/A	12 inches

For poured or installed foam or rubber surfaces, the materials must meet the ASTM F1292 requirements. Verify through a written statement from the manufacturer.

Indicator

Continued from page 61.

space at one time, but all should have the opportunity to freely use the space for at least 1 hour a day in a program operating more than 4 hours per day. The 1 hour a day does not have to be provided all at one time. One half hour is required in programs operating 4 hours or less. (See Indicator 3.1.)

In addition to such outdoor space, ***some indoor space*** that can be used for gross motor activity must be available for use. Examples are a special gymnasium, a gross motor room, or an all-purpose room. Classroom or hallway space can count as "some indoor space" only if the space is reasonably large and open (through moving furniture, if necessary). In some areas, where the climate is never extreme, a covered outdoor area that can be used year-round can also count as some indoor space.

Both indoor and outdoor spaces do not have to be used on the same day, but both must be available for use when needed. For example, in bad weather, the outdoor space might not be used, while the indoor space would be.

7.5.2 a Outdoor space is not easily accessible when children must reach it by using long steep stairs.

5.2 ***Space*** means all spaces, indoors and outdoors, which are regularly used for gross motor play.

Space is ***easily accessible*** means that children can get to the space(s) used for gross motor play without undue effort or complications. The space is reasonably close to the classroom used by the children, and there are few, if any, barriers, so that the time and challenges required to access the space are minimized. If it is difficult to access the space in any way, score 5.2 "No."

This indicator applies to accessing the gross motor area, but not to specific spaces within the gross motor area.

Examples of conditions that make gross motor space difficult to access include children having to:

- Use a steep or long staircase or an elevator
- Walk long distances, either indoors or outdoors
- Go through other classrooms or rooms that are currently in use

If the gross motor space is easily accessible for most children enrolled in the group, but not all children, for example, due to barriers that prevent access to children with disabilities enrolled in the group, credit cannot be given for this indicator. (See photos 7.5.2 a–c.)

7.5.2 b Classrooms that open directly into the playground are easily accessible.

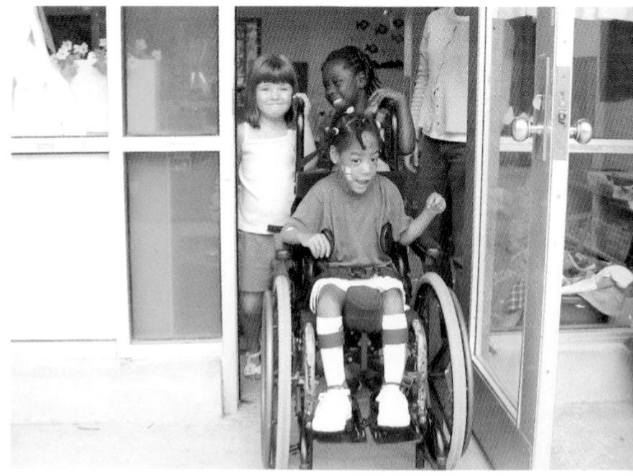

7.5.2 c Even though this classroom opens directly onto the playground, the round door knob makes the gross motor space inaccessible to the child with a physical disability.

5.3 The intent of this indicator is to allow gross motor play to occur safely in the gross motor space, with minimal disruption from the various activities that go on in the space or from the traffic patterns within the space. The observer must evaluate how equipment and materials are placed, what areas are used for the different types of activities that may be happening in the space,

Indicator

the traffic patterns, and the interrelationships among all of these. In doing this, all areas accessible to the children in the space and all types of activities that occur (even the non-gross motor activities) must be considered.

Organized so that different types of activities do not interfere with one another means that each activity can take place without undue disruption from other activities or from people moving through the activity spaces. It is required that play space is set up with areas for different types of play, and that the pathways used most frequently by those on the playground do not go through activities. For example:

7.5.3 The trike path is located in a separate area so that it does not interfere with other outdoor activities, such as the outdoor music area.

- Ball play and activities with other portable gross motor equipment are separated from stationary equipment.
- Tricycles and other wheel toys are not used in the major pathways between activities or between the building and the play area. (See photo 7.5.3.)
- The more quiet activities that occur in the gross motor space (such as art, books, blocks, or sand/water) are separated from very active play.
- Gardens are protected from active play.
- Pathways to different areas are separated from swings or other moving equipment.
- Portable materials and equipment are kept separate from the areas used for climbing equipment (especially fall zones).
- Gross motor play indoors, such as a bean bag toss, are separated from other non-gross motor activities in the room.

To score this indicator, observe to see that the various activities in the gross motor space do not disrupt each other. For example, be sure that children are not in great danger of tripping over toys as they run across the space, that children coming down a slide will not run into anything, that children climbing will not fall onto anything placed in the fall zone, or that wheel toys do not usually go through areas with other types of play and "run people down."

Of course, even when gross motor spaces are well organized, children will still want to cross borders. They will want to move tricycles away from the wheel toy area and bring portable equipment onto climbers. To give credit for this indicator, staff should supervise to minimize interference due to this crossing of borders, but perfection (in terms of keeping things where they are supposed to be) is not expected.

7.1 The term ***surface*** generally means the covering on the ground where children can carry out their gross motor activities, such as the soil, sand, grass, gravel, black-top, or cement.

In order to give credit for a ***variety of surfaces,*** determine whether the surfaces in the outdoor space(s) enable children to successfully participate in different types of active play. For example, wheel toys, and bouncing balls require a hard surface while rolling, balancing on a balance beam, or playing catch are fine on a soft surface. Running, jumping rope, and some ball games work well on either type.

7 Space for gross motor play

Indicator

7.7.2 a

7.7.2 b

7.7.2 a–b Trees and awnings are used for protection from sun and/or rain.

Children gain information about how their world works as they try out various activities on different surfaces. They also have better chances for successful practice of gross motor skills when the surface matches the activity.

Each different surface must be large enough to permit a type of play without much interruption from other activities. At least one hard and one soft play surface must be accessible daily outdoors.

Surfaces in the fall zones of equipment are not counted to meet the requirements of this indicator, because no other activity can occur in a fall zone, restricting the chances for various types of play on the accessible surfaces. However, if a soft surface extends beyond the fall zone of equipment, and is large enough to permit another type of gross motor play, then that area can be counted as the soft surface.

7.2 The elements are the natural conditions that cause discomfort or problems in the outdoor space. Examples of elements are:

- The sun in hot weather
- The wind in cold, dusty, or sandy areas
- Rain, snow, or other precipitation
- Water, causing pooled water or erosion

Protection from the elements for outdoor areas relieves discomfort or problems caused by the elements. For example, protection from the sun comes from things that provide shade, such as trees, buildings, partial roofs, or awnings. (See photos 7.7.2 a–b.) Solid fences or rows of trees provide windbreaks. Open areas allow sun to warm spaces on cold days. Covered areas protect from precipitation. Drainage helps to prevent large puddles or standing water.

To give credit for 7.2, the most necessary protection for the location and season must be provided. For example, on very hot summer days in a warm location, shade must be provided. If the gross motor space is located in a place with frequent rain, drainage must be provided, so children will be able to use the play area during non-rainy days.

Only one example of such protection must be observed to give credit for 7.2. But the protection observed must match the most prevalent adverse conditions caused by the elements in the local area. For example, the provision of shade would not be

Indicator

7.7.3 a

7.7.3 b

7.7.3 a–b Water fountains and hose outlets count as convenient features in outdoor areas.

acceptable as a protection from the elements in a place where it was rarely sunny, or drainage would not be credited in a place where rain was very unusual, but hot sun was commonplace.

7.3 ***Convenient features*** are provisions in the gross motor space that make the area easier to use by children and staff. In some cases, the feature may encourage children to be more independent in caring for themselves. In others, it might make the care and supervision of the children easier for the staff. Examples of such features are provided in the indicator, but other examples might include:

- Special place where a first aid kit, tissues, and sanitizing solution, are stored
- Water sources for drinking, play, or handwashing (See photos 7.7.3 a–b.)
- Portable telephone or other communication device for staff to use in emergencies
- Special place to put coats or other clothing

To give credit for 7.3, at least two such features must be observed. If necessary, ask questions of staff to gather information to supplement observed information.

8 Gross motor equipment

General information about this item

During the preschool and kindergarten years, children continue to develop their large muscle coordination through active play. There are many types of equipment that are used to encourage the development of large muscle skill and coordination. Some pieces of equipment are more appropriate for this age group than others, in terms of the challenge provided and the safety features.

This item covers the appropriateness of gross motor equipment for the children who use it, to ensure that children have safe opportunities to fully practice necessary skills. Since gross motor challenge and safety are inter-related, the condition and appropriateness of equipment used for gross motor play is considered at the lower levels of quality in this item. Because individual children have differing needs and interests, requirements for variation in challenge are included at the higher quality levels, in addition to ensuring that plenty of equipment is present for children to use.

Gross motor equipment includes *anything* provided for or regularly permitted by the staff to be used for stimulating gross motor activity. This includes manufactured, custom-made, and/or natural objects used for climbing, sliding, balancing, or other gross motor activity. It does not include objects meant to be used for other purposes, such as benches to sit on, shade trees, or shelves children are not supposed to climb on, unless children are encouraged to use these for active physical play. (See photos 8 A–C.)

There are two types of gross motor equipment to be considered in scoring this item—***stationary*** and ***portable***.

Stationary equipment is that which has been installed on a playground or is anchored. However, this also includes non-anchored equipment that

8 A Outdoor items such as benches and the trellis are not considered gross motor equipment, unless staff allow children to use them as such.

8 B This table is not considered gross motor equipment because children do not use it for climbing or other gross motor play.

8 C Even though this water play provision is located on the playground, it is not considered gross motor equipment.

8 Gross motor equipment

Indicator

8 D

8 E

8 D–E Both of these climbing structures are considered stationary equipment because they are anchored into the ground.

8 F Even though this climber is not anchored in the ground it is considered stationary equipment because children cannot move the structure.

8 G Trikes, which are meant to be moved, are considered portable equipment.

can be moved by adults, but that is too heavy for children to move as part of play. (See photos 8 D–F.)

Portable equipment is that which is meant to be moved or arranged by children as part of their gross motor play. (See photos 8 G–H.) This is not to be confused with other types of play materials, such as dramatic play props, sand or water toys, or outdoor blocks, because the primary use of such playthings is not for gross motor activities.

Examples of stationary and portable equipment are found in the "Notes for Clarification" in the ECERS-R, on page 16.

In scoring this item, decisions should be based on observation of how both ***indoor and outdoor*** gross

8 H Rocking boats and tumbling mats are considered portable gross motor equipment.

Indicator

motor equipment functions with regard to the children who are using it. Especially with unusual, natural, or innovative play opportunities, which may vary greatly, it is essential to observe carefully to see how children use the provisions and if they encounter problems.

A closer look at each indicator

1.1 Indicator 1.1 is scored "Yes" if:

- There is ***very little gross motor equipment*** that children can choose from during gross motor times. Even though there is enough time when children are allowed to use gross motor equipment (either stationary or portable), there are few choices. The result might be that children are bored, unchallenged, have to wait for long periods before getting a chance, or fight over what may be available.
- There is adequate, or even much, gross motor equipment present in the program, but there are strict limitations on the extent to which it is ***used for play.*** The chance to use the equipment is very limited. For example, if gross motor equipment is located outdoors, and children rarely go outdoors, 1.1 would be true, unless gross motor equipment was provided indoors, and children were allowed to use it.

Very little will depend on the number of children present, with fewer children requiring less gross motor equipment.

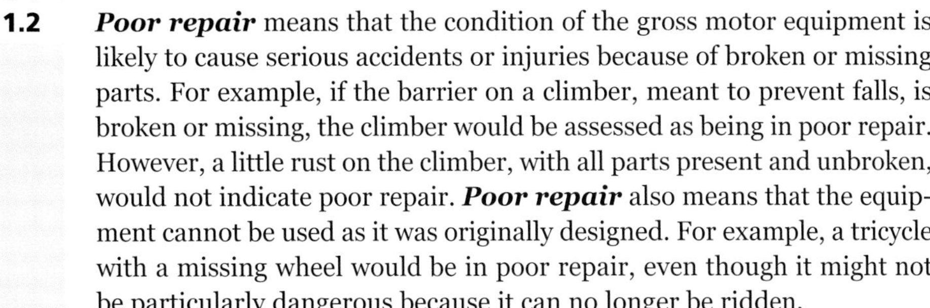

1.2 ***Poor repair*** means that the condition of the gross motor equipment is likely to cause serious accidents or injuries because of broken or missing parts. For example, if the barrier on a climber, meant to prevent falls, is broken or missing, the climber would be assessed as being in poor repair. However, a little rust on the climber, with all parts present and unbroken, would not indicate poor repair. ***Poor repair*** also means that the equipment cannot be used as it was originally designed. For example, a tricycle with a missing wheel would be in poor repair, even though it might not be particularly dangerous because it can no longer be ridden.

Generally in poor repair means that the *majority* of gross motor equipment (either portable or stationary) is broken or missing parts. There may be some equipment that is not broken or missing parts, but for the most part, few pieces of equipment are in good shape.

To score the indicator, *all* gross motor equipment that is used by children must be evaluated for condition, including both indoor and outdoor, both portable and stationary equipment.

If the majority of gross motor equipment is in such poor repair that accidents or injuries could occur, score 1.2 "Yes." If there is some equipment in poor repair, but not the majority of equipment for use by children, score 1.2 "No."

1.3 ***Age-appropriate*** gross motor equipment challenges children to develop and practice large muscle skills safely. Equipment that is too easy for children to use, too difficult, or not safe, is ***not*** age-appropriate. (See photos 8.1.3 a–c.) Both indoor and outdoor gross motor equipment should be

8.1.3 a Children can easily get their fingers caught between the slats. Equipment that is unsafe is considered to be inappropriate.

8.1.3 b This piece of climbing equipment is not appropriate for preschoolers because it is too high.

8.1.3 c Open "S" hooks on swings are a safety concern because children's clothing can be easily caught on the hooks.

Indicator

8.1.3 d

8.1.3 e

8.1.3 d–e Consider the ages and abilities of the children to determine whether the gross motor equipment is age-appropriate. A younger child is frustrated or endangered when using this equipment because it is too large. However, it may be age-appropriate for children who are older.

considered when determining how to score this indicator. Both stationary and portable equipment, if present, should also be considered.

Too easy or too difficult

Equipment that is "too easy" for children to use does not challenge them. Children tend to become bored with too-easy equipment or ignore it or misuse it. For example, a no-pedal tricycle that would challenge a toddler would not be of much interest to a preschool-aged child. The size would make it difficult to use properly, and the challenge would be limited. Similarly, a climber that is 6 to 12 inches high, with a simple ramp to reach the platform, would not provide interesting challenge for preschool-aged children, while it would probably appeal to crawling babies or toddlers.

Equipment that is "too difficult" frustrates children and encourages accidents. (See photos 8.1.3 d–e.) Equipment, such as tall firefighter poles or hanging rings, is inappropriate because it requires upper body strength that young preschoolers have not developed yet. Swings, that most preschoolers cannot use properly without help (they usually need to be pushed because they can not yet pump), cause accidents if children fall or are hit by them. Portable equipment meant for older children, such as bicycles (two wheelers) or high narrow balance beams are also too difficult for most preschoolers.

Characteristics of "safe"

The Consumer Product Safety Commission (CPSC) provides guidelines for determining whether outdoor anchored equipment is safe for children in the publication, "Handbook for Public Playground Safety." The complete handbook is available at no cost when downloaded from the internet website: http://www.cpsc.gov.

The major points covered in the Handbook are summarized in the "Playground Information Sheet" which is included in Item 7, Space for gross motor play. (See pages 62–63)

It should be noted that CPSC only provides guidelines for outdoor anchored equipment. Anchored equipment means stationary equipment that is fixed in the ground

Indicator

so that it cannot be moved. However, similar standards should be applied in determining whether other gross motor equipment with similar characteristics is safe for the children who use it. For example, a high indoor climber will require protective barriers, guardrails to prevent falls, just as an outdoor anchored structure would, even though the indoor climber is not anchored and could be moved by the staff.

Portable equipment should also be evaluated for safety hazards. It should not be broken, have missing parts, or present serious threats to preschool-aged children. For example, plastic bats should be used in place of wooden or metal bats, balls should be lighter in weight than balls used by older children, jump ropes should not be so flexible that they can be knotted or tangled and strangle a preschooler.

Note that safety of the gross motor space, as opposed to safety of the equipment, is considered in Item 7, Space for gross motor play. In addition to being considered here, safety issues that are related to gross motor equipment are also considered in Item 14, Safety practices.

Score 1.3 "Yes" if ***most*** of the gross motor equipment children use (including indoors and outdoors, stationary and portable), is ***not appropriate*** for the ages and abilities of the children in the group being observed. In determining whether ***most*** is true, consider the frequency of use, the other more appropriate options that are available for use simultaneously, and the seriousness of any safety hazards associated with use of the equipment.

In addition, consider non-traditional provisions that children are encouraged to use as gross motor equipment. For example if children *are encouraged or allowed* by staff to climb on benches or trees and jump from them, consider the appropriateness of that type of provision.

3.1 ***Gross motor equipment*** is defined in the General Information section for this item. To give credit for this indicator, the equipment can be either indoors or outdoors and portable or stationary.

In addition, the equipment must be ***accessible***—children must be able to reach and use the equipment.

Accessibility is required for at least ***1 hour per day*** (give or take a few minutes) in a program of 4 hours or more. This amount of time can include access to gross motor equipment indoors, outdoors, or a combination of both. Every child does not have to have access at the same time, but all children should have access for 1 hour during each day. As stated in the scale, for programs of less than 4 hours, at least ½ hour of access is required.

The time for accessibility is required even if the weather does not permit outdoor play. In the case when there is inclement weather, and children are unable to go outside, then some gross motor equipment should be provided indoors. For example, beanbags for tossing into boxes, parachutes for lifting, mats for tumbling, or soft foam balls for passing games.

Some means that all children can have access to equipment, during the gross motor time. For example, credit would not be given if the only gross motor equipment options were two tricycles and four balls when the group had 12 children who were supposed to have access during the gross motor time.

Often, gross motor equipment includes a climber or other stationary equipment meant to be used by several children at one time. To give credit when this is the *only* option, there should be no crowding or long waits for access.

Indicator

3.2 ***Good repair*** means that the condition of the gross motor equipment is not likely to cause serious accidents or injuries because of broken or missing parts. In addition, the children can use the equipment as it was originally designed to be used.

Generally means that the vast majority of equipment (indoors and outdoors, stationary and portable) is in reasonable condition so it is safe and usable. To evaluate whether ***generally*** is true, consider the number of children who use it, and the frequency of use. For example, if a major piece of equipment that is often used by children is not in good repair, but several other smaller or less popular pieces are in good repair, it is likely that credit for ***generally*** would not be given. However, if problems are minor and do not create a serious safety hazard, then give credit for this indicator. For example, if a ball is deflated or there is a little rust on a climber, but no other problems are observed, do not count off for these small things.

3.3 ***Appropriate for the age and ability of children*** is discussed in Indicator 1.3, on page 71.

In a mixed-aged group, appropriate equipment must be available for the different abilities represented. In a same-age group, there should also be some range in the challenge presented by the equipment, but less is required. When determining whether the equipment is appropriate, consider especially the stationary equipment, such as climbers, since they are permanent installations and usually accessible. Since equipment is often used by several age groups, consider the appropriateness for the age and ability level of the group currently being observed.

Most means approximately 75% or more of the stationary equipment is ***appropriate for the age and ability of the children*** in the group being observed. It is not required for the observer to count pieces of equipment, however, to figure a percentage that is appropriate. Instead, all equipment should be considered in terms of appropriateness, and the observer should determine whether the vast majority meets the children's needs for challenge safely.

5.1 ***Enough*** in this indicator is in contrast to "some" in 3.1. In 3.1 "some" means that each child can use equipment without having to wait with *no other* gross motor option. ***Enough,*** however, means that children do not have to wait long periods of time to use the equipment they *choose* to use. In other words, there are enough pieces of popular equipment so children do not have to compete or wait, and there are enough interesting options so that no one thing is overwhelmingly popular. For example, there are enough tricycles or other wheel toys so children do not feel competitive pressure when wanting to ride. There are enough balls so children wanting to play alone do not have to share. (See photo 8.5.1 a, next page.) The climbing structure is large enough to accommodate the number of children wishing to use it, or there are several climbing structures. (See photo 8.5.1 b, next page.)

When observing to see if this indicator is true, determine whether competition over equipment is caused by a lack of popular pieces of equipment or whether competition is really being caused by social issues between children. For example, if two children are fighting over using a tricycle, and there are similar tricycles accessible for use, give credit for ***enough***. However, if two children are competing over a tricycle, and there are no other tricycles accessible that provide the same level of challenge, and this sort of problem occurs several times during the observation, no credit should be given for 5.1.

Consider both portable and stationary equipment when determining whether there is enough equipment.

Indicator

8.5.1 a There are enough balls provided so that children do not need to argue.

8.5.1 b Children are crowded and have to wait because this is the only piece of gross motor equipment available.

5.2 ***Equipment stimulates skills*** requires that the gross motor equipment encourages children to use their large muscles is certain ways. The nature of the equipment causes this large muscle use. For example, steps on a climber invite a child to practice climbing. A tricycle encourages the child to practice pedaling and steering, and to coordinate the two.

The intent of this indicator is for the equipment to stimulate a variety of skills, rather than a limited set. A limited set of skills is encouraged when there are only a few types of equipment for children to use. For example, if a slide and some balls are the only gross motor equipment, the primary skills to be stimulated would be climbing and sliding, throwing, kicking, and catching. However, if there is a more complex climber, with a slide and several ways to climb up, plus balls of various sizes, with a basketball hoop, then more variety is provided. Generally one piece of equipment will not provide the required variety, but in the case of a very complex climber, with many skill options, the indicator might be true.

Note that there is an expectation that the skills being encouraged would be developmentally challenging for the children in the group being observed. For example, if older preschoolers use equipment that is designed for toddlers, it is unlikely that credit would be given for this indicator. Thus, when observing preschoolers, the observer would look for equipment more challenging than very low climbers, toddler push toys, or no-pedal riding toys.

To meet the requirement for a ***variety of skills***, there should be seven to nine different developmentally appropriate skills that are obviously encouraged *by the equipment children can use*. These skills should be *in addition* to the running, jumping, hopping, or other gross motor actions that a flat surface with no additional equipment allows.

Other examples of skills encouraged by equipment, besides those listed in the 5.2 example, might include pulling/pushing, pulling up by arms, swinging, jumping, hopping, using a jump rope, using a hula hoop, tossing, catching, throwing, or kicking balls.

To score, observe to see how many skills the equipment encourages and list them. Consider both portable and stationary equipment.

8 Gross motor equipment

Indicator

5.3 Score "NA" if there are no children in the group with diagnosed disabilities that require adaptations to equipment or special gross motor equipment.

The definition of ***adaptations or special equipment*** is provided in the original item in the ECERS-R. Note that the adaptation may be provided in the form of adult help. For example, staff help by holding a child's hand while she climbs up the stairs to the slide.

To score, observe to ensure that all children have some appropriate gross motor challenge. If there is a child with special needs that requires special help in gross motor activities, pay close attention to see if there are options that make use of the skills the child can practice. Even in cases where a child has very few gross motor skills, active physical play should not be ignored, for example, by keeping the child inside while others go out, or by leaving the child with nothing to do in a stroller or wheel chair while others participate in active physical play.

Score 5.3 "Yes" when all children, including those with special needs, can participate in active physical play to the extent possible. Extra equipment, adaptations, or help from staff should be provided to allow a child to participate as fully as possible, even though some children will not be able to participate in the same way as their typically developing peers.

8.7.1 A stationary climber and portable hula-hoops are among the gross motor options during this play time.

7.1 ***Stationary equipment and portable equipment*** are defined in the ECERS-R item and above, in the General Information section of this item.

To give credit for ***both*** types of ***equipment used***, each type must be *accessible daily* to the children during at least one active playtime. (See photo 8.7.1.) If one or the other type of equipment is not used during the observation, ask staff whether such equipment is ever used, and if so, how often and for how long. To give credit, the active play time(s) when each type of equipment is accessible must total at least 1 hour a day in a program of 4 or more hours per day, or ½ an hour in programs of less than 4 hours.

7.2. Indicator 5.2 requires that a variety of skills are encouraged by the equipment children can use for gross motor activity. This indicator requires that the variety provided by the gross motor equipment meets the individual needs of the children in the group. This means that there are both easier and more challenging options for the children to choose from. (See photo 8.7.2.)

8.7.2 Different kinds of riding toys ensure that differing needs of all children in a group will be met. Wheel toys with and without pedals are included. Some encourage carrying an extra passenger, which requires more strength.

There are examples of such options listed in the ECERS-R indicator for this item. Other examples might include basketball hoops of varying heights, lightweight baseball bats of different sizes, balance beams of varying widths or heights, or various ways of climbing onto a stationary play structure, such as stairs, a stationary ladder, a swinging ladder, or cargo net.

To score 7.2, consider the ages of the children in the group being observed and what challenges each child may experience to determine whether equipment stimulates skills on different levels.

Personal Care Routines

9 Greeting/departing

General information about this item

This item has a social/emotional rationale, but also is based in safety. From the social/emotional point of view, greeting of children helps them feel welcome in the classroom and sets the tone for the whole day. It is often difficult for children to separate from people they love. Pleasant greetings from staff remind them that they are also valued in their early childhood program. In addition, staff can help children with the transition from home to school by giving them interesting play options upon arrival.

Greeting of parents helps to build the relationship of trust that allows them to leave their children in the care of others, makes them feel at ease so they can linger to see what happens in the classroom. Greeting also provides the time needed for parents and staff to share required information about the child.

Similarly, pleasant, organized departures help the children move smoothly from school to home. Things are not rushed, frantic searches for important possessions are minimized, and everyone gets the message that they will be happy to see one another the next day.

From the safety point of view, greeting and departing helps all adults, both staff and parents, to formally realize that responsibility for the child is officially transferred. Through greeting, staff register in their minds that each child is present. At departure, staff know who picked up a child, and when the child left.

In this item, we evaluate the extent to which staff use greeting and departure times to meet the requirements for both the social-emotional and the safety components for children and adults.

Observation of greeting and departure of each child in the class is not required to score the item. Scores can be based on greetings and/or departures observed and information generalized to come to a scoring decision. In some situations only one or two greetings will be observed; use this small sample to score this item.

If some greetings are observed, but not departures, base the score on what is observed, and ask questions to collect information about how departures are handled. Do not consider answers to questions that are not supported by what was observed. For example, if it is observed that greeting procedures are chaotic, or staff seem detached, it is unlikely that departure procedures will differ substantially, even if the staff report that they are.

9 Greeting/departing

Indicator

A closer look at each indicator

1.1 For this indicator, ***greeting*** requires that the children entering the classroom upon arrival at the center, or when entering a new classroom when they have been in another, will be acknowledged in some way—in other words, welcomed to the classroom. The requirement for a greeting is meant to help children make the change from home to the center, from the care of the parent (or other responsible adult) to classroom staff, so they feel more comfortable about coming into the classroom. Being greeted helps children to feel valued by staff, and also assures that staff know the child has entered their area of responsibility.

Children who are upset about leaving their parents are likely to feel less anxiety from separation if their arrival is handled with a greeting. Children are also more likely to enjoy coming to school if the staff greet them in some way.

Greetings can vary in intensity and content. The quality required of the greeting for this item becomes more demanding as the quality level increases. At the lower quality levels, it is only required that children entering the classroom are acknowledged by the classroom staff in some way that is either positive or neutral, but *not* negative. For example, staff might greet children using non-verbal communication, such as making eye contact and nodding hello without talking. Or staff might use words as a greeting, for example by saying "Hi" or "Good morning." At the lower levels of quality it is not necessary to do more than to acknowledge the arrival in some way that is not negative.

Negative messages that are given to the children—acknowledgements used by staff that make children feel unwelcome in the class, are not considered "greetings." For example, the following are not counted as greetings:

- Staff member says coldly, "I see you finally showed up."
- Staff member frowns at the child and looks displeased that he or she has arrived.
- Staff member is rude to child.

To determine if greeting is neglected, it is best to keep track of arrivals, noting specifics. See Chart 1 for a sample of a tracking system.

Indicator 1.1 is true (scored "Yes") when children are usually (75% of the time) *not* acknowledged by staff, either verbally or non-verbally, either positively or neutrally, upon entering the classroom, or very soon after their arrival (within 1–2 minutes).

Chart 1

Child Arrived	Child greeted/ other interactions
1	No, missed child entering room
2	Yes, teacher waves to child
3	No, teacher talked to parent but not child
4	No, never saw child
5	Teacher reprimands child for running into room; no greeting

Indicator

This chart shows that at least 75% of the time children are not greeted. In this case, 1.1 would be scored "Yes."

1.2 Departure is the time when children change from the care of the classroom staff back to that of their parent or other responsible caregiver. Most often children will be going home, but departure may also be followed by such activities as shopping with the parent, going out to eat, or visits to the doctor. Departure usually happens close to the time a center closes at the end of the day, but some departures are at irregular times, and sometimes the child returns to the classroom at a later time that day.

In programs such as Head Start, some children go home by bus. Providing communication with the driver ensures a well organized departure; for example, staff make sure that messages are given to the driver as needed, verify with the driver that all children are safely on the bus, or help children gather things from their cubbies before getting onto the bus.

In centers where children go to an afternoon program (extended-day, wrap-around program) instead of being picked up by a parent or guardian, staff should help children to gather belongings and ensure that supervision is transferred from one provider to the next.

It is important for parents and children to have a familiar routine regarding departure from the center or classroom. If departure is well organized, children and parents have an easier time making the change from center to home. For example, there will be less time spent in searching for and gathering up the child's belongings or putting play materials away. In addition, staff and parents are assured that the transfer of responsibility for the child has been handled carefully, and children do not become "lost." Parents, children, and staff are usually tired out by the time departure comes. An organized departure eliminates confusion at this stressful time.

Score 1.2 "Yes" if there is evidence that departure is ***not well organized,*** such as:

- During the observation, a parent enters the classroom, picks up the child, and leaves without being noticed or acknowledged by staff.
- There is no obvious place for parents to find their children's belongings.
- There is no routine to ensure the safe exchange of responsibility for the child (e.g., sign-out list indicating who picked up the child and when, or another system).
- Parents have difficulties finding where their children are, and no one can easily tell them.
- Inadequate supervision is provided at pick-up time, so things are chaotic.
- There is no communication between bus driver and staff.

1.3 It is important to have parents ***bring their children into the classroom*** for several reasons. First, parents are considered to be the primary monitors of what happens to their children in early childhood programs. If they do not experience the classroom on a regular basis, they will not be adequately informed to make judgements about whether the program is meeting their children's needs. Parents should be able to go into the classroom to see what their child is able to experience during the day in terms of materials, display, space, staff, or friends. Parents should have

Indicator

the opportunity to make sure they approve of everything that their children have access to while they are in the program.

Second, the safety of the child is best ensured when the parent turns over responsibility for the child directly to the child's teachers. Possibilities for the child becoming "lost" are minimized when parents bring the child directly into the classroom.

Third, parents can learn from and profit by seeing what happens in the classroom, and hearing what staff have to say, while staff can learn from the information and suggestions offered by parents.

Fourth, when parents do not come into the classroom, they have less to share with their children about what the child has been doing while in care. Shared experiences between child and parent are minimized. In addition, the child never gets the message that the parent knows about the classroom and thinks it is OK.

And finally, when parents are not allowed to enter the classroom, the natural interactions that can occur between parent and staff are restricted to communications by phone, notes, formal conferences, or other less naturally occurring methods. Parents might be less aware of important information such as field trips, particular problems, or new children and staff. If a teacher must relay this information, there is no guarantee that the information gets to the parent. With the responsibility of many children, information can easily get lost or forgotten along the way.

In some programs such as Head Start or public school pre-kindergarten some children are picked up at home by bus. However, parents are still allowed the option to bring their child into the classroom, as for example, when a child has missed the bus or arrives late because of a morning doctor's appointment. If the program provides bus transportation for some or all of the children, ask questions about whether the center has a policy prohibiting parents from bringing or picking up their children.

Score 1.1 "Yes" if parents are generally *not* allowed to bring their children into the classroom, for example, if they must drop them at the entrance to the building with no option of entering the room with the child.

3.1 A ***warm*** greeting acknowledges the child's arrival, and must be positive rather than negative or neutral. There are many different ways that a child can be warmly greeted, either verbally ("Hello." "Hi there." "How are you?" "So nice to see you." "I see you brought Teddy with you this morning."), non-verbally (a hug, handshake, or being picked up), or a combination of both. The child's name may be used in the warm greeting, but it is not required at this level of quality, as long as the greeting is positive. The most important thing is that a staff member recognizes the child's arrival in the classroom and does not reject or ignore the child. The children should know that the staff member realizes they are there and is happy to see them.

Sometimes a group of children is being supervised by one person who has already greeted them, and then a new staff member joins the group to either take over or share in responsibility for the children. In this case, the new staff member must greet the children in some way, but not necessarily individually. It is sufficient for the new person to greet the group as a whole.

To determine whether ***most*** of the children are greeted warmly, as is required in this indicator, it helps to keep track of each child as he or she enters the room and to note whether each is warmly greeted or not. See Chart 2 for a sample of a tracking system.

Indicator

Chart 2

Child arrived	Child greeted/ other interactions
1	No
2	Yes, hug
3	Yes, said hi
4	Yes, child's name
5	Yes, smiles, child's name
6	Yes, child's name
	Assistant arrived and greeted the group

Most requires that at least 75% of the children are greeted warmly, and any new staff member greets the children as well. In this example, all but one of the children observed entering the class were warmly greeted, and the assistant greeted the group upon arrival. Since at least 75% represents ***most***, credit can be given for the indicator.

3.2 A ***well organized departure*** requires the following:

- The safe transfer of child to parent (or other authorized person) must be ensured. This means that there is a system working that ensures both parents and staff know who has picked up each child, every day. Often there is a sign-out system in place, with a list of the people who are authorized by the parents to pick up their child. (See photo 9.3.2 a.)
- Staff can help parents immediately locate their children if needed.
- Children are adequately supervised until they leave the classroom or center.
- The child's personal belongings are collected together in an individual space, so things do not usually have to be found at the last moment. (See photo 9.3.2 b.)

9.3.2 a Parents sign out children as a regular part of departure.

9.3.2 b Throughout the day, children's things are placed in their cubbies and ready to go at departure.

9 Greeting/departing

Indicator

3.3 This indicator requires that parents are not prevented from bringing their children into the classroom. They must be able to come into the room with their child, if they wish, and feel free to move around the room. (See photo 9.3.3.) Parents can be prevented from coming into the classroom in varied ways. If there is a policy or a drop-off procedure that prevents parents from entering the classroom, then this indicator is not true (score "No"). In addition, if staff are impolite or forbidding to the extent that it makes it extremely difficult for most parents to enter the classroom, also score "No."

9.3.3 Parents can come into the room with their children and feel free to visit.

The indicator does *not* require that all parents bring their children into the classroom, but that they are allowed to do so any time they wish. There can be nothing preventing this practice. In some programs, all children gather in a "community" room before their regular classroom teacher arrives. If parents bring their children into a community room before their children's classrooms are open, the staff in the community room should greet them and their children. Parents should still have access to the classroom normally used by their child. If the regularly used classroom is locked and parents are unable to enter, then this indicator should be scored "No."

The importance of allowing parents to enter the classroom is described in Indicator 1.3 of this item.

5.1 ***Greeted individually*** means that, in addition to acknowledging the child's arrival in a positive way, the greeting must be personalized, or directed to the specific child in some way. (See photo 9.5.1.) To give credit for the indicator (score "Yes"), look for evidence such as that listed below, but remember that there are other ways to provide individual greetings as well:

- Use of child's name
- Child greeted in his/ her primary language
- Child greeted with eye contact, smile, and/ or physical contact such as a hug or pat on the head
- Child greeted and asked something personal, such as about their previous evening, family members, or pets
- Child told something about what they will be doing that day

9.5.1 Staff take responsibility for greeting *all* children.

Sometimes a group of children is being supervised by one person who has already greeted them, and then a new staff member joins the group either to take over or to share in responsibility for the children. In this case, the new staff member must greet the children in some way, but not necessarily individually. It is sufficient for the new person to greet the group as a whole.

To give credit for this indicator, every child should be warmly greeted upon first arrival into the classroom, and no lapses or long delays in greeting of a child can be observed. It helps to keep track of each child as he or she enters the room and to note whether *each* was individually greeted or not. Entering the room can occur

Indicator

at any time of the day. For example, if a child enters the room just for naptime or as the first step to making the transition to a new classroom, the child should be greeted personally upon entry.

Use of the child's name in the greeting is preferred, but not required, as long as the greeting is personalized in some way. Use the same tracking system shown in Charts 1 and 2, but add notes on how each greeting is individualized. See Chart 3 for a sample; notice that every child is ***greeted individually.***

Chart 3

Child arrived	Child greeted/ other interactions
1	Yes ("Hi" with name)
2	Yes ("¡Hola!," name in Spanish)
3	Yes ("[Name], we missed you yesterday.")
4	Yes ("Hey, how was your weekend?")
	Teacher arrived at 9AM, greeted group and some individuals
5	Yes (Look at and talk about toy child brought in)
6	Yes ("Hello there!" with a hug)

In Chart 3, credit would be given for the indicator (score "Yes"). If even one child were not greeted in a personalized way, the score would be "No."

5.2 A ***pleasant departure*** improves the relationship between parents and staff, just as a pleasant greeting does. It encourages parents to feel comfortable leaving their children during the day, and children get that message, easing any worries about leaving their parents.

A ***pleasant departure*** requires that there is a familiar routine for parents, so that they can pick up their child easily. The time should allow for either a quick departure or a more relaxed one, depending on what the parents and children want. Parents should have a choice of being able to linger if they wish, and children can finish up what they are doing. If a parent is running late, the staff should be ready to help smooth the exit from the classroom. Any disagreements between parents and staff should be handled in a professional and fair way. Arguments should be avoided at departure time. If further discussion is needed, a telephone call or conference should be arranged.

5.3 To meet this indicator, it is necessary for staff to go beyond acknowledging a parent's presence, by greeting the parent warmly as well as the child. (See photo 9.5.3.) To give credit, each parent does not have to be ***greeted warmly*** during the observation, but it must be obvious that, in general (approximately 75% of the time), parents are treated in this way. Some neutral greetings are acceptable, but there can be no negative interactions.

9.5.3 Staff help parents feel welcome and comfortable in the classroom.

Staff members may represent different personality types, with some being more social and enthusiastic, while others are more

9 Greeting/departing

Indicator

9.7.1 a When parents leave, children sometimes become upset.

9.7.1 b Extra attention is needed at this time to help children recover.

reserved or calm. Despite these differences, staff must make the parents feel at ease while they are in the room. Parents should not be afraid to look around, ask questions, or share information about their child.

Not all staff members need to take part in personally greeting parents as long as one staff member takes responsibility for greetings.

As indicated in the "Notes for Clarification" in the ECERS-R (note †, page 17), "NA" is permitted if children are not brought into the program by their parents. In such cases, parent communication should be rated in Item 38, Provisions for parents.

9.7.1 c Getting children involved in activities helps with the transitions between home and school.

7.1 Children need to get settled when they arrive in the classroom. Some can do this easily, while it is more difficult for others. (See photos 9.7.1 a–c.) If children are not encouraged to get out materials, participate in an activity, or play with their peers, they are more likely to become upset at drop-off times. This is especially true at the beginning of the school year, when a child is new to the class, or after the child has missed some days in the program due to vacation or illness.

To give credit (score "Yes") for this indicator, it must be observed that children do become involved and do not wander, show distress, or sit with nothing to do. They might become involved either with, or without, interaction with staff.

Children can be ***helped to become involved*** by actions the staff take. First, staff should provide interesting activities for children to do. This means that there are materials accessible for children to choose, or that there are special activities going on. Staff have arranged for these activities to be available for the children when they arrive. If there are no problems with children becoming involved because the children are engaged in classroom activities easily, score the indicator "Yes."

Second, staff should be able to work directly with the children who are having more trouble getting involved. They might ask parents to help with this if it works well

Indicator

for the child. For example, sometimes it helps if a story is read, or an adult participates in play until the child becomes comfortable and engages in an activity. A staff member might also help a reluctant child become involved by designating the child as her "helper" in whatever she is doing (getting ready for snack, feeding the class pet, taking attendance, or setting up a center for teacher-directed activities).

Whatever help is given, the indicator requires that the staff pay attention to uninvolved children, work with them in a positive, very personal way, and help them through the change from home to the center. Staff might leave a reluctant child alone for a short period to see if this helps, but they should return and gently encourage the child to progress towards involvement in classroom activity.

Helping a child to become involved should never include forced or negative treatment. For example, if all children are forced to sit quietly and watch TV, and some do not want to, this would *not* count as helping children to become involved, except for those who enjoyed the TV activity. If negative attempts to get a child involved are observed, no credit should be given for the indicator (score "No").

7.2 ***Busily involved*** means that children are participating in activities they appear to enjoy—not waiting with "nothing" to do until they are picked up. For example, children sitting at a table waiting to be picked up in a classroom where all materials have been put away, would not meet the requirements of the indicator; nor would children watching TV with no other activities available in case they became bored.

If a child has to wait at the end of the day with nothing to do, discipline problems are more likely to occur. Children are more likely to be bored, to have conflicts with one another, or do things that are not permitted in the classroom, setting the stage for negative relationships between adults and children.

There are a variety of ways in which children can be kept ***busily involved*** until they are picked up. Look for evidence of the following:

- Children play outdoors until they depart.
- Free play is provided in all areas of the classroom or in a few areas that are interesting to the children.
- Group times are offered with stories or music/movement for interested children.
- Some children clean up and/or help staff get ready for the next day while others choose activities.

7.3 It is important that parents and staff have contact so that they can both share information about the child. Being able to talk with the staff, in person, ensures that parents get a chance to hear how their children are doing while in the program. Receiving this information firsthand assures parents that they are getting accurate news about their child's behavior, mood, health, safety, interactions, and learning experiences. (See photo 9.7.3.)

9.7.3 Staff share information with parents during greeting and departing times.

Equally important, parents can help the staff know and understand the children to better meet their needs. Staff need to know about parents' preferences, how they feel about things, and the important events that might be going on in the child's life at home.

9 Greeting/departing

Indicator

The expectation for this indicator is that staff are available to talk with parents both during greeting and departure so that during this time staff and parents ***share information***.

Staff are the adults who are responsible for the care of the children when they arrive and for departure. In many cases, greeting and departure are handled by the regular classroom teacher, but it could include other adults. Some programs have a "community" room, where children from several classrooms gather together in the mornings or late afternoon when the attendance numbers are low. Therefore, in this situation the ***staff*** may be other adults who are not the child's regular classroom teachers, but the expectations are the same.

As indicated in the "Notes for Clarification" in the ECERS-R, "NA" is permitted if children are not brought into the program by their parents. Rate the communication between parents and staff under Item 38, Provisions for parents if this is the case.

10 Meals/snacks

General information about this item

In preschool care and education programs, we have an opportunity to help children develop healthful food habits that will benefit them through their lifetime. Thus, nutritious foods should be offered to children throughout the day to ensure that they are getting the foods they need for healthful growth and development. Without the energy that nutritious meals/snacks give the children, they are not able to get the most out of their learning opportunities. In addition, when offered a variety of healthful foods, children become used to eating foods that might not be offered in their homes, and that they therefore would not choose on their own.

Eating times are also social times in our society. Providing pleasant meals and snacks for children, where they can enjoy the company of friends, helps children to learn the social skills they need to get along well with others. In addition, during meals and snacks, children can develop self-help skills such as setting the table, serving themselves, clearing their place, and handwashing before and after eating.

This item must be observed to score and the observer should be present for one or more meals/snacks.

A closer look at each indicator

1.1 For this indicator, the appropriateness of the ***meal/snack schedule*** is judged by observing when children are actually served meals and snacks. The written schedule posted in the classroom is not to be used as evidence to judge whether meals/snacks are served at the correct times, unless the schedule is consistent with what has been observed.

A ***meal/snack schedule is inappropriate*** (score "Yes") if children are fed less often than is required by the U.S. Department of Agriculture (USDA) Child and Adult Care Food Program or national standards adopted by other nations. These standards are to be used whether or not the program is participating in the USDA Child and Adult Care Food Program (or alternative in another country). According to the U.S. standards (which represent the minimum basic requirements), children should be given nutritious food (meals and/or snacks) often, i.e., every 2 to 3 hours, unless they are sleeping. This means that programs of up to 4 hours in length are required to provide one meal or a snack; of 4–6 hours require one meal; of 6–12 hours require one meal and two snacks or two meals and one snack; of more than 12 hours require two meals and two snacks. Any supplementary foods served in addition to the required meals/snacks do not have to meet the required food group components.

An ***inappropriate schedule*** also means that children are not offered food when they need them. For example, if children are fed too early, they might not be hungry

Indicator

enough to eat all they need for healthful growth. If snack and lunch are too close together, the same thing might happen. If meals/snacks are too late, the children will have to wait too long and may be too tired and cranky to eat.

Young children have different appetites and food interests, so flexibility in the schedule is important. One child might be going through a growth spurt and will require more calories, while another might be going through a slower growth period and be less interested in meals and snacks. A more active child will need to eat more to make up for all of the calories he/she has expended. If there is no flexibility in the meal/snack schedule, and one or more children show obvious signs of distress (such as hunger or fatigue) because of this, then the indicator should be scored "Yes."

This does not mean that children need to be fed every time they say they are hungry or request food. (They should always have access to water or be given water on request, however.) Children can usually wait for the next meal or snack if the wait is not too long, and staff need to ensure that when meals and snacks are served, the children will be interested in eating. When judging the meal/snack schedule, observers should watch for signs that children are *so* hungry that they are not able to become involved in interesting activities, but rather whine or cry until they are fed. In this case, 1.1 would be scored "Yes."

1.2 The USDA Meal Guidelines for ages 1–12 should be inserted into the front or back cover of the ECERS-R so observers can easily reference it during an observation. These guidelines will allow the observer to determine whether or not a program's meals/snacks are nutritionally adequate for the children.

A copy of these guidelines can be found in on page 91.

If the proper components required by the Guidelines are *not* served at observed meals/snacks, score Indicator 1.2 "Yes."

Personal dietary preferences of the observer (e.g., whole grain vs. white bread, fresh vs. canned vegetables, high vs. low sugar or fat content, etc.) are not to be used in determining the quality of the foods served.

The program is not required to *supply* the food for the meals or snacks, but they are required to make sure food is offered to the children. Often parents supply food for their own children or take turns providing snacks. However, in scoring the indicator, the observer must make sure that whatever food is served, it must meet the USDA guidelines for nutritional adequacy. Staff are responsible for ensuring that children's nutritional needs are met, even if the foods parents have provided must be supplemented by the program.

Although the major judgment about this indicator is based on observation of the foods/beverages served at meals and snacks, menus for the classroom should also be examined to ensure that the observed meals/snacks are similar in nutritional adequacy to others served.

1.3 Many illnesses, such as diarrhea or other gastrointestinal diseases, are spread in group care and education settings. These illnesses can be reduced substantially by consistent use of basic sanitary procedures before, during, and after meals/snacks.

To score this indicator, *careful* observation of the complete meal/snack procedure is required, including preparation, eating, and clean-up. During an observation,

Indicator

Meal Guidelines – Ages 1-12

Source: Child and Adult Care Food Program, USDA Food and Nutrition Service ***Updated 9/25/00***
www.nal.usda.gov/childcare/Cacfp/index.html

BREAKFAST

Food Components	Ages 1-2	Ages 3-5	Ages 6-12[1]
1 serving milk fluid milk……	½ cup……	¾ cup……	1 cup
1 serving fruit/vegetable juice[2], fruit and/or vegetable….	¼ cup……	½ cup……	½ cup
1 serving grains/bread[3]			
bread or……	½ slice……	½ slice……	1 slice
Cornbread, biscuit, roll or muffin, or……	½ serving……	½ serving……	1 serving
Cold dry cereal or……	¼ cup……	1/3 cup……	¾ cup
Hot cooked cereal or……	¼ cup……	¼ cup……	½ cup
Pasta, noodles or grains……	¼ cup……	¼ cup……	½ cup

LUNCH OR SUPPER

Food Components	Ages 1-2	Ages 3-5	Ages 6-12[1]
1 serving milk fluid milk……	½ cup……	¾ cup……	1 cup
2 servings fruit/vegetable juice[2], fruit and/or vegetable…	¼ cup……	½ cup……	¾ cup
1 serving grains/bread[3]			
bread or……	½ slice……	½ slice……	1 slice
Cornbread, biscuit, roll or muffin, or……	½ serving……	½ serving……	1 serving
Cold dry cereal or……	¼ cup……	1/3 cup……	¾ cup
Hot cooked cereal or……	¼ cup……	¼ cup……	½ cup
Pasta, noodles or grains……	¼ cup……	¼ cup……	½ cup
1 serving meat/meat alternative			
meat, poultry or fish[4], or……	1 oz……	1½ oz……	2 oz.
alternate protein product or……	1 oz……	1½ oz……	2 oz.
cheese or……	1 oz……	1½ oz……	2 oz.
egg or……	½……	¾……	1
cooked dry beans or peas, or……	¼ cup……	3/8 cup……	½ cup
nuts and/or seeds[5], or……	½ oz……	¾ oz……	1 oz.
Peanut or other nut or seed butters, or……	2 tablespoons…	3 tablespoons…	4 tablespoons
Yogurt[6] ……	4 oz……	6 oz……	8 oz.

SNACK: *Choose 2 of the 4 components*

Food Components	Ages 1-2	Ages 3-5	Ages 6-12[1]
1 serving milk fluid milk……	½ cup……	½ cup……	1 cup
1 serving fruit/vegetable juice[2], fruit and/or vegetable…	½ cup……	½ cup……	¾ cup
1 serving grains/bread[3]			
bread or……	½ slice……	½ slice……	1 slice
Cornbread, biscuit, roll or muffin, or……	½ serving……	½ serving……	1 serving
cold dry cereal or……	¼ cup……	1/3 cup……	¾ cup
hot cooked cereal or……	¼ cup……	¼ cup……	½ cup
pasta, noodles or grains……	¼ cup……	¼ cup……	½ cup
1 serving meat/meat alternative			
meat, poultry or fish[4], or……	½ oz……	½ oz……	1 oz.
alternate protein product……	½ oz……	½ oz……	1 oz.
cheese or……	½ oz……	½ oz……	1 oz.
egg or……	½……	½……	½
cooked dry beans or peas, or……	1/8 cup……	1/8 cup……	¼ cup
nuts and/or seeds, or……	½ oz……	½ oz……	1 oz.
peanut or other nut or seed butters, or……	1 tablespoon….	1 tablespoon….	2 tablespoons
yogurt[6]……	2 oz……	2 oz……	4 oz.

Footnotes

1 Children age 12 and older may be served larger portions based on their greater food needs. They may not be served less than the minimum quantities listed in this column.
2 Fruit or vegetable juice must be full-strength. Juice cannot be counted as the second snack-item if the other snack-item is milk.
3 Breads and grains must be made from whole-grain or enriched meal or flour. Cereal must be whole-grain or enriched or fortified.
4 A serving consists of the edible portion of cooked lean meat or poultry or fish.
5 Nuts and seeds may comprise only half of a meat/meat alternative serving and must be combined with another meat/meat alternative to fulfill the lunch or supper requirement.
6 Yogurt may be plain or flavored, unsweetened or sweetened.

Indicator

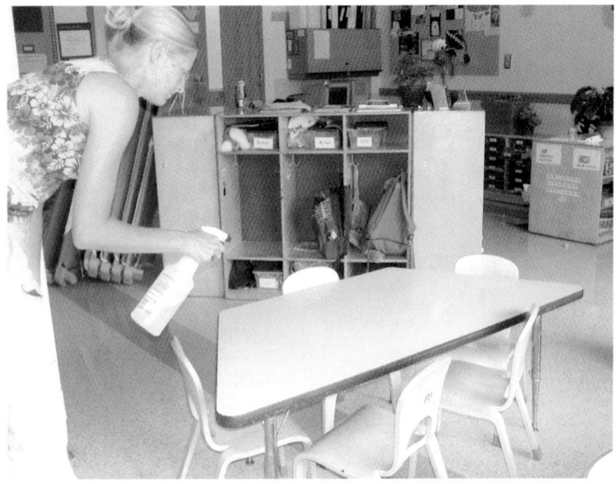

10.1.3 a After washing the tables, staff sanitize tables by spraying a bleach-water solution and allowing time for it to kill germs.

10.1.3 b Staff then use a clean disposable towel to dry tables.

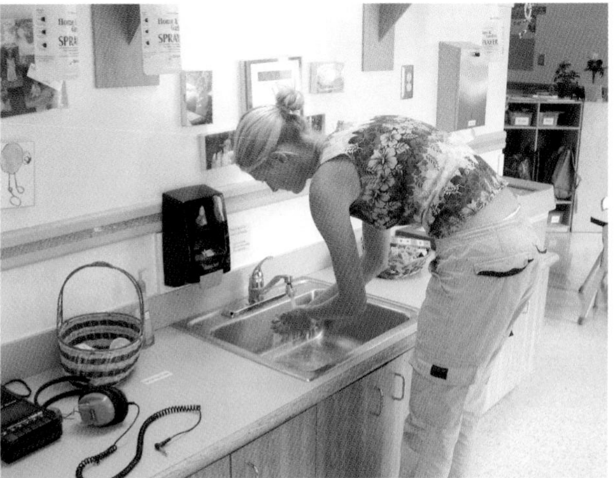

10.1.3 c Staff wash hands after wiping tables and before serving food.

10.1.3 d Turning off facets using a paper towel helps reduce the spread of disease and illness.

there will only be a few chances to watch how each of these is handled. While the teacher is preparing for a meal or snack, make sure to pay close attention to the preparation of the eating area, such as the cleaning and sanitizing of tables and the washing of hands by children and staff. Avoid going through the materials or looking at the display during the meal/snack preparation time because, without careful observation, very important information will be missed. Photos 10.1.3 a–d show the types of practices observers should be sure to notice.

To score this indicator, the following should be considered. If there is little evidence that these sanitary conditions are a regular practice, score 1.3 "Yes."

Handwashing is the most important way to reduce the spread of intestinal infections. Studies have shown that unwashed or improperly washed hands are the primary carriers of disease. Handwashing for children and staff requires that both hands be washed with liquid soap and rinsed thoroughly under warm running water for about 10 seconds (sing "Row, Row, Row Your Boat" once). Hands should be dried with individual paper towels that are not shared, or air-dried with a blower. Using gloves, wipes, or antiseptic waterless washes does not count as substitutes for handwashing.

Indicator

Care must be taken so that hands (or gloves) are not recontaminated before handling or eating food. For example, children should not be allowed to touch the floor or play with toys between handwashing and eating. Staff with washed hands, with or without gloves, should keep from touching children, toys, materials, the floor, and other things that would contaminate the gloves. (See photo 10.1.3 e.) Faucets that can be turned off without the use of hands (e.g., with a foot pedal or automatic sensor) are best because they prevent the recontamination of hands. If these are not available, the best thing to do to prevent recontamination is to use a disposable paper towel to turn the water off.

10.1.3 e Before helping children with food, gloves will have to be removed and hands washed.

If children touch food or finger feed themselves during meals, then they must have hands washed after eating to prevent the growth of germs and contamination of the many surfaces around the classroom. Faces should also be wiped.

To determine whether there are lapses in handwashing for this indicator, it helps to keep track of each child and adult, and to note whether each person washes hands as required or if significant recontamination takes place. The following is an example of an easy way to keep track on the score sheet.

Child	Hands washed?	Recontaminated?
1	yes	no
2	yes	no
3	yes	no
4	yes	no
5	no	
6	yes	no
7	yes	no
8	yes	no
9	yes	no
10	yes	no
11	yes	no
12	yes	yes
13	yes	no

Adult	Hands washed?	Recontaminated?
1	yes	no
2	yes	no

In this example, handwashing, without recontamination, is clearly a part of the program. There was only one miss in children's handwashing, one example of a child's hands being recontaminated, and no lapses in the adults' practices.

Eating equipment, surfaces, and foods themselves, must be kept clean to avoid the spread of disease. Tables should be washed to remove gross soil and sanitized with a bleach-water solution before and after being used for meals/snacks. To allow the

Indicator

bleach-water solution to do its job—to kill the germs—it should be allowed to sit for at least 10 seconds before being wiped dry. Allowing the solution to sit for at least 2 minutes before wiping dry is preferable, and the table can be allowed to air dry. However, only at least 10 seconds is required to give credit for this aspect of maintaining sanitary procedures for this item.

Sponges should not be used for sanitizing tables because they soak bacteria away from the surface of the sponge, which then cannot easily be reached by a sanitizing agent. If wet cloths are used, a separate cloth is required for each table, and cloths cannot be returned to soak in the bleach-water solution. Food spills on the floor should also be cleaned up.

Food and beverages should be served with sanitary utensils. Clean dishes, cups, utensils, and napkins should be used for eating. Disposable supplies should not be reused. Reusable plates, cups, utensils, etc. must be washed and sanitized before reuse. Foods should not be served directly onto the table top. No contaminated foods should be eaten, such as food that can spoil which has been un-refrigerated for more than an hour or not kept hot enough, or foods that have been dropped on the floor.

In the case where meal or snack times are flexible and children come and go throughout a period of time, the same sanitary conditions are required (e.g., table sanitized between children using same places, children's hands washed, etc.)

In scoring what would be considered sanitary food service for the children, the observer should think of what he or she would expect in terms of cleanliness in a restaurant. Would a customer want to eat food that had fallen onto the restaurant table top or the seat of the booth, or want waiters to touch the food with their hands? The issue of spreading germs from one individual to another and from one family to another is the same for adults and children.

1.4 Score this indicator "Yes" when meals or snacks are generally chaotic or cause children to be very anxious or unhappy. Examples of a ***negative social atmosphere*** might include:

- Not allowing children to talk during meals/snacks;
- Rigid control over children or use of harsh punishment to enforce manners, such as making children eat by themselves, withholding any food or beverages, yelling at children, embarrassing or teasing children;
- Chaotic atmosphere, with children fighting, screaming, and annoying one another;
- Forcing children to eat;
- Staff responding negatively or harshly to food accidents, such as children spilling their drinks or dropping food, eating or serving utensils.

Note that observing a single, minor negative staff-child interaction would not merit a score of "Yes." Watch the children to see whether they are frightened, rigidly controlled, or generally unhappy during meals/snacks.

1.5 To score this indicator, look for a list of children with their ***food allergies*** specified. This may be posted in the classroom or in another space used for eating. If there are children with food allergies listed, but proper food substitutions are not made as needed, credit cannot be given.

Indicator

If no list is observed, during the interview time, ask staff the questions listed in the ECERS-R to collect the information needed to score this indicator. Then ask if they make any accommodations for those children.

If no children in the program have food allergies, this indicator should be scored "NA."

3.1 See Indicator 1.1 for information needed to score whether the meal/snack schedule is ***appropriate***.

3.2 Use the USDA nutrition guidelines (see Indicator 1.2) to determine whether meals/snacks are ***well-balanced***. Personal preferences cannot be used when assessing the quality of the food. Consider only the guidelines, and as long as they are met, give credit. To give credit, no meal or snack served to children can be out of compliance with the guidelines. It should be noted that the guidelines represent the minimum requirements for children, and that larger servings or more food choices are permissible, in addition to the minimum requirements.

Any additional food/beverages served after the program has met the USDA requirements does not need to have the required components. For example, if children are given a cupcake because of a birthday in the class, it does not have to meet any nutritional guidelines as long as the requirements have already been met in the other meals/snacks.

3.3 To score whether ***sanitary conditions are usually maintained*** for meals/snacks, see information about Indicator 1.3.

If the proper sanitary measures are clearly practiced as part of the child care program, but an occasional lapse does occur, credit can still be given. (See photo 10.3.3.)

3.4 ***Non-punitive atmosphere*** during meals/snacks means that staff are either positive or neutral in their interactions with the children. They are not negative and do not punish children during meal/snack time. Look for evidence of children who are not afraid and are relaxed.

3.5 "NA" is permitted if there are no children in the program with a food allergy.

See information for Indicator 1.5 to score.

10.3.3 Children wash hands with soap and water and, after drying with a paper towel, go directly to the table to minimize the recontamination of hands.

10.3.6 A special chair allows a child with physical disabilities to eat lunch with her friends.

Indicator

10.5.1 a

10.5.1 b

10.5.1 c

10.5.1 d

10.5.1 a–d Staff who sit with children at mealtimes act as good role models and supervise for health and safety.

3.6 The law prohibits discrimination based on the disability of a child. Furthermore, studies show that children with disabilities who are included in activities such as meals/snacks with their peers have increased self-esteem and social skills. Children without special needs become more understanding and accepting of differences among people if they interact with them. (See photo 10.3.6, preceding page.)

"NA" is permitted if there are no children with disabilities enrolled in the class being observed.

Score 3.6 "No" if a child with a disability is separated from the other children during meals/snacks. Every attempt should be made to include children with disabilities with their peers at eating times. This means that they should be sitting at the table with the others, eating the same foods (to the extent possible), and having the opportunity to socialize. If needed, adaptive equipment should be provided to allow this inclusion. When a child with a severe disability requires feeding by an adult, whenever possible this should be done as part of the group meal/snack, with the child's peers.

5.1 Having ***staff sit with the children during meals/snacks*** provides several benefits. First, staff who are pleasant and polite act as good role models for social interaction. The children watch, listen, and learn how one is supposed to act when eating with others. An additional benefit is gained if the staff enjoy the foods the

Indicator

10.5.2 a

10.5.2 a–b Pleasant mealtimes are enjoyed by children and staff.

10.5.2 b

children are eating, show enthusiasm for healthful foods, and try those they might not prefer. Furthermore, when staff sit with the children, they are better able to prevent any discipline problems that are typical during meal/snack time (e.g., throwing food, children taking other children's food, doing "yucky things" with food in their mouths). Staff are also more likely to see, prevent, or quickly handle safety problems, such as choking or allergic reactions. (See photos 10.5.1 a–d.)

Most requires that it is *more likely* for staff to be sitting with the children during meals and group snacks than not. All staff do not have to be sitting with children at the same time, and it is possible that most staff will be sitting with the children while another staff member is not, if there are more than two teachers. It is fine for staff to get up once in a while, for example, to get more food or to help a child, but for the most part, they should be sitting with the children, not standing and watching or tending to other tasks. Usually, once a child or two are finished eating, at least one staff member will have to leave the table to tend to their needs, such as clearing places, throwing away trash, handwashing, and getting children involved in the next activity. However, when most children are still eating, as many staff as possible should remain sitting with them.

If there are not enough staff members to sit at each table, then they should arrange eating areas so that the staff member sitting at one table is close enough to another table to see, hear, and respond to problems that might occur.

5.2 Meal/snack times can be a great time for socializing if handled appropriately. (See photos 10.5.2 a–b.) The major requirements for ***pleasant social atmosphere*** are:

- Children are obviously relaxed during the eating times.
- Conversations (when staff and the children talk about things that interest them and when children talk among themselves) are encouraged and take place.
- Manners are practiced and modeled by staff but not strictly enforced. Staff are patient and understand that it takes a long time to develop manners, and that the best way for children to learn is to watch adults model manners. They gently and politely guide children to use good manners, not emphasizing this aspect of meals/snacks.

Indicator

10.5.3 a

10.5.3 b

10.5.3 c

10.5.3 d

10.5.3 e

10.5.3 a–e Children are encouraged to eat independently according to their abilities.

5.3 Children, who are ***encouraged to eat independently***, are helped by staff when they need help, but allowed to eat on their own, in a way that matches their abilities. (See photos 10.5.3 a–e.) Younger preschool-aged children will usually be able to drink from a cup independently, use a spoon for some easier foods, but still use their hands quite a bit. Older preschoolers will be able to use spoons or forks more, but not perfectly. All children will be able to wipe their mouths with a napkin, but younger ones will need more help with this task. Staff will need to gently remind and encourage children to practice their developing eating skills.

Children, who are ***encouraged to eat independently***, are also helped by being provided with sturdy, appropriately-sized eating utensils, tableware, cups, plates, and bowls that they can manage by themselves, and eat at a table of appropriate size where they can easily reach and handle foods/beverages. Children with disabilities need to be provided with any necessary adaptations required to allow them to eat as independently as they can. For example, a child with difficulty using hands and

Indicator

fingers might be provided with a special spoon or cup, and the plate/bowl might be put onto a non-slip surface so it does not slip or tip over when the child is trying to eat.

10.7.1 a

5.4 There can be a number of reasons for families to have ***dietary restrictions.*** These reasons include:

- Religious beliefs (for example, members of a religious group do not eat certain foods, do not eat certain combinations of certain foods, require special preparation of certain foods, or are restricted to certain foods on particular days)
- Health issues (for example, because of health history in a family, certain special dietary guidelines are followed, such as low sugar or low fat diets)
- Personal beliefs (for example, the belief that a vegetarian diet is more healthful or ethically responsible)
- Cultural customs (for example, people of a specific culture do not eat certain foods)

These restrictions and values should be respected by the staff, and the guidelines given by families should be followed to ensure that the children are eating only the foods that their parents want them to eat. Substitutions need to be made so that the children receive food that still meets the nutritional guidelines.

Score this item "NA" if none of the children have family dietary restrictions.

10.7.1 b

7.1 The extent to which ***children can help during meals/snacks*** will vary, based on the ages and abilities of the children in the group. Closer, more active staff guidance will be needed to make helping possible for younger or inexperienced preschoolers, while older, more experienced preschoolers will need less active adult help, but still require close supervision.

When scoring this indicator, credit can be given if any example of helping, such as those listed below, is observed for younger children (2½-year-olds and 3's), while at least three examples would be required to give credit for a group with older preschoolers (4-year-olds through kindergarten).

Children should be encouraged to help in the following ways:

- Set the tables by putting out cups, napkins, plates, or utensils. They can take turns doing this for the group or set their own places, individually. Older preschoolers can also help to put foods onto the table. It is important that children who are chosen to help during meal/ snack time are supervised closely so that sanitary conditions are always maintained. For example, hands must be washed and remain clean (not become recontaminated) when children are handling cups, eating utensils, napkins, foods, etc. that will be used by the group. (See photos 10.7.1 a–c.)

10.7.1 c

10.7.1 a–c With supervision, preschoolers are capable of setting the table.

Indicator

- Clear their own places after eating. When children are finished eating, they should be able to throw away their own plates or utensils or place washable items in a tray or bin. They should then be able to wash their hands and go to another activity. The amount of staff supervision and help needed to enable children do these tasks properly should be provided.
- Serve themselves. Even younger preschoolers should be able to serve themselves easy-to-handle foods, such as slices of fresh fruit, crackers, or pieces of bread. Helping children learn to serve themselves without contaminating the foods and to serve reasonable portions requires a great deal of staff guidance. The age and ability of a child should be taken into account when deciding how to handle self-serving. Younger children might need staff to go through the motions with them physically (e.g., hold his/her hand while serving from the bowl, lift the pitcher while the child brings his/her cup towards it) so they have more control. Any physical help should be accompanied by a verbal description of the actions. Older children may only need a little extra supervision, and staff can talk them through or physically assist if any problems do arise.
- Pass foods and other meal/snack necessities to others. Staff will have to help children ask one another to pass things, as well as help children hear and respond to the various requests.
- Clean up spills and help clean the table or floor after meals/snacks. Staff need to participate to ensure that sanitary conditions are maintained and that the job is done thoroughly.

7.2 Children develop self-help skills as well as fine motor skills when they are encouraged to serve themselves at meals/snacks. To make self-help easier, children should be provided with sturdy ***child-sized*** serving utensils, plates, or bowls, and beverage containers that encourage them to serve themselves independently. To be ***child-sized***, the serving equipment must generally be smaller than that routinely used by adults. For example, an adult can easily handle a half-gallon or gallon-sized milk container, while preschoolers require a pitcher or other container that holds only up to a quart, with younger children using even smaller pitchers. (See photos 10.7.2 a–b, next page.) While adults can serve using large serving spoons, preschoolers can manage tablespoon-sized utensils for serving. The beverage and food serving pieces should not be filled up to the top in order to avoid spills.

In some cases, children are able to do some, but not all, of the serving at meals/snacks. For example, in some classrooms, staff are required to provide children with first servings of each component of the nutrition guidelines, and children are then encouraged to serve second helpings as they wish. Or some classrooms allow children to serve certain foods themselves, but not others.

Credit can be given for this indicator when the children can do some or all of the serving *and* when some child-sized serving utensils (spoons, forks, bowls, plates, pitchers, etc.) are provided for and used by the children.

Using child-sized serving bowls, pitchers, and other serving implements will require that staff observe to see when serving containers become empty and refill as needed.

It is important that children who are serving themselves are closely supervised to ensure sanitary conditions. If sanitary conditions are not maintained sufficiently as children serve themselves, consider this under Indicators 1.3 and 3.3.

Indicator

10.7.2 a–b These quart-sized containers can be handled by these older preschoolers, but smaller pitchers would be needed for younger children. The serving spoon in 10.7.2a is too long for children to handle easily.

7.3 ***Conversation*** adds to meal/snack times by making them more relaxing and fun for the children. ***Conversation at meals*** is a great way to improve the relationship between staff and children. Meal/snack time conversations allow staff to incorporate learning of many kinds into a routine care activity.

It should be noted, however, that ***conversations*** do *not* include quizzing children on facts, but rather talking with them about the things they have done or plan to do in play, things they enjoy, current events in their lives, or problems they want to solve. Conversations should include exchanges of information and turn-taking between staff and children, and children and their peers.

Staff can start talking about concepts such as colors ("What color is your broccoli?"), numbers ("How many pieces of sausage to you have?"), quantity ("How much more is left on your plate?"), and science ("Is our cereal hot or cold this morning? How about your milk?"). Staff can encourage children's language development, using expansion ("The orange is very juicy, with lots of seeds that might get stuck in your teeth.") and reasoning ("You both want another piece of apple, and there is only one piece left. What should we do so you both get more?"). However, children should not be forced to take part in the conversation, but should do so because they choose to, and they enjoy it. This means that the mealtime atmosphere should be kept casual and friendly in tone.

11 Nap/rest

General information about this item

During ***nap/rest***, children either sleep or relax quietly. Since so much of a child's day in an early childhood program is spent being active with other children, a regularly scheduled time where each child can be alone to rest or just wind down during a quiet activity is beneficial.

Younger children (2's and 3's) tend to need more nap or rest time than older children do, and they are more likely to sleep during this period of the day. The oldest preschoolers have often (but not always) outgrown their need for sleep during the day but still benefit from a quiet rest time where they can relax and do quiet activities. It is important to understand that the amount of sleep or rest that children need varies substantially, some children requiring more rest or sleep than others of the same age.

For this item, the appropriateness of the *schedule* is judged by observing when children are actually provided with nap/rest time. A written schedule posted in the classroom is not to be used as evidence to judge whether nap/rest is provided at the correct times, unless the schedule is consistent with what has been observed.

To score this item, it is best to observe how nap/rest is handled. At a minimum, the observer should observe the beginning of the nap/rest time. If nap/rest time is not observed, the observer should ask the questions provided for the item during the staff questioning time.

This item does not apply (score "NA") to programs of 4 hours or less that do not provide a nap/rest time. It does apply to all programs of more than 4 hours in duration.

Preschool-aged children should be provided with a regular time, everyday, when they are encouraged, but not forced, to nap or rest. The time should be regularly scheduled, so that it happens at about the same time each day.

A closer look at each indicator

1.1 ***Schedule is inappropriate*** means that nap/rest usually does not meet the needs of most of the children in the group. At the lower levels of quality, it is not required that a nap/rest schedule meet each individual child's needs. Therefore, to score 1.1 "Yes," the nap/rest schedule must be problematic enough to negatively affect most children in the group. To score 1.1 "Yes," look for the following types of problems that impact most children, remembering that in general, younger preschoolers will require more rest than older children:

- Nap/rest time is too late. Evidence would be that the children are generally tired and cranky for a long period and unable to become positively engaged

Indicator

in activities. They may rub their eyes or fall asleep on the floor or while sitting at a table. If most of the children are yawning, tired and cranky, or are falling asleep, but staff keep them up, score this indicator "Yes."

- Nap/rest time is too early. Evidence would be that most children are not tired enough to settle down for the quiet time. Even after 15–20 minutes into the nap/rest time, most children remain actively awake, do not appear to be able to relax, or complain about having to rest. A certain amount of "fooling around" is to be expected as children begin to settle for nap/rest. However, if many children are getting upset or into trouble long after a reasonable "settling down" time has passed, and appear not to be tired, score 1.1 "Yes."
- Nap/rest time is too long. Children should not sleep too long, or for a period that is longer than 2½ hours in a full-day program. When children get too much sleep in the afternoon it is likely that they will be wide awake late into the night, causing problems between children and their parents who must try to put them to bed. Score 1.1 "Yes" if children are left to sleep for a period longer than 2½ hours or if older children are required to nap/rest for a period that is far longer than they need. When nap is not observed, the observer must determine the actual length of nap/rest time. Look at the written schedule if it is an accurate depiction of what has been observed to occur during the day, or ask staff questions during the questioning time. If the accurate written schedule or teacher report indicates more than 2½ hours for nap/rest score 1.1 "Yes."
- Nap/rest time is too short. Most children do not want to wake up or are groggy and cranky when required to wake up. If nap/rest lasts for less than an hour in a full-day program, or if children obviously need more sleep when required to get up, score 1.1 "Yes."
- Nap/rest time is not dependable. There is no regular time in the daily schedule when children know they will be napping or resting. Nap does not come at a particular place in the sequence of events that children experience in the program. For example, nap might be at 11:30 one day and 1:00 the next, or nap may follow lunch one day and follow outdoor play the next day. If there is no regular daily nap/rest schedule that children can count on, score 1.1 "Yes."

1.2 ***Unsanitary*** means unclean to the extent that the spread of disease from child to child is not minimized. Children in the group are put at increased risk of disease because cleanliness is not maintained properly. For example, lice infestation, scabies, and ringworm are among the most common health problems in child care. These diseases are transmitted through direct skin contact or by sharing personal articles, such as bedding. If children's bedding is kept separate, the spread of these infectious diseases will decrease. Although children interact with each other and can transmit these diseases while they are awake, if they are further apart while sleeping, they will have less overall exposure.

Below are listed the major requirements for *sanitary provisions* of nap/rest. Score 1.2 "Yes" if there are problems with any of the following during nap/rest, indicating that sanitary conditions are *not* maintained:

- All children sleep on a special, clean nap/rest surface, such as a cot or mat, and do not rest directly on the floor or sitting at tables. Bed linens, such as blankets or sheets, cannot be used as a substitute for a cot or mat.

Indicator

- Nap/rest area is not crowded, with most cots/mats at least 18" apart or separated by a solid barrier. Even if children sleep head-to-toe, so their faces are not close, the mats must still be placed 18" apart. (See photos 11.1.2 a–b.)
- Children are provided with clean, individual bedding and do not share the same bedding or sleep surface (for example, cot/mat, blankets, sheets, pillows) with another child. If the same bedding is used by two or more children, it must be washed between use by each child. There are no visible signs of recent stains, dried food, or mulch/sand from the outdoor area on the sleeping surfaces.
- Children's bedding is stored separately, so that personal items are not touching one another. In addition, sleeping surfaces of cots/mats must be kept clean, not touching one another or touching the floor or the floor-side of other children's sleeping surfaces. (See photo 11.1.2 c.)
- Mats/cots must be covered with material that makes them easy to wash and sanitize. They must be sanitized after they have been contaminated (such as by vomit, mucous, blood, or toileting accidents).

1.3 Children who are resting or sleeping still need to be within sight and hearing of a supervising adult. An adult needs to be there in case some children are still awake, an emergency occurs, or a child suddenly wakes up and is frightened or is feeling sick. In addition, sufficient staff must be present to help in case of emergency, such as an evacuation due to fire.

Little supervision is true (score "Yes") when there is *not* a staff member in the room, actively supervising, during naptime. If regular, required staff-child ratios are not maintained during nap/rest times, at least one staff member must be in the room with the children, and additional staff to meet ratio requirements must be immediately available, in case of emergencies or if children wake up and need attention. The additional staff available for emergencies cannot be another teacher who is solely responsible for watching her own group of children. When groups of children are combined for nap (for example, all children in several classrooms nap together in one big nap room), more than one staff member is required to supervise the increased number of children.

The staff member(s) must remain in the room with the children at all times—not go out into the hall, attend meetings that are not in the room, or leave the room for personal reasons unless someone else takes over the supervision in the nap/rest room. Supervising staff must be awake and alert, with primary interest in ensuring the safety and comfort of the napping or resting children. There can be *no* lapses in supervision to score 1.3 "No."

1.3 is also true (score "Yes") if supervision during nap/rest is harsh. For this indicator, ***harsh supervision*** means that staff

11.1.2 a

11.1.2 b

11.1.2 a–b In these nap arrangements, children are too close together. Germs are spread more easily and it is difficult for staff to access children in the event of an emergency.

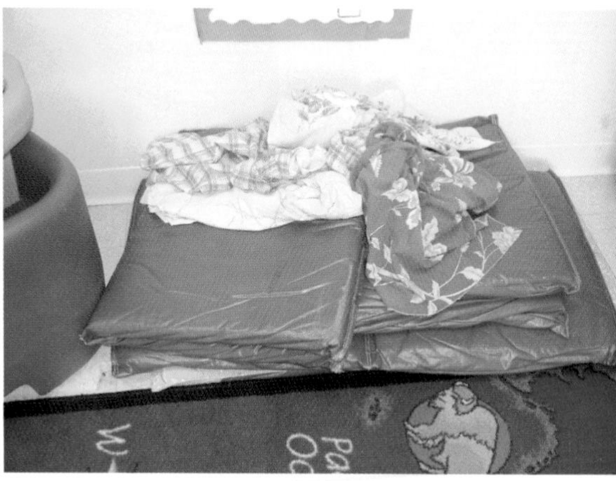

11.1.2 c The children's bed linens are all stored together in a pile, causing health concerns such as the transmission of lice, scabies, or ringworm.

Indicator

yell at children, threaten them, frighten them, handle them roughly, or use physical punishment of any type. If *any* child is supervised harshly, 1.3 is scored "Yes." Firmness is permitted as long as it is not harsh enough to upset children. The observer should watch children carefully to see if their response indicates harsh supervision. If any child appears frightened or extremely upset due to staff harshness, then 1.3 is true.

3.1 ***Scheduled appropriately*** means that nap is not too early, too late, too long, too short, or irregularly scheduled from day to day. See 1.1 for more information on each.

At the minimal (3) level of quality, it is not required that a nap/rest schedule meet each child's individual needs. Therefore, to score 3.1 "Yes," the nap/rest schedule must be reasonable for ***most*** (almost all or the vast majority) of the children in the group being observed, even if a few children seem to be having difficulties with the schedule or are reported by staff to have difficulties. Remember that in general, younger preschoolers will require more rest than older ones.

Look primarily for evidence that ***most of the children*** in the group are able to go to sleep during nap time or rest quietly with little difficulty.

3.2 ***Sanitary provisions*** requires that all cots/mats or sleeping surfaces are at least 18" apart unless separated by a solid barrier. In addition, bedding and sleep surfaces (for example, cot/mat, blankets, sheets, pillows) must be clean, meeting the requirements described in 1.2. (See photos 11.3.2 a–c, this page, and 11.3.2 d, next page.)

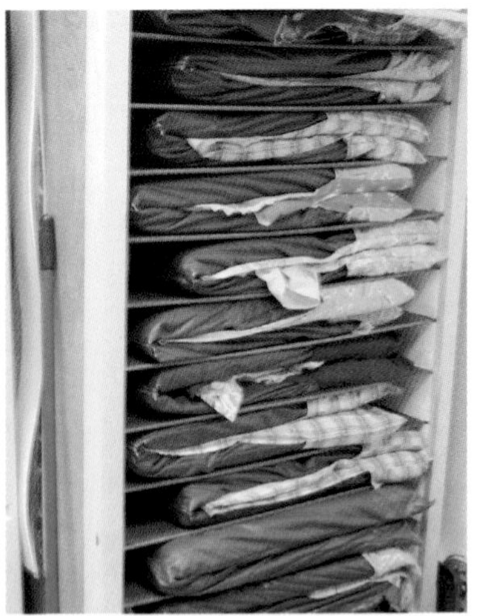

11.3.2 a

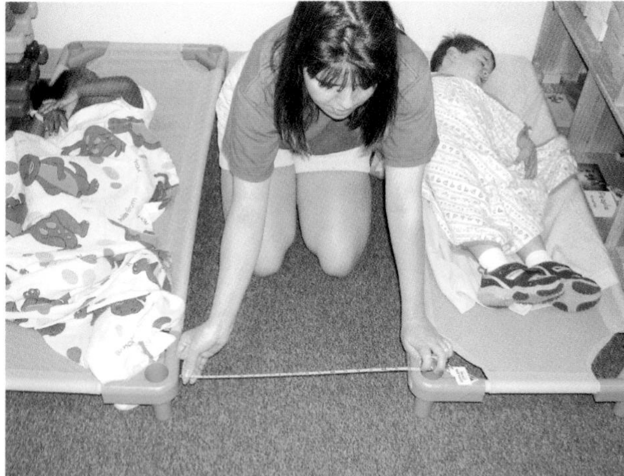

11.3.2 b

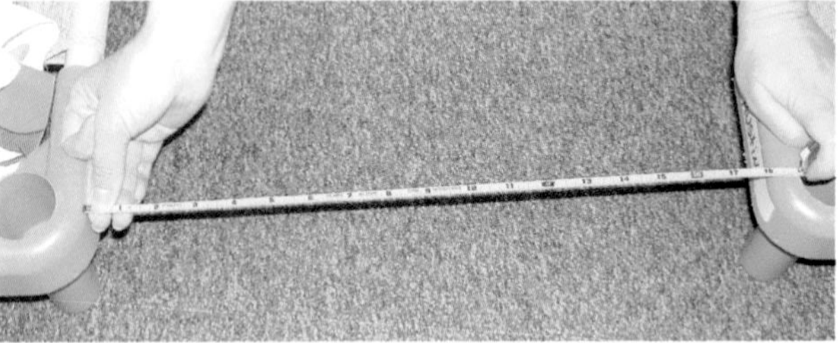

11.3.2 c

11.3.2 a Children's mats and linens are stored in individual, labeled shelves to reduce the spread of germs and illness.

11.3.2 b–c Meeting minimum requirements for sanitary provisions requires that cots/mats are placed at least 18 inches apart.

Indicator

11.3.2 d A shelf can be used as a solid barrier between cots.

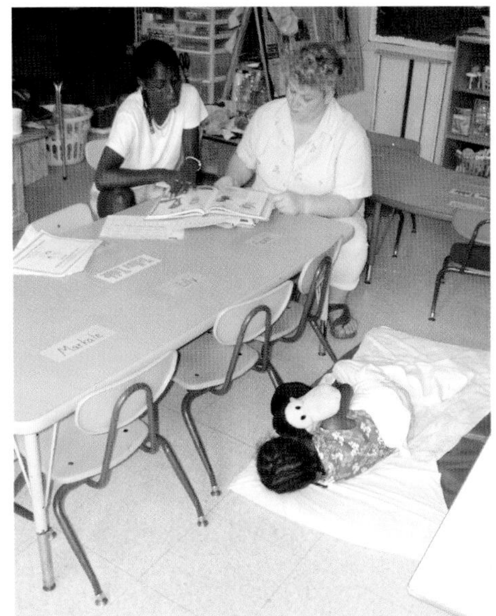

11.3.3 Staff closely supervise children during nap.

3.3 ***Sufficient supervision*** means that enough staff are present in the room to protect the children's safety in case of an emergency and to handle children who may be awake. At least one alert staff member is always in the room, actively supervising the children with no lapses. (See photo 11.3.3.) In cases of very large groups of children sharing a nap room, more staff are required. More staff may also be required when the needs of one or several children require most of the attention of the staff present.

See 1.3 for more information on ***sufficient supervision.***

3.4 Relaxed, pleasant supervision inspires confidence in children and helps them sleep. If children are forced to lie down, or if nap is used as a punishment, then they will resent naptime and more problems will arise. To score "Yes," no harsh treatment can be used.

Observe the beginning or a portion of naptime to determine if supervision is calm and supportive.

5.1 All children benefit from methods that help them relax for nap/rest. Children can be ***helped to relax*** in a variety of ways. If any of the following is used, 5.1 is true and can be scored "Yes":

- Same routine is used each day to get children settled, such as lights dimmed and children are helped onto cots. Staff take time to get each child settled and covered, allow a favorite toy if requested, put on soft music, and remind children to have a good rest.
- Soft music or a relaxing story on tape is used.
- Staff rub children's backs. (See photo 11.5.1 a.)
- Staff sit next to children who have trouble settling down and talk quietly to them.

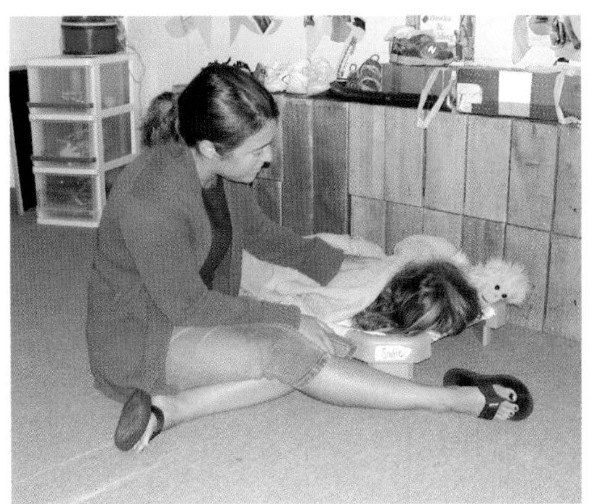

11.5.1 a Staff help children relax for nap by rubbing their backs or sitting next to them.

Indicator

11.5.1 b This child is relaxing by reading a book before falling asleep.

11.5.2 Closing the blinds to dim the room helps make the nap area conducive to resting.

- Staff tell or read a relaxing story.
- Staff sing a lullaby to the children.
- Children are allowed to have a soft toy or special blanket for sleep (as long as it does not pose any safety hazards).
- Children are allowed to read a book or play quietly with a toy while on their cots/mats until they are ready to sleep. (See photo 11.5.1 b.)

5.2 For space to be ***conducive to resting,*** the following provisions are helpful. If some of these things are implemented and children seem to rest well, then give credit (score "Yes") for this indicator:

- Lights are turned down and/or blinds closed to dim the room. However, the room must remain light enough to permit appropriate supervision. (See photo 11.5.2.)
- Cots/mats are put in the same place every day so children can go to the same spot as part of their routine.
- Cots/mats of more active children are separated from those who sleep, and more active children are also separated from one another.
- The room is quiet.
- Problems are handled very calmly and gently by staff.

5.3 Spacing cots/mats at least ***three feet apart or separated by a solid barrier*** will help reduce the spread of respiratory illness and other diseases in child care centers. This distance reduces the total amount of exposure to germs children face during the entire day.

A ***separation of at least three feet*** also provides easy access to the children if staff need to get to them in an emergency situation. If the facility uses screens or other solid barriers, the staff must still be able to see the children and be able to easily reach them if an emergency should arise.

All cots or mats means that the distance of three feet or separation by a solid barrier is required between *each* child's cot or mat. To score 5.3 "Yes," placement

Indicator

of *all* cots/mats must meet the requirement. If even one mat is placed closer than three feet to another child's mat without separation by a solid barrier, then score 5.3 "No." (See photos 11.5.3. a–b.)

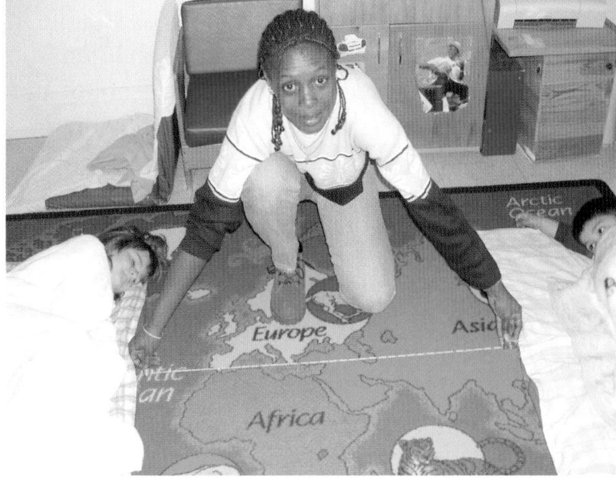

11.5.3 a

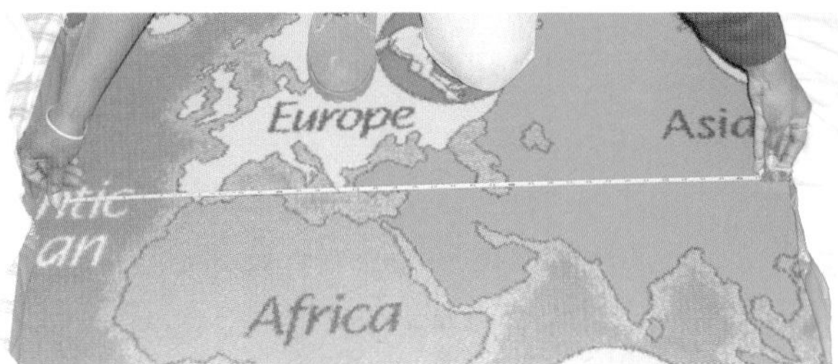

11.5.3 b

11.5.3 a–b Meeting high standards for sanitary provisions requires that cots/mats are placed at least three feet apart.

7.1 There is almost always one child, or even a few, in a group who, for some reason, have trouble dealing with a nap/rest schedule that is appropriate for all others in the group. In a program that handles nap/rest at the highest levels of quality, accommodations are made to meet the needs of such children. Problems with the nap/rest schedule tend to occur most often when:

- A child is less able to sleep than usual (for example, because she woke up later than on other days, has become afraid of something new, such as a frightening movie character, or is new to the group).
- A child is more tired than usual (for example, because he woke up earlier than on other days, did not sleep well the night before or went to bed too late, had an especially tiring morning, or is becoming ill or just getting over being sick).
- A child simply needs either more, or less, sleep than the other children do.
- The classroom consists of a mixed age group (such as 2–3-, or 3–5-year-olds), where the younger children may need more sleep than the older children.

These situations may not occur during the observation, but the observer should ask the teacher the questions suggested in the item to get information needed to score 7.1 and 7.2.

To score 7.1 "Yes," the nap/rest schedule must be ***flexible to meet the individual needs*** of all the children. Staff must accommodate individual needs, for example, by letting one child go to sleep earlier than others or another to stay up through some or all of nap. Flexibility can also be provided as staff give attention to a particular child for a longer period of time than is needed by others, to help that child relax.

This requirement is different from that described in Indicator 1.1 because meeting the needs of individual children requires responding to an exception rather than the rule. If most children are having a hard time going to sleep or staying awake everyday, then there is a problem with the schedule for most children (considered in 1.1 or 1.3). If only one or two children have difficulties with the schedule, the meeting of their individual needs is considered in 7.1.

7.2 ***Early risers and non-nappers*** are those children who sleep less than the others in the group, and who are ready to get up and do an activity while others sleep. Whether a child is an early riser or a non-napper can be determined by the individual child's need for less sleep or by parents' requests that their preschoolers have either shorter naps or no naps at all, so that they sleep well at night.

Indicator

Programs that handle nap/rest at the highest levels of quality make ***provisions*** for these children who sleep less than others. Rather than making early risers or non-nappers stay quietly on their cots/mats, with nothing to do, staff provide a way for the children to be appropriately involved and supervised while others are sleeping. To score 7.2 "Yes," the observer should look for evidence of provisions such as the following:

- Children are encouraged to quietly read books or play quietly with toys on their mats or cots.
- Children can read or play quietly in a separate part of the room that is away from sleeping children. (See photo 11.7.2.)
- Children are allowed to go to another room where non-nappers or early risers can participate in interesting activities, with the necessary supervision.
- Children can go outside where they can participate in either free play or specific activities, supervised by staff.

11.7.2 Two early risers can play quietly while the others nap.

If no situation involving early risers or non-nappers is observed, then questions about how this is handled should be asked during the staff interview, using the suggested questions in the scale.

Indicator

12 Toileting/diapering

General information about this item

Maintaining sanitary conditions during toileting/diapering routines is necessary to minimize the spread of germs in the early childhood classroom. Having so many children sharing space, equipment, and materials for a large part of the day makes it easy to spread germs among both children and adults. In terms of toileting/diapering, the diseases spread most frequently are those that are passed from contaminated hands to the mouth, especially intestinal diseases that cause diarrhea.

A vast amount of contamination can occur during toileting/diapering routines in early childhood programs. Early childhood programs are often looked upon as being the place into which germs are carried, transferred to others, and then spread out into the community. However, studies have shown that infections can be reduced by half when proper sanitary procedures are used in early childhood programs. Such procedures help prevent the spread of disease within a program and limit the spread outside the program as well. So it is important for every child and staff member that sanitary procedures be carried out consistently and correctly to protect the health of the staff, the children, their families, and greater community.

In addition to basic health concerns, this item examines the social-emotional and learning aspects of toileting/diapering. How well children are supervised, whether these routine care times are pleasant for the children, and whether children are helped to learn the skills needed for independence are also considered.

A closer look at each indicator

1.1 ***Sanitary conditions of the area*** means the space and equipment used for toileting and/or diapering of the children in the group. The area may be located within the classroom space or elsewhere in the building in which the classroom is housed, for example, down a hallway or within another classroom. More than one area might be used, and the requirements for "sanitary conditions" must be met in all toileting/diapering areas used by the children.

Maintaining ***sanitary conditions*** requires the following:

- Ideally, a separate sink should be used only for handwashing after toileting/diapering to prevent the spread of infectious agents in the feces and urine. If staff or children touch sink faucets while washing their hands after they have used the toilet or taken part in diapering, germs from feces or urine will get on the faucets and in the sink. Therefore, a separate sink is required for toileting/diapering use. Ideally, this sink should not be used for any other purpose. If it is possible to designate sinks for specific purposes, then this should be done (for example, sinks near toilets should be used only for handwashing

Indicator

after toileting, while other sinks in the classroom should be used for all other handwashing). If the same sink is used by either children or adults for both diapering/toileting and food-related routines (including brushing teeth) or for other purposes (for example, to wash toys or other classroom equipment), it must be sanitized after diaper/toileting use by spraying the sinks and faucets with a bleach solution. (See photo 12.1.1.) All use of the sink for one purpose can be completed before the sink needs to be sanitized for another use. It is not required that the sink be sanitized before diapering/toileting use. However, the sink should be sanitized after use for toileting/diapering, before using the same sink for other purposes.

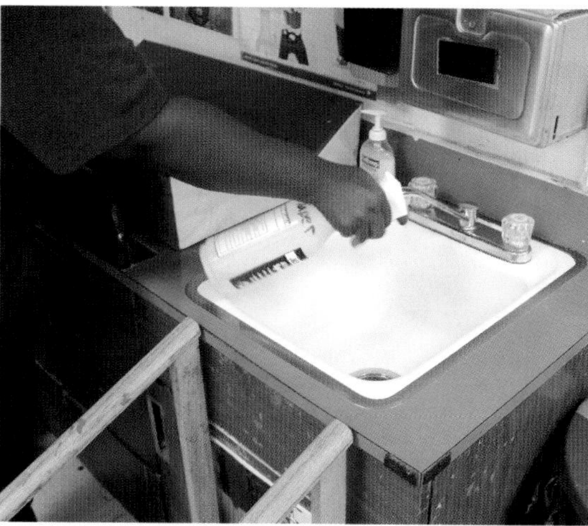

12.1.1 Sanitize sinks and faucets after toileting use and before using the same sink for other purposes.

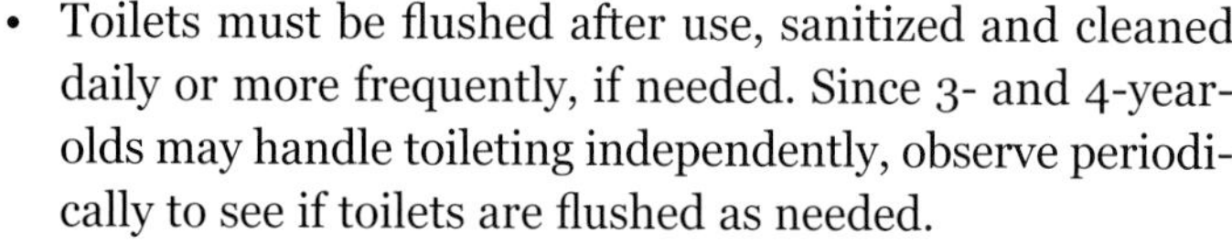

- Toilets must be flushed after use, sanitized and cleaned daily or more frequently, if needed. Since 3- and 4-year-olds may handle toileting independently, observe periodically to see if toilets are flushed as needed.
- If potty chairs are used, required sanitary procedures must occur immediately after each use. The contents of potty chairs must be disposed of in the toilet, which is flushed. After emptying, they must be rinsed/washed in a special sink, designated for that use only, and sanitized.
- Toileting/diapering area(s) must be kept clean. Floors, doors, and walls should be well maintained and obviously clean. No trash (paper towels, toilet paper), built-up grime, or spills should be on the floor. The area should not be dominated by the smell of urine. If an area is obviously old and more difficult to maintain, the requirements for cleanliness must still be met.
- Trash, including paper towels, must be disposed of properly.

Also, ***sanitary*** conditions to avoid contamination during diapering require following the practices listed in the chart on page 113.

If problems are observed with the sanitary requirements listed above, score 1.1 "Yes."

If no major problems are observed, or only two or three minor problems, score 1.1 "No."

1.2 ***Basic provisions*** for diapering include the equipment and supplies needed to change children properly, including a diapering surface that can be sanitized, a sink with warm running water, liquid soap, wipes, bleach and water (or other approved sanitizing) solution, diapers, plastic bags for soiled clothes, and individual or disposable towels. ***Basic provisions*** for toileting include toilet (or less preferably, potty chairs), toilet paper, sink with running warm water, liquid soap, plastic bags for soiled clothes, and individual or disposable towels.

Supplies needed for staff and children in the toileting or diapering areas must be within easy reach to encourage proper personal hygiene and to minimize the spread of disease. If provisions are not readily available, children and staff will be less likely to use them. Also, if staff and children have to move from one area to another to access needed supplies, they are more likely to spread contamination into other areas of the classroom.

Indicator

I. Preparing for Diapering

To minimize contamination outside of the diapering area, prepare for a diaper change *before* bringing the child to diapering area, for example, by having ready:

- Changing table paper (if used) to cover the table from the child's shoulders to heels (in case it becomes soiled and must be folded over to give a clean surface during the change)
- Enough wipes for the diaper change (including wiping the bottom and hands after taking the soiled diaper away from the child's skin)
- A clean diaper, plastic bag for soiled clothes, and clean clothes if soiled clothing is anticipated
- Non-porous gloves if they will be used, and a dab of diaper cream on a disposable piece of paper or tissue if cream is being used

Supplies should have been removed from their containers and placed near, but not directly on, the diapering surface before starting the diaper change.

II. Diapering Procedure

1. Prepare for diapering as indicated above.
2. Place child on diapering table. Remove clothing to access diaper. If soiled, place clothes into plastic bag.
3. Remove soiled diaper and place into lined, hands-free trash container. (To limit odor, seal in a plastic bag before placing into trash container.)
4. Use wipes to clean child's bottom from front to back.
5. Use a wipe to remove soil from adult's hands.
6. Use another wipe to remove soil from child's hands.
7. Throw soiled wipes into lined, hands-free trash container.
8. Put on clean diaper and redress child.
9. Place child at sink and wash hands following the "handwashing procedure." [See next page.]
10. Spray diapering surface with bleach-water solution and wait more than 10 seconds before wiping with disposable towel or allow to air dry. It should be noted that the recommended practice is to wait for 2 minutes to allow the solution to kill germs. However, if there is a delay of at least 10 seconds before the solution is wiped from the surface, this will be considered adequate. The surface cannot be sprayed and immediately wiped.
11. Adult washes hands using the "handwashing procedure," without contaminating any other surfaces.

Additional Precautions

- The diapering surface must be sanitized after each diaper change with a bleach-water or other approved sanitizing solution (all surfaces must be able to be sanitized—e.g., no quilted pads or safety straps, no containers that are stored on the diapering surface). The bleach-water solution must be allowed to stay on the surface for more than 10 seconds, and ideally 2 minutes, to kill the germs. So it is best for staff to spray the surface as the last step of the diapering procedure before washing their own hands. After the time lapse, the surface can be dried (no additional handwashing required at this time) or allowed to air dry (and wiped dry if still damp) before use with another child.
- Diapers are disposed of in a hands-free covered can (usually one that has a step pedal that lifts the lid) to prevent further contamination of surfaces.
- Toys that are played with or objects that are touched, while children's diapers are changed, must be put aside to be sanitized.
- Note: Both child's and staff's hands must be washed after the diapering procedure is completed (see 1.3 for information).

Indicator

Disposable towels are preferred because shared cloth towels transmit infectious disease. If a cloth towel is assigned to each child, the observer must watch carefully to be sure that each child uses only the assigned towel and that the towels never touch. Preventing shared use is difficult, and children usually tend to use the towel that is most readily accessible, unless carefully supervised by staff. Disposable towels prevent this problem completely if they are thrown away after being used and are not reused.

Lack of basic provisions is true (score 1.2 "Yes") when any of the toileting/diapering equipment or supplies that are obviously needed are not observed to be readily accessible to staff and/or children. For example, if no soap is accessible during any time that it is needed during the observation, or if staff do not take immediate action to replace the soap when it is needed, then 1.2 would be true.

If no problems are observed, score 1.2 "No."

1.3 ***Handwashing*** is the most important way to reduce the spread of intestinal diseases. Studies have shown that unwashed or improperly washed hands are the primary carriers of disease.

Handwashing for children and staff requires that both hands be washed with liquid soap and rinsed thoroughly under warm running water for *about* 10 seconds (sing "Row, Row, Row Your Boat" once). Hands should be dried with disposable paper towels that are not shared or air-dried with a blower. (See "Handwashing Procedure," below.)

Note that handwashing does not have to be timed by observers. Rather, the observer should watch to be sure that the proper handwashing steps have taken place, including wetting hands, applying liquid soap, rubbing together fronts, backs, and between fingers, and rinsing thoroughly. Then the hands should be dried.

Using wipes or antiseptic waterless washes do not count as substitutes for handwashing.

Handwashing Procedure

The handwashing procedure should be completed immediately after toileting and/or diapering and before touching other objects in the room. Handwashing at the sink should be conducted individually. For example, each child should wash hands, not having to share the sink and water, and the teacher should not consider that her hands have been washed because she washes the hands of a child. The teacher, as well as the child, should independently wash hands using the following procedure:

1. Moisten hands with warm water and use liquid soap.
2. Rub hands together for 10 seconds (sing 1 verse of "Row, Row, Row Your Boat").
3. Rinse hands free of soap under running water.
4. Dry hands with a clean, disposable paper towel or air dry with a blower.
5. Throw the used paper towel into a hands-free trash container.

Indicator

12.1.3 a Using a disposable paper towel to turn faucets off will help reduce the spread of germs and illnesses.

12.1.3 b Children are taught how to turn off faucets using a disposable paper towel.

Gloves do not take the place of handwashing. Teachers are not required to wear gloves, but gloves may reduce soil on caregivers' hands and underneath fingernails. Teachers who wear gloves during toileting/diapering must remove their gloves, dispose of them properly, and wash their hands to reduce the spread of germs. Gloves must be changed *after use with each child.*

Children who are diapered require the same handwashing procedure as children who use the toilet because their hands become contaminated in the diapering area or during play. Washing at diapering time reduces the amount of all types of germs on a regular basis. Staff who assist children in toileting or diapering, or who check diapers, also need to follow correct handwashing procedures after helping each child.

The handwashing procedure must minimize recontamination of hands from toileting/diapering germs that are on the sinks and faucets. Faucets that can be turned off without the use of hands (e.g., with a foot pedal or automatic sensors) are best because they prevent the recontamination of hands. If these are not available, faucets should be turned off with a disposable paper towel. (See photos 12.1.3 a–b.)

If children use the toilet, wash hands, and then immediately sit down for meals/snacks, contamination of children's hands at the toileting sink must be minimized by having children turn off the faucets with a paper towel or having adults turn off the faucet. Children do not have to wash their hands twice, once at the toileting sink and once at the food sink if one of these measures is taken.

Handwashing for this item is considered ***often neglected*** when adults' and children's hands are washed less than 75% of the time when needed. Score 1.3 "Yes" when most (more than 75%) children and adults do not wash their hands after toileting/diapering and in situations where it is obvious that there is clearly no system in place for washing hands after toileting or diapering.

To gather the evidence needed to score this indicator, keep a chart as handwashing by children and staff is observed so it is clear at the end of the observation how many children and staff washed hands properly.

It is not necessary to observe every handwashing instance if many take place throughout the observation. A sample can be used, as long as it represents the

Indicator

regular practice of each staff member and of the children. Note the handwashing until a clearly representative sample is observed. After that point, any handwashing that represents new information should be added to the sample. For example, new cases would be needed in the sample when a new teacher or additional children arrive in the classroom who were not observed earlier, or if children use the toilet independently, whereas they had been supervised earlier in the day.

Handwashing for adults should be observed and calculated separately from that required for children. Calculate if the number of proper handwashings observed is less than 75% by dividing the number of handwashings completed by the number observed.

Chart 1
Tracking handwashing after toileting

	Child	Teacher (if needed)
1	Yes	No (zipped pants)
2	No (no soap)	N/A
3	No (not long)	Yes (helped child pull up pants)
4	Yes	Yes (helped child pull up pants)
5	No (no soap)	N/A
6	No (washed with teacher)	No (washed with child)

This tracking system shows that there were six opportunities observed when children's hands needed to be washed. However, children's hands were properly washed only two out of the six times needed. Use this calculation to determine the percentage (2 ÷ 6 = 33%). The required percentage required to receive a "No" for Indicator 1.3 is 75%. This requirement also applies separately to the teacher's handwashing. Again, the tracking system shows that the teacher's hands were washed two out of the four times needed, or 50% (2 ÷ 4). There was an attempt to carry out handwashing properly for the children, but many inadequate practices were observed, such as no soap used or hands not washed adequately. Even though there was an attempt to wash hands adequately, this indicator must be scored "Yes."

Since there could be many occasions during an observation when handwashing must be documented, keeping a record system such as Chart 1 will help to determine how to score handwashing indicators.

1.4 ***Inadequate supervision*** means that staff do not monitor to protect the children or ensure that sanitary procedures (e.g., handwashing) are carried out. For toileting, staff do not keep an eye on children using the toilet to ensure that toilet paper is used, toilets are flushed, or hands are washed as needed. Or staff do not notice when children are using the toileting area inappropriately (such as splashing water, unrolling all the toilet paper, playing in the toilet, or rough-housing) when they should be using the toilet. For diapering, inadequate supervision means that staff do not pay sufficient attention to the child, for example, by leaving a child who is on the diapering table for any amount of time.

The amount of close supervision required will depend on the ages and abilities of the children being observed, with closer, more helpful supervision required for

Indicator

younger or less able children. However, if it is observed that older children do not usually complete toileting procedures correctly and responsibly, supervision must be considered inadequate.

Children develop differently socially, emotionally, and physically. All of these aspects will affect their ability to control their bodily functions. It is important that staff are patient with children even when they have accidents, so that the children and their self-esteem do not suffer. Staff should encourage children to try to control their bodily functions and praise them when they do. This will instill pride and confidence in them, but if they do have accidents, encouragement is still needed so that the children are not afraid or embarrassed, thus learning to hate bathroom time.

Unpleasant supervision means that staff are observed using any of the following:

- Responding harshly or negatively to toileting accidents
- Using rigid control or harsh punishment to manage the children during toileting/diapering routines, such as embarrassing or teasing children, yelling at them, handling them roughly, or using any physical punishment
- Not allowing children to use toilet when needed, for example, by telling them to "hold it" when this causes the child distress
- Not providing help when children request or obviously need it, but rather belittling children and making them feel incompetent because they need help
- Showing a negative response to children's diapering/toileting needs or experiences, such as complaining about lifting a child to the diapering table or commenting negatively about a soiled diaper
- Putting undue pressure on children to be toilet-trained, such as forcing children to use the toilet when they do not want to or making them sit on the toilet for a long time to "try"

Base the score for this indicator on what is generally observed. One or two minor lapses in supervision do not require that 1.4 be scored "Yes." However, if the usual practice is to provide inadequate or unpleasant supervision, score "Yes" for this indicator.

3.1 Making toileting/diapering a consistent procedure, that is completed the same way each time it is done, makes it easier to maintain the necessary sanitary conditions for both the children and the staff. Completing the same procedures correctly, over and over again, turns good practices into a habit.

For information on the requirements of ***sanitary conditions*** see 1.1.

It is important for observers to check the children's toileting and/or diapering area several times during the observation to be sure sanitary conditions are maintained, such as toilets flushed, spills cleaned up, trash removed from floors, and sinks cleaned. (See photo 12.3.1.)

12.3.1 Staff maintain the restroom area by replenishing supplies, cleaning up spills and sanitizing toilets.

Indicator

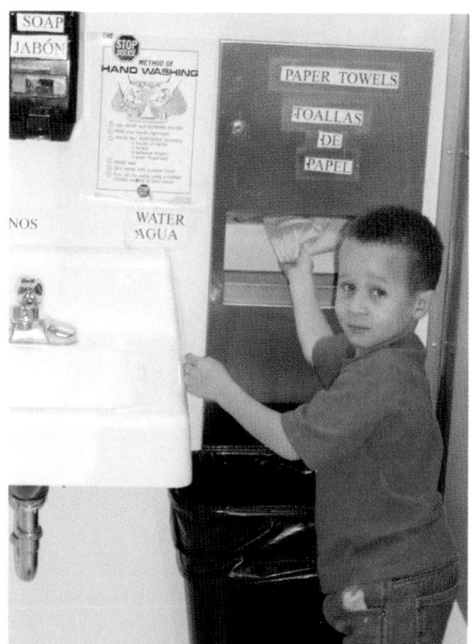

12.3.2 Liquid soap and paper towels are basic provisions needed so children can successfully wash hands after toileting.

12.3.4 When children are expected to use the restroom as a whole group, it does not allow for individual needs.

Indicator 3.1 is true (score "Yes") when no major problems are observed with one or more of the sanitary requirements listed in 1.1, or only one minor problem.

3.2 See Indicator 1.2 for the requirements of ***basic provisions***.

The observer should check the toileting and/or diapering areas when there are no children using the toilet or being changed to make sure that they have enough toilet paper, warm running water, soap, and towels. (See photo 12.3.2.)

3.3 Watch carefully during toileting/diapering times to make sure that children and staff are washing their hands properly. If less than 75% of children or staff wash their hands when needed, credit cannot be given (score 3.3 "No"). Keep track of how many handwashings are needed and the number completed properly, as shown in Chart 1 on page 116. The observer should watch a sample of the times when handwashing is needed until evidence is obtained to document the usual practice (as explained in 1.1). If more than one staff member handles toileting/diapering during the observation, be sure to watch and collect evidence on all staff.

3.4 The way in which toileting is scheduled in a classroom will depend on the ages and abilities of the children, the number of children and staff, the location or convenience of the toileting/diapering facilities, and the beliefs of the staff.

The ***toileting schedule*** can be handled in several ways:

- Whole group routine (includes everyone at the same time, whether needed or not)
- Small group routines (includes a few children at the same time, but not all)
- Individually (includes only the child who needs to use the toilet)
- Combination (whole or small group go together, but individuals are allowed to use toilet when needed)

Indicator

A whole group approach might be used when a staff member is by herself with young children and the bathroom is down the hall, because going to the bathroom as a group would be the only option to ensure proper supervision. (See photo 12.3.4, previous page.) Two or more teachers who work with the same group might decide to use another type of schedule, for example, with one staff member being responsible for taking the children individually or in small groups to use the bathroom while the other stays in the room.

Whatever the reasons for the type of schedule selected and used, obviously the individual schedule can best meet the toileting needs of each child (as long as it is well carried out), and the whole group schedule meets individual needs the least well. A small group schedule or combinations of the whole group and individual schedule can also meet individual needs.

To score this indicator, the observer must consider what is observed, in terms of the toileting schedule (what children experience as a time sequence, rather than what is printed on the classroom schedule), and observe how well the schedule that is carried out meets the toileting needs of each child in the group.

When the toileting schedule appears to be individualized, observe to be sure that all children are encouraged to use the toilet at some time during the observation and that toileting accidents do not occur due to lack of attention on the part of the staff. If a whole group approach is used, observe to see whether children are forced to use the toilet when not needed or if children can also use the toilet whenever needed, so they are not uncomfortable.

Determine whether the needs of each child are being met without having to wait or be forced to use the toilet, and with few accidents, if any. If these conditions are true for each child, score 3.4 "Yes." If there are problems with the schedule for any child in the group, score 3.4 "No."

3.5 ***Adequate supervision*** means that staff monitor to protect the children or ensure that sanitary procedures (e.g., handwashing) are carried out. For toileting, staff keep an eye on all children using the toilet to ensure that toilet paper is used, toilets are flushed, and hands washed as needed. Staff notice and take action when children are using the toileting area inappropriately (such as splashing water, unrolling all the toilet paper, playing in the toilet, rough-housing) when they should be using the toilet. For diapering, adequate supervision means that staff pay sufficient attention to the child, for example, by never leaving a child who is on the diapering table unattended for any amount of time.

The amount of close supervision required will depend on the ages and abilities of the children being observed, with closer, more helpful supervision required for younger or less able children. Supervision can be considered adequate only when it is observed that children usually complete toileting procedures correctly and responsibly.

Most young children need the close supervision of an adult during toileting to make sure they are washing their hands properly and flushing toilets. Children who go to the bathroom without proper supervision often do not wash their hands, even if reminded by staff who are not directly supervising them, or they will do some of what is required but not all.

To give credit for this indicator, supervision cannot be unpleasant or inadequate. However, supervision can be neutral in affect (for example, staff are not unpleas-

Indicator

ant, but they are not particularly pleasant; warmth is not obvious, but neither is harshness or coldness); it is not required that supervision be pleasant. Score this indicator "No" if preschoolers go into bathroom, close the door, and staff cannot see the children to monitor them.

5.1 Sanitary conditions are ***easy to maintain*** when the area (such as floors and walls) is uncluttered and easy-to-clean. Equipment (such as toilets, sinks, and diapering surfaces) must also be easy-to-clean. There is warm running water in the area and easily accessible supplies, such as liquid soap, toilet paper, paper towels for all to use, and bleach-water solution, gloves and wipes for adults. Replacement supplies are also readily accessible as needed. When these sanitary conditions are present, staff and children are less likely to contaminate other areas of the classroom during the completion of toileting/diapering routines.

Since potty chairs are a health hazard, they should be avoided for general use. In the rare case when a special need requires the use of a potty chair, it may only be used for the child with special needs, and it must be cleaned and disinfected after each use (as described in 1.1). If potty chairs are for general use, score 5.1 "No."

5.2 The ***provisions*** considered in this indicator include the equipment and supplies needed by the children to complete toileting and/or diapering. ***Convenient and accessible*** means that the provisions are easy to reach and use, with minimal difficulty. For example, the observer should look for:

- Accommodations to make the sinks or toilets easy to use (such as steps or platform near sink so that children can wash hands independently, sit securely on toilet). (See photo 12.5.2.) Child-sized toilets and sinks fulfill this requirement, and if used, should also be credited in Indicator 7.1.
- Handrails or other adaptations provided for children with disabilities that require them.
- Toilet area adjacent to room or within room used by children.
- Faucets and flushing mechanisms that are easy to manage.
- Supplies, such as toilet paper, paper towels, and liquid soap are easy to reach and use.

12.5.2 Children use steps so that they can easily use the sink and soap.

Helping children to independently manage toileting, and some parts of diapering, gives the children a sense of competence and accomplishment, besides encouraging good health habits. When the required procedures are easy to carry out, because of convenient arrangements, it is far more likely for those important things to occur consistently.

5.3 ***Pleasant staff-child interactions*** during toileting/diapering are neither unpleasant (see 1.3) nor neutral (see 3.5). To give credit for 5.3, any staff member helping with toileting/diapering should be observed paying positive attention to the children during the routine and showing patience, encouragement, and support. The observer should watch the children's responses to the interactions of the adult and look for relaxed children who are not anxious and who seem to trust the staff to be understanding of their needs. If an adult teases or shames a child for wetting pants or uses any other negative approach, score this indicator "No."

Indicator

12.7.1 a

12.7.1 b

12.7.1 a–b Child-sized toilets and sinks make it easier for children to independently use the facilities.

7.1 ***Providing child-sized toilets and sinks*** encourages children to independently complete toileting/diapering routines. (See photos 12.7.1. a–b.) In addition, there is less physical stress on staff who do not have to lift or support children as they use the equipment. It is also easier to maintain the health and safety conditions for children when child-sized equipment is used. For example, children will not fall from steps, steps will not present extra cleaning challenges, and children will be less likely to have accidents when they can reach the provisions easily.

To score 7.1 "Yes," toilets and sinks must be smaller than adult-sized equipment and usable by at least 75% of the children, with no extra adult help (such as lifting) or adaptations (such as steps or toilet seats), unless required by special needs.

7.2 ***Self-help*** means that children can manage tasks on their own to the extent possible, with little adult assistance. The extent to which children will be able to help themselves in toileting/diapering routines will depend on a variety of factors, such as their ages and abilities, the convenience of the provisions, and the difficulty of managing their clothing. Generally, younger children or children with certain disabilities will require more staff assistance than older children or those who are typically developing.

To score 7.2, the observer must determine:

- The extent to which self-help is possible for the children, based on ages and abilities
- Whether the environment is set up to encourage self-help
- Whether staff are teaching children the required skills as needed
- Whether staff follow up on their teaching by supervising adequately and helping when needed (for example, staff remind the children to flush toilets, wash their hands, use paper towels, and turn off faucets, and staff check to be sure they do.)

12 Toileting/diapering

Indicator

Credit can be given for this indicator (score "Yes") when children appear to manage their toileting routines as independently as they should be able to, considering their ages and abilities. If staff help much too much or far too little, or if the basic provisions required to allow children to handle toileting/diapering routines are not present, credit should not be given (score "No").

13 Health practices

General information about this item

This item considers health-related issues other than those required for toileting/diapering, meals/snacks, and nap/rest, which are handled in the respective items.

Therefore, in scoring this item it is important to listen and watch very carefully for examples of how ***staff act to cut down on the spread of germs*** throughout the day.

Keeping spaces, materials, and equipment clean:

- All surfaces that come into contact with potentially infectious body fluids (such as blood, saliva, vomit, urine, feces, oozing from wounds or infections, mucous) must be cleaned up and disinfected (with a bleach and water solution) immediately, and children's and staff's hands must be washed properly without contaminating any other surfaces. The possibility of contamination from bloodborne pathogens, such as the hepatitis B virus, HIV, or hepatitis C must be minimized. Since it is unknown whether any person is a carrier of these diseases, precautions must be taken with the assumption that each person is infected. Toys that have been soiled or mouthed must be set aside and washed.
- Toothbrushes must be stored to avoid contamination (brushes not touching and stored in a container to prevent touching other surfaces), and air dried.

Toothpaste for each child must be uncontaminated, for example, by using individual tubes or putting pea-sized dots of paste onto an individual piece of clean paper for each child to use. Toothpaste containers must not be contaminated by contact with multiple toothbrushes.

- Using a hands-free trash container, for example, with a foot pedal, will minimize contamination of hands.
- Individual paper towels, disposable tissues, and liquid soap should be accessible. No towels, tissues, or wash cloths should be used by more than one child or staff member.
- Dirty floors and play surfaces should be cleaned up after messy play.
- Indoor and outdoor areas used for children should be free of animal contamination.
- Dress-up clothes should be cleaned on a regular basis and when soiled.

Ensuring proper handwashing:

Proper handwashing procedures are followed when needed (do not consider handwashing for diapering/toileting and meals/snacks).

Handwashing for children and staff requires that both hands be washed with liquid soap and rinsed thoroughly under warm running water for about 10 seconds (sing one verse of "Row, Row, Row Your Boat"). Hands should be dried with individual

Indicator

13 A Children should wash their hands after touching trash can lids.

13 B Hands-free or foot-pedal cans prevent contamination of hands

paper towels that are not shared or air-dried with a blower. Using gloves, wipes, or antiseptic waterless washes does not count as substitutes for handwashing. An exception is that if handwashing is required on the playground (after wiping noses, for example), use of a wipe is acceptable.

Examples of categories when proper handwashing is needed include:

To avoid spreading household germs:

For example,

- Upon arrival into the classroom
- After touching trash cans or lids (See photos 13 A–B.)
- After cleaning up spills
- When hands are otherwise contaminated

After messy play:

For example,

- After using sand outdoors
- After being outdoors, and hands are noticeably soiled
- After messy play such as painting or gluing
- After gardening
- After cooking activities (and before as well)
- After playing with pets

To avoid spreading diseases through bodily fluids or skin contact:

For example,

- Before and after group water play in the same water table or other container
- After sneezing or coughing when hands are contaminated
- After wiping noses (See photos 13 C–D, next page.)
- Before and after applying sunscreen to a child
- Before and after dealing with cuts, scrapes, or other health needs
- After cleaning up bodily fluid spills

Indicator

13 C

13 D

13 C–D Children wash hands after blowing noses to avoid spreading diseases and illness.

To score, observers should be aware of times that cleaning, sanitizing, and handwashing are carried out when needed. This means that the observer should watch and listen. For example, observers should listen for coughing or sneezing by the children and staff, or watch for noses that need wiping to see that the proper procedures are carried out. Notes should be taken on the score sheet to indicate when needed cleaning or sanitizing has been ignored. It is equally important, however, to recognize when it has been carried out properly.

To collect the necessary information on handwashing, it helps to keep track of whether it was or was not completed as needed. A small chart, such as Chart 1, should be made to describe when handwashing is needed, and whether or not it is carried out properly.

Chart 1
Keeping track of handwashing

	Adult		**Child**	
Times when needed:	**YES**	**No**	**YES**	**NO**
• Upon arrival in the classroom/ When re-entering classroom after outdoor play	✓✓✓✓	X X X	✓✓ ✓✓✓	X X X X X X
• After messy or sand/ water play	✓✓		✓✓✓✓ ✓✓✓✓	X X X X X X
• After dealing with bodily fluids (e.g., running noses, sneezes) or making significant skin contact (e.g., applying lotions, medications)	✓✓✓✓ ✓✓✓✓		✓✓✓✓	X X X X X X
• After touching contaminated objects (trashcan lids, the floor) or pets	✓✓✓✓ ✓✓	X X X X X	✓✓	X X X X X X X X X X

Indicator

13.1.2 a Ashtrays and cigarette butts should not be permitted in spaces used by children.

13.1.2 b Look for cigarette butts on the playground to determine if smoking ever happens in child care areas.

A closer look at each indicator

1.1 ***Staff do not act to cut down on the spread of germs*** means that staff rarely do any of the procedures listed on page 125. Do not score 1.1 "Yes" unless serious health problems are observed during the observation, and very little staff attention is given to health requirements such as those listed.

Since this item does not handle issues related to toileting/diapering, the examples in the ECERS-R related to toileting/diapering should be omitted in scoring this indicator.

1.2 Since inhaling second-hand cigarette smoke has been shown to be harmful, children and non-smoking adults should not be exposed to smoking. In addition, no tobacco or waste from smoking should be accessible to children.

Smoking is allowed in child care areas means that either smoking (of any substance, such as cigarettes, pipes, or cigars) is permitted in spaces used by children, indoors or outdoors, or that there are signs that smoking occurs in these spaces. (See photos 13.1.2 a–b.)

Observe to see if there are signs that smoking occurs in areas used by children. For example, look for ashtrays or cigarette butts in children's spaces. No cigarette butts should be found on playgrounds used by children or spaces they use at any time while supervised on-site by program staff.

If any signs of smoking or tobacco use are observed in areas used by children, score this indicator "Yes."

If no signs are observed, ask staff if smoking is allowed in any of the areas used by children, indoors or out. If the answer is "Yes" score this indicator "Yes."

3.1 Since ***handwashing*** at meals/snacks and after toileting/diapering is handled in other items, rate 3.1 based on all other handwashing required, as described in 1.1.

Give credit for 3.1 only if it is observed that both staff's and children's hands are washed 75% of the time when needed. Look across all categories listed in the General Information section for this item to determine if staff and children are

Indicator

properly washing hands when needed. Make sure to notice when attempts are made to reduce contamination and as well as times when no action is taken. If either children's or staff members' hands are washed less than 75% of the time when needed, do not give credit for 3.1 (score "No").

3.2 Staff ***action*** includes ensuring that both staff and children cut down on the spread of germs, as described in the General Information section of this item with issues related to keeping spaces, materials, and equipment clean. Handwashing issues are addressed in indicator 3.1 and not in this indicator.

Usually means that staff cut down on the spread of germs more often than not. If staff take action to cut down on the spread of germs without many lapses (completed at least 75% of the times needed) during the observation, then score 3.2 "Yes."

If many lapses occur (more than 25% of the times when needed), or there are any major problems, such as bodily fluid spills not being cleaned up immediately or signs of animal contamination in children's play spaces, score 3.2 "No."

3.3 See 1.2 for information on ***smoking*** to score this indicator. If there is ***no smoking*** allowed in spaces used by children, indoors or outdoors, and there are no signs of smoking in these spaces, score 3.3 "Yes."

3.4 ***Procedures used to minimize spread of contagious disease*** are those that are carried out *in addition* to the types of procedures required to cut down on the spread of germs described in the General Information section. These procedures include:

- Carrying out an exclusion policy so children who are ill do not attend, or if they become ill, they are isolated from other children until picked up by parents
- Ensuring that children are immunized as required
- Ensuring that staff are in good physical health and do not carry communicable diseases
- Alerting parents to the presence of a communicable disease within the group (See photo 13.3.4.)

To score this indicator, the observer should *first* look for evidence to see whether or not the requirement is met. For example, if a child who is obviously sick is present in the group (such as with high temperature, diarrhea, vomiting, or unidentified rash), and staff take no action to isolate the child or contact the parents, score the indicator "No."

If no obvious evidence can be observed to score the indicator, staff should be asked general questions such as "Do you have any health requirements for children and staff?" or "How do you handle children who are sick?" These questions will usually elicit the information needed to score.

If a substantial number of procedures are used to minimize spread of contagious diseases, give credit (score "Yes") for this indicator. Not all examples in the indicator are required.

13.3.4 Notice of classroom illnesses is posted in an obvious place, near other parent information.

5.1 ***Children are dressed properly*** means that children wear clothing that allows freedom of movement, while protecting health and safety.

Indicator

13.5.1 a

13.5.1 b

13.5.1 a–b Warm weather requires cool clothing.

13.5.1 c Cold weather requires warm clothes including hats and mittens.

13.5.2 Teachers eat healthful foods when joining children for meals.

Children should be dressed appropriately for all weather conditions. During the summer, children should have clothing that will keep them as cool as possible, especially when the children go outdoors. (See photos 13.5.1 a–b.)

If it is a rainy day and children go outside, they should be dressed in boots or raincoats or use umbrellas if needed. If the children do get wet outside, and it is cold or chilly, they should be changed into dry, warm clothes when they get inside.

When it is cold outside, children should be dressed in coats, mittens, scarves, and winter hats or caps as necessary. If the weather is snowy, boots should be worn to keep the children's feet warm and dry. (See photo 13.5.1 c.)

Indoors, children should be neither too warm nor too cold. When clothes become wet, they should be changed.

If shoes are *not* worn, walking surfaces must be safe for bare feet. The floor covering or outdoor areas should be clear of sharp objects and extremely hot surfaces, and there should be no other risks, such as a risk of hookworm.

The observer cannot judge whether children are dressed properly based on their own comfort indoors or out. Observers generally move around much less than the

Indicator

children, so children tend to remain warmer than the observers do. In addition, children can often adjust better to warmer temperatures than some adults can. To score this indicator, observers should look to see whether children appear to be comfortable and are protected to ensure health and safety. Observers should listen to hear if children are complaining of being too cold or hot and see if providers are taking action to make them more comfortable, such as putting on warmer clothes or adjusting the room temperature.

If any child lacks needed clothing, staff must be able to supply the child with the required clothing. If it is *observed* that *any* child is not dressed properly (such as wet clothes not changed or no coat provided for cold weather), and supplemental clothing is not provided, score 5.1 "No."

If *all* children are observed to be dressed to meet their comfort, health, and safety needs throughout the observation, score 5.1 "Yes."

5.2 Staff who clearly care for their own health needs while in the presence of children are ***good models of health practices***. Children learn much about how to care for their health when they watch what staff do, in terms of their own health habits.

Score this indicator "Yes" if it is observed that staff generally show children that they care for their own health by doing these types of things:

- Washing hands as needed
- Eating healthful foods, not candy or other sweets in front of children (See photo 13.5.2, preceding page.)
- Drinking water, juice, or milk, but not sodas
- Being active and getting exercise
- Brushing teeth after meals
- Not smoking
- Checking and flushing toilets in the children's bathroom
- Keeping things clean
- Appearing to be reasonably well rested

If staff obviously give children the message that they do not try to care for their own health, score 5.2 "No."

5.3 ***Care given to children's appearance*** means that staff generally notice when children need help with their personal grooming and follow through as needed. The amount of help required from staff will vary depending on the ages and abilities of the children and the complexity of what is needed. All aspects of grooming are considered in this indicator, including issues related to meals/snacks, toileting/diapering, and nap, as well as outdoor and indoor play.

To score "Yes" for this indicator, staff must generally take action when needed throughout the observation. Watch to see if staff remind a child to put on an apron or smock before a messy art activity and follow up to make sure it is done. Staff may have to provide substantial help for children who cannot manage the tasks on their own (such as helping to change wet clothes or combing hair).

Indicator

13.5.3 Children wear large shirts to protect their clothing.

13.7.1 a Staff help children learn how to properly wash hands.

The observer should see evidence of staff guiding or helping children with the following types of tasks:

- If a child's face has become messy while eating or doing art, staff make sure the child's face is cleaned properly.
- If a child has a toileting accident, staff make sure the child is cleaned up and clothes are changed.
- If children's clothes become very soiled or wet, staff ensure that clothes are changed.
- If children participate in a messy activity, aprons/smocks are used to prevent or reduce the soil that gets on children's clothes. (See photo 13.5.3.)
- If a child has a runny nose, staff make sure it is wiped properly.
- If a child's hair becomes very messy, staff help with combing or brushing with the child's personal comb/brush, replacing barrettes, etc.

7.1 ***Health practices*** considered for this indicator include all children's personal care, such as handwashing, putting on or removing clothes, keeping clean, brushing teeth, caring for hair, or wiping noses.

Manage independently means that children are encouraged to do as much as they can to carry out health practices by themselves.

Children can be ***taught to manage health practices independently,*** either by having staff show them how to complete the actual health practices properly, or by using educational materials about the health practices with the children.

Staff can guide children to complete health-related tasks, follow up to be sure the tasks are completed, and provide help as needed. Examples include:

- Staff teach children to wash their hands by showing them initially, then reminding them to "make bubbles" and sing "Row, Row, Row Your Boat" or count to 10 while they wash. (See photo 13.7.1 a.)
- Staff make tissues accessible, show children where they are, and help them with nose blowing/wiping as needed, then follow up with handwashing.
- Staff show children how to flush toilets and periodically check to make sure it is being done.

Indicator

13.7.1 b A nutrition poster leads to conversation about healthful foods.

13.7.1 c Staff and children discuss the importance of good oral hygiene.

- Staff put smocks near the art and messy play areas and remind or help children to use them.
- Staff show children how to fasten clothes or put on or take off clothing.

Examples of teaching materials used with children to encourage independence in health practices include:

Displayed posters or pictures:

- Handwashing poster next to the sink that shows pictures of the handwashing steps (with or without printed words)
- Nutrition poster reminds children about healthful foods (See photo 13.7.1 b.)
- Poster showing how to brush teeth. (See photo 13.7.1 c.)

13.7.1 d Children learn more about bathing through water play activities.

Books used with or by the children on topics such as:

- Eating or cooking healthful foods
- Personal grooming, such as getting dressed, sequences to follow in handwashing
- Toileting or toilet training
- Daily personal care routine sequences, such as bathing, eating, resting, or playing
- Going to the doctor, dentist, or hospital
- Caring for injuries

Games or activities:

- Including nutritious play fruits and vegetables in the pretend play area
- Washing baby dolls or doll clothes in soapy water. (See photo 13.7.1 d.)
- Providing puzzles that show healthful personal care routines or foods
- Providing the props needed to act out doctor/nurse/patient roles in pretend play
- Offering cooking activities where healthful foods are prepared
- Discussing appropriate clothing for different types of weather

Indicator

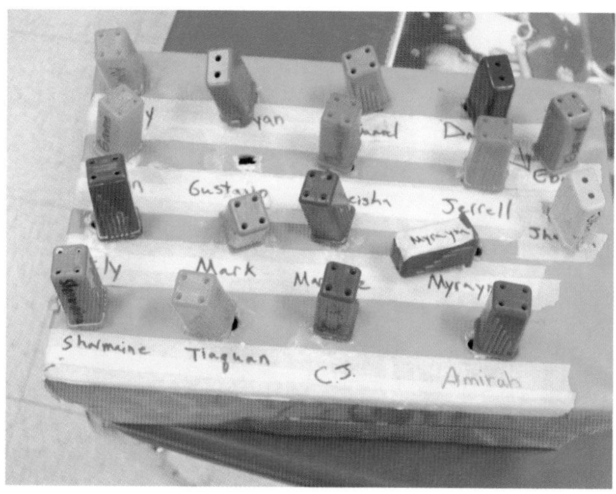

13.7.2 a

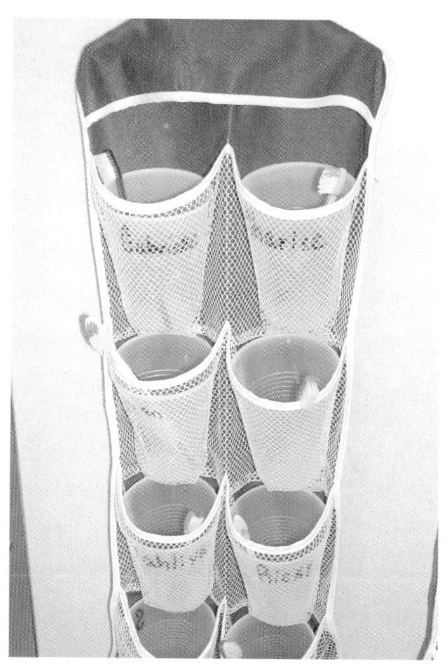

13.7.2 b

13.7.2 a–b Toothbrushes can be stored individually in a variety of ways.

If children generally carry out health practices properly by themselves, with little help or supervision from staff, then credit can be given for 7.1 (score "Yes") because it is assumed that much teaching occurs that was not observed during the time period.

If children obviously need help and supervision to carry out health procedures (they do not properly do the procedures independently), to score 7.1 "Yes," there must be evidence of teacher help and follow through (described on pages 129–130, Indicator 5.3). In addition, evidence of some teaching through activities or materials must be observed or reported by the staff.

7.2 A score of "NA" is permitted for programs open six hours or less per day.

Properly labeled means that each child has his/her own toothbrush with name on it, so that the toothbrush will not be used by any other child. Labels ensure that everyone knows which toothbrush belongs to each child, and sharing of toothbrushes does not occur. If children were to share a toothbrush, bacteria and germs would be spread among the children.

Properly stored means that:

- Children store their toothbrushes in storing devises (such as commercial or homemade racks for storing many toothbrushes or in individual cups), with the bristles up so that they can air dry. (See photos 13.7.2 a–b.)
- Toothbrush bristles should not be touching the bristles on another toothbrush or any contaminated surface.
- The storing devices should be washed and sanitized or replaced whenever they become visibly dirty.

Used at least once a day requires that children brush teeth daily, preferably after eating. Toothpaste is not necessary for children to use since food and plaque can be removed from the teeth without toothpaste.

Indicator

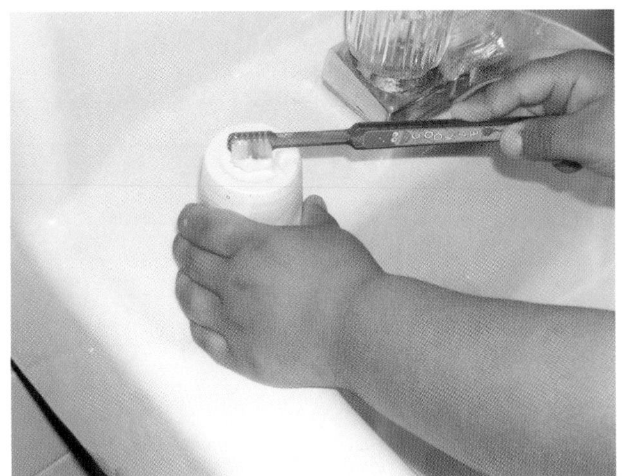

13.7. 2 c

13.7.2 d

13.7.2 c–d Cups, toothbrushes, and a small amount of paste are provided so that children can independently brush their teeth.

If staff choose to use toothpaste, only a pea-sized amount should be used for each child, and the toothpaste should not be contaminated. Contamination of toothpaste can be avoided by providing each child with his or her own small, labeled tube, not to be shared. Or staff can put the small amount of toothpaste on a piece of paper or cup for children to use. (See photos 13.7.2 c–d.) Children should not squeeze the toothpaste from the same tube directly on to their brush.

Score 7.2 "Yes" if most children brush their teeth at least once daily, and if sanitary procedures are maintained.

If the "same sink" is used for both tooth brushing and handwashing after toileting, without sanitizing, consider this sanitation problem under Item 12. Toileting/diapering and not in this item.

14 Safety practices

General information about this item

When serious accidents happen to young children, adults feel sorrow and guilt. Everyone knows that young children must be protected by adults because they do not have the understanding or experience that is needed to know what might be dangerous. No one wants a young child to be seriously injured or killed, especially while they are responsible for the child.

Hazards that could result in serious injury are dangers in the physical environment that might cause accidents for young children and require a hospital or doctor visit for treatment. Often these hazards do not appear to be very dangerous to adults because they do not cause accidents very often, and adults have the experience with the world to know how to avoid injury. But many dangers are not clear to preschool-aged children because they are too young to understand how things work in the world. For example, they will not know that an electrical outlet poses a serious threat if they push something into the holes. It does not look dangerous to the child, as a growling, frightening dog might.

Young children are learning about the world by exploring and trying things out. Even if they have been told that something is dangerous, they can easily forget. It is up to responsible adults to protect the children in their care, to minimize hazards present in a child's space, and to also supervise carefully. Supervision cannot take the place of minimizing hazards. No assumptions can be made, such as saying, "I know it is dangerous, but the children know not to go near it," or, "We have never had a child fall from that place," or, "We are always watching." Accidents will happen.

The "Notes for Clarification" (ECERS-R, page 22) for this item list indoor and outdoor hazards that could result in serious injury, such as lack of safety caps on electrical outlets or poisonous substances that are not locked away.

A closer look at each indicator

1.1 This indicator requires that all hazards found in the ***indoor*** spaces used by children be evaluated. ***Indoors*** includes the classroom(s) that are used by children at any time, and any other spaces children access such as multi-purpose rooms, gymnasiums, rest rooms, storage areas, cafeterias, hallways, or stairwells. To score this indicator, the observer should look through all the indoor areas used by, or accessible to, children for hazards. (See photos 14.1.1 a–c, next page.) The "Notes for Clarification" list does not include all possible indoor hazards—there are many

Indicator

14.1.1 a Bleach-water solution should be stored out of children's reach.

14.1.1 b Uncovered electrical outlets pose a safety hazard to young children

others that could cause serious injury, and if observed, they should be listed on the score sheet and considered in scoring. For example:

- Bleach and water solution, used to sanitize surfaces, does not have to be locked away, but it must be stored out of reach of young children. It cannot be sprayed when it will be breathed in by children, for example, if children are sitting around the table while the table is being sprayed.
- Any electrical outlets or wires present where children are allowed to play must be safe—outlets covered, cords secured. When special safety outlets are used in a program, ask the teacher or director how they are operated to ensure child safety, and check to be sure operation rules are followed correctly. Flip covers on outdoor outlets are acceptable as safety caps as long as they are kept closed when not in use. Computer wires should not be within view or easy reach of children.

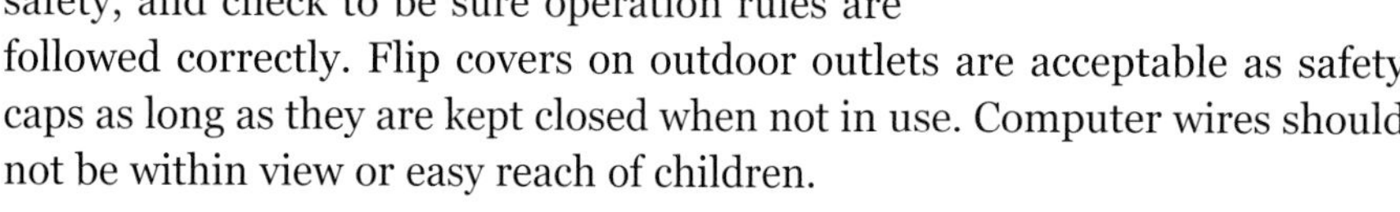

14.1.1 c This area is potentially dangerous because the climbing equipment is placed too close to furniture and there is insufficient cushioning.

Indicator 1.1 is true (score "Yes") when the observer can list two or more very serious hazards seen in indoor spaces used by the children. If no serious hazards are observed, (or only one), score 1.1 "No."

Minor hazards (such as a loose carpet edge, splinters on a shelf, or bleach-water solution stored within children's reach), which are unlikely to cause *serious* injury and require hospitalization or a visit to the doctor, are not considered in scoring this indicator, unless there are more than five observed. If more than five are listed during the observation, score 1.1 "Yes."

1.2 ***Hazards that could result in serious injury*** are defined in the General Information section for this item. See the General Information section for an explanation of why this indicator is important. In this indicator all hazards present in the ***outdoor*** area(s) used by children must be evaluated. ***Outdoors*** includes all playgrounds that are used by children at any time, and any other outdoor spaces children access such as patios, semi-shelters, storage areas, and even parking lots if they are ever used for activities.

Indicator

14.1.2 a This play area is not safe because there is no soft cushioning under the equipment.

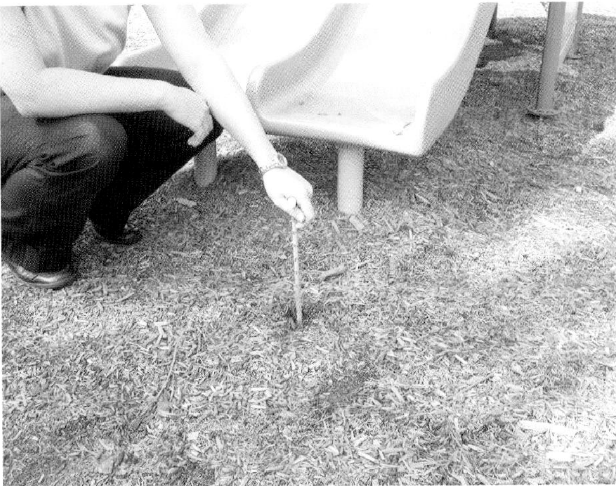

14.1.2 b

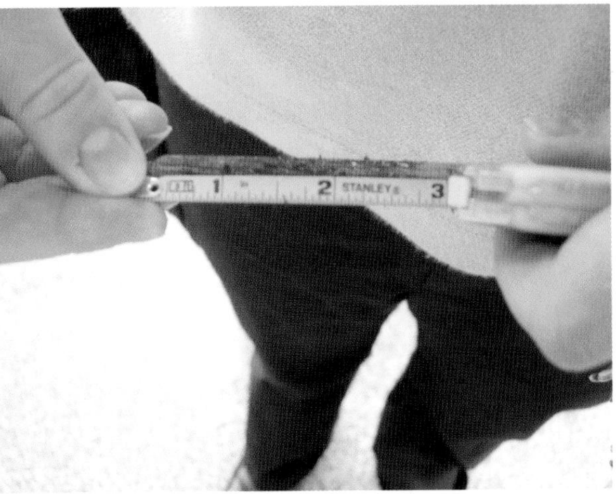

14.1.2 c

14.1.2 b–c A probe is used to find the depth of the cushioning materials. Then the probe is measured to see whether the cushioning material is sufficient.

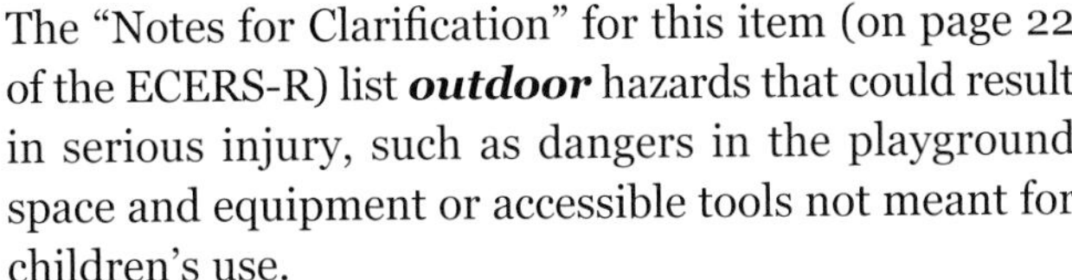

The "Notes for Clarification" for this item (on page 22 of the ECERS-R) list ***outdoor*** hazards that could result in serious injury, such as dangers in the playground space and equipment or accessible tools not meant for children's use.

To score this indicator, the observer should look through all the outdoor areas used by, or accessible to, children for such hazards. (See photos 14.1.2 a–c.) The "Notes for Clarification" list does not include all hazards—there are many others that could cause serious injury, and if observed, they should be listed on the score sheet and considered in scoring. For example:

- A fence that has sharp prongs or long exposed bolts within easy reach of children, on which children could become caught
- Unprotected water, such as pools, deep puddles, bogs, creeks, or rivers, accessible to children
- Children allowed to climb on rocks or in trees without adequate safety precautions, such as resilient ground covers in fall zones

Indicator 1.2 is true (score "Yes") when the observer can list two or more *very* serious hazards seen in the outdoor space(s) used by the children. If no hazards are observed (or only one), score 1.2 "No."

Minor outdoor hazards (such as tree roots that might cause tripping, very shallow puddles, or a little sand on a sidewalk), which are unlikely to cause serious injury and require hospitalization or a visit to the doctor, are not considered in scoring this indicator, unless there are more than five. If six or more are listed during the observation, score 1.2 "Yes."

1.3 The requirements of this indicator are based on ***supervision,*** (watching and protecting children from danger) provided by staff during both indoor and outdoor times.

To score this indicator, consider the supervision to protect children provided by *all* observed staff supervising indoors or outdoors. Concentrate primarily on the

Indicator

staff and children in the group being observed, but if groups mix at any time (for example, several classes are sharing the same outdoor space), consider *all* observed children of similar age/abilities as those in the class being observed and *all* staff supervising in that area.

Notice whether there are enough staff to watch all areas used and whether adults are supervising the most hazardous areas/activities adequately. (See photo 14.1.3.)

14.1.3 While the teacher is on one side of the classroom helping children, this child is left unsupervised.

Meeting or not meeting certain recommended staff-child ratio requirements does not automatically mean that 1.3 is true or false. Ratio requirements vary substantially (for example, by state or agency). It is the *combination* of factors (number of staff to children, stringency of the supervision, the needs of the children, and the nature of the environment) that will determine the score for 1.3.

Inadequate supervision means that staff severely compromise children's safety needs by not watching, guiding, or intervening as is required by the children's abilities or the nature of the hazards present. More diligent supervision is required for younger children or in more dangerous circumstances. For example, an older 4- or 5-year-old might be considered adequately supervised when using a stapler by himself, but a 2-year old, or an older impulsive child, would be considered inadequately supervised under similar circumstances.

The score for this item must be based on what is seen throughout the observation. The observation must be long enough to provide a range of circumstances, including quiet and more active times, group times and free play, routine and play times, and more or less stressful periods of the day. For example, to score accurately, the observer should observe supervision early in the morning, when children and staff are fresh, and continue to observe to see the more stressful times of the day, such as before lunch or nap, when people are hungry or tired.

Indicator 1.3 should be scored "Yes" if staff leave children and *no* adult is present to supervise them, even for short periods of time. Inadequate supervision may also be true (score "Yes") when there are too few staff for the number of children or hazards present, inattentive staff who ignore children or attend to other interests. When children leave the area supervised by staff, and are completely unsupervised (for example, leave the classroom unnoticed and no adult realizes the child's absence), score this indicator "Yes."

If 1.3 is scored "Yes," then it is likely that the Supervision Items, 29 and 30, will also receive scores of 1. Note that to score this indicator "Yes," supervision must be inadequate both ***indoors and outdoors***.

3.1 See 1.1 and 1.2 for definition of major safety hazards indoors and outdoors.

To score 3.1 "Yes" there can be *no* safety hazards present, indoors and outdoors, which could cause serious injury that would require treatment by a hospital or doctor. There must also be less than six minor hazards observed.

3.2 ***Adequate supervision to protect children's safety*** requires that there are enough staff present to watch children during both routines and play. The staff are positioned to see all areas where children may be playing, move around as needed to keep a close eye on children, and are attentive to children's basic safety needs. There is always an adult present, supervising, and children are never left unsupervised, for any amount of time. See photos 14.3.2 a–b, on next page, for a contrast between supervised and unsupervised.

Indicator

14.3.2 a Staff closely supervise children when they are using the climbing equipment.

14.3.2 b Staff have moved away, leaving the climbing equipment unsupervised.

To give credit for this indicator, staff must intervene when problems occur that could seriously compromise a child's safety (e.g., to stop children from hurting themselves or others or to ensure that all children remain within view of adults). They must pay extra attention in more hazardous situations, such as when children are doing certain cooking activities, playing around water, climbing on high equipment, or using carpentry tools or sharp objects.

14.3.2 c Staff use a "zone" approach to ensure all areas on the playground are adequately supervised.

Strategies used to help ensure adequate supervision by staff include:

- Adjusting supervision for ages and abilities of children
- Standing where all of the children are easily seen, and moving close to areas where they are playing
- When helping one child, keeping an eye on the others and being available to step in when needed
- Knowing where the potentially dangerous areas are indoors and outdoors, and supervising these areas more closely
- Establishing safety rules that are realistic and easy to follow
- Using a "zone" approach to supervising for safety, where each staff member has primary responsibility for certain areas. If there are no children in an area, staff move to help supervise another area, until children return to their supervision zone (See photo 14.3.2 c.)

If there are any serious lapses in supervision, or many minor lapses, score 3.2 "No."

3.3 ***Essentials to handle emergencies*** are the provisions needed to deal with accidents, fire, or other dangers that require immediate action. (See photos 14.3.3 a–b, next page.) The examples listed in this indicator do not include every essential required for every classroom. They only provide some of the things the observer

Indicator

should consider in scoring the indicator. For example, a fire alarm, working fire extinguisher, and evacuation system are not listed, but the observer should consider such essentials also.

Often the requirement for essentials needed to handle emergencies will depend on local conditions. For example, in an area where earthquakes are possible, procedures to follow in case of earthquakes would be required. Or if an enrolled child tends to have special medical needs, such as seizures or severe allergies, the essentials needed to handle such cases would be required.

Additional information to consider about the essentials listed in the examples for 3.3 follows:

- ***Access to a telephone*** means that the phone must be on-site and easily accessible, but not necessarily in the room. If a portable phone is used, staff must know its location. If the phone is in another room, the room must be unlocked so staff can use the phone when needed.
- Emergency numbers must be posted, so they are easily found and used by staff, parents, substitutes, or even sometimes by older children. To get credit, the numbers cannot be hidden (such as in drawers or cabinets).
- A substitute for staff must be immediately available when called upon in an emergency. The substitute must be on-site. Arrangements for staff to share supervision responsibilities in emergencies are acceptable, but the remaining staff must be able to supervise all children.
- The first aid kit must be well stocked, with items required for emergencies (such as disposable non-porous gloves, scissors, tweezers, thermometer, bandages and tape, sterile gauze pads, roller gauze, various band-aids, safety pins, eye dressings, cold pack, and a current first aid instruction chart). If all such items are not stored together in one kit, staff should have easy access to them, and know where they are stored. For example, cold packs might be stored in the kitchen freezer, rather than in the first aid kit.

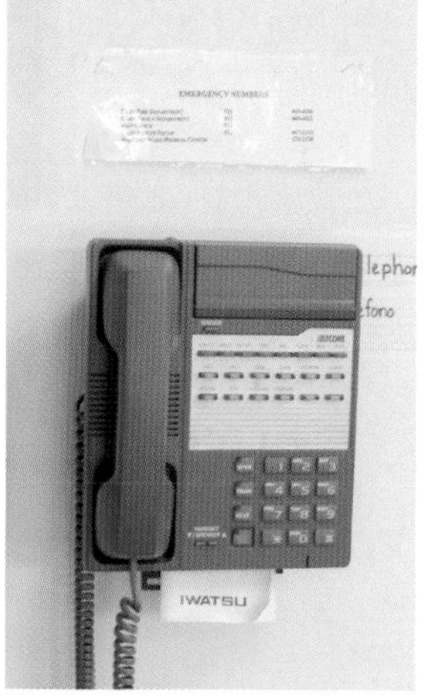

14.3.3 a Emergency numbers are posted above the phone.

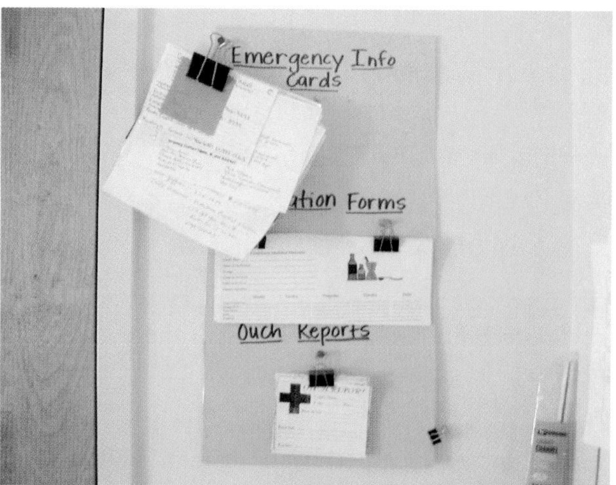

14.3.3 b Emergency information is posted where teachers, parents, and substitutes can easily see it.

Indicator

- Transportation must be readily available to transport an injured child for medical treatment. Transportation can be called (for example, by dialing 911 for an ambulance) or provided by staff.
- Written emergency procedures must be clear, indicating, for example, the sequence for how emergencies will be handled, who will take responsibility, and who will be called.

To give credit for 3.3, observe to ensure that essentials are present, and ask staff for information not observed.

14.5.1 Staff remind children to keep trikes on trike path so they do not interfere with other gross motor activities.

5.1 ***Staff anticipate and take action to prevent safety problems*** means that staff recognize possible hazards in the areas used by children, and correct the problems before accidents happen. (See photo 14.5.1.) Some examples of such precautions are listed in 5.1. Other examples include:

- Removing broken toys and equipment that might cause injury
- Removing trash from children's play areas
- Securing cords or wires that are loose
- Putting heavy objects out of the reach of children
- Anchoring wobbly furniture or placing it in a safe position so it will not fall
- Tying children's shoes so that falls are less likely to occur
- Sweeping sand off walking and running surfaces or stairs
- Limiting the number of children on certain climbing equipment where having too many children could increase risk of pushing and falling
- Stopping children who are fighting before it becomes serious
- Placing possibly dangerous tools used by children and staff (knives, scissors, hammers, saws) out of reach when not being supervised in use
- Preventing children from running in front of swings
- Ensuring gates or doors are closed

Score 5.1 "Yes" if there are one or more obvious attempts by staff to prevent safety problems during the observation. If safety problems generally go unnoticed, score 5.1 "No." If all areas are completely safe, and no possible problems arise, give credit for this indicator.

5.2 ***Safety rules*** for children must be understood by them to be effective. Reasons for safety precautions are needed to help children understand the importance of what they view as restrictions to their desire to explore and try things out.

When staff only tell children what they cannot do, with no explanations, children feel overly controlled by adults, and may want to rebel against rules. Reminding children about how important their safety is to themselves, their parents, and the staff helps them feel that rules are not so limiting, or if there are limits, they are worth following.

Providing ***reasons for safety rules*** does not mean that staff have to give long lectures or use harsh tones. The reasons can be provided both informally, when a problem is about to happen, or at more formal times, for example, through activities or discussions with the children.

Indicator

When reasons are explained informally, during a time when a possible accident is being prevented, the dangers associated with a hazard must be quickly and clearly stated to the child.

Here are some examples of explaining safety rules informally to children:

- "Please sit on the chair. I am afraid you will fall and get hurt."
- "Walk far away from the swings, not in front of them. You might be hit and hurt because the swing can't stop."
- "Please don't hurry her to go down the slide. She might fall and get hurt."
- "Don't touch; it's hot and will burn you."
- "Use the knife carefully, on the cutting board, like this. You might cut your finger."
- "Stay with me. I might lose you."

The observer should watch and listen carefully during the observation to decide whether only rules are provided or whether reasons are also given. It is not required that every limitation or rule used by staff is associated with a reason, as long as some reasons are observed being given to the children. It helps to note examples on the score sheet.

Reasons for rules can also be given to children during more formal activities or discussions. Here are some examples to look for, but many other possibilities are acceptable to meet the requirements of the indicator:

- Discussing the reasons for fire safety and the fire drills practiced in the center while doing a curriculum unit on the topic
- Having group discussions of classroom safety rules, such as why children should use blocks carefully, never leave the classroom without an adult, follow special rules while on fieldtrips, etc.
- Talking about puzzles or pictures illustrating safety precautions
- Reading a book on a safety topic at group time

Simply having toys or materials accessible that illustrate safety rules does not meet the requirements of the indicator. To give credit, staff must be observed discussing or explaining safety rules.

Formal activities, such as those listed above, should be considered in scoring 5.2, but these do not substitute for the immediate, less formal, explanations required if staff must take action to prevent accidents.

7.1 ***Play areas*** should be ***arranged to avoid safety problems***, both indoors and outdoors. In arranging both indoor and outdoor areas, staff should consider furniture/equipment placement, traffic pathways, the materials that are accessible in each area, the characteristics of the children who will use the space, and the hidden messages children might get from the arrangement.

A few examples of the types of arrangements to consider in scoring are included in the indicator. However, many other possibilities exist and should be considered. For example, to avoid safety problems indoors:

Indicator

- Pathways do not encourage running indoors; there are natural obstacles (such as furnishings) that prevent obvious running places.
- There are no large, wide-open spaces that encourage roughhousing or wrestling.
- Active play areas are placed away from quite play areas, especially those that have fragile or breakable materials.
- Soft cozy areas are not designed to invite jumping on others.
- Water and messy play areas are placed so the floors can be easily cleaned and dried.
- Furnishings are placed and used so they do not invite climbing.

14.7.1 Large climbing equipment is located in a separate area so that other activities, such as balls and swings, do not interfere with the use of this equipment.

Examples for avoiding safety problems outdoors include:

- Different types of activities are placed to avoid safety problems; for example, swings are not in usual path of running children; wheel toy area is separated from pedestrian pathways or other activities. (See photo 14.7.1.)
- Areas for more quiet activity are separated from more active areas.
- Ball and block play are separate from other activity areas.
- No activities are located in fall zones of equipment. When sand is used as a cushioning surface for a fall zone, another separate area is provided just for sand play.

7.2 It is unlikely that all children will always ***follow*** all ***safety rules***. ***Generally*** means that children follow the rules during most of the observation, even if there are a few lapses in following rules. Credit can be given for 7.2 if children listen to staff when they remind children about safety rules, or if no safety problems with children are observed because children follow safety rules by themselves.

Language-Reasoning

15 Books and pictures

General information about this item

Helping preschoolers and kindergartners develop a close and enjoyable relationship with books is a vital step towards literacy. Children who regularly have books read to them progress from turning the pages and studying the pictures intently to selecting favorite stories, anticipating the next action in a story, telling the story themselves, and finally reading on their own. The early childhood program staff have an important role to play in preparing a child for lifelong literacy.

In this language item, as in all items involving any types of interactions, ***staff*** refers to those adults who are in the classroom with the children for a ***substantial portion of the day*** (1/3 of the time the program is open). This can include volunteers, if they are in the classroom the required amount of time. Adults who are in the classroom for shorter periods of the day, or who are not a regular part of the classroom, do not count in evaluating whether the requirements for this item are met. For example, if a therapist, parent, or a director of a program comes into the classroom and interacts with the children for short or irregular periods, these interactions do not count in scoring language items, unless the interactions are extremely negative. As an exception, in a parent cooperative or lab school, in which the usual staffing patterns include different people as teaching assistants daily, these assistants are counted as staff.

For this item, the observer should focus on all books that are in the classroom for children to use. In order to count as a ***book***, the cover and pages must be intact, and the pages are not so torn or defaced that they cannot be read. In addition to commercially produced books, books made by staff and children can be counted. For example, the children might draw pictures of their Halloween costumes and dictate captions that the teacher writes on the pages, which are then made into a book and placed with the other books. Or a class photo album can count as a homemade book.

In a high quality classroom, staff not only have planned story times daily, but also read books to children spontaneously, as the occasion arises. When the staff want to extend something the children have done, a relevant book is useful as a follow-up. Children also feel free to ask to have a favorite story read to them outside of planned story time in a classroom where interest in books is evidenced throughout the day.

Each time a staff member reads or tells a story to the children, it should be an interesting and rewarding experience, so that the children form pleasant associations with literature. Planned story time, initiated by the staff, should be limited in length and matched to the interest level of the group. Since it is usually easier to hold the attention of a small group of young preschoolers, reading to the whole

Indicator

15.1.1 a This reading center has very few books accessible to the children and there are no books in any other areas.

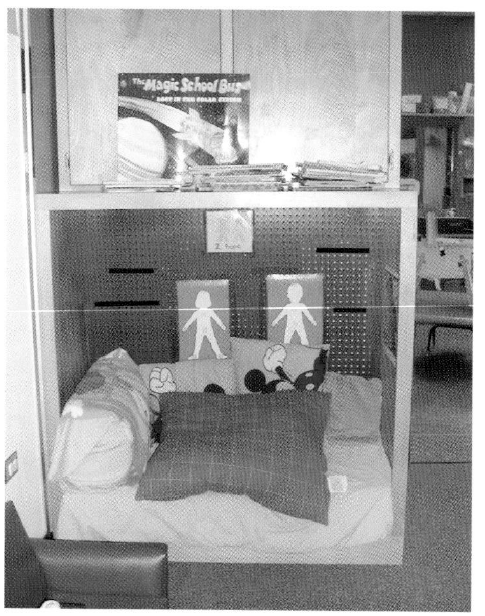

15.1.1 b

15.1.1 c

15.1.1 b–c There are very few books and they are too high to be accessible to the children.

group should be reserved for 4-year-olds and kindergartners, if needed. When books are read to individuals or a relatively small group, the children and staff are able to discuss points of interest in the story.

In addition to having a large and varied collection of books accessible to children, additional storytelling materials, such as puppets, flannel board stories, and recorded stories help in the growth of literacy and are considered in this item.

A closer look at each indicator

1.1 ***Very few books accessible*** means that there are fewer than five intact books for children to use. (See photo 15.1.1 a.) ***Accessible*** means that the children can reach the books and are allowed to use them. (See photos 15.1.1 b–c.) Give credit only

Indicator

for children's books or magazines, either commercial or teacher-made, designed to be read or used by children. Do not give credit for magazines meant for adults or equipment catalogs that are stored to be cut up and used in other activities, for example, in a collage art project. Score 1.1 "Yes" if fewer than five intact books are accessible to the children or if the accessible books can be used for less than one hour per day in a full-day program. Less time is required in a part time program of less than 6 hours (see 3.1 below).

15.3.1 In order to be accessible, the books must be easy for the child to reach. Books may be placed on a book shelf, put in a basket, out on a table, or made accessible in another way.

1.2 ***Rarely read to children*** means that staff hardly ever read to children. There is no daily story time initiated by the staff in which most of the children can participate or any daily response to children's interests or requests. Reading is extremely infrequent (less than once a day) for the whole group, for smaller groups, or for individuals. If story time is listed in the posted schedule, and the rest of the schedule is fairly well carried out, but no reading occurred during the observation, ask the teacher if story time is part of the daily schedule and how often it occurs. Score 1.2 "Yes" if children are not read to at least once a day, except under unusual circumstances.

3.1 ***Some books accessible*** means that there are enough books within easy reach that the children can use so that few, if any conflicts over books occur due to scarcity. (See photo 15.3.1.) Generally there should be enough books accessible for at least half the number of children who are allowed to attend on any day, to score this indicator "Yes." Thus, in a group with a maximum attendance of 20, at least 10 books must be accessible. Remember to count only books that are meant for children and that are in reasonably good repair.

To give credit the books must be accessible for at least an hour per day in a program of 8 hours or more. This does not require that all children be able to use the books at the same time or that each child has a full hour to use the materials. However, it is required that children would have a reasonable chance to use books at some time if they wished.

Less time is required for programs operating less than 8 hours a day, with the amount of time calculated proportionally, based on the ratio of 1 hour for programs of 8 hours or more. For example, if a program operated for 6 hours a day, this would be 3/4 of a full-day program, so the time required would be 3/4 of the 1 hour. If the program operated 4 hours a day, the requirement would be 1/2 hour.

3.2 ***Staff-initiated*** means that the staff conduct the activity. ***Receptive language activity*** means that the staff provide an activity to help children learn to listen to and understand language. For example, staff might read a story, tell a story using puppets, or tell a story using flannel board pieces or dolls. ***Time daily*** means that the receptive language activity is provided as a regular part of the scheduled daily activities. (See photos 15.3.2 a–b, next page.)

5.1 ***A wide selection of books*** includes both a relatively large quantity of books and a variety of topics. All books that children use in the room must be included in scoring. Look around to see whether there might be books accessible in a number of areas, such as the dramatic play area, science area, cozy area, or private area, as well as in the main reading center. To score 5.1 "Yes," there should be 20 books easily accessible in the room for a group of 15 children or less and at least 1 extra book for each additional child over that number permitted to attend. Thus, a group

Indicator

15.3.2 a

15.3.2 b

15.3.2 a–b A staff-initiated daily receptive language activity may include book reading, story telling, and/or using a flannel board or puppets to tell a story. It must be a daily planned, staff-initiated activity that all children have access to. It may be carried out in small groups, as long as all children can participate, if they wish to.

in which 25 children are enrolled and might attend should have at least 30 books accessible daily.

A wide selection also means that a variety of topics are included in the accessible books. Look to see whether there are books accessible for children to use in the categories listed in the ECERS-R item. Credit may be given if one category has fewer books and another has more books, but all must be represented. In some cases, one book might be representative of more than one category. For example, an illustrated book about how the body works might also show people of different races in the illustrations. Give credit for each category the book represents. (See photos 15.5.1 a–c, next page.)

The ECERS-R categories are:

- Fantasy (pretend stories about people and animals)
- Factual information (books with pictures of real animals, facts about real life of animals and plants, or other real life experiences)
- Nature and science (such as how the five senses work, the human body, houses of different animals)
- Different races and cultures (historical and contemporary stories about people from different races and cultures or books in other languages, even if they are also available in English)
- Different abilities (individuals with disabilities and how they might use aids such as eyeglasses, a hearing aid, a wheelchair or crutches)

In order to tell what an unfamiliar book is about, it is necessary to leaf through the book, not just to look at the cover. In most cases it will be possible to leaf through all books accessible to the children. Although it is fairly unusual, there are instances where a very large number of books is accessible to the children. Such a large collection is often placed on shelves with only the spine showing so that there is no hint about the subject matter contained in the books. Since it is unreasonable to take the time to look at every book, the observer should randomly sample the

Indicator

15.5.1 a

15.5.1 a–b These bookcases both make a wide selection of books accessible to the children. The selections include factual books, fantasy books, and books about people of different races, cultures, ages and abilities. In addition, photo 15.5.1a meets indicator 7.2 because there are some books related to the current theme, which is Fall.

15.5.1 b In order to see if the program meets the entire indicator, the schedule needs to be checked for the amount of time the books are accessible.

15.5.1 c This bookcase does not contain a wide selection of books because most of the books are fantasy books and there are no books about people of different races, cultures and abilities.

required number of books to see if all the categories are present. Check only the books and pictures that are accessible to the children. It is not necessary to check the materials that are not meant for use as books by the children such as magazines being saved for art projects. Also, do not check books stored in a space used only for teachers' books.

Keeping a list of examples of each of these categories is helpful for keeping track of information and to justify scores as well as for staff improvement. On the list, include the following categories:

- Fantasy
- Fact
- Nature/science
- Different races and cultures
- Abilities

While looking at the accessible books, also note and record other information needed to score other indicators. These include:

- Books or pictures accessible to the children that show graphic violence against people or animals or depict other frightening content that are to be scored under Indicator 5.4 in Books and pictures
- Math/number books which could be given credit also in Item 26, Math/number

Indicator

- Books about nature/science for credit in Item 25, Nature/science
- Cultural diversity for credit in Item 28, Promoting acceptance of diversity

Accessible for a substantial portion of the day means that the children have easy access to the wide selection of books for 1/3 of the time the program is open for any children to attend. If other areas of the facility are used for the children in this group before and/or after they are in their own room, look to see if there are appropriate books available in those areas, and ask when they are accessible to the children in the group during the times they are in those areas. Include all the times books are accessible to the children in any of the areas used by the group being observed as you calculate whether they have access for a substantial portion of the day. (See "Calculating 'Substantial Portion of Day,'" at the end of the chapter on pages 156–158.)

5.2 ***Some additional language materials used daily*** means that at least two materials, in addition to books, that encourage language learning are accessible daily. For example, look for accessible recorded stories and songs, a listening center, flannel board stories, picture card games such as lotto, and/or puppets out for use by children. (See photos 15.5.2 a–e, next page.) Also observe whether posters and/or pictures are used by the staff to encourage language learning daily. To give credit, the materials must be accessible at least 1 hour daily in a full-day program.

5.3 ***Organized in a reading center*** means that the books are easily accessible in a place for reading which contains books for the children and a suitable place for reading, such as a small table and chairs, a rug area, or cushions or other soft seating. ***A reading center*** should be out of traffic so that children can read without constant interruption. Having books on a bookshelf or in a large basket is not sufficient to give credit for having a reading center. Score 5.3 "Yes" only if a suitable space to use the materials has been set up conveniently nearby. (See 15.5.3 a–c, on page 154.)

5.4 ***Appropriate*** means that the books, language materials, and activities are age and developmentally appropriate for the children in the group. Younger children need simpler books and picture games; older preschoolers and kindergartners enjoy more complex stories and games they find challenging. If children are enrolled who speak a primary language that differs from that used in the class, there should be books and songs accessible in that language. Children who have special needs should have materials that are appropriate for them, such as materials with large print, recorded stories, or books with different textures for children with visual impairment.

Books and other language materials that contain graphic violence or frightening content are not considered appropriate for any preschool-kindergarten children. Children of this age often cannot distinguish between imaginary and real occurrences, and therefore many young children find violence in books very upsetting or get an incorrect message about how to behave. Young children empathize with imaginary people, animals, or other creatures who are depicted as the victims of

Continued on page 154.

15.5.2 a A flannel board story is an enjoyable experience that children can recreate by themselves later, if the story pieces are accessible.

15.5.2 b Puppets and a flannel board story are accessible for daily use in this reading center.

15.5.2 c A staff member helps the younger children listen to a recorded story.

15.5.2 d

15.5.2 e

15.5.2 d–e This 4-year-old can use the recorded stories independently.

Indicator

15.5.3 a

15.5.3 b

15.5.3 a–c A reading center needs to have a bookshelf with books displayed so they are easily accessible to children, and a convenient place to use the books. Additional language materials, such as a flannel board with flannel board stories, puppets, or a listening center with earphones, are acceptable if they do not overcrowd or disrupt the book center.

15.5.3 c

Continued from page 152.

violence and may become concerned for their own safety if such books are read to them or they look at violent pictures. In order to judge the appropriateness of the books and language materials accessible to children, look at those materials that are obviously meant to be used as language materials by the children. Do not look through stacks of magazines that may be stored for other activities, for example, to be cut up for use in collage or materials in storage spaces.

5.5 ***Read informally*** means that staff read books to children at various times during the day in addition to any scheduled or formal staff-initiated group story time. (See photos 15.5.5 a–b, on next page.) Examples of informal reading may include staff reading to an individual child or very small group during:

- Free play
- At naptime
- As an extension of an activity (See photos 15.5.5 c–d, on next page.)
- If child is having difficulty (e.g., leaving his parent)
- If requested by the child

At least one instance of informal reading must be observed to score 5.5 "Yes." The full observation time of 2½ to 3 hours must be allowed before determining whether staff read informally to children.

7.1 ***Rotated*** means that different books and language materials are added or exchanged periodically with the accessible materials in the classroom, in order to keep the children interested in looking at books. Children are attracted to and excited by new things to explore. Since this indicator is difficult to observe, a suggested question to ask the staff is included in the item. The staff may talk about the

Indicator

15.5.5 a

15.5.5 b

15.5.5 a–b Informal reading is a satisfying experience for an individual or a small group, during free play, upon arrival or before naptime.

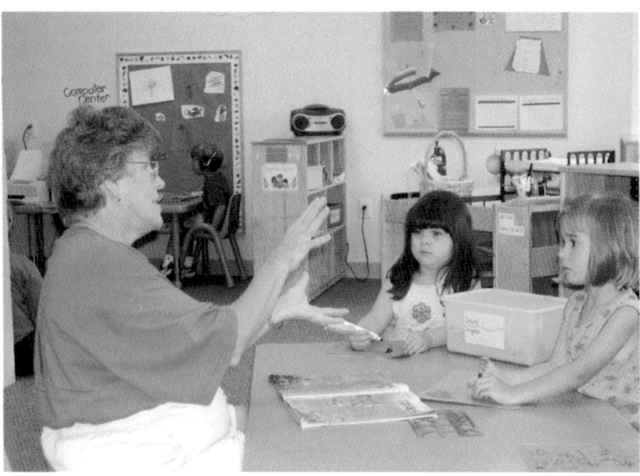

15.5.5 c

15.5.5 d

15.5.5 c–d Informal reading can extend an activity by adding information. Here a staff member is reading a book about fish to two girls who are drawing fish pictures.

materials or show where they are stored. Ask how often books are rotated. Sometimes children are taken on regular visits to the library to pick out new books, and this information may be obtained through a question as well. In order to give credit for this indicator, some books must be rotated or added at least monthly.

7.2 ***Some books relate to current activities or themes*** means that three or more of the accessible books clearly are about the current theme or major focal topic of interest. ***Current*** means a theme that is being studied now or has been studied during the past month. Often, a dated monthly plan is posted in the room that can be used to help with this indicator. Such a posted plan may only be used if it represents what is currently being carried out with the children. If there is no plan posted, ask the staff if they have a written curriculum plan and, if so, ask to see it. If the staff do not have a written plan, ask the open-ended question suggested in the item for Indicator 7.2. Score "Yes" if three or more books relate to a theme studied during the past month. If themes (or units or topic projects) are not changed as part of the children's learning experience for example, the main content of the curriculum is always shapes, colors, the alphabet, and/or numbers, and books are observed on these unchanging topics, credit is not given for 7.2 (score "No").

15 Books and pictures

Indicator

Calculating "Substantial Portion of the Day"

Example 1

This schedule is based on an observation period of 4.5 hours (from 8:00 AM – 12:30 PM) and information collected during the teacher interview about how unobserved time during the day is used and what is accessible to the children.

Time	Scheduled activity	Time to use books
6:30 – 8:00	Breakfast in cafeteria and TV time for those who are finished with breakfast	
8:00 – 8:30	Children go to regular classrooms and play with table and rug toys (puzzles; legos; duplos with cars, people, and trucks; stringing beads and cards; pegboards)	
8:30 – 8:45	Prepare for breakfast/children wash hands	
8:45 – 9:15	Breakfast	
9:15 – 9:45	Circle (teacher reading time)	
9:45 – 10:45	Centers (housekeeping, art, sand and water, nature/science, writing table, blocks, music, computer and cozy book area)	**1 hour**
10:45 – 11:15	Outdoor play (gross motor activities only)	
11:15 – 12:15	Prepare for and eat lunch	
12:15 – 12:30	Story, put out cots, prepare for nap	
12:30 – 2:45	Nap	
2:45 – 3:00	Wake up from nap; bathroom	
3:00 – 3:25	Snack and story	
3:25 – 4:25	Centers (housekeeping, nature/science, writing table, computer, fine motor area and cozy book area)	**1 hour**
4:25 – 5:30	Outdoors or indoor gross motor	
5:30 – 6:30	Table and rug toys (puzzles; legos; duplos with cars, people, and trucks; stringing beads and cards; pegboards) Prepare for departure	

1. Figure the total number of hours that children are allowed to attend.

   (6:30AM to 6:30 PM = 12 hours)

2. Calculate 1/3 of the operating hours to determine "Substantial Portion of the Day."

   (12 hours ÷ 3 = 4 hours)

3. Add up all times that children have access to books.

   (see shaded times on schedule = 2 hours)

4. Compare the amount of time children have access to books to the time requirement for substantial portion of the day. If the amount of time children have access to books is the same or greater, then score "Yes." If the amount of time children have access to books is less than the time requirement for substantial portion of the day, then score "No." For example, the schedule above indicates:

   2 hours (access to books) **is less than 4 hours** (time requirement for substantial portion of day), and therefore the time requirement for substantial portion of the day is not met.

Calculating "Substantial Portion of the Day"

Example 2

This schedule is based on an observation period of 4 hours (from 9:00 AM – 1:00 PM) and information collected during the teacher interview about how unobserved time during the day is used and what is accessible to the children.

Time	Scheduled activity	Time to use books
9:00 – 9:30	Arrival/quiet centers open (cozy book area, computer, writing table, math, science and fine motor)	**30 minutes**
9:30 – 9:45	Snack	
9:45 – 10:00	Clean up snack/bathroom/wash hands	
10:00 – 11:00	Outside (gross motor activities only)	
11:00 – 11:45	Free choice of centers (fine motor, art, blocks, dramatic play, nature/science, math, sensory table, computer, writing table and cozy book area)	**45 minutes**
11:45 – 12:15	Large group activity (M,W,F is music/movement and Tu,Th is art activity)	
12:15 – 12:45	Prepare for and eat lunch	
12:45 – 1:00	Clean up/bathroom/prepare for quiet time	
1:00 – 1:45	Quiet time/quiet centers available (cozy book area, fine motor, math, and science)	**45 minutes**
1:45 – 2:00	Clean up all centers and prepare for departure	

1. Figure the total number of hours that children are allowed to attend.

   (9 AM to 2 PM = 5 hours)

2. Calculate 1/3 of the operating hours to determine "Substantial Portion of the Day."

   (5 hours ÷ 3 = 1 hour and 40 minutes)

3. Add up all times that children have access to books.

   (see shaded times on schedule = 2 hours)

4. Compare the amount of time children have access to books to the time requirement for substantial portion of the day. If the amount of time children have access to books is the same or greater, then score "Yes." If the amount of time children have access to books is less than the time requirement for substantial portion of the day, then score "No." For example, the schedule above indicates:

   2 hours (access to books) **is greater than 1 hour and 40 minutes** (time requirement for substantial portion of day), and therefore the time requirement for substantial portion of the day is met.

Indicator

Calculating "Substantial Portion of the Day"

Example 3

This schedule is based on an observation period of 3.5 hours (from 9AM –12:30 PM) and information collected during the teacher interview about whether what was observed represents the typical daily practice.

Time	Scheduled activity	Time to use books
9:00 – 9:20	Arrival/group time to discuss activities for the day	
9:20 – 9:45	Whole group art activity	
9:45 – 10:00	Whole group reading time (teacher-directed)	
10:00 – 10:45	Outside time (gross motor activities only)	
10:45 – 11:30	Free choice of centers (fine motor, art, blocks, dramatic play, nature/science, math, sensory table, computer, writing table and books)	**45 minutes**
11:30 – 11:45	Clean up/bathroom/prepare for lunch time	
11:45 – 12:15	Prepare for and eat lunch	
12:15 – 12:30	Clean up/bathroom/prepare for departure	

1. Figure the total number of hours that children are allowed to attend.

   (9 AM to 12:30 PM = 3 hours and 30 minutes)

2. Calculate 1/3 of the operating hours to determine "Substantial Portion of the Day."

   (3 hours and 30 minutes ÷ 3 = 1 hour and 10 minutes)

3. Add up all times that children have access to books.

   (see shaded times on schedule = 45 minutes)

4. Compare the amount of time children may have access to books to the time requirement for substantial portion of the day. If the amount of time children may have access to books is the same or greater, then score "Yes." If the amount of time children may have access to books is less than the time requirement for substantial portion of the day, then score "No." For example, the schedule above indicates:

   45 minutes (access to books) **is less than 1 hour and 10 minutes** (time requirement for substantial portion of day), and therefore the time requirement for substantial portion of the day is not met.

16 Encouraging children to communicate

General information about this item

Children need to learn to use language to communicate with others in order to express their needs, desires, and interests. When children learn to use expressive language, they can share their ideas with others and negotiate solutions to problems effectively. A child learning to speak, instead of hitting or grabbing, to achieve a desired outcome is a big step forward socially. A child using language to describe what he or she has made, ask questions, and share information has taken a big step forward intellectually.

Children talk when they have something interesting to talk about. That is why communication is lively in the dramatic play and block areas. Materials such as toy telephones, puppets and flannel boards, dolls and dramatic play props, and small barns, fire stations, or dollhouses create lots of conversation among children as they assume many different roles. Children also talk when there is an interested person who listens to them. Thus, the staff in a high quality early childhood classroom use both activities and materials to encourage growth in communication skills.

In this language item, as in all items involving any types of interactions, ***staff*** refers to those adults who are in the classroom with the children for a substantial portion of the day (1/3 of the time the program is open). This can include volunteers, if they are in the classroom the required amount of time. Adults who are in the classroom for shorter periods of the day, or who are not a regular part of the classroom, do not count in evaluating whether the requirements for this item are met. For example, if a therapist, parent, or a director of a program comes into the classroom and interacts with the children for short or irregular periods, these interactions do not count in scoring in language items, unless the interactions are extremely negative. As an exception, in a parent cooperative or lab school, in which the usual staffing patterns include different people as teaching assistants daily, these assistants are counted as staff.

In order to give credit for activities that encourage communication, the observer must see the staff actively encouraging children to communicate verbally (or nonverbally if a disability does not permit verbal communication), for example, by asking questions about what they have created during ***free play*** or leading children in songs or finger-plays during ***large group time***.

Free play, according to the definition in the ECERS-R, means that the "child is permitted to select materials and companions, and as far as possible manage play independently. Adult interaction is in response to the child's needs. Situations in which the children are assigned to centers by staff, or staff select the materials that individual children may use do not count as free play." ***Large group time*** means that all or many children in the classroom are gathered together to participate in one activity, with the expectation that all children will participate.

Indicator

Children who use nonverbal communication, such as pointing or making sounds, can be helped to communicate more effectively if the staff model for them by saying appropriate words. Younger children or those with delayed verbal ability benefit from having a teacher who talks about what the children see, feel, do, or want. A teacher who provides a running verbal commentary helps link language to children's thoughts and actions. Praising children for trying to say words and helping them promptly achieve their goals encourages nonverbal children to use language, because it gets results. Staff also need to actively draw communication from children who already use language. This is accomplished by listening to what children say, asking questions, leading children in songs, and reciting finger-plays, as well as providing materials in a wide variety of areas that stimulate communication among children.

The issue often arises that all staff members may not be equally verbal or communicative in their interactions with children. For example, one staff member might be relatively uncommunicative while the other is extremely communicative. How does this discrepancy between staff members affect the score on this item and other items in the Language-Reasoning subscale?

In the ECERS-R, scoring is not based on what each staff member produces but rather the amount of encouragement to communicate that the children get from the whole staff. An analogy that might help is to think of something physical the children experience in the classroom, for example, the temperature of the room. Suppose it is warm enough in the room even though we discover that only one air vent is producing all the heat and the other is partially blocked and not functioning at all. It is still warm enough for the children despite the poorly functioning vent. We are concerned with the overall temperature, not which of the vents is pumping out the air. Similarly, in this item we are scoring the overall encouragement to communicate produced jointly by staff. If the one communicative teacher is supplying enough encouragement for children's communication, then the classroom will meet certain requirements. If staff members' communication with children fails to meet the children's needs, either alone or in combinatin with other staff, requirements will not be met.

Since communication may vary throughout the observation, it is best to score this item at the end of the observation period. Jotting down how staff encourage children to communicate during the observation will help provide enough information for accurate scoring. The scoresheet or another piece of paper can be used for these notes.

A closer look at each indicator

1.1 ***No activities*** to encourage communication means that staff do most of the talking and do not try to draw communication from the children either during group time or free play. Encouraging children to communicate can include staff-initiated activities during group time and free play such as:

- Singing songs at circle time
- Doing finger-plays or repeating rhymes with a group
- Asking children to share ideas about a story being read
- Asking children to tell about something from their own experiences, such as their pet or their favorite breakfast
- Circulating around the room during free play and discussing with children what they have been doing

Indicator

- Asking children to tell about their art work or block constructions

In order to be given credit for ***activities to encourage communication,*** the staff have to take action to draw communication from children. To count, ***activities*** do not have to be planned or formal, such as a song or discussion at circle time. They can be informal and spontaneous, such as when staff circulate around the room during free play and stop to ask about and discuss the various activities children are engaged in. Score 1.1 "Yes" if no such activities are observed throughout the observation.

1.2 ***Materials that encourage communication*** are those that promote talking through their use. For example, a toy telephone encourages a child to pretend to answer the phone with words and to do some "telephone talk." A puppet might encourage a child to pretend to talk, taking on the puppet's personality, or the child might talk to a puppet another person is using. Dramatic play materials, such as dolls, housekeeping toys, and other props encourage children to act out roles, talking to one another and to the toys, as they play. Small figures and animals, flannel board pieces, and language board games are also materials that stimulate communication among children.

Very few materials means little or no materials. ***Accessible*** means within easy reach for the children to use.

Look around the room to see what materials are out and accessible for children to play with when talking is allowed. An insufficient quantity of materials causes children to miss out on communication activities and may cause conflict and negative interactions. If children with special communication needs are enrolled, look to see whether they have the equipment they need in order to communicate, such as a communication board.

Score 1.2 "Yes" if almost no materials are accessible for children to use, or accessibility of the materials is limited to a very short time period of the day. In other words, children rarely get to use the materials.

16.3.1 a

3.1 ***Some activities*** means that throughout the observation, instances where staff actively elicit communication from children during group and/or free play occur, but they are relatively infrequent. (See 1.1 for the meaning of ***activities.***)

To give credit for this indicator (score "Yes"), at least four instances must be observed during the 2½ to 3 hour observation, some during group time and some during free play. For example, during circle time the staff might lead songs or finger-plays or ask children questions requiring an answer. (See photos 16.3.1 a–b.) During free play staff might ask children about what they are doing or making.

3.2 ***Some materials accessible*** means that there are enough materials to encourage communication without competition and conflict due to scarcity. Watch to see if some constructive play is possible, particularly with materials that encourage role-taking and social play and materials that two or more children can play with at one time, since these are important to encourage communication.

16.3.1 b

16.3.1 a–b During these circle times children are encouraged to communicate by singing action songs and doing fingerplays.

Indicator

To give credit, the materials must be accessible for at least an hour per day in a program of 8 hours or more. This does not require that all children be able to use the materials at the same time or that each child have a full hour to use the materials. However, it is required that children would have a reasonable chance to use the materials at some time if they wished.

Less time is required for programs operating less than 8 hours a day, with the amount of time calculated proportionally, based on the ratio of 1 hour for programs of 8 hours or more. For example, if a program operated for 6 hours a day, this would be ¾ of a full-day program, so the time required would be ¾ of the 1 hour. If the program operated 4 hours a day, the requirement would be ½ hour.

3.3 ***Generally appropriate*** means that the great majority, or most, of the ***communication activities,*** are suitable for children and on the right level of difficulty so that they participate with interest and success.

During group time activities, watch to see if the questions children are being asked are simple enough for them to understand and answer. Do most of the children give the right answer or does the teacher have to give the answer after children experience failure?

Children who speak a primary language that differs from that used in the class and are just learning the new language must have some opportunities to use their own language as well as the language of the majority of the group. In addition, none of the words to the songs and/or poems and chants used may be violent, sexually explicit, or culturally biased, because such material is not appropriate.

Score 3.3 "Yes" if most of the communication activities, with very few exceptions, are appropriate.

5.1 Communication activities must be observed ***taking place during both free play and group time*** (see definitions of these terms in the General Information section for this item). Since this indicator is at the good level, numerous instances throughout the observation must be seen during both free play and group time.

Look for instances where staff draw communication from children by asking them questions, listening to their answers, and asking for further details to get longer and more complex answers. At ***group time***, look for lively participation involving many of the children in response to questions asked by the staff, as well as group songs and finger-plays. During ***free play*** look for staff moving around to ask different children to tell them about their play, encouraging children to dictate a story about their completed drawings or paintings, and generally expressing interest in various activities so that the children talk frequently to the staff about what they are doing. Questions should be possible for most children to answer correctly.

To give credit for this indicator (score "Yes"), such instances should obviously be the usual, rather than the unusual, practice, *throughout the observation* during *both* free play and group times. (See photos 16.5.1 a–h, pages 163–164.)

5.2 ***Materials that encourage communication are accessible in a variety of interest centers*** requires that the classroom be well stocked with many different types of materials that encourage engagement in play that stimulates interaction with other children.

Dramatic play materials, such as dress-up clothes, dolls, and child-sized household furnishings, encourage children to talk as they act out family roles. Props that go

Continued on page 164.

Communication activities during free play and group times

16.5.1 a

16.5.1 b

16.5.1 a–b During group time, children are eager to talk about something they have experienced recently, a trip to a farm. Many ideas are contributed by the children and recorded by the teacher near the photos they took at the farm.

16.5.1 c These children have a lot to say about the farm they have created with small animals.

16.5.1 d Children and staff talk about what goes in the barn during free play.

16.5.1 e Outdoors there are plants to discuss—how they look, feel, smell.

16.5.1 f A few questions from the teacher make the puppet show more elaborate.

Indicator

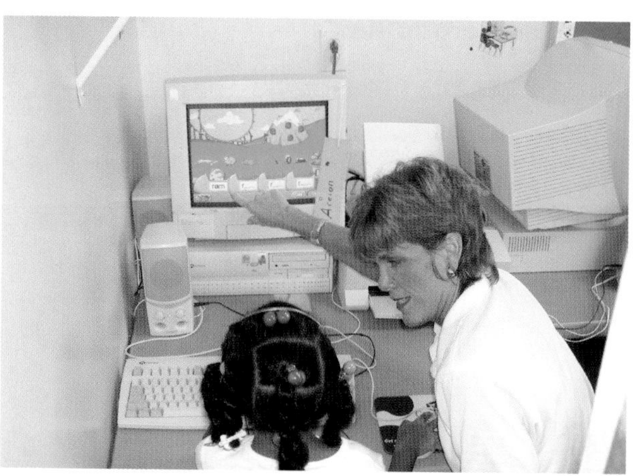

16.5.1 g A computer program can provide a lot of discussion between teacher and child.

16.5.1 h At the drawing table, each child has a story to tell about his/her drawing.

Continued from page 162.
beyond housekeeping allow children to broaden their range of discussion topics. For example, props such as a tent or backpack help children discuss vacations; a white coat and doctor's bag with a stethoscope suggest hospital play. Doll houses, farms, castles, and other small structures with appropriately sized accessories also encourage broader pretend play. (See photos 16.5.2 a–b, next page.)

Block structures created by the children can become garages, airports, or farms that the children will talk about with the addition of the appropriate vehicles, airplanes, or farm animals from the various block accessory boxes. (See photo 16.5.2 c, next page.)

Having flannel board story sets in the *book* area also encourages lots of talking as the children tell the stories while moving the flannel pieces. Puppets can also be used in this area to encourage children's talk.

Imaginative play areas outdoors, with dramatic play props or blocks and accessories, are usually accompanied by lots of language as children assume roles and weave a story line. (See photo 16.5.2 d, next page.)

7.1 ***Staff balance listening and talking appropriately*** means that the staff demonstrates that the purpose of their questions and comments is to stimulate child-talk, while introducing new words and understanding to the children. Since both of these are necessary as children learn to communicate, staff must be sure to do each, as needed by the children in the group. The amount of talking done by the staff, as opposed to listening to the children, will depend on a number of factors.

First, older, or more verbal, children will need more time to do the talking, while younger, or less verbal, children will need more adult talk so they can learn the words they need for later use. Leaving ample time for *all* children to respond and elaborate is essential, however. Younger or less verbal children may need more language modeling, requiring staff to verbalize more for them or expand on their nonverbal communication.

Second, when introducing new concepts or ideas, more adult talk is needed for all children so that they expand their vocabularies and sentence structures.

The balance between the adult's listening and talking should be suited to the needs of the various children, usually with more staff talk for the younger children and

Indicator

16.5.2 a

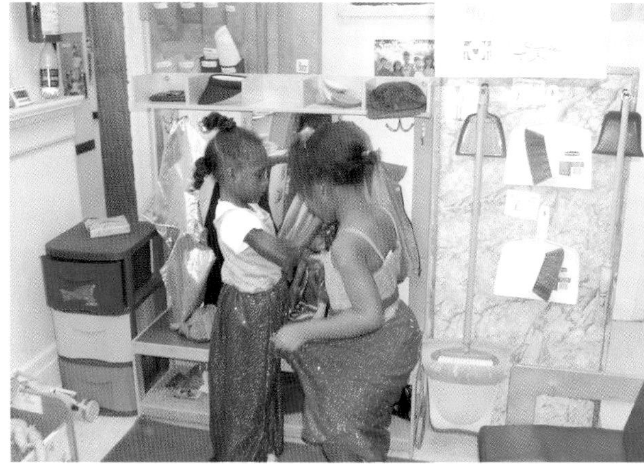

16.5.2 b

16.5.2 a–b A wide variety of materials in the dramatic play center encourages communication about many different scenarios.

16.5.2 c Blocks and accessories stimulate communication among these children who are building a zoo.

16.5.2 d Construction workers talk in the outdoor sand area.

more staff listening with the more verbal, older children. Score this indicator "Yes" if staff create the balance needed by the children as a usual practice in the group being observed. (See photo 16.7.1.)

16.7.1 The teacher listens to a child explaining the book he has just completed.

7.2 When staff write down what children say and read it back to them, they ***link children's spoken communication with written language***. This connection between what is said and the words written on the paper is clearest if the child dictates what is to be written, and it is read back immediately.

Many appropriate occasions to link speech to print occur daily in an early childhood setting where children are busy and creative. For example:

- Watching to see when a child finishes a piece of artwork and then asking the child to tell about it. At the very least, a short caption identifying the object can be printed on the work. When the staff read the children's words back to them, a strong link is created between spoken and written language (See photos 16.7.2 a–d, on page 167.)

Indicator

- Writing notes to parents, dictated by the child, for example, to remind them to do something or to tell them about something the child did
- Helping to write and post reminders for the classroom, for example, to remind the class to buy new fish food or to remember the first aid kit for a fieldtrip
- Creating charts that record the main points in a group discussion, which can help children remember what was said, as well as reinforce the value of writing things down so that they can be read later (See photos 16.7.2 e–f.)
- Using other communication, such as something of particular interest that a child talks about that can be written down, read back and either posted, added to a teacher made book, or sent home

If an example of staff linking writing to spoken language is not observed, evidence of this practice observed in the classroom may be used to give credit for this indicator, including:

- Children's work on display with written captions
- Captions on children's work included in a teacher made book that is in the room
- Posted charts that record in writing a group discussion that children have had

Do *not* give credit for picture word labels on shelves or labels posted on other objects in the room such as a label that says "door" on the door. Also, if staff only write children's names on their work, no credit is given for this indicator, even if staff read the names back to the children.

If no examples of staff linking writing to spoken language are observed nor any evidence seen in the classroom, ask staff the question provided for this indicator in the ECERS-R. If the answer provided shows that linking children's talking to written language is a *regular practice,* rather than an unusual occurrence, give credit. It is best to request specific examples of what is done, and how often. Be sure to ask to see examples of what has been done.

The intent of this indicator is to give credit only for experiences that actively demonstrate to children the relationship between what they say and what is written down. Score 7.2 "Yes" if this is clearly the case as part of the usual practices used in the classroom.

Indicator

16.7.2 a

16.7.2 b

16.7.2 a–b A child dictates the story that goes with the pictures he made with collage and drawing.

16.7.2 c The children have drawn pictures and dictated captions for this Thanksgiving book.

16.7.2 d This child is trying to write some words to go with the picture she drew. She can write some of the letters but needs help spelling out the words.

16.7.2 e

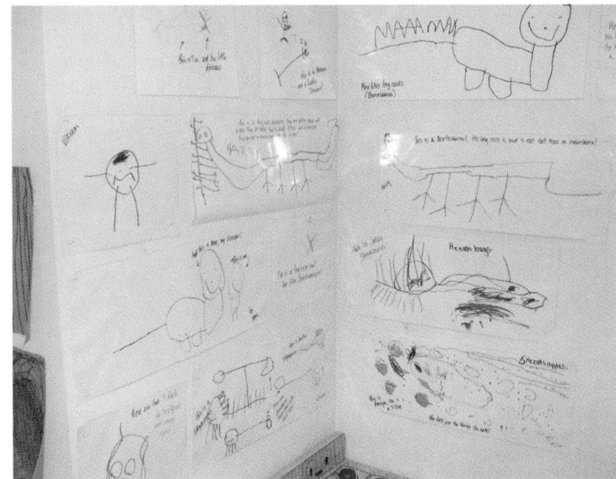

16.7.2 f

16.7.2 e–f Displays of charts resulting from a previous discussion and children's drawings with captions are evidence that staff link written with spoken language.

17 Using language to develop reasoning skills

General information about this item

Language not only serves the function of communication with others, it also provides the framework to help us think about and understand ourselves and the world around us. Children have to learn basic logical concepts (e.g., same/different, cause/effect) that adults take for granted. They do this from repeated concrete experiences that we label for them with words. A young child can recognize his favorite blanket (as opposed to a substitute) long before he understands the concept of same/different.

During the preschool years children are developing concepts or logical structures that help them organize what they see, hear, feel, smell, taste—their perceptions. Concepts are abstract, organizing ideas that identify how things are related. How are things the same or different from one another? Which categories do animals of different kinds belong in? How does counting work? Children need many experiences so they can form abstract concepts, both from daily practical life and from playing with educational materials designed for this purpose.

The classroom staff can help children develop concepts by pointing out key features and talking about them using the appropriate words, while children are dealing with daily life as well as while they are playing with materials.

In our eagerness to help children learn concepts and the words used to represent them, we must not forget that young children learn best from repeated, hands-on, engaging experiences that are enhanced by what staff say to children about them. We must not forget that there is a developmental component in learning concepts.

Teaching children to parrot words through daily drill, before they have had sufficient hands-on experiences or time to mature, is neither appropriate nor effective. On the other hand, children benefit from sensitive adult interest and verbal input while they are developing abstract concepts through experiences.

Since all the indicators in this item are based on observation, it is best to score this item toward the end of the observation period. Keeping notes with specific examples helps in accurate scoring.

A closer look at each indicator

1.1 This indicator, at the inadequate level, describes a classroom where ***staff***, that is, the adults who are with the children daily or almost daily for a substantial portion of the day (1/3 of the time the program is open), do not talk with children about logical relationships at all. Staff do not point out examples of ***logical relationships*** such as size, shape, and number, things that are the same or different, cause and effect, or so on.

Notice if there are *no* instances either while children play with materials or at other times in the program such as routines. An observer might see examples of

Indicator

staff ignoring children's questions that could lead to pointing out concepts, such as if a child asks when they are going out, which is a question about the sequence of daily events, or why something happened, which is a cause/effect question. If no examples are seen during the observation, score 1.1 "Yes."

1.2 ***Concepts***, as used in this item, include the logical thinking structures identified in the work of Piaget. Children gradually learn to distinguish:

- ***same/different***, which is the basis of many matching games
- ***classifying*** what belongs together based on one or more characteristics
- ***sequencing***, putting one thing after another based on a particular characteristic
- ***one-to-one correspondence*** which is the basis for counting
- ***spatial relationships*** such as up/down, in/out
- ***cause and effect***

Staff can encourage development of concepts appropriately, taking advantage of children's real experiences to help them think. For example, clean-up is a good time for staff to encourage matching as children replace blocks by matching them to an outline on shelves, or practice classifying objects by putting the right things in specific places in the dramatic play or fine motor areas. To count as introducing concepts, the staff need to follow through and see that the children actually match the blocks and sort and classify the dramatic play materials or manipulatives, not just give the order to "put things back in the right place."

17.1.2 Concepts such as recognizing letters, numbers, shapes, or colors are introduced without concrete experience and taught by rote repetition.

Introduced inappropriately means that concepts, which are abstractions, are introduced either before children are developmentally ready or by using teaching methods that lack concrete experiences. This results in inappropriate activities that are neither interesting nor meaningful for the children. (See photo 17.1.2.)

In some early childhood classrooms, drills with worksheets or a daily group session of repeating together numbers and/or letters, shapes, and colors by rote are the main approaches used to help young children develop concepts. If these methods are used exclusively or for a long period of time during the observation with preschool children, score 1.2 "Yes."

3.1 ***Staff sometimes talk about logical relationships*** means that during the observation (of at least 2½ to 3 hours) staff make comments at least *twice* that relate to logical concepts.

These comments may be made casually, such as recalling the sequence of daily events or mentioning the size, shape, or color of objects. They might also be made under more formal circumstances, such as at circle time, when children count to find out how many children are present.

Note on the score sheet when such comments are observed to help in scoring. Score 3.1 "Yes" if at least two instances are observed. (See photos 17.3.1 a–c.)

17.3.1 a Staff explain matching an object to the same color to a young preschooler.

Indicator

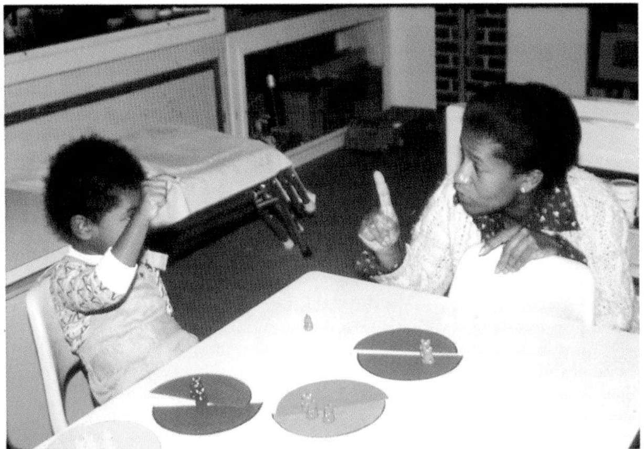

17.3.1 b Color matching and numbers are introduced with concrete objects.

17.3.1 c Children are encouraged to play with the materials on their own.

17.3.2 a As this child builds with blocks, she is experiencing differences in shape and size.

17.3.2 b Staff point out and name the different shapes. Each shape has several different sizes in the building.

3.2 ***Some*** concepts are ***introduced appropriately*** means that the ages and abilities of the children are taken into consideration when staff introduce or point out relationships. Concrete experiences with real objects are used as the main teaching method, and exact words are used to describe the relationships.

Concepts may be introduced by staff as children play or observe natural events. For example, staff point out or explain why water is evaporating and creating steam on a hot sidewalk, or call a child's attention to the different sizes and shapes of blocks he is playing with.

If at least two such instances are observed during the observation (of at least 2½ to 3 hours), score 3.2 "Yes." (See photos 17.3.2 a–c.)

17.3.2 c Different sizes of measuring cups in the sand table leads to a discussion of same and different quantities.

5.1 At this level of quality, ***talking about logical relationships*** requires that staff explain the concept illustrated in particular ***materials*** designed to ***stimulate reasoning***. A wide variety of concept-driven educational games and materials are currently available, and

17.5.1 a Staff set up activities using materials that stimulate reasoning as a basis for introducing concepts.

17.5.1 b The child tries out balancing, making one side heavier and the other lighter.

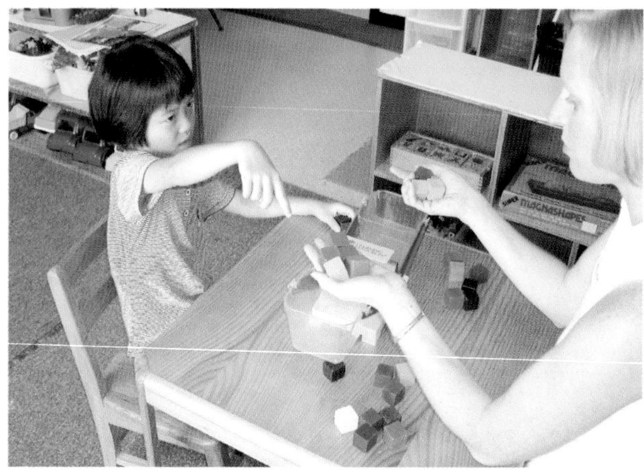

17.5.1 c Teacher talks about more and less.

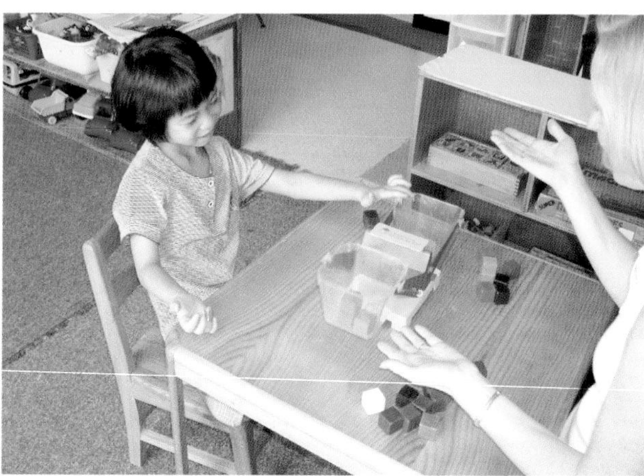

17.5.1 d Teacher explains why the scale goes down more on the heavier side.

many classrooms include them among their puzzles, manipulatives, and math materials. For example, a puzzle showing crayons of different length in a sequence can be used to explain sequencing by size. In order to assure that children understand the concept inherent in such materials and know the words to describe the concept, staff need to talk to the children and explain the concept while children are using the materials.

Examples of ***materials that stimulate reasoning*** include sequencing cards, matching games, balance scales with things to weigh, objects for counting and sorting, and number/object matching puzzles. These materials may either be manufactured or homemade. Even natural objects can be used, such as pinecones of different sizes to put into a sequence or to sort by size.

17.5.1 e Child experiments with balancing more cubes.

Unfortunately, these types of materials often are found sitting on the classroom shelf unused, or are observed being used in inappropriate ways. In many classrooms, staff do not explain how to use these materials and do not "feature" them during small group time while staff help is available. A notable exception is the Montessori

Indicator

17.5.2 a Teacher asks child to explain how she got both sides to balance.

17.5.2 b This 4-year-old can recognize and name numbers in sequence when playing a game with the teacher.

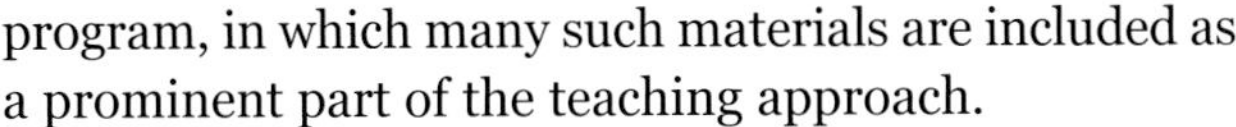

program, in which many such materials are included as a prominent part of the teaching approach.

In order to give 5.1 a score of "Yes," at least one instance must be observed, during the 2½ to 3 hours observation, where staff explain the logical concept inherent in a material designed for that purpose, while a child is playing with the material. (See photos 17.5.1 a–e.)

5.2 This indicator requires that staff ***encourage children to explain their reasoning*** when they have solved a logical problem ***using materials that stimulate reasoning*** as described in 5.1. For example, if a child has sorted red, blue, and green "counting bears" into three bowls, which were set up as a small group activity, staff might ask why all the red/blue/green bears were put in separate bowls. If a child has completed a puzzle with the number on one piece and the correct number of dots on the other, the staff would ask them why they match. Staff might follow up by asking if the child can find five blocks and bring them, and play a "finding five" game.

17.5.2 c She can also explain to the teacher that five has one more peg than four.

By listening to the child's explanation, the staff will know how much the child understands about the concept, in this case number, and can determine whether to bring out easier or harder games based on the same concept.

In order to give 5.2 a score of "Yes," at least two instances, such as those described, must be observed during the 2½ to 3 hours observation. (See photos 17.5.2 a–c.)

7.1 ***Reason throughout the day*** means that staff use real events and experiences (other than those with the materials described in Indicators 5.1 and 5.2) to get children to talk about concepts, on many occasions, during the observation. For example, when the group is doing a cooking project, children may be asked whether the steps in the recipe always have to be done in the same order or whether they can be varied. The children can try variations and find out if they work. (See photos 17.7.1 a–d, page 174.)

The staff would be observed using "how" and "why" questions frequently with older

Indicator

17.7.1a

17.7.1 b

17.7.1 a A cooking activity that follows a picture and word recipe is used often in this class of older preschoolers.

17.7.1 c

17.7.1 d

17.7.1 c–d The concept of sequencing is reinforced as children follow steps in a cooking recipe, one step after another.

preschoolers and simpler questions with younger children, such as "What comes first, putting on your socks or shoes?" "Setting the table or eating?"

To give credit for 7.1, at least two examples of such interactions must be observed during the 2½ to 3 hours observation, that are not related to children's use of play materials that encourage reasoning.

7.2 When children face problems, staff ***introduce concepts in response*** to children's ***need to solve problems***. This indicator does *not* relate to staff helping children resolve the social problems that they have with one another. Instead, it focuses on problems children face in their physical world. For example, children might have trouble balancing a block structure or negotiating a curve while pulling a wagon. Staff can show and explain why the block structure or wagon fell, thus adding to the child's experience in solving problems. (See photo 17.7.2, next page.)

Watch to see if the staff use a problem solving approach that involves the children in thinking things through, or whether they ignore such problems or simply give children the answers. For example, if children are helping to set the table, the staff might suggest that older children count the number of places needed or that

Indicator

younger children put a spoon and napkin on the table in front of each chair (one-to-one correspondence). If a child is pulling a wagon that gets turned over rounding a corner, do staff help the child see the cause and how to avoid the problem next time?

At least two instances should be observed during the 2½ to 3 hours observation to give credit for this indicator.

17.7.2 Problems with balancing the tall tower lead to consideration of cause and effect.

18 Informal use of language

General information about this item

Language is used by staff in many ways throughout the day, including to comfort, inform, direct, socialize, complain, protect, converse, negotiate, question, anticipate, and recall. For relatively short periods, usually at circle time or in a group setting, staff have a *formal* plan that guides the language they use. But in reality, most of the language stimulation provided by staff to the children throughout the day occurs ***informally***, in response to situations that arise spontaneously. The way that staff use language informally has a significant effect on the social and intellectual climate of the classroom.

In this scale, ***staff*** is used to refer to all the adults who work directly with the children in the classroom daily (or almost daily) for a substantial portion of the day, defined as 1/3 of the time the center is open. Commonly, there are at least two staff members working with a group at the same time, each one with a unique personality and possibly a different way of using language with children. When deciding on a score for this item, look at the overall impact on the children, of the collective informal communication of all staff members. If one staff member is quiet and non-communicative, but the other is very dynamic and meets the children's needs for conversation and information, then the score on this item will be high because the children's needs for informal language are being met by the collective *staff*.

In scoring this item, the focus should be on whether the children's needs for informal language are being met, rather than which staff member is producing the informal language. Although it will not affect the score, if the purpose for the observation is to improve classroom practice and teacher competence, it will be necessary to help the non-communicative staff member improve her informal use of language.

When scoring this item, look at each indicator in terms of all the informal language being produced by the staff throughout the observation. Because language use changes, depending on many variables, such as activity or fatigue in children and staff, this item should always be scored at, or near, the end of the complete observation. This ensures that the use of informal language is accurately evaluated, under the varying circumstances that naturally occur.

A closer look at each indicator

1.1 This indicator describes a classroom where staff use language ***only to control*** children's behavior and ***manage routines***. Please note that this item addresses only the content of the verbal communication, not the tone used by the staff which is scored in the Interaction subscale (Items 29, Supervision of gross motor activities; 30, General supervision of children; 31, Discipline; 32, Staff-child interactions;

Indicator

and/or 33, Interactions among children). Staff may be pleasant and use a conversational tone of voice, but the content of what is said may ***only control behavior and manage routines***.

Common statements to control children might include:

- "Use your indoor voice."
- "Walk don't run."
- "Excuse me, who's talking now?"
- "Keep your hands to yourself."
- "Could you please bring that here?"

Common statements to manage routines might be:

- "Go wash your hands before snack."
- "You need to put your coat on before you go out."
- "Time to line up to go outside."
- "Put your things in your cubby."
- "Let's remember to flush the toilet."

18.1.1 Staff use language only to control children's behavior and manage routines.

At the end of the observation if the overwhelming impression is that staff use language for extreme verbal control, rather than for socializing, providing information, or encouraging children to talk, score this indicator "Yes." (See photo 18.1.1.)

1.2 ***Rarely respond to children's talk*** means that the staff frequently ignore children's requests, questions, and comments. By staff response, we mean listening to children talk (or taking notice of nonverbal communication, such as holding out hands to be picked up) and answering in some way. For example, staff may try to meet a request or explain why it cannot be met,and/or offer an alternative. Or staff might add more information to something a child has expressed interest in.

Staff response can be verbal or nonverbal, but must be clearly linked to something said by a child. In some cases when children attempt to communicate nonverbally, staff are expected to respond to such nonverbal use of communication as they would when children talk to them.

Score 1.2 "Yes" if little or no response on the part of the staff to children's communication (verbal or nonverbal) is observed.

1.3 ***Children's talk is discouraged*** means that children are expected to be quiet, mainly listen, and not talk to one another or to the staff. ***Much of the day*** means that this occurs during most of the observation.

Children can be ***discouraged*** from talking informally with staff or other children in many ways. For example:

- They can be told talking is not allowed at particular times, such as during lunch, circle time, when they line up to go outside, or walk in the hallway.
- They can also be discouraged from talking informally by being kept in teacher dominated groups for long periods where they either have to listen to staff or respond in a predetermined way, such as reciting the alphabet or numbers.
- They might be punished for talking, and so rarely talk.
- They might be isolated, so there is no one to talk with, as when children must sit at individual desks.

Indicator

This indicator is scored "Yes" if there is very little chance during the observation for children to talk informally to staff or to one another.

3.1 ***Some staff-child conversation*** means that there is a little bit of mutual listening and talking or dialogue between staff and children during the observation.

In order to give credit for ***conversation***, there must be some talking between a staff member and an individual child, or a small group of children, one listening, the other communicating either verbally or nonverbally. There must also be a common topic or interest for the conversation, something both staff and child are mutually attending to.

The dialogue may consist only of very short questions and one word answers, or there may be only two or three examples of very short conversations observed to score "Yes" on 3.1, at this minimal level. Jot down the examples to justify scoring. (See photos 18.3.1 a–b.)

3.2 Children ***allowed*** to talk means that the staff do not stop the children from talking with one another or with staff, or become angry if they do. They may ask for quieter "inside voices" if children get very noisy, but talk is not discouraged. See Indicator 1.3 for examples of discouraging children from talking.

Judge what happens ***much of the day***, or most of the time, based on what is seen and heard during the observation. To score 3.2 "Yes," children must be permitted to talk most of the time during the observation. (See photo 18.3.2.)

5.1 ***Many staff-child conversations*** means that there is mutual listening and talking involving turn-taking for children and staff, and this is seen throughout the observation.

In cases where children are younger or less verbal, the conversation may include responses from the children in gestures, or sign language may be used by both parties, if needed. Conversations should be observed both during ***free play,*** when children may choose their activities, and during ***routines*** such as meals/snacks or preparing for nap (e.g., making up cots, undressing).

To score, watch for examples of informal conversations including verbal give and take. Examples of such conversations include talking about what a child has created and for whom he has created the work, home or family events of importance to the child, things he has seen or experienced either inside or outside of school, the child's and staff's pets, and events of the day.

18.3.1 a A child and teacher have a conversation about the child's drawing.

18.3.1 b While children work with materials, there is some conversation along with instructions for managing the materials.

18.3.2 Children are allowed to talk much of the day. Their voices are heard during routine care and play times, indoors and outdoors.

Indicator

18.5.1 a Staff circulate around the room during free play so many conversations occur.

18.5.1 b There is also lively conversation during lunch time at each table.

The conversation may be initiated by either the staff or the child, but *both staff and child must take turns for the interaction to be considered a* ***conversation***. If such communication takes place as the usual (not the exceptional) practice, throughout the observation, give credit for 5.1 (score "Yes"). (See photos 18.5.1 a–b.)

5.2 The requirement of this indicator is that informal language be used by staff ***primarily*** (which means usually or mostly) to ***exchange information with children and for social interaction***. This describes a classroom where language may be used occasionally to control behavior or manage routines, but where language is used much more frequently—or most often—to exchange information about things of interest to the children and to interact with them socially.

Staff use language to ***exchange information*** means that staff are observed talking to children and adding information about things that children ask about or express interest in. For example, a child might be looking at a collection of shells in the nature/science area and a staff member might go over and explain about the function of shells (a protective place to live), identify the different creatures that live in shells, and where they live (ocean, fresh water), show how two parts of a clam shell fit together, and so on. If the staff member brings over a book and reads it to the child, reading the book informally would be given credit in Item 15, Books and pictures, Indicator 5.5, and not here. However, conversation about the information in the book and verbal explanation in addition to what is read would be given credit here. Often credit for both items can be given based on such an example.

Staff can also bring up new ideas when exchanging information with children. For example, during outdoor play, a staff member might point out that she sees leaf buds on the trees, and this means spring is coming. The weather will get warmer and the trees will have new leaves.

Credit can be given for verbal exchange of information between staff and a small group of children, as well as with an individual child, if each child feels free to participate. The intent of this indicator is to give credit for staff who use language frequently to provide information to children while the children are active and interested.

To meet this indicator, staff should also use language with children for ***social interaction***. ***Social interaction*** means that staff will respond to and discuss

Indicator

18.5.2 a

18.5.2 b

18.5.2 a–c Language is primarily used to exchange information and for social interaction.

matters of human interest children bring up, such as family events, their pets, toys, friends, problems, and concerns. Staff may also discuss with children something positive they saw them do that day, for example, the fine block structure several girls built in the block area, or how nice it was that one child helped another find the book he brought to school and thought was lost. Recognizing and discussing positive actions creates a bond between staff and children, and as staff get to know the children's families better, their social conversations will become richer in content. (See photos 18.5.2 a–c.)

18.5.2 c

In order to decide on a score for this indicator, consider the amount of language staff use to manage routines and control behavior in relationship to the amount of language used to exchange information and interact socially. If a far greater amount is used for information exchange and social discussion (about 75%) than for control and management, give 5.2 a score of "Yes."

5.3 This indicator requires that staff add information to or ***expand*** on ideas as they talk to children. ***Expansion*** means that staff add details or new, more exact words to build on ideas children are expressing.

Listen to find out whether a conversation between staff and children includes more that one round of turn-taking, where the staff member elaborates, rephrases, or adds details. When a child with restricted verbal ability points to something or uses one word, listen to whether the staff member uses only one or two words in response to name the object, or whether she uses more words to add information about the properties and uses of the object, in addition to the name.

Only the elaborate answer that uses more words is given credit in this indicator. For example, let's contrast how two teachers might deal with the same situation. Let's pretend that a child with limited verbal ability points to a ball another child is playing with.

Indicator

Teacher 1 might say, "That's a ball. Can you say 'ball'?"

Teacher 2 might say, "Would you like to play with a big ball like the one Peter has? That's a big, round, red ball. Let's go find one for you to play with."

We would not give credit to Teacher 1 for expansion because she used very few words, and in essence only named the object. Teacher 2 would get credit for expansion because she used several descriptive words about the ball ("big, round, red"). She also verbalized the child's intention ("play with a ball like the one Peter has") and suggested a solution ("find one for you to play with").

Another example might be a situation where a more verbal child responds to a teacher's question about whether soccer is over by saying, "Yes, we got a trophy."

Teacher 1 might say, "That's nice," and end the conversation.

Teacher 2 might continue with "A trophy—why did you get a trophy?" The child might say, "Because it was the end of the year," and the teacher might add, "I bet you and the rest of the team were good players and tried very hard, and played very well. That's why you got a trophy."

This example illustrates that we can give credit for expansion even if the teacher initiates the topic, if, in the course of the conversation, she adds more information, words, and ideas to expand on what the child says during the conversation. (See photos 18.5.3 a–c, next page.)

In order to give credit for this indicator, at least two instances of expansion must be observed during the 2½ to 3 hour observation. An observer should write down the instances observed to justify the score.

5.4 This indicator focuses on what the staff do to ***encourage communication*** among all children in the group, including those with disabilities if any children with disabilities are included. Inclusion of a child with disabilities is not required to score this indicator. However, if a child with disabilities is enrolled, the score must reflect that child's experience as well as that of the others in the group.

Staff can use a number of different approaches to ***encourage children to communicate*** with their classmates:

- They can model or demonstrate good listening behaviors throughout the day by looking at the child who is speaking, listening respectfully to what he has to say and responding appropriately.
- During group time, staff can make sure that shy or less verbal children get a chance to talk, explain the reasons for taking turns with listening and talking, establish a system for turn-taking that the group can use, and praise them for doing so. It helps 3-year-olds to have something to hold onto or wear when it is their turn, like a "talker's" hat or a "turn" yarn ball. Four-year-olds and kindergartners can learn to quietly hold up one finger to be recognized for a turn, and listen to the talker. As with all group activity, it helps to have fewer children and keep the group time short.
- During meals and snacks, staff can encourage conversation among children. Topics might include what is being served that day, what the children have been doing at various centers, and other spontaneous interests. Meal/snack times should not be times for "No talking."
- During free play, having many different activities accessible that encourage

Indicator

18.5.3 a Staff add to the information these children have about snakes and other reptiles as they talk to her about the toys they are playing with.

18.5.3 b This staff member adds ideas to expand on the children's camping play.

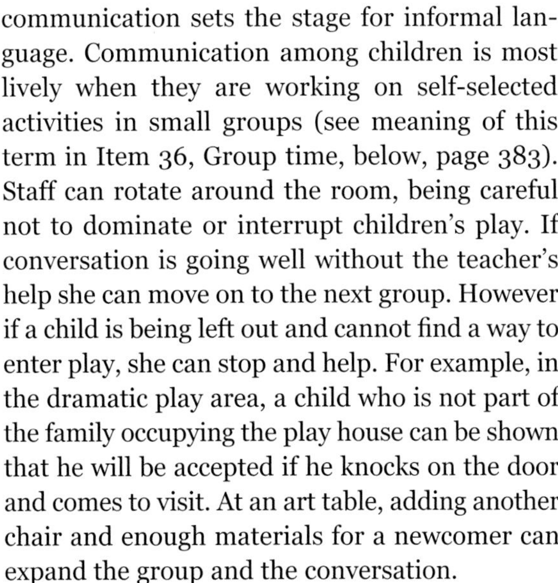

communication sets the stage for informal language. Communication among children is most lively when they are working on self-selected activities in small groups (see meaning of this term in Item 36, Group time, below, page 383). Staff can rotate around the room, being careful not to dominate or interrupt children's play. If conversation is going well without the teacher's help she can move on to the next group. However if a child is being left out and cannot find a way to enter play, she can stop and help. For example, in the dramatic play area, a child who is not part of the family occupying the play house can be shown that he will be accepted if he knocks on the door and comes to visit. At an art table, adding another chair and enough materials for a newcomer can expand the group and the conversation.

18.5.3 c She and the children then make a pretend fire of colored cellophane to warm the campers on a cold day.

- If children with special needs are included, staff must make additional efforts to bring these children into close contact with the others. Children with physical disabilities must have special equipment, if it is needed, so that they can join the other children at table and floor activities. Staff must stay with the group in order to act as a facilitator to encourage interaction and communication. The children in the group may need some help and be shown how to interact appropriately with a child who has severe disabilities: How do you give him toys? What must you do so he can hear or see you? Including a child with special needs is a commitment to supply whatever is needed to help the child join the group as fully as possible without reducing what any other child receives. Inclusion creates valuable learning experiences for the typically developing children as well as children with disabilities. (See photo 18.5.4, next page.)

Score 5.4 "Yes" if encouraging communication among children is seen as a usual practice (rather than only once in a while). The encouragement is evidenced both in *how* the setting is structured (Is talking allowed? Does the grouping of children

Indicator

encourage talk?) and *action taken by staff* when interacting with children.

7.1 This indicator requires that ***staff*** be observed ***having individual conversations*** with ***most*** of the children. Individual conversations means that the staff member makes eye contact or shares a focus on something that interests both of them and is obviously engaging the child in conversation. The conversation does not have to be restricted to one child alone. The staff member can have individual conversations with a small group if each child seems personally involved and is free to make comments. During the observation, ***most*** of the children should be given the personal attention of an individual conversation. This indicator requires that several instances, at least three or four, be observed throughout the observation as a sample of the ongoing behavior that staff exhibit towards all children, sometime during the day. It is not necessary for the observer to make sure that every child has the experience during the observation, but if it is generally true that many individual conversations occur and several instances are observed, give credit for this indicator. (See photos 18.7.1 a–c.)

18.5.4 If a child with a disability is included in the group, staff encourage communication among all children, and make a special effort to facilitate communication, if needed.

18.7.1 a

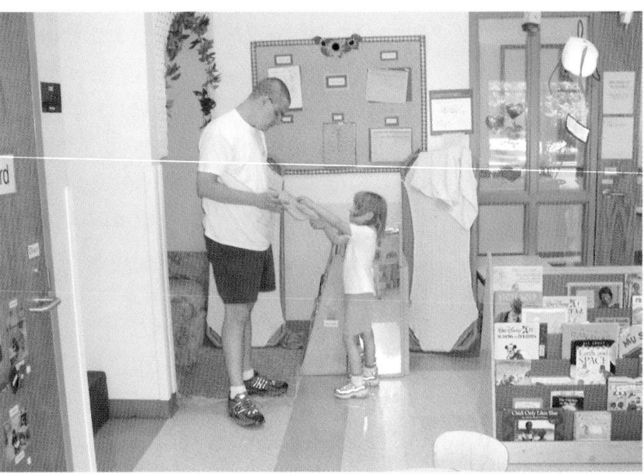

18.7.1 b

18.7.1 a–b Staff have individual conversations with most of the children.

18.7.1 c Individual conversations can occur with a small group of children, if each child is personally involved.

Indicator

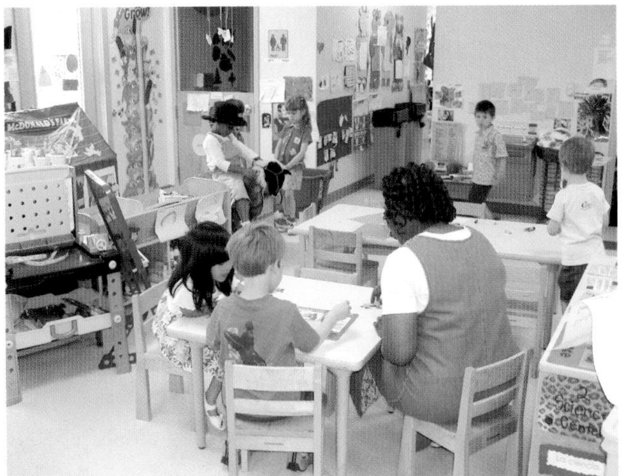

18.7.2 a Children are asked questions to encourage longer and more complex explanations of their work.

18.7.2 b

18.7.2 c

18.7.2 b–c As teachers circulate around the room, they stop to ask many different children about their work, being careful not to interrupt them.

7.2 Asking questions can be a good way to ***encourage children to give longer and more complex answers***. It all depends on what questions are asked and the tone that is used by staff.

Questions that are asked for effect, but not to get an answer, stop conversation. For example, if a staff member finds a child doing something that is unacceptable, and she asks in an annoyed tone, "What do you think you're doing?" this is obviously not a prompt to have the child add information.

To give credit for questions that enhance conversations, observe to see if the staff member is making eye contact and/or showing interest in what the child has been doing or looking at, and seems pleased.

Questions starting with "how" require longer answers because they ask about a process (e.g., "How did you make this tall tower?") Questions starting with "why" or "what do you think" also require longer answers ("What do you think you might do if it snows today?") Factual questions starting with "what," "where," or "who" call for short answers and are particularly useful with younger children. They can also be interspersed in a longer conversation with older children when specific information is needed. However, if most questions only call for one word answers, and the children are capable of longer answers, do not give credit. (See photos 18.7.2 a–c.)

Questions can encourage more rounds of turn-taking and prolong conversations. Note the questions that are typically used by staff throughout the observation and the children's answers. If questions are sometimes used to encourage longer answers, and this seems to be a regular, usual practice rather than an exception, give credit for 7.2 (score "Yes").

Activities

19 Fine motor

General information about this item

Fine motor activities are those that encourage the development of eye-hand coordination—using the fingers and eyes together to manipulate objects. Good eye-hand coordination is very important as preschool children learn self-help skills and also become ready for many of the academic tasks they will meet in the future, such as writing. It takes years to become adept at coordinating the eyes and hands, with each task requiring practice, and some being more difficult to achieve than others.

The types of activities and materials children can access will determine the kinds of fine motor skills they can practice. Art materials develop some skills while manipulative toys encourage others. This item requires that children be provided access to a variety of challenging fine motor materials that they enjoy using.

Fine motor materials help children practice the skills required to handle or manipulate small objects with their fingers, especially the fingers and thumb working together. Using fine motor materials usually means that children will use their sight to guide their finger movements, such as looking to see where the hole is in a bead in order to push the string through.

Different types of fine motor materials are considered in this item. Here are examples of each type, but look for others, as well:

19 A One example of small building toys is interlocking blocks.

Small building toys:

- Interlocking blocks (See photo 19 A.)
- Lincoln Logs
- Small blocks, inch cubes
- Bristle blocks
- Tinker Toys
- Magnetic blocks

19 B Art supplies such as scissors, markers, and crayons give children the opportunity to develop their eye-hand coordination.

Art materials:

- Crayons, watercolor markers, either wide or narrow (See photo 19B.)
- Pencils (colored or black, large or small)
- Paints (tempera or watercolors) with brushes, finger paints
- Paper, (various sizes and colors, construction, painting, drawing papers)

Indicator

19 C Children select colors and shapes of beads to string bead patterns.

19 D This floor puzzle is more challenging than a simple puzzle in a frame.

- Tools, such as hole punches, safe, child-sized scissors, rulers, stencils, tape
- Collage materials, such as glue, paste, string, yarn, paper scraps, fabric scraps, cardboard or styrofoam pieces, glitter, stickers
- Play dough, clay

Manipulatives:

- Beads and strings in various sizes, colors, shapes (See photo 19 C)
- Lacing cards with strings
- Pegs with peg boards (various sizes, colors, shapes are available)
- Parquet shapes or other shapes used to make designs
- Zip, snap, and button toys, such as dolls with clothes to fasten or dressing frames
- Gears with interlocking plates and connectors
- Snap blocks
- Sticks with connectors for building
- Links
- Nuts and bolts
- Other toys with pieces to link or fit together, such as pop beads, snap cubes, magnetic blocks, Mr. Potato Head, toy train tracks

Puzzles:

- Picture puzzles in frames with differing numbers of pieces, with or without knobs to grasp; easier puzzles have each piece as an individual picture while more difficult puzzles require a combination of pieces to complete the picture with interlocking pieces
- Puzzles without frames, such as floor puzzles, jigsaw puzzles (See photo 19 D.)

Indicator

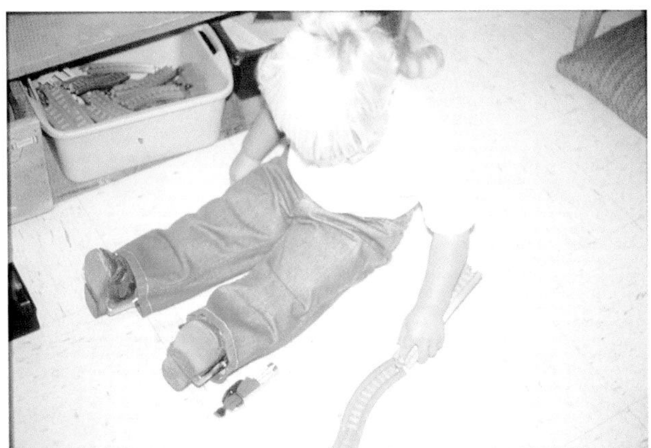

19.1.1 a Teachers make manipulatives accessible by placing materials on a low, open shelf.

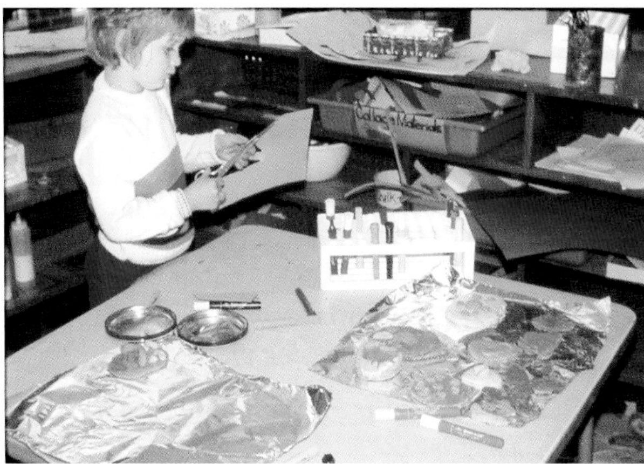

19.1.1 b Children are free to take materials off the shelf in the art center.

19.1.1 c The teacher makes art supplies accessible by placing them on the table.

A closer look at each indicator

1.1 ***Very few*** of these materials means that there is little opportunity for children to develop fine motor skills in the classroom. Only a few examples of one or two types of materials might be present, or, if there are more, the pieces needed for using them are so scattered that it would be impossible for a child to play successfully.

Developmentally appropriate means that the materials interest and challenge children, in terms of their ages and abilities, without being frustrating. The best way to determine if materials are developmentally appropriate is to observe children using the materials and notice whether the materials are too difficult or easy, and whether children maintain interest while using them.

Accessible means that children can reach and use materials by themselves. For materials to be considered accessible, they must be within view of younger preschoolers (2½ to 4 years). For older preschoolers and kindergartners (4 to 6 years), if materials are stored in closed spaces, they can be considered accessible only if it is observed that children can freely access and use the materials.

Observers should be sure to find out whether toys stored on open shelves are actually ***accessible*** to the children. This is usually discovered as children are allowed or encouraged to take toys from open shelves. (See photos 19.1.1 a–b.) However, when children do not seem to feel free to take toys from shelves, ask how and when materials are used and whether there are rules about special times when children are allowed to access them. For example, in some cases, staff may control the fine motor toy choices children can make by taking certain toys out and placing them on a table. (See photo 19.1.1 c.) A rule in one classroom might be that only the toys on the table can be used, while in another classroom, children are allowed to use the other toys in addition to the table top toys. The observer must determine how and when fine motor materials are accessible to score this item.

Indicator

Accessible daily means that the above is true every day. To get credit for accessible daily, children should have access to materials for some time during the day.

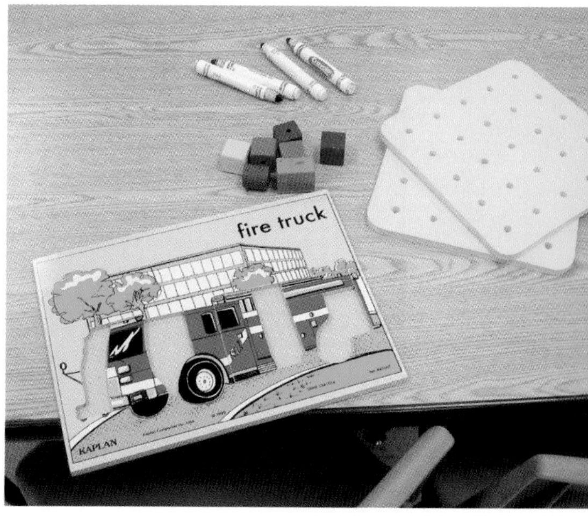

19.1.2 These fine motor materials are incomplete. The puzzles are missing pieces, no pegs for pegboards, no strings to use with beads, and markers are dried out.

1.2 ***In poor repair or incomplete*** means that fine motor toys and materials cannot be used properly because too many pieces are missing, parts are broken, or other problems exist. (See photo 19.1.2.) For example, the watercolor markers are dried out, pegboards are missing pegs, beads are missing strings, or puzzles are missing pieces.

Generally in poor repair or incomplete means that *most* (about 80%) of the materials cannot be used properly because of their poor condition.

3.1. ***Some of each type*** means more than one example of each type is accessible to the children for approximately 1 hour on a daily basis.

Each example must be complete enough to allow the type of activity for which the material was designed. For example, drawing paper must accompany crayons to count as one example. Markers cannot be dried out and must have drawing paper with them. Interlocking blocks must consist of a set with enough blocks to build something. (See photo 19.3.1.) A puzzle must have all its pieces to be counted as one example. Also, to count as an example, the set, rather than the individual piece is considered. For example, crayons count as one example of art materials, a set of beads with strings counts as one manipulative example, and a puzzle with all pieces counts as one puzzle example.

19.3.1 This sample of materials meets the requirement for some of each type.

To give credit, the materials must be ***accessible*** for approximately 1 hour daily in full-day programs of 8 hours or more. (See example in 19.3.1.) The 1 hour may take place at one time, or be a combination of times throughout the day. All types of materials do not have to be accessible at the same time, but children should have access to fine motor materials from each type for approximately 1 hour per day. For example, art materials might be available during special art activity times when other types of fine motor materials are not accessible. The other types (small building toys, manipulatives, and puzzles) might then be available at other times of the day.

Less time is required for programs operating less than 8 hours a day, with the amount of time calculated proportionally, based on the ratio of 1 hour for programs of 8 hours or more. For example, if a program operated for 6 hours a day, this would be ¾ of a full-day program, so the time required would be ¾ of the 1 hour. If the program operated 4 hours a day, the requirement would be ½ hour.

3.2. ***Complete and in good repair*** is true as long as ***most*** (about 80%) of the fine motor materials/toys are in good shape, unbroken, have all their pieces, and can be used by the children. This indicator does not require that all fine motor toys and materials be complete and in good repair, as long as most are.

Credit can be given for this indicator even if there are some fine motor materials with missing pieces or in poor repair. For example, in a classroom that contains

Indicator

many smaller building toys, many and varied art materials, and manipulatives, but the stringing cards are missing strings, credit can be given because most of the fine motor materials are in good repair and complete. However, in a classroom that has limited fine motor materials for the number of children enrolled, several puzzles are missing pieces, the markers are dried out, and strings are missing from the few stringing cards, then credit could not be given for this indicator. To determine if 80% of the materials are in good repair, make a list of the fine motor materials and categorize them into the types listed in 3.1. Put an "X" next to the materials that are either in poor repair or missing pieces. Evaluate the list to determine if this indicator is true.

5.1. ***Many*** requires at least three examples of each type of the fine motor materials listed in the General Information section. See 3.1 for additional information to use in scoring.

Accessible for a substantial portion of the day refers to the ***many*** (not just some) fine motor toys/materials. Accessible for a substantial portion of the day means that the materials are within the child's reach and children are allowed to use them for 1/3 of the center's operating hours. Many items representing each type do not have to be out and accessible at the same time. However, a combination of these materials should be accessible for the substantial portion of the day and children should have experiences with many fine motor materials.

See sample schedules showing calculations of whether fine motor materials are accessible for a substantial portion of the day (on pages 196–198).

5.2 ***Well organized*** means that each of the fine motor materials is stored with all its pieces in an area designated for its use, so that children know where to find the materials they need for an activity and can easily put them away. (See photo 19.5.2.) Children are able to easily see and access these materials with little or no help from the staff. Well organized also means that materials for a specific activity are stored together so that a child can easily access the materials without undue effort. For example, the chalk is stored with the chalk boards, the paint brushes are stored with the paint sets, and the peg boards are stored with the pegs that fit the board.

Fine motor materials containing many small pieces should be stored in individual containers. If pieces of different fine motor materials are all jumbled together, so that it would be difficult to find the pieces needed for a certain activity, or if puzzles are stored without their pieces in place, do not give credit for 5.2 (score "No"). If the vast majority of fine motor materials are stored so it is easy to use them and put them away, score "Yes." Perfection is not required to score "Yes," and all fine motor materials do not have to be stored together in the same area of the room. However, most should be in one area, and sets with many pieces stored in their own containers.

5.3 ***Different levels of difficulty*** means that there are some fine motor materials which are more challenging and some that are less

19.5.2 Open shelves, baskets, and containers are used to keep materials well organized by type.

19.5.3 These puzzles represent different levels of difficulty.

Indicator

challenging to the children in the group. (See photo 19.5.3, preceding page.) The less challenging materials require less advanced eye-hand coordination, while the more difficult materials require higher levels of skill. Since children's fine motor skills will vary, it is important to have a variety of materials so children are not frustrated with difficult-to-use materials or uninterested in materials that are too easy.

Examples of materials that are of different levels of difficulty include:

Easier	More challenging
Knobbed puzzles	Puzzles without knobs
Puzzles with few, large pieces	Puzzles with many smaller pieces
Puzzles in a frame	Jigsaw puzzles with no frame
Zipper toys	Button toys
Large interlocking blocks	Small interlocking blocks
Large beads with string	Small beads with string
Big water color markers	Thin fine-point markers
Sewing cards with large holes and shoelaces	Real sewing activities with darning needles and yarn

7.1 ***Rotating materials*** means that the fine motor toys that are accessible to children are changed so children can practice different skills, find new interests, and use toys

19.7.1 a Materials no longer interesting to the children are removed from the shelf.

19.7.1 b They are put in storage and new materials are brought out.

19.7.1 c Old materials are replaced with new materials.

Indicator

that they have used before, but in a new way. Rotating toys keeps children from becoming bored with the choices they can make for play and adds new learning opportunities. (See photos 19.7.1 a–c.)

Toy rotation should occur when children become bored with the materials because they no longer find them interesting or challenging. The materials should then be put away and different materials brought out. Toys should also be rotated to provide new types of experiences and to relate to certain projects or themes.

Calling children's attention to a fine motor material that is regularly accessible to children does not count as "rotating materials." For example, when staff take pop beads off the shelf where accessible toys are stored and place the beads on the table for children to use at free play time, credit for "rotation" is not given. Credit is given only when toys are removed from the accessible shelves in the classroom, and replaced with toys that were formerly inaccessible.

Inaccessible materials can be made accessible as either special projects or for free play. The rotated fine motor materials can be brought from storage or other classrooms or newly purchased.

To give credit, some toys should be rotated at least monthly.

7.2 Containers as well as storage shelves must have ***labels*** to give credit for this indicator. This allows children (and adults) to put materials away in the correct places by matching.

Labels ***encourage self-help*** only when the label's meaning is clear to the user. Since the labels are used primarily by preschool-aged children, they must consist of something children can easily understand. For example, labels can consist of pictures of the toys that belong on a particular shelf or in a container. (See photo 19.7.2 a–b.) Words can be added to the pictures, but words alone as labels are not acceptable for this age group.

Other labeling systems are acceptable as long as the meaning is clear to children. For example, a container might have a shape label that should be matched to the same shape label on a shelf. This would tell the child where the container must be placed during clean-up.

19.7.2 a

19.7.2 b

19.7.2 a–b Labeling systems with pictures in addition to written descriptions help children independently access and clean up fine motor materials.

Indicator

Calculating "Substantial Portion of the Day"

Example 1

This schedule is based on an observation period of 4.5 hours (from 8AM – 12:30PM) and information collected during the teacher interview about how unobserved time during the day is used and what is accessible to the children.

Time	Scheduled activity	Time to use fine motor materials
6:30 – 8:00	Breakfast in cafeteria and TV time for those who are finished with breakfast	
8:00 – 8:30	Children go to regular classrooms and play with table and rug toys (puzzles; legos; duplos with cars, people, and trucks; stringing beads and cards; pegboards)	**30 minutes**
8:30 – 8:45	Prepare for breakfast/children wash hands	
8:45 – 9:15	Breakfast	
9:15 – 9:45	Circle (teacher reading time)	
9:45 – 10:45	Centers (housekeeping, art, sand and water, nature/science, writing table, blocks, music, computer and cozy book area)	**1 hour**
10:45 – 11:15	Outdoor play (gross motor activities only)	
11:15 – 12:15	Prepare for and eat lunch	
12:15 – 12:30	Story, put out cots, prepare for nap	
12:30 – 2:45	Nap	
2:45 – 3:00	Wake up from nap; bathroom	
3:00 – 3:25	Snack and story	
3:25 – 4:25	Centers (housekeeping, nature/science, writing table, computer, fine motor area and cozy book area)	**1 hour**
4:25 – 5:30	Outdoors or indoor gross motor	
5:30 – 6:30	Table and rug toys (puzzles; legos; duplos with cars, people, and trucks; stringing beads and cards; pegboards) Prepare for departure	**1 hour**

1. Figure the total number of hours that children are allowed to attend.

   (6:30AM to 6:30 PM = 12 hours)

2. Calculate 1/3 of the operating hours to determine "Substantial Portion of the Day."

   (12 hours ÷ 3 = 4 hours)

3. Add up all times that children have access to fine motor materials.

   (see shaded times on schedule = 3 hours and 30 minutes)

4. Compare the amount of time children may have access to fine motor materials to the time requirement for substantial portion of the day. If the amount of time children may have access to fine motor materials is the same or greater, then score "Yes." If the amount of time is less than the time requirement for substantial portion of the day, then score "No." For example, the schedule above indicates:

   3 hours and 30 minutes (access to fine motor materials) **is less than 4 hours** (time requirement for substantial portion of day), and therefore the time requirement for substantial portion of the day is not met.

Indicator

Calculating "Substantial Portion of the Day"

Example 2

This schedule is based on an observation period of 4 hours (from 9AM – 1PM) and information collected during the teacher interview about how unobserved time during the day is used and what is accessible to the children.

Time	Scheduled activity	Time to use fine motor materials
9:00 – 9:30	Arrival/quiet centers open (cozy book area, computer, writing table, math, science and fine motor)	**30 minutes**
9:30 – 9:45	Snack	
9:45 – 10:00	Clean up snack/bathroom/wash hands	
10:00 – 11:00	Outside (gross motor activities only)	
11:00 – 11:45	Free choice of centers (fine motor, art, blocks, dramatic play, nature/science, math, sensory table, computer, writing table and cozy book area)	**45 minutes**
11:45 – 12:15	Large group activity (M,W,F is music/movement and T,Th is art activity)	
12:15 – 12:45	Prepare for and eat lunch	
12:45 – 1:00	Clean up/bathroom/prepare for quiet time	
1:00 – 1:45	Quiet time/quiet centers available (cozy book area, fine motor, math, and science)	**45 minutes**
1:45 – 2:00	Clean up all centers and prepare for departure	

1. Figure the total number of hours that children are allowed to attend.

   (9 AM to 2 PM = 5 hours)

2. Calculate 1/3 of the operating hours to determine "Substantial Portion of the Day."

   (5 hours ÷ 3 = 1 hour and 40 minutes)

3. Add up all times that children have access to fine motor materials.

   (see shaded times on schedule = 2 hours)

4. Compare the amount of time children may have access to fine motor materials to the time requirement for substantial portion of the day. If the amount of time children may have access to fine motor materials is the same or greater, then score "Yes." If the amount of time is less than the time requirement for substantial portion of the day, then score "No." For example, the schedule above indicates:

   2 hours (access to fine motor materials) **is greater than 1 hour and 40 minutes** (time requirement for substantial portion of day), and therefore the time requirement for substantial portion of the day is met.

Indicator

Calculating "Substantial Portion of the Day"

Example 3

This schedule is based on an observation period of 3.5 hours (from 9AM –12:30 PM) and information collected during the teacher interview about whether what was observed represents the typical daily practice.

Time	Scheduled activity	Time to use fine motor materials
9:00 – 9:20	Arrival/group time to discuss activities for the day	
9:20 – 9:45	Whole group art activity	**25 minutes**
9:45 – 10:00	Whole group reading time (teacher directed)	
10:00 – 10:45	Outside time (gross motor activities only)	
10:45 – 11:30	Free choice of centers (fine motor, art, blocks, dramatic play, nature/science, math, sensory table, computer, writing table and books)	**45 minutes**
11:30 – 11:45	Clean up/bathroom/prepare for lunch time	
11:45 – 12:15	Prepare for and eat lunch	
12:15 – 12:30	Clean up/bathroom/prepare for departure	

1. Figure the total number of hours that children are allowed to attend.

   (9 AM to 12:30 PM = 3 hours and 30 minutes)

2. Calculate 1/3 of the operating hours to determine "Substantial Portion of the Day."

   (3 hours and 30 minutes ÷ 3 = 1 hour and 10 minutes)

3. Add up all times that children have access to fine motor materials.

   (see shaded times on schedule = 1 hour and 10 minutes)

4. Compare the amount of time children may have access to fine motor materials to the time requirement for substantial portion of the day. If the amount of time children may have access to fine motor materials is the same or greater, then score "Yes." If the amount of time is less than the time requirement for substantial portion of the day, then score "No." For example, the schedule above indicates:

   1 hour and 10 minutes (access to fine motor materials) **is equal to 1 hour and 10 minutes** (time requirement for substantial portion of day), and therefore the time requirement for substantial portion of the day is met.

Indicator

20 Art

General information about this item

Art activities for young children encourage the development of a variety of skills. First, using art materials allows children to practice important fine motor skills, which are necessary in later challenges, such as learning to write and being successful in many self-help skills. Second, art allows children to experiment with shapes, lines, and space, and the combinations of colors; in this way, art is like science and math. Third, art allows children to develop their own creative expression, by being able to use materials in a process that they control and make a product only they could have created. Art also gives the children (especially older children) an opportunity to show how they see things—to represent their ideas and interests for themselves and for others. Their ideas become more understandable to others as children gain the skills to depict things more realistically.

The benefits children receive from art experiences will depend on how art is provided to them—the time children have to use the materials, the variety of materials they can use, the restriction or freedom children experience in their use of materials, and the extent to which they can experiment or create following their own ideas. The indicators at the lower quality levels in this item describe situations that will not provide the kinds of experiences needed to optimize children's learning opportunities, while at the higher levels, chances for benefiting from art are greatly increased.

A closer look at each indicator

1.1 An ***art activity*** is an experience a child has when using art materials (see 3.1 for definition of art materials).

Rarely available means that activities with art materials are offered less than once a day, or if offered daily, all children do not have the opportunity to participate if they wish, or the time offered is too short to be satisfying to the children. Children should be able to choose to do an art activity on a regular basis daily, or almost daily, to score 1.1 "No."

1.2 ***Individual expression*** means that children can use art materials in their own creative way. In doing this, children are free to express their own ideas, using the skills that they currently possess.

No individual expression means that children are not given the opportunity to select the subject matter and/or the medium to be used in an art activity or use their own ideas in creating the product. Topics for artwork, the art materials to be used and the way in which they are used are selected by the adult. Typical examples are

Indicator

20.1.2 a Children have no individual expression in art activities when staff select the art materials and subject.

20.1.2 b These children are using their own ideas to create art. They are free to choose the materials and can paint or draw any topic.

adult-created pictures that children are supposed to color (e.g., coloring book pages, work sheets) or craft-type activities in which children make an object by copying an adult-created model. Another type of example includes activities in which art materials are used to complete a specified task, such as cutting strips of paper into squares or punching holes around a precut design. When no individual expression is present in art activities, the work of many children looks quite similar.

Photo 20.1.2 a shows no individual expression by children in their artwork, contrasted with the example shown in 20.1.2 b where children can paint in their own way.

3.1 ***Art materials*** include the following categories: Drawing materials, Paints, Three-dimensional materials, Collage materials, and Tools. The following are examples of each:

1. *Drawing materials*: things used to draw/scribble—crayons, water color markers, felt-tip markers, pens, pencils, colored pencils, chalk; things to draw/scribble on—various types, shapes and sizes of paper, chalk boards, paper plates, dry-erase boards
2. *Paint materials:* finger paints, tempera paints, water-color paint sets with appropriate brushes and paper
3. *Three-dimensional materials:* play dough, clay, wood for gluing or for carpentry, pipe cleaners, modeling compound
4. *Collage materials:* paste or glue, various types, colors, and shapes of paper, cardboard shapes and pieces, felt remnants, magazine pictures, yarn/string, cotton balls, pom-poms, sequins, gems, feathers, buttons, glitter, natural objects, varied safe "junk" such as cardboard tubes, egg cartons
5. *Tools:* safe scissors, staplers, hole punches, tape dispensers with tape, tools to use with play dough, stencils, sponge painters, rollers, brushes of various sizes and shapes

Indicator

20.3.1 a Art materials are stored on open shelves for easy access and an easel is set up for children to use independently.

20.3.1 b Art materials are placed on the table to encourage children's use.

Note that foods *are not counted as art materials* for the following reasons:

First, children usually eat the foods used in art projects (even hard macaroni). This food is not eaten under the necessary sanitary conditions. Second, using foods for art is confusing to children, who are trying to learn the proper uses of food and art materials (one is to eat, the other is not; one is for messy play, the other is not). Finally, food is in short supply in many children's families, and should not be wasted, but eaten.

Accessible means that children can reach and use art materials. For example, art materials are placed on open shelves, or an easel is set up with paint that children can use independently. (See photo 20.3.1 a–b.)

At least 1 hour a day requires that the minimum amount of time art materials should be accessible for *all* children to participate if they wish, is 1 hour daily. This does not require that all children be able to participate at one time, however. The 1 hour can be provided all at one time or as a combination of several periods throughout the day. For example, art materials might be accessible to children for 30 minutes in the morning for a special art activity and then again for 30 minutes in the afternoon. The materials do not have to be provided as a free choice activity but do have to be accessible for this time period.

Less time is required for programs operating less than 8 hours a day, with the amount of time calculated proportionally, based on the ratio of 1 hour for programs of 8 hours or more. For example, if a program operates for 6 hours a day, this would be 3/4 of a full-day program, so the time required would be 3/4 of the 1 hour. If the program operates 4 hours a day, the requirement would be 1/2 hour.

Some art materials means that there is at least one *usable* example observed that will allow children to complete artwork (e.g., crayons with paper; paper, paste, and scraps for collage work; or paints with paper and brushes). For example, if there are usable markers and paper, credit can be given. However, if the markers are dry and not usable and are the only art material option, credit cannot be given.

3.2 If ***individual expression*** is permitted in an art activity, the observer should get a sense of what the children are able to create on their own, using their own

Indicator

20.3.2 a During this art activity children are expected to follow the model on the cards to complete a task. If most classroom activities are handled this way, where the staff select the medium and subject, score indicator 3.2 "No."

20.3.2 b The teacher has provided the art materials for children to use, but children are free to create their own artwork.

ideas and abilities. Much of the artwork that young children create on their own is scribble pictures or abstract work. As children become older, at 4 or 5 years of age, recognizable shapes are quite often created, although scribbling or abstract work is still seen frequently.

To meet the requirement of ***individual expression***, the child must be allowed to select the subject matter of the art activity and/or the art medium (types of art materials) to be used. The best example of individual expression being encouraged is when children can use any art materials they choose and draw or create anything they wish. The only restriction on the child would be that the art materials are used in a constructive manner, within the limits of how art materials should be used.

Art materials that can be used with the most flexibility (that do not carry with them a certain expectation) are those that encourage the most creative expression. Examples of activities that carry certain expectations for a pre-determined product are drawing with stencils, using cookie cutters with play dough, or painting by rolling marbles around in a pan. (See photo 20.3.2 a.) Materials that allow more flexibility, for example, drawing materials and paints with plain paper, a variety of collage materials, and three-dimensional materials such as play dough and clay to be modeled with the hands, *without* cookie cutters or rolling pins, are more likely to encourage children's individual expression. (See photo 20.3.2 b.)

There is some flexibility allowed when determining whether individual expression is encouraged.

First, the adult can offer a certain art material for children to use, and as long as children can choose the topic of the work and create what they wish, credit should be given. For example, the teacher might put out two colors of paint with paper. If children can paint whatever they wish with the materials, credit would be given.

Next, the topic of the work can be assigned, but children must be able to choose the art materials to use to carry out the work in their own way. For example, the teacher may tell children to make pumpkins in art. Some may decide to make play dough pumpkins, others may decide to use markers to draw them, and others may paint pumpkins at the easel. All pumpkins should not look alike in this case, and credit would be given for this indicator.

Indicator

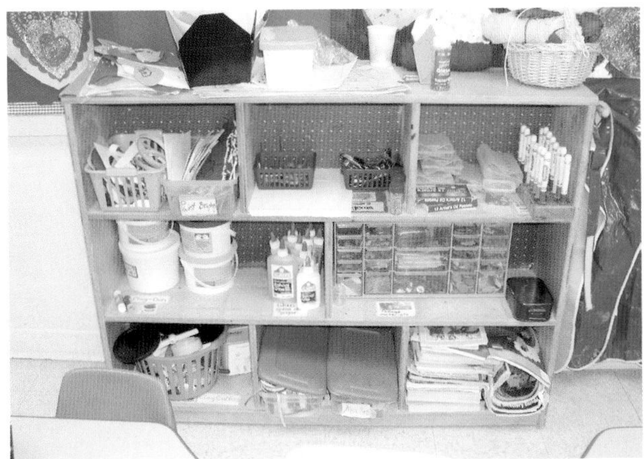
20.5.1 Children can choose from a wide variety of art materials

20.5.2 In this classroom, children's artwork is varied and individual. Children are encouraged to use individual expression in most art activities.

Finally, credit can be given if the basic subject matter and medium are suggested by the adult, but there is much room for individual expression in how the child creates the work. The children do not have to do the work to meet adult expectations, and can freely choose to do something different with the materials. For example, if children are asked to draw pictures of the people in their families using markers and paper, individual expression can be given credit if they can choose how to represent their families in their own way. All pictures will look quite different.

Some individual expression means that children are sometimes permitted to use art materials with very little instruction or direction from the teacher. However, there could also be occasions when the teacher will dictate how the art activities should be completed as well as some time when children can choose the topic and/or art materials they want to use. For example, the teacher provides a pre-cut shape of an apple but the children are free to choose from markers, paint, or crayons to complete their drawings on the pre-cut shape in their own way. **Some** individual expression may be observed when the daily schedule offers time for teacher-directed as well as child-initiated art activities.

5.1 ***Many and varied*** means that there are three to five different art materials accessible from at least four of the five categories listed in 3.1, on page 200, and drawing materials is required as one of the four. (See photo 20.5.1.)

Substantial portion of the day means that children have access to the materials daily for 1/3 of the program's operating hours. See sample schedules showing calculations of whether art materials are accessible for a substantial portion of day (on pages 207–209).

5.2 See 3.2 for definition of ***individual expression***.

Much individual expression means that there are very few, if any, teacher-directed activities, and most of the time when art materials are used (about 85%) the children can do "free art" and are not required or expected to follow an example. Most of the time, children will use the more flexible art materials with no expected product. (See photo 20.5.2.)

Indicator

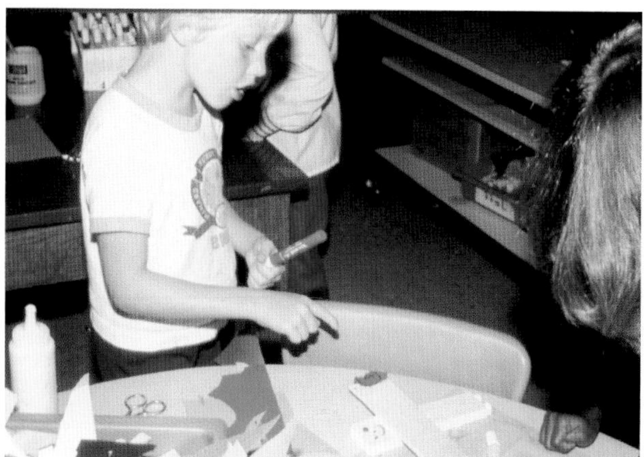

20.7.1 a

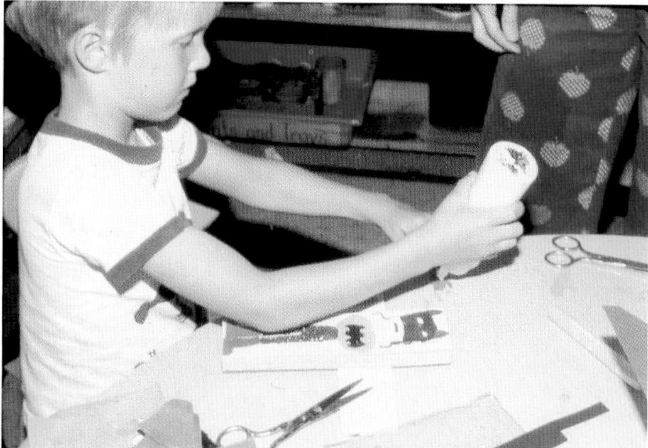

20.7.1 b

Observers should look to see whether children have access to the art materials and if they actually use them in their own creative way. Evidence of creativity (or lack of it) may also be found in the art work displayed in the room. If many teacher-directed projects are displayed, and little individual work is being done by the children during the observation, do not give credit for this indicator. If not sure, the observer should ask the teacher how often projects like those in the display are done. If projects that meet the requirements of 3.2 are used *no more than* once or twice a week, and many instances of children using art materials in a creative way are observed, credit can be given for this indicator, even if much of the work displayed is of the "project" variety. Additional questions such as, "How do you choose what to put on the bulletin board?" may also be helpful.

20.7.1 c

20.7.1 a–c Children in these photos are building their 3-dimensional figures using wood, glue, clay, and other art materials.

7.1 ***Three-dimensional*** means that the art objects that have been created have height, depth, and width. Gluing small three-dimensional objects (such as styrofoam chips, pieces of egg cartons, art sticks) to a flat surface does not count as three-dimensional work, unless the work is built up substantially, away from the base surface. Art materials used to create three-dimensional objects include modeling clay, play dough, papier maché, woodwork, and "junk" (such as cardboard tubes, paper boxes, packing materials, etc.) to make sculptures. (See photos 20.7.1 a–c.)

7.2 During the preschool years, children are developing the abilities to express what they think about how they see the world, and to tell others about these thoughts. They can show their ideas in the artwork that they create, as well as with their words and other actions. When art activities are ***related to other classroom activities***, children have the chance to consider what they are experiencing, and to show their ideas through their own creative abilities. This is true primarily when children create their own work, through individual expression rather than attempting to copy the work of an adult.

Art activities ***related to other classroom experiences***, in this indicator, should allow children to do art in their own ways, while considering a topic being discussed and experienced in the class. The art experience, under these condi-

Indicator

20.7.2 a

20.7.2 b

20.7.2 a–e In this series of photographs, staff and children in the classroom are talking and reading about dinosaurs. Children use art to extend their ideas.

tions, will help the children tell what they think about the topic through their creations or add to what they think by looking at the topic from another point of view. Therefore, staff can provide materials that relate to a specific topic. For example, in November, the staff provide leaves to make leaf prints or fall-colored paints at the easel while talking about the characteristics of the season. Or when discussing families, children are encouraged to create pictures of their own family members. Other examples include encouraging children to draw pictures to illustrate their daily journals, to draw about the nature/science planting activity that they completed earlier in the day, or to make portraits of the new classroom pet.

The extent to which children will be able to represent their thinking about a topic will differ by age. Younger preschoolers will best be able to relate their artwork to a classroom topic by using special colors in their scribble works that relate to the topic or by using special collage materials. Older preschoolers may be able to add drawings that represent a topic more exactly. (See photos 20.7.2 a–e.)

7.3 When older preschoolers are encouraged to ***extend an art activity***, they have an opportunity to do more complex artwork that requires the completion of stages, while having the opportunity to think about an art project over a period of more than just one art activity time. They can think back on what they have already done and think ahead to consider what will come next. Such an experience encourages a longer attention span while allowing a child to delay the completion of a work.

20.7.2 c

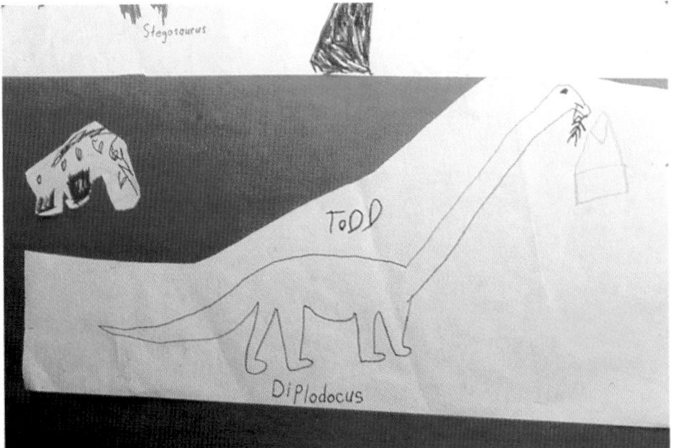

20.7.2 d [above]
20.7.2 e [below]

Indicator

It can also give children the opportunity to experience more stages of the process.

Examples of extended art activities that could be observed or reported by the staff include creating papier maché objects that require a process of gluing, drying, and decorating; woodworking projects that use carpentry skills followed by painting; book-making or sewing projects that last over several days; or large group murals that last for several days. (See photos 20.7.3 a–e.)

Indicator 7.3 can be scored "NA" if all children enrolled in the classroom are under 4 years of age.

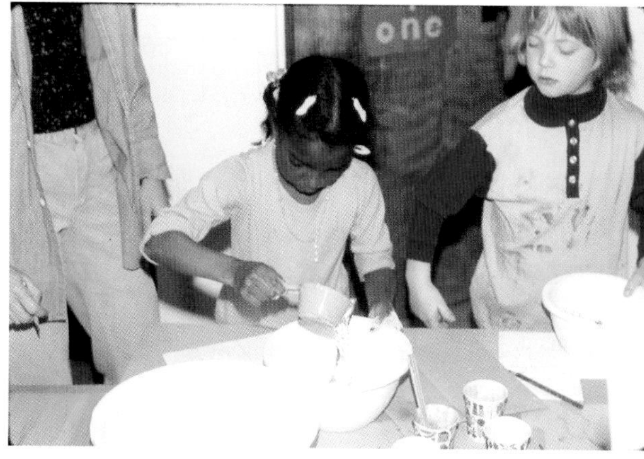

20.7.3 a Children are participating in an art project that lasts over several days. On the first day, the children prepare the dough mixture.

20.7.3 b To finish the dough, children add color and knead.

20.7.3 c Making objects with the dough comes next.

20.7.3 d Several days later the objects are hard and ready to decorate.

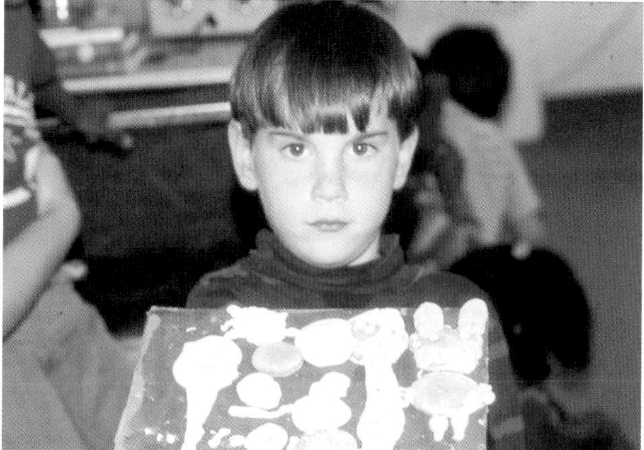

20.7.3 e The children have carried the process through several days.

Indicator

Calculating "Substantial Portion of the Day"

Example 1

This schedule is based on an observation period of 4.5 hours (from 8AM – 12:30PM) and information collected during the teacher interview about how unobserved time during the day is used and what is accessible to the children.

Time	Scheduled activity	Time to use art materials
6:30 – 8:00	Breakfast in cafeteria and TV time for those who are finished with breakfast	
8:00 – 8:30	Children go to regular classrooms and play with table and rug toys (puzzles; legos; duplos with cars, people, and trucks; stringing beads and cards; pegboards)	
8:30 – 8:45	Prepare for breakfast/children wash hands	
8:45 – 9:15	Breakfast	
9:15 – 9:45	Circle (teacher reading time)	
9:45 – 10:45	Centers (housekeeping, art, sand and water, nature/science, writing table (with markers, colored pencils, and paper), blocks, music, computer and cozy book area)	**1 hour**
10:45 – 11:15	Outdoor play (gross motor activities only)	
11:15 – 12:15	Prepare for and eat lunch	
12:15 – 12:30	Story, put out cots, prepare for nap	
12:30 – 2:45	Nap	
2:45 – 3:00	Wake up from nap; bathroom	
3:00 – 3:25	Snack and story	
3:25 – 4:25	Centers (housekeeping, nature/science, writing table (with markers, colored pencils, and paper), computer, fine motor, and cozy book area)	**1 hour**
4:25 – 5:30	Outdoors or indoor gross motor	
5:30 – 6:30	Table and rug toys (puzzles; legos; duplos with cars, people, and trucks; stringing beads and cards; pegboards) Prepare for departure	

1. Figure the total number of hours that children are allowed to attend.

   (6:30AM to 6:30 PM = 12 hours)

2. Calculate 1/3 of the operating hours to determine "Substantial Portion of the Day."

   (12 hours ÷ 3 = 4 hours)

3. Add up all times that children have access to art materials.

   (see shaded times on schedule = 2 hours)

4. Compare the amount of time children may have access to art materials to the time requirement for substantial portion of the day. If the amount of time children may have access to art materials is the same or greater, then score "Yes." If the amount of time is less than the time requirement for substantial portion of the day, then score "No." For example, the schedule above indicates:

   2 hours (access to art materials) **is less than 4 hours** (time requirement for substantial portion of day), and therefore the time requirement for substantial portion of the day is not met.

Indicator

Calculating "Substantial Portion of the Day"

Example 2

This schedule is based on an observation period of 4 hours (from 9AM – 1PM) and information collected during the teacher interview about how unobserved time during the day is used and what is accessible to the children.

Time	Scheduled activity	Time to use art materials
9:00 – 9:30	Arrival/quiet centers open (cozy book area, computer, writing table, math, science and fine motor)	**30 minutes**
9:30 – 9:45	Snack	
9:45 – 10:00	Clean up snack/bathroom/wash hands	
10:00 – 11:00	Outside (gross motor activities only)	
11:00 – 11:45	Free choice of centers (fine motor, art, blocks, dramatic play, nature/science, math, sensory table, computer, writing table and cozy book area)	**45 minutes**
11:45 – 12:15	Large group activity (M,W,F is music/movement and T,Th is art activity)	
12:15 – 12:45	Prepare for and eat lunch	
12:45 – 1:00	Clean up/bathroom/prepare for quiet time	
1:00 – 1:45	Quiet time/quiet centers available (cozy book area, fine motor, math, and science)	
1:45 – 2:00	Clean up all centers and prepare for departure	

1. Figure the total number of hours that children are allowed to attend.

   (9 AM to 2 PM = 5 hours)

2. Calculate 1/3 of the operating hours to determine "Substantial Portion of the Day."

   (5 hours ÷ 3 = 1 hour and 40 minutes)

3. Add up all times that children have access to art materials on a daily basis. Since the 30 minute large group art activity is not offered on a daily basis, the time cannot be counted toward the substantial portion of the day.

   (see shaded times on schedule = 1 hour and 15 minutes)

4. Compare the amount of time children may have access to art materials to the time requirement for substantial portion of the day. If the amount of time children may have access to art materials is the same or greater, then score "Yes." If the amount of time is less than the time requirement for substantial portion of the day, then score "No." For example, the schedule above indicates:

   1 hour and 15 minutes (access to art materials) **is less than 1 hour and 40 minutes** (time requirement for substantial portion of day), and therefore the time requirement for substantial portion of the day is not met.

Indicator

Calculating "Substantial Portion of the Day" for Item 20, Art

Example 3

This schedule is based on an observation period of 3.5 hours (from 9AM –12:30 PM) and information collected during the teacher interview about whether what was observed represents the typical daily practice.

Time	Scheduled activity	Time to use art materials
9:00 – 9:20	Arrival/group time to discuss activities for the day	
9:20 – 9:45	Whole group art activity	**25 minutes**
9:45 – 10:00	Whole group reading time (teacher-directed)	
10:00 – 10:45	Outside time (gross motor activities only)	
10:45 – 11:30	Free choice of centers (fine motor, art, blocks, dramatic play, nature/science, math, sensory table, computer, writing table and books)	**45 minutes**
11:30 – 11:45	Clean up/bathroom/prepare for lunch time	
11:45 – 12:15	Prepare for and eat lunch	
12:15 – 12:30	Clean up/bathroom/prepare for departure	

1. Figure the total number of hours that children are allowed to attend.

   (9 AM to 12:30 PM = 3 hours and 30 minutes)

2. Calculate 1/3 of the operating hours to determine "Substantial Portion of the Day."

   (3 hours and 30 minutes ÷ 3 = 1 hour and 10 minutes)

3. Add up all times that children have access to art materials.

   (see shaded times on schedule = 1 hour and 10 minutes)

4. Compare the amount of time children may have access to art materials to the time requirement for substantial portion of the day. If the amount of time children may have access to art materials is the same or greater, then score "Yes." If the amount of time is less than the time requirement for substantial portion of the day, then score "No." For example, the schedule above indicates:

   1 hour and 10 minutes (access to art materials) **is equal to 1 hour and 10 minutes** (time requirement for substantial portion of day), and therefore the time requirement for substantial portion of the day is met.

21 Music/movement

General information about this item

Music includes both producing and listening to music. Examples of producing music include singing existing songs, chants, or nursery rhymes; making up new songs; making sounds with different musical instruments and music toys; and listening to recorded music on tapes, records, or CD players as well as on radios, computers, TV, or video. Recorded music can be listened to with or without headphones.

Examples of ***music activities*** for preschoolers include:

- Singing songs with children while they transition from group time to snack
- Playing soft music at naptime
- Singing a good morning song, and other songs, at circle time (See photo 21 A.)
- Singing a "clean-up" song to encourage children to help
- Allowing a child to listen to a recording of songs, using headphones, during free play
- Having children play rhythm instruments to different kinds of music during circle time (See photo 21 B.)
- Bringing musical instruments outside so that children can have a very active and noisy musical experience
- Allowing children to freely access and use pleasant sounding music instruments in a music center

21 A Singing together is a music activity often done in a group.

Movement includes dancing, marching, or exercising to music or rhythms, or acting out the content of songs, rhymes, or chants with large muscle body actions. Do not give credit for finger plays because these activities do not require movement using arms and legs. Movement activities can be teacher- or child-initiated. They can be done as a group or individually. Movement activities might require that children do prescribed body actions or create their own individual motions.

Examples of some ***movement activities*** include:

- Encouraging dancing to recorded music as a free choice activity during free play
- Encouraging a small group of children to exercise with a music exercise video

21 B Playing simple music instruments is a music activity.

Indicator

- Encouraging children to dance or move to recorded music in the way that shows how the music makes them feel
- Encouraging children to clap to different rhythms at circle time
- Playing freeze dancing, where children dance until the music stops, then begin dancing again when the music starts
- Singing songs that have movements to go along with the words, such as "Hokey Pokey" or "I'm a Little Teapot"
- Dancing with musical instruments or scarves as a group activity. (See photo 21 C.)

Music activities include music and/or movement as the primary content. They can be offered at both group and free play times. Music activities can be teacher- or child-initiated. Music can be done by a group or individually.

21 C Dancing with musical instruments is a movement activity.

A closer look at each indicator

1.1 Score this indicator "Yes" if the children in the group do *not experience any* of the music or movement experiences such as those described on pages 211–212 *at least once a day.*

1.2. ***Loud background music*** is music played at a level that adds significantly to the general noisiness within the classroom.

Such music ***interferes with ongoing activities*** when the children and staff have a difficult time hearing one another. For example, the music prevents children from being able to hear and follow directions, which may cause a variety of problems. In addition, children will not be able to hear the talking that is going on in the room, which is so important to their own language development.

Loud background music also causes children to become easily distracted so that if they are trying to work on a quiet activity that requires concentration, such as a puzzle, they lose their focus more easily.

If it is observed that people in the classroom are forced to speak loudly to be heard, or if music seems to be adding to a chaotic atmosphere in the room, then it would be considered to ***interfere with ongoing activities.***

Often, outside observers might be irritated by music, because they are concentrating on observing. This is not enough to consider the music in the room to be "interfering with ongoing activities." It is important for the observer to be aware of the use of music and to judge its effect based on the behavior of the children and staff.

Much of the day means the majority of the time the children are in the program. For this indicator, however, if loud music is on for most of a 2½ to 3 hour observation, the requirement for ***much of the day*** would be met.

Score this indicator "No" if no loud music is used, but quiet music is played, even for much of the day. The indicator is also scored "No" if loud music is used, but only for a small portion of the day. This is done even if the loud music interferes with ongoing activities for the short period.

Indicator

21.3.1 a Tape players, with microphones for children to use as they sing along, are accessible to these children.

21.3.1 b These music materials are located on low, open shelves, making them accessible to children.

21.3.1 c Accessible music materials include a variety of instruments, tapes, CDs, and a player.

3.1 ***Music materials*** are anything that children can use to create or listen to music. This can include *musical instruments* such as drums, electric keyboards, bells, a piano, triangles, xylophones, harmonicas, or rhythm sticks. The instruments can be homemade or commercially produced.

The materials must be provided specifically for children to use for music. Furnishings or non-music objects are not counted for this item, even if children are allowed to use them to create music (for example, allowing a child to tap on the table with a spoon while waiting for lunch).

Note: If children use musical instruments with their mouths, such as harmonicas or kazoos, the spread of germs between children must be minimized. This does not affect the scoring of *this* item, but should be considered in scoring Item 13, Health practices.

Materials can also include the things needed for children to listen to recorded music, such as tape or CD players (see photo 21.3.1 a), or some software for computers that offer extensive musical content, such as complete songs and/or passages of music. Do not give credit for very short musical sound patterns on the computer.

Accessible means that children can reach and use materials by themselves. For materials to be considered accessible, they must be within view of younger preschoolers (2½ to 4 years). For older preschoolers and kindergartners (4 to 6 years), if materials are stored in closed spaces, they can be considered accessible *only* if it is *observed* that children can freely access and use the materials. For example, a tape player is considered accessible to a group of older children (majority of children are 4 years and older) if children can use the equipment and tapes independently, but in younger groups help may be needed from the teacher. (See photos 21.3.1 b–e.)

Some requires *more than one* example of ***music materials*** to be accessible to children for at least 1 hour per day. For example, a tape player might be accessible for use by children in the early morning hours, plus a set of bells for the children to use.

Indicator

21.3.1 d This cabinet must be opened by staff for music materials to be considered accessible to younger children.

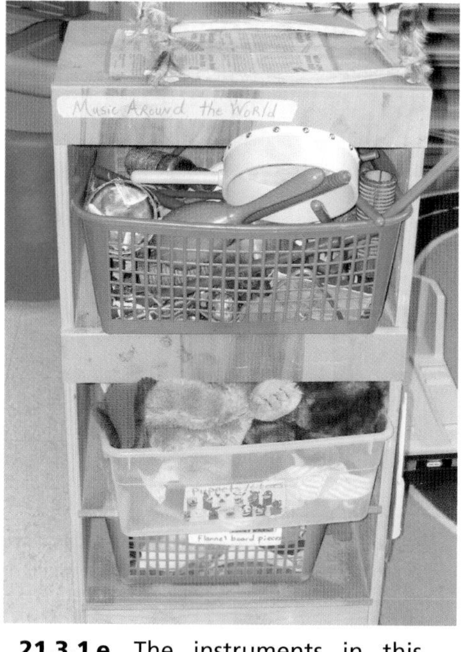

21.3.1 e The instruments in this basket are more difficult for children to access than those stored on less crowded open shelves.

Less time is required for programs operating less than 8 hours a day, with the amount of time calculated proportionally, based on the ratio of 1 hour for programs of 8 hours or more. For example, if a program operates for 6 hours a day, this would be 3/4 of a full-day program, so the time required would be 3/4 of the 1 hour. If the program operates 4 hours a day, the requirement would be 1/2 hour.

21.3.2 Teachers get out musical instruments to initiate dance time.

3.2 ***Staff*** refers to those adults that are in the classroom and who work with the children daily (or almost daily), for a substantial part of the day. This can include volunteers, if they are in the classroom for the required amount of time. Adults who are in the classroom for irregular periods of the day, or who are not a regular daily part of the classroom, do not count in evaluating whether the requirements of the item are met. For example, if a therapist, parent, or director of a program comes into the classroom and interacts with children for short or irregular periods, these interactions do not count in scoring the item, unless the interaction is very negative. As an exception, in parent co-operatives or lab schools, in which the usual staffing pattern includes different people as teaching assistants daily, these assistants should be counted as staff.

When a special music teacher is used in the classroom, for example once a week, this person can substitute for the regular staff when scoring indicators that require staff-initiated music activities. However, on days when this music teacher is not present, regular staff must meet such requirements.

Music activities are discussed in the General Information section for this item.

Indicator

21.5.1 This program has music instruments outdoors, as well as inside. All are considered when determining "many."

Staff initiate means that the staff think of and start the music activity, and the children then participate in some way. Examples are provided in the indicator, but additional examples might include staff putting on music for children to dance to, handing out rhythm instruments for children to play at circle time, or singing a "clean-up" song to end free play time. (See photo 21.3.2.)

To give credit for this indicator (score "Yes), at least one music activity *each day* must be started by the *staff for children's participation*. The activity may be done formally or informally, as a part of a group time, free play, or routine.

Score "Yes" if a music activity is initiated by the staff during the observation. If no staff-initiated music activity is observed, ask staff whether music is ever used with the children. If the response is "Yes," ask how it is handled and how often. Activity plans and daily schedules can also be used in trying to discover the information needed to score, but only if they reasonably match what is observed during the observation period.

3.3 ***Movement activities*** are discussed in the General Information section for this item.

Some movement activities requires at least one activity.

To give credit for 3.3 (score "Yes"), children must be able to do one movement activity at least once per week.

5.1 ***Music materials*** are defined in 3.1.

To give credit for ***many*** music materials, there must be enough musical instruments for at least half of the children to use at once *plus* some music to listen to, such as a tape player with tapes or music on a computer program that has extensive musical content (for example with complete songs, and/or passages of music). Do not give credit for very short musical sound patterns on the computer, as found in many computer games. (See photo 21.5.1.)

Dance props, if accessible, must be accompanied by something that makes music, such as a recorded music, child-created music, or adult-created music. For a tape player to be considered accessible in a group of older children (majority of children are 4 years and older), children should be able to use the tapes independently, but in younger groups, help may be needed from the teacher.

Refer to Indicator 3.1 for the definition of ***accessible.***

To score this indicator "Yes," the ***many*** music materials must be ***accessible*** for at least 1 hour daily. The 1 hour can be provided at one time, or as a combination of several periods. The music materials can be accessible either indoors or outdoors, or in both places and either as a whole group activity or individually as an informal, child-initiated activity.

Indicator

21.7.1 a This group singing activity is led by the teacher.

21.7.1 b This child can choose to participate in a free choice music activity or a group music activity.

5.2 Examples of various types of music are provided in the indicator. However a more comprehensive list of examples includes:

- Classical
- Popular
- Children's songs
- Jazz
- Rock
- Reggae
- Rhythm and blues
- Music characteristic of different cultures
- Songs in different languages
- Lullabies
- Rap
- Folk songs
- Country and western

Any music counted as a "type" for this indicator must be appropriate for use with children, in that the music contains no violent or sexually explicit material or language that is unacceptable according to typical societal standards. Much of the music that has been composed for adults is usually appropriate, as well as most children's songs.

Various types of music can also include instrumental or sung, and active or quiet music.

To score this indicator "Yes," *at least three different types* of music must be used regularly with the children. Often this is observable, but to score this indicator, the observer might have to look through the recorded music options, such as records, tapes, and compact disks, and question staff using the question provided for 5.2 on page 29 of the ECERS-R.

Indicator

21.7.2 a The variety of instruments in this outdoor music center allows children to experiment with sounds without noise limitations.

21.7.2 b The arrangement of different-sized drums, that make different tones, allows children to experiment systematically.

7.1 Refer to the definition of ***music*** given in Indicator 1.1. For this indicator, movement activities can be included as part of music.

For this indicator, a ***group activity*** means an activity *done with a small or large group of children, and led by the teacher*. The teacher gathers the children together into a group and initiates a musical activity. (See photos 21.7.1 a–b.)

Free choice occurs when children decide what they want to do and with whom.

To give credit for 7.1, (score "Yes") both options (i.e., for group activities and free choice) must be offered to the children each day. Often these two options can be observed during the observation, but questioning of staff might be required if the information needed to score is not observed.

21.7.3 These children are encouraged to be creative as they dance in their own way.

7.2 Preschool children should have more advanced experiences that help ***extend their understanding of music***. These experiences help children to learn more about how music is created, the many different instruments that are used, different uses of music, and how to distinguish the major characteristics of music, such as loud and soft, fast and slow, high and low tones. Examples of such activities are provided as part of the indicator. Additional examples include:

- Guitar player invited to come in and play songs as children sing along
- Music lessons provided for some instruments
- Music to a song displayed where children can see it so they can see what written notes look like as they sing
- Games played, with direct help from staff, where children distinguish fast and slow, loud and soft

Indicator

- Clapping along to changing rhythms offered to children as an activity, with explanations by staff about timing
- An outdoor music center that allows children to experiment with sounds without noise limitations (See photo 21.7.2 a, preceding page.)
- The same instrument of different sizes available at the music center to compare and contrast their sounds (See photo 21.7.2 b, preceding page.)

Occasionally, as noted in the item, means at least 3-4 times per year.

7.3 ***Creativity*** is the unique or new production of an individual or group of individuals who work together. During the early years, children are beginning to think independently and to express *themselves*. We see their creativity in the individual ways they use their art, language, dramatic play, and movement. Creativity is shown in music/movement as children make up and sing their own songs and dance in their own ways.

To give credit for this indicator, staff must ***encourage creativity in music***, by setting up activities that allow children to do things in their own unique way, rather than in activities that have children copy something that has already been done (see photo 21.7.3, preceding page). Examples of such encouragement are provided in the indicator. Other examples might include:

- Asking children how many different ways they can play an instrument
- Encouraging children to make up many different dances to a song
- Having children make up their own songs
- Giving children free (but not destructive) use of musical instruments so they can experiment with the sounds they can make

If no activities are observed that encourage creativity in music, ask staff the question provided on page 29 of the ECERS-R for 7.3 to get the information needed to score. Creative music must be a *daily option (or almost daily)* to give credit.

22 Blocks

General information about this item

Blocks are materials that children use to build various types of structures. The complexity of the structures children build with blocks varies, based on interest, age, and ability. For example, 2-year-olds usually create simple structures, either stacking the blocks in a tower or lining them up end to end to build roads. They like to watch when the blocks fall down. As children become older, their structures become far more complex, with bridges, well-balanced buildings with many parts, and roads that intersect and go to many imaginary places. When the buildings of older preschoolers fall, there is often frustration, especially if another child has caused the structure to collapse. Whatever the interest or ability level, all children have a far better chance to use blocks successfully when the blocks are plentiful, organized, easy to access, and in a play space out of traffic.

22 A Wooden unit blocks allow children to experience different sizes and shapes and see relationships that exist among different types.

In the ECERS-R, blocks do not include small blocks (sometimes called table blocks), or any size of plastic interlocking blocks that fit together. These are considered fine motor materials and are included in Item 19, Fine motor. Blocks are building materials that do not restrict children by having to fit pieces together in a special way, but challenge children to carefully place and balance the materials to create a variety of structures.

Blocks can be made of different materials—wood, plastic, cardboard, cloth-covered or vinyl-covered foam. They include both solid and hollow versions.

Types of blocks:

- *Unit Blocks*

Unit blocks come in sets with different sizes and shapes, such as triangles, squares, rectangles, cylinders, and arches. (See photos 22 A–B.) The important thing about unit blocks is the size relationship of each block to the others. The smaller blocks represent fractions of the larger blocks. For example, two smaller square blocks equal the size of one longer, medium sized rectangular block. A child could place two medium rectangular blocks on top of one long rectangular block to find that they take up the same space. This helps children learn about math concepts as they play with blocks. Children can use the different sizes and shapes to create structures that range from very simple to intricate.

22 B Children also enjoy using foam unit blocks.

The most common sets of unit blocks are usually made of smooth hard wood, but unit blocks made of plastic are also acceptable.

Indicator

22 C Hollow blocks allow children to build larger structures.

22 D These homemade blocks on the top shelf are made from shoe boxes covered with wrapping paper.

- *Large Hollow Blocks*

These blocks are often 1 foot in length or longer, about the size of cinder blocks. (See photo 22 C.) However, smaller sizes are also available to be used with the larger blocks. Usually the blocks are made of wood, cardboard, or hard plastic. Since these blocks are hollow, they are easy to lift, despite their size. They allow children to build bigger, sturdier structures than they can build with the smaller unit blocks. Children often create houses for themselves with such blocks and use them with dramatic play props such as dolls, play furniture, shopping or grocery store props. They also use them to build big roads that they can walk along or to build cars, buses, or trains for transportation play. Because of their size, they require more space for good use and are often used outdoors.

- *Homemade Blocks*

Homemade blocks can be made from food boxes, larger cardboard boxes, plastic containers, foam containers, tissue boxes, wood cut into block shapes, or other stackable objects. (See photo 22 D.) Whatever they are made of, children should be able to use the homemade materials as they would use blocks—to stack and build sizable structures. Any safety concerns that might come up when children use such materials (such as splinters, staples, sharp edges) should be considered under Item 14, Safety practices.

A closer look at each indicator

1.1 ***Few blocks*** means that there are either no blocks for children to use *or* fewer blocks than are needed for two children to each build a sizable structure. (See photo 22.1.1, next page.) There may be one or two types of blocks but not enough for children to have experiences such as balancing, stacking, or creating structures. Take into consideration the age of the children when deciding whether there are enough blocks for two children to use. The actual number of blocks required to build sizable structures will vary, based on children's developmental level, with fewer blocks required for younger children and more for older preschoolers.

Accessible for play means the blocks are within the children's reach. Materials should be accessible on a regular basis daily, or almost daily, to score 1.1 "No." Observers should look for blocks in any area regularly used for children's play—in the classroom where children spend most of their day and in other rooms that

Indicator

22.1.1 Having only a few blocks to use limits the possibilities for play.

22.3.1 a There are enough blocks for children to build larger structures, but no accessories.

children use during certain parts of a day, such as the space used in early morning or later afternoon, a gross motor room, or outdoors. Any one or a combination of these spaces can be used to provide block materials as long as children can reach and use the blocks.

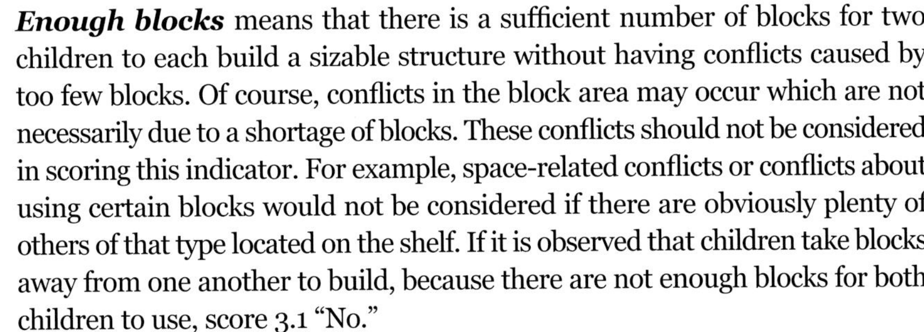

3.1 ***Enough blocks*** means that there is a sufficient number of blocks for two children to each build a sizable structure without having conflicts caused by too few blocks. Of course, conflicts in the block area may occur which are not necessarily due to a shortage of blocks. These conflicts should not be considered in scoring this indicator. For example, space-related conflicts or conflicts about using certain blocks would not be considered if there are obviously plenty of others of that type located on the shelf. If it is observed that children take blocks away from one another to build, because there are not enough blocks for both children to use, score 3.1 "No."

Enough blocks also means that there are sufficient blocks of a specific type that can be used together to make a sizable structure. Very different sets of blocks, with fewer than 10–20 blocks of each type (depending on size), would not be considered enough blocks. For example, if an observer sees 3–5 large cardboard blocks, 8 two-inch cube blocks, and fewer than 10 unit blocks, credit would not be given for this indicator because two children would have difficulty creating sizable structures with the accessible blocks.

22.3.1 b Accessories consist of plastic animals and wooden people stored with blocks.

Accessories are toys used with blocks to stimulate or expand block play. These include toys such as small trucks, cars, trains, road signs, small toy people, and small toy animals. Accessories should add to, rather than detract from, block play. Accessories, therefore, should not be of a type that would disrupt or take attention from block play, such as woodworking benches with tools, riding toys, shopping carts, very large stuffed animals, child-sized furniture, or toy buildings.

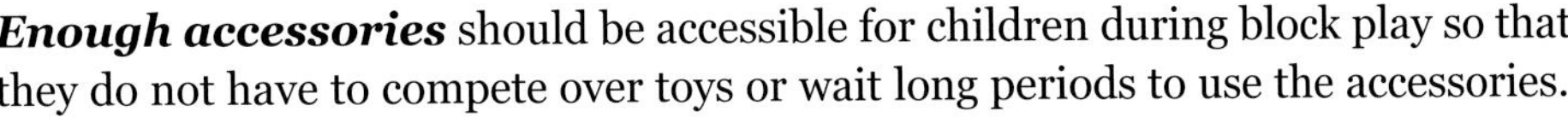

Enough accessories should be accessible for children during block play so that they do not have to compete over toys or wait long periods to use the accessories.

To give credit, the block accessories must be stored near the blocks so children easily recognize that the materials can be used together. If they are not stored near the blocks, it must be obvious that children use the materials together. Photo 22.3.1 a shows an example that does not meet the requirement, while that shown in 22.3.1 b does.

Indicator

22.3.2 At the minimal level of quality there is some space for block play.

22.3.3 a

22.3.3 b

22.3.3 a–b Blocks and accessories are accessible daily to children when they are within easy reach and can be used.

An ***independent structure*** is one that can be considered a complete work by itself. It is not dependent on another child's building, so that a child can build creatively, in his or her own way, without having to share blocks with another child. Examples of independent structures include a house, tower, or other building; a road, and fences for toy animals. Two or more children may certainly be observed cooperating in creating one independent structure, but the observer must be sure that the possibility exists for two children to build sizable independent structures without having problems over sharing too few blocks.

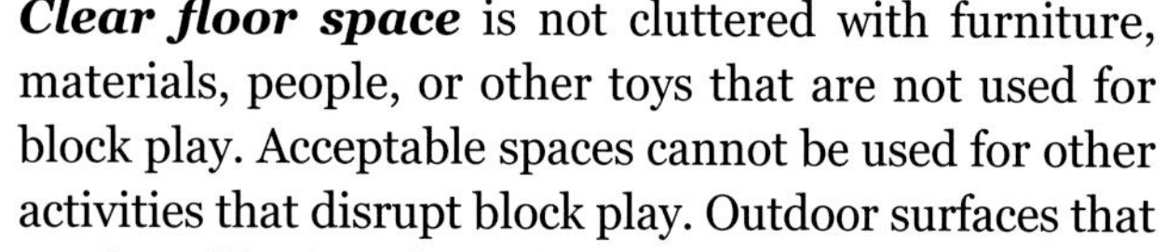

3.2 ***Clear floor space*** is not cluttered with furniture, materials, people, or other toys that are not used for block play. Acceptable spaces cannot be used for other activities that disrupt block play. Outdoor surfaces that are floor-like (steady and somewhat hard) can count as clear floor space, if they are not cluttered or used for active physical play that is not block-related.

Some means that the space, although not necessarily large, does allow children to successfully balance, build, and create structures in their block play. The space size would allow two children to build successfully without undue interference from one another or from others. (See photo 22.3.2.)

3.3 The definition of ***blocks*** is found in the General Information section for this item. The definition of ***accessories*** is found in the information provided for Indicator 3.1.

Accessible for daily use requires that the blocks can be reached and used by children for at least 1 hour per day in a full-day program (less time is required in a part-day program), with very few exceptions, such as on the day of a field trip. (See photos 22.3.3 a–b.) This does not require that all children be able to use the blocks at the same time or that each child has a full hour to use the blocks. However, it is required that children would have a reasonable chance to use blocks at some time if they wished.

Indicator

The 1 hour can be provided all at one time or as a combination of several periods throughout the day. For example, blocks might be accessible to children for 30 minutes in the morning during free play time and then again for 30 minutes in the afternoon. The materials do not have to be provided as a free choice activity but do have to be accessible for this time period. For example, children might be assigned to the center where the materials are accessible for them to use.

Less time is required for programs operating less than 8 hours a day, with the amount of time calculated proportionally, based on the ratio of 1 hour for programs of 8 hours or more. For example, if a program operates for 6 hours a day, this would be ¾ of a full-day program, so the time required would be ¾ of the 1 hour. If the program operates 4 hours a day, the requirement would be ½ hour.

5.1 Add the word "space" to this indicator so that it reads "Enough space, blocks, and accessories. . . ." The word "space" has already been added to the indicator in the more recent printings of the scale.

Enough space means that the area used for block play is large enough to allow ***at least three*** children to successfully balance, build, and create structures independently. The space size would allow three children to build successfully without undue interference from one another or from others. In addition, there would be enough space to accommodate the larger structures children might want to build, such as long roads or large buildings, without having to compete for space.

It should be noted that even in a sufficiently large space, children might still have trouble sharing the space. This is not due to the space being too small, but rather to the children's inability to solve problems related to sharing. In order to score this indicator, the observer must first evaluate whether the space would accommodate the creative block play of three or more children, and second, if problems are observed, determine whether the problems are due to the space being too small or to children's immature social skills.

Enough blocks for three or more children can vary in the actual number of blocks needed, depending on the children's ages and ability to build complex structures. The number of blocks required for younger children may be less since older 2's will tend to use blocks simply, for example, by placing them side by side or stacking only a few blocks. However, older children, especially 4's and 5's, may be capable of building large structures requiring more blocks. The size of blocks should be considered when determining if there are enough blocks for three or more children to play. More blocks would be needed if the sizes were smaller (4 x 4 inches); if the blocks were larger (12 x 4 inches), then fewer would be required.

To score the indicator, observe the children to see if they get along well when playing in the block area without having to compete for blocks. It should be noted however, that sometimes children fight over certain blocks when there are actually plenty more of the type needed on the block shelf. In this case, credit should be given for "enough blocks." However, if there were plenty of blocks, but a scarcity of a favorite type (such as only a few very long rectangular blocks or arches), and this caused excessive competition among children, credit would not be given.

Photos 22.5.1 a–c (next page) show examples of enough space and blocks for three or more children to use at one time.

Indicator

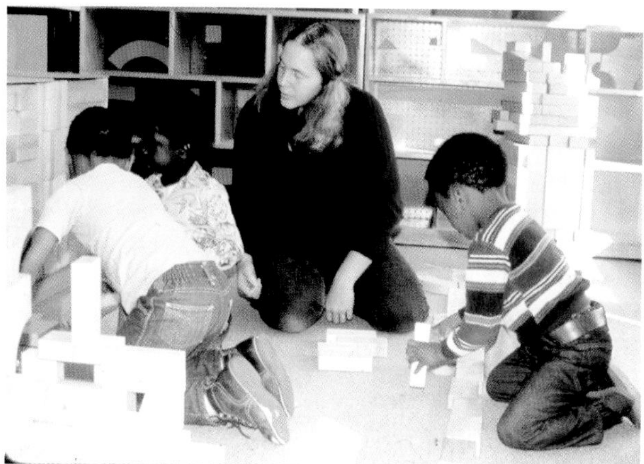

22.5.1 a

22.5.1 b

22.5.1 c

22.5.1 a–c When there is enough space for block play, the options are unlimited.

22.5.2 Blocks are organized by type, and accessories are each stored separately, so that children can clearly see the various materials.

Enough accessories requires that there are sufficient accessories for at least three children to use in their block play without undue competition over certain types.

5.2 ***Blocks organized according to type*** means that different kinds of blocks (such as wooden unit blocks, large cardboard blocks, and plastic blocks) are not mixed together in storage on shelves or in containers. Children should be able to clearly see the type of block they can choose to use and should not have to search through mixed blocks and/or other toys to find more blocks of the same type. Ideally, blocks should be organized by type, size, and shape. But simple organization by type is acceptable to give credit. For example, large hollow blocks are stored separately from wooden unit blocks or plastic unit blocks.

Accessories organized according to type requires that the different kinds of accessories used with blocks (such as small people, zoo animals, farm animals, larger or smaller cars and trucks, and road signs) are each stored separately, either in their own containers or on divided shelves. (See photo 22.5.2.) Children should be able to clearly see the type of accessories they can choose to use and should not have to search through blocks or mixed toys to find more accessories of the same type.

5.3 A ***special block area*** is a space that is arranged to allow children to play with blocks and accessories with minimal interruptions. The space is set up to encourage children's block play, rather than to discourage it. For example, the blocks

Indicator

and accessories are stored so they can be taken out and used on the floor directly next to the storage. (See photo 22.5.3.)

22.5.3 This area is used only for block play and not interrupted by other activities.

Materials in the space must be specifically for block play, and they cannot include other types of toys or equipment that might interfere with building structures by taking up needed space or causing children to walk through the blocks to access the other materials. The block area may include small blocks, such as interlocking blocks or other fine motor building materials. However, to receive credit for "special block area set aside," the use of such materials cannot interfere with block play. When other materials, such as fine motor toys, art, pretend play materials, or carpentry tools, are included in the block area, it will distract or take away from the possibilities of block play and therefore credit cannot be given for this indicator. The vast majority of materials in this "special" area should be blocks and block accessories.

Storage can consist of shelves or containers for blocks and accessories. The storage must be next to and facing the floor space to be used for block play.

A ***suitable building surface*** requires a level, steady surface so that blocks can be balanced effectively and are less likely to fall over. An unsteady, cluttered space for block play prevents the careful placement of blocks and leads to frustration so that children quickly lose interest in the materials or use them in inappropriate ways. Unsuitable floor spaces include those that are cluttered with toys or are covered with soft foam mats or bumpy carpet. Unsuitable outdoor surfaces include those that are uneven or unsteady, such as grass or sand, so that the block structures constantly fall over.

5.4. ***Accessible for a substantial portion of the day*** means that children can choose to use the special block area where blocks and accessories are placed on open shelves or in containers and can play with the blocks daily, for 1/3 of the program's operating hours. If more than one block area is considered in calculating accessibility for a substantial portion of the day, all block areas must meet the requirements for 5.1, 5.2, and 5.3. This includes an outdoor block area as well as indoor areas.

See the sample classroom schedules on pages 228–230 for examples of calculating substantial portion of the day for block times.

7.1. ***Two types of blocks*** requires access to blocks from two of the categories listed in General Information section for this item. The two types must have different characteristics (such as weight, size, texture, forms, and shapes), so that the children can have varied building experiences. (See photos 22.7.1 a–c, next page.)

A variety of accessories means that there are differences among the accessories that children can use daily and can choose from at one time. For example, small people, various types of animals, cars, and trucks, and road signs would be accessible for children to choose from to allow many different themes in block play.

7.2. ***Open shelves*** allow children to see and reach blocks and accessories independently without having to ask for help. They also encourage children to be able to clean up blocks independently. If block shelves are "closed" in some way, for

Indicator

22.7.1 a Cardboard blocks and larger hollow blocks represent only one type of block, so another type would be needed to grive credit for 7.1.

22.7.1 b Smaller unit blocks and larger hollow wood blocks are provided, representing two types.

example, with doors, curtains, a stop sign, or turned to the wall, they must be made obviously open during the time assigned for children's use to receive credit.

Labeled block shelves require a system that allows the clear organization of blocks and accessories. To give credit, blocks and accessories must, for the most part, be stored according to the system. However, perfectly organized storage is not required to give credit. Block storage labels can consist of pictures or outlines of the blocks, with words added as an option. (See photo 22.7.2 a.) The use of printed words only, without the graphic representation of the blocks, is not given credit in this indicator, since the preschool-aged children considered in the ECERS-R are not expected to be able to read.

Labels for accessories can be placed on storage containers or directly onto storage shelves. Perfectly organized storage is not required, but most accessories

22.7.1 c Smaller unit blocks and larger hollow cardboard blocks are provided for children, representing two types.

22.7.2 a Outlines of the various shapes are used to organize blocks so that children can easily find and return blocks to the shelves.

22.7.2 b Photos help keep accessories used for block play organized.

Indicator

should be stored according to the labeling system. (See photo 22.7.2 b.)

7.3 ***Some block play available outdoors*** means that the children have opportunities for more active block play without the space and noise restrictions associated with being indoors. Large numbers of blocks are not required but there should be enough blocks so children can explore, build, and experiment without difficulty. The outdoor blocks do not need to be accessible daily but should be available for the teacher to add to the other outdoor activities. If the outdoor blocks are in *addition* to those blocks used daily indoors to meet requirements of 5.2, 5.3, and 5.4, they do not have to meet these requirements. (See photo 22.7.3.)

22.7.3 In addition to blocks indoors, children have opportunities for more active and noisy play with blocks outdoors. Both interlocking and smooth blocks are shown, but only the non-interlocking blocks are credited in this item.

Calculating "Substantial Portion of the Day"

Example 1

This schedule is based on an observation period of 4.5 hours (from 8AM – 12:30PM) and information collected during the teacher interview about how unobserved time during the day is used and what is accessible to the children.

Time	Scheduled activity	Time to use block area
6:30 – 8:00	Breakfast in cafeteria and TV time for those who are finished with breakfast	
8:00 – 8:30	Children go to regular classrooms and play with table and rug toys (puzzles; legos; duplos with cars, people, and trucks; stringing beads and cards; pegboards)	
8:30 – 8:45	Prepare for breakfast/children wash hands	
8:45 – 9:15	Breakfast	
9:15 – 9:45	Circle (teacher reading time)	
9:45 – 10:45	Centers (housekeeping, art, sand and water, nature/science, writing table, block area, music, computer and cozy book area)	**1 hour**
10:45 – 11:15	Outdoor play (gross motor activities only)	
11:15 – 12:15	Prepare for and eat lunch	
12:15 – 12:30	Story, put out cots, prepare for nap	
12:30 – 2:45	Nap	
2:45 – 3:00	Wake up from nap; bathroom	
3:00 – 3:25	Snack and story	
3:25 – 4:25	Centers (housekeeping, nature/science, writing table, computer, fine motor area and cozy book area)	
4:25 – 5:30	Outdoors or indoor gross motor	
5:30 – 6:30	Table and rug toys (puzzles; legos; duplos with cars, people, and trucks; stringing beads and cards; pegboards) Prepare for departure	

1. Figure the total number of hours that children are allowed to attend.

   (6:30AM to 6:30 PM = 12 hours)

2. Calculate 1/3 of the operating hours to determine "Substantial Portion of the Day."

   (12 hours ÷ 3 = 4 hours)

3. Add up all times that children have access to the block area.

   (see shaded times on schedule = 1 hour)

4. Compare the amount of time children may have access to the block area to the time requirement for substantial portion of the day. If the amount of time children may have access to the block area is the same or greater, then score "Yes." If the amount of time is less than the time requirement for substantial portion of the day, then score "No." For example, the schedule above indicates:

   1 hour (access to block area) **is less than 4 hours** (time requirement for substantial portion of day), and therefore the time requirement for substantial portion of the day is not met.

Indicator

Calculating "Substantial Portion of the Day"

Example 2

This schedule is based on an observation period of 4 hours (from 9AM – 1PM) and information collected during the teacher interview about how unobserved time during the day is used and what is accessible to the children.

Time	Scheduled activity	Time to use block area
9:00 – 9:30	Arrival/quiet centers open (cozy book area, computer, writing table, math, science and fine motor)	
9:30 – 9:45	Snack	
9:45 – 10:00	Clean up snack/bathroom/wash hands	
10:00 – 11:00	Outside (gross motor activities and large hollow blocks)	**1 hour**
11:00 – 11:45	Free choice of centers (fine motor, art, block area, dramatic play, nature/science, math, sensory table, computer, writing table and cozy book area)	**45 minutes**
11:45 – 12:15	Large group activity (M,W,F is music/movement and T,Th is art activity)	
12:15 – 12:45	Prepare for and eat lunch	
12:45 – 1:00	Clean up/bathroom/prepare for quiet time	
1:00 – 1:45	Quiet time/quiet centers available (cozy book area, fine motor, math, and science)	
1:45 – 2:00	Clean up all centers and prepare for departure	

1. Figure the total number of hours that children are allowed to attend.

   (9 AM to 2 PM = 5 hours)

2. Calculate 1/3 of the operating hours to determine "Substantial Portion of the Day."

   (5 hours ÷ 3 = 1 hour and 40 minutes)

3. Add up all times that children have access to the block area.

   (see shaded times on schedule = 1 hour and 45 minutes)

4. Compare the amount of time children may have access to the block area to the time requirement for substantial portion of the day. If the amount of time children may have access to the block area is the same or greater, then score "Yes." If the amount of time is less than the time requirement for substantial portion of the day, then score "No." For example, the schedule above indicates:

   1 hour and 45 minutes (access to block area) **is more than 1 hour and 40 minutes** (time requirement for substantial portion of day), and therefore the time requirement for substantial portion of the day is met.

Indicator

Calculating "Substantial Portion of the Day"

Example 3

This schedule is based on an observation period of 3.5 hours (from 9AM –12:30 PM) and information collected during the teacher interview about whether what was observed represents the typical daily practice.

Time	Scheduled activity	Time to use block area
9:00 – 9:20	Arrival/group time to discuss activities for the day	
9:20 – 9:45	Whole group art activity	
9:45 – 10:00	Whole group reading time (teacher directed)	
10:00 – 10:45	Outside time (gross motor activities only)	
10:45 – 11:30	Free choice of centers (fine motor, art, block area, dramatic play, nature/science, math, sensory table, computer, writing table, blocks and books)	**45 minutes**
11:30 – 11:45	Clean up/bathroom/prepare for lunch time	
11:45 – 12:15	Prepare for and eat lunch	
12:15 – 12:30	Clean up/bathroom/prepare for departure	

1. Figure the total number of hours that children are allowed to attend.

   (9 AM to 12:30 PM = 3 hours and 30 minutes)

2. Calculate 1/3 of the operating hours to determine "Substantial Portion of the Day."

   (3 hours and 30 minutes ÷ 3 = 1 hour and 10 minutes)

3. Add up all times that children have access to the block area.

   (see shaded times on schedule = 45 minutes)

4. Compare the amount of time children may have access to the block area to the time requirement for substantial portion of the day. If the amount of time children may have access to the block area is the same or greater, then score "Yes." If the amount of time is less than the time requirement for substantial portion of the day, then score "No." For example, the schedule above indicates:

   45 minutes (access to block area) **is less than 1 hour and 10 minutes** (time requirement for substantial portion of day), and therefore the time requirement for substantial portion of the day is not met.

23 Sand/water

General information about this item

Children, like many adults, enjoy playing in sand and water. That is why beaches are one of our most popular vacation destinations. For many of us, sand and water activities are relaxing and stress-reducing. Early childhood staff often notice that very active children tend to calm down while running sand through their fingers or pouring from one container to another. The stress reducing characteristic of sand and water play make it a valuable activity in the preschool to counteract the pressure of attending programs with many other young children.

However, that is not the only benefit of providing sand/water play. By experimenting with sand and water, children learn about measurement and natural science.

Providing the equipment and materials needed for sand and water play is emphasized in this item. Typically, centers have sand outdoors, but it can also be provided indoors as an interest center or special activity. Water play is associated with outdoor warm weather activities, but can also be provided indoors.

As with most play opportunities, learning is enhanced when there is variety possible in what children experience. The toys provided for sand/water play can encourage many types of experimenting and play with these simple, flexible open-ended materials.

A closer look at each indicator

1.1 ***Provision*** means that staff have made accessible the equipment and materials needed for children to be able to play in sand and/or water (or substitutes), in a meaningful way. Children need to be able to dig, scoop, pour, fill containers, and experiment with the material.

There are various options for holding sand/water: sand boxes, sand pits, various types of sand/water tables, dishpans, plastic bins, tubs, buckets, or sinks. (See photos 23.1.1 a–f, pages 232–233.)

There are various materials that meet the requirements for this item in place of sand and water (see photo 23.1.1 g, page 233.) Examples are given in the item's "Notes for Clarification," but other safe materials are also acceptable. There should be a sufficient quantity of the material so children can dig, scoop, pour, fill, and empty containers. Often, materials are observed in sand/water tables that *cannot* be used for digging, measuring, *and* pouring, such as styrofoam packing materials, natural objects (e.g., pine cones, acorns, leaves for children to examine), or gelatinous sensory materials (e.g., goop, jello) Such materials cannot be counted as sand/water substitutes.

No provision means that neither sand nor water (or acceptable substitute material) is ever provided for children's use. Even if sand/water containers or materials are present, but staff never use them for sand/water play, then 1.1 is scored "Yes." For example, if a sand table is in the room, but it is obviously only used for storage

23 Sand/water

Indicator

23.1.1 a Two large outdoor sand tables on wheels are used for sand play.

23.1.1 b An outdoor sandbox is used as a provision for sand play.

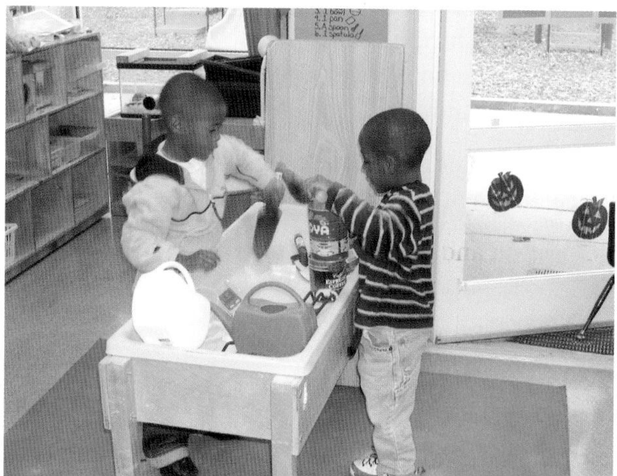

23.1.1 c Children in this classroom enjoy sand play using the wooden sand table with a plastic liner.

23.1.1 d Children have opportunities to use the water table located indoors.

or for sensory activities that do not meet the sand/water requirements, then 1.1 is true, and scored "Yes." Also, if children manage to play in sand or water, for example by playing at the sink when washing hands, or digging in dirt with a stick on the playground, but staff do not make appropriate provision to support such activity, then "no provision" is also true.

1.2 ***Toys to use for sand and water play*** include those that children can use to dig, scoop, fill, pour, and experiment with the material as well as toys that extend sand/water play into the area of dramatic play.

Examples of sand toys most often observed include: measuring cups and other unbreakable containers, funnels, plastic tubes, molds, shovels, scoops, trowels, pails, rakes, sifters, sand/water-wheels, pipes, and toys that make patterns in sand, such as wide-toothed combs.

Dramatic play toys include animals, dinosaurs, small trucks and cars, small people and figurines, large trucks and diggers, and housekeeping cooking props, such as pots, pans, pitchers, dishes, bowls, cups, and spoons.

Many of the sand toys listed above can also be used for water play, as well as sponges, things that sink or float, turkey basters, spray bottles, pumps to experiment with, and fantasy toys, such as animals, sea creatures, dolls, and boats.

Indicator

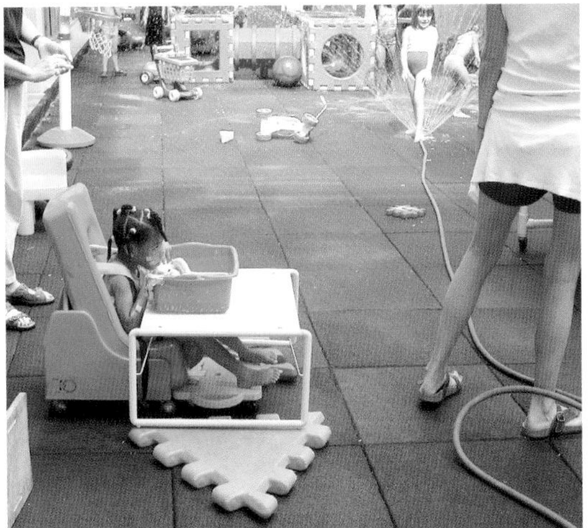

23.1.1 e Small plastic containers as well as outdoor water sprinkler can be used.

23.1.1 f Plastic tables are used to provide water play outdoors.

3.1 ***Some provision*** means that staff have made accessible the equipment and materials needed for children to be able to play in sand and/or water (or a substitute), in a meaningful way.

Accessible means that children can reach and use the provision by themselves. If the water, sand or sand substitute is stored in a closed space, it can be considered ***accessible*** only if the staff bring these materials out at some time for children to freely access and use. If the material is located outdoors, then children should be able to freely access and use them when outdoors.

To give credit for 3.1, the access does not need to be provided on a daily basis, but should be a regular part of the program, for example, at least for ½ hour twice a week. Both sand and water are not required. If only one of these materials is accessible, credit can be given. However, there must be a sufficient quantity of the material so that children can pour, fill, and empty containers.

23.1.1 g Beans are often used as a substitute for sand, but this is not a wise use of food and they pose a safety threat to preschoolers.

3.2 This indicator should read "Some sand/water toys accessible."

Some sand/water toys means that there are at least two or more toys for children to use with sand or water. The toys should meet the requirements of sand/water toys stated in 1.2. (See photo 23.3.2.)

These toys must be ***accessible*** for children to use freely during the time that sand and water play is provided.

23.3.2 The presence of one scoop and one block does not meet the requirement for "some" because only the scoop can be used for meaningful experiences with sand.

5.1 This indicator requires provision for both ***sand and water***. This means that staff make each of these materials available for children to use at some time. The two materials do not have to be provided at the same time or in the same place.

Indicator

23.5.2 a A variety of toys are used including cups, funnels, wheels, boats, and molds.

23.5.2 b In the outdoor sandbox children have access to a variety of sand toys such as trucks, buckets, shovels, scoops, and rakes.

There can be substantial flexibility in the way both sand and water are provided for children's play. For example, one container might be used for both sand and water, but at different times—one material is in the container at a time. Or there can be two separate containers—one for sand and the other for water. One might be indoors while the other is outdoors. For example, water play might occasionally be in dishpans indoors, while sand might be outdoors in a sandbox for daily use. As long as children have regular experiences with both materials, credit can be given.

5.2 The intent of the requirement for ***variety*** is that children have many different opportunities to experiment, explore, and learn while using sand and water. For ***variety*** consider the differences among the toys that children can use in sand/water play. Variety may be represented in characteristics of the toys, such as use, size, transparency, shape, color, or challenge level. All these characteristics should be considered in determining whether variety is present, but use of the toys is the most important characteristic. (See photos 23.5.2 a–b.)

Number of toys accessible for play is also considered when determining ***variety***. For example, when fewer children use the toys at one time, fewer toys are required for ***variety***, as long as the toys can be used for different purposes. When more children must share, more toys of different types are needed.

If there are duplicates of one toy (e.g. many spoons, but no other toys to use), then the requirement for ***variety*** is not met since the children's experiences are limited to the type of play that the one toy provides. For example variety is not present when only shovels are present in the sand box or only cups are used in a water table.

If both sand and water are accessible, ***variety*** in toys must be provided for both, but many of the same toys can be used for both sand and water play. If provisions for sand and/or water are present both indoors and outdoors, ***variety*** of toys is required in both locations.

The ***variety*** in toys does not have to be provided all at one time. If many different examples of one type of toy is used at a time, then variety can be provided through regular rotation of toys. For example, different types of measuring toys (e.g., cups of different sizes, measuring spoons) could be used, and at another time the water table could be turned into an ocean with a variety of toy fish and boats in blue water. If the teacher reports that toys are rotated, then ask to see the toys. Find out how they are used and how often they are changed. If toys are actually rotated very infrequently, credit should not be given.

Indicator

For definition of ***accessible***, see 3.1.

5.3 The time requirement, ***for at least 1 hour daily***, means that water or sand play must be accessible to children every day for no less than 1 hour. Both materials are not required for this amount of time. A combination of sand for a portion of the time and water for the other portion is acceptable, as long as the total time is 1 hour or more. The hour can consist of a combination of time periods or one period by itself. It must occur every day, with only very few lapses (such as bad weather or a fieldtrip which prevents the 1 hour access).

For programs of 4 hours or less, the requirement of 1 hour of access is changed to ½ hour.

7.1 This indicator requires that both ***sand and water*** play must be accessible ***indoors*** as well as ***outdoors***. For example, a sand box might be provided outdoors and a sand table indoors; hoses for water play outdoors and basins for water play indoors.

Separate provisions for indoor use and outdoor use for sand and water play must be provided. Credit cannot be given if the teacher has to move the provision (for example a sand/water table) from indoors to outdoors every day. This causes an inconvenience for the teacher, and changing the material in one container to allow for the provision of both sand and water is difficult. Therefore, dual use of one piece of equipment is unlikely to occur.

7.2 ***Different activities*** with sand and water are required to give children broader experiences from which to learn and develop skills. To give credit, staff must provide a variety of materials and/or toys to change what the children can do with sand and water. Providing the same toys to use with sand and water every day will not meet this requirement, even if there is variety in the toys provided. The activities must give children a different experience. (See photo 23.7.2.) Examples of different activities include:

23.7.2 Adding water to the sand box gives children experiences with both wet and dry sand.

Water:

- Bubbles added
- Color added
- Wooden or plastic boats used
- Sink and float experiment done with water play
- Sponges and non-porous objects used to compare
- Shells or toy sea creatures added
- Small water droppers and large basters used
- Water table used to wash baby dolls or doll clothes
- Sprinkler used on hot day
- Plastic pipes used to route water

Sand:

- Wet sand used instead of dry, with toys that can be used to mold sand
- Cars and trucks added
- Small people added
- Another material used, such as bird seed or sterilized potting soil
- Tools to make differing designs in sand provided
- Small animal toys used

24 Dramatic play

General information about this item

According to the ECERS-R, "***Dramatic play*** is pretending or making believe. This type of play occurs when children act out roles themselves and when they manipulate figures such as small toy people in a dollhouse." In doing so, children practice many skills and attempt to understand what happens in their world.

Dramatic play is the activity in which children practice the most language skills in the classroom and also develop their social skills. As children pretend play, they use talking to tell about their ideas, either talking to themselves or to those they are playing with. Listening and talking become more important in dramatic play as children become older preschoolers because they begin to take on roles and coordinate them with each other in a more elaborate story line or plot.

Children go through obvious, well documented developmental stages in their play. Younger children tend to play alone, while 2-year-olds do lots of parallel play, not yet cooperating, but doing similar things next to one another. Preschoolers begin to use cooperation in their pretend play, taking on complementary roles. One child may say, "I'll be the Mommy and you be the baby." The other child might respond, "No, I want to be the Daddy." And then they agree and play out the roles they have selected, with much talking, cooperating, and coordinating.

Children who are successful in such play have a good chance for success in school because of their language and social skills, both of which are very important in kindergarten and throughout the school years.

As children represent what they know about the world, they are often imitating what they have experienced and trying to make sense of things they do not yet understand very well. In this way, many emotional issues can be resolved through dramatic play. Such play is good for all children, but it is also used to help children with emotional difficulties to work through some of their issues, as in play therapy.

Because of these benefits, dramatic play is a very valuable experience for young children. It helps to bring about a wide range of development.

Dramatic play usually takes place during free play times, both indoors and outdoors. Even when materials and equipment are not provided for dramatic play, children will pretend with whatever they might find. One child might use sticks picked up on the playground as airplanes that make noises and fly through the air. Another child might use a crayon, indoors, for the same purpose. However, when ***materials and equipment*** are provided especially for dramatic play, children have far more opportunities to pretend in a more complex way.

In this item, the materials used in dramatic play are often called ***props***. The terms ***materials and equipment*** are also used in the item. All refer to the objects

24 Dramatic play

24 A These boys are pretending using hardhats.

24 B Dolls and hats are used as materials in pretend play.

that children use in pretending. ***Very few*** props or materials will limit the type of play children can carry out. More props allow richer play, with more meaning to the children. A variety of props encourage children to play out more roles, with increased options for what can happen. (See photos 24 A–C.)

24 C Furnishings are used to create a housekeeping center.

Children use their imagination and understanding to go beyond the props, but these props (or materials and equipment) get them started. For example, a two-year-old might pick up a spoon and pot and show an understanding of how he has seen such things used by stirring imaginary food in the pot. Without these props, it is unlikely that the child would have done this.

Meaningful play is more likely when props can be used together in play. A wider range of props extends possibilities for children to pretend. For example, if a child has a doll, she might act out a role of Mommy, by

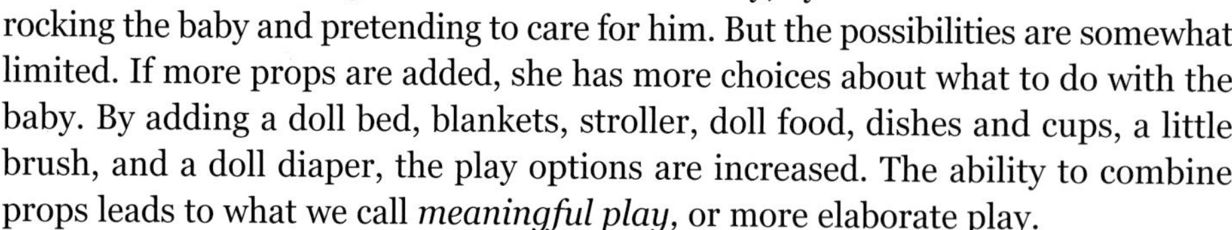

rocking the baby and pretending to care for him. But the possibilities are somewhat limited. If more props are added, she has more choices about what to do with the baby. By adding a doll bed, blankets, stroller, doll food, dishes and cups, a little brush, and a doll diaper, the play options are increased. The ability to combine props leads to what we call *meaningful play,* or more elaborate play.

Examples of ***materials and equipment*** (including props) for dramatic play are provided in the "Notes for Clarification" in the ECERS-R item. The examples are given for four different themes, including housekeeping, different kinds of work, fantasy, and leisure. Additional examples for each type are provided in Indicator 1.1.

To get the most out of dramatic play, children must be free to use materials and equipment (props) in their *own* way, as part of their self-created make-believe. Props that encourage a variety of themes allow children a wide range of play opportunities. *It should be noted that activities used to teach children to follow specific sequences* and not their imaginations, in order to properly complete household chores, such as table washing or silver polishing activities, *are not counted to meet the requirements of this item.* Although the same materials may be used, the intent of the activity and the children's experiences are completely different.

Indicator

A closer look at each indicator

1.1 ***Materials or equipment*** for dress-up or dramatic play are those items that children use in order to act out roles and situations. These can include:

Dress-up clothes

Dress-up clothes enhance children's dramatic play by allowing them to wear different things for the different roles they might play. For example, if the children are pretending to go on vacation, they might dress-up using cameras, sunglasses, purses, ski jackets, or bathing suits. Likewise, children will be able to try out different gender and occupation roles with proper dress-up materials. Special dress-up clothes can be provided for the four different types of themes, for example:

- Shirts/blouses for both men and women
- Dresses, skirts, pants, jackets
- Footwear, such as boots, sandals, slippers, various shoes
- Ties, scarves
- Aprons for cooking or for using tools
- Uniforms of various work roles (medical, firefighter, postal worker, office)
- Hats of many types, for men and women, including hard hats and other hats used in different jobs, hats for different kinds of weather, hats for leisure
- Accessories, such as jewelry, hair clips, purses, tote bags, briefcases, glasses (no lenses), sunglasses

Themes about Housekeeping

Materials and equipment/props for housekeeping allow children to take on the roles that are most familiar to them—those carried out at home. It is through such play that children represent what they know about family life. They act out things that have happened in their own world, and also try out things that they have learned about but not actually experienced.

- Child-sized furniture, such as kitchen sink, stove/oven, washer/dryer, refrigerator, ironing board with iron, couch, table and chairs
- Cooking/eating equipment, such as pots/pans, utensils, dishes, tea set, wok, toaster, microwave oven
- Play foods, including different ethnic foods
- Dolls, such as baby dolls, dolls representing adults, small dolls for doll-houses, paper dolls, wooden dolls, people figures to use with blocks or building sets; showing racial diversity
- Doll furniture, such as a baby doll-sized bed, high chair and stroller, cars, other furnishings to use with dolls including equipment used by people with disabilities, such as walkers or wheelchairs
- Doll clothes
- Stuffed animals
- Telephones
- Mirror
- Play houses

Themes about Different Kinds of Work

Props used in different kinds of work allow children to act out what they know about occupations or jobs that they have observed during their lives, that they have seen in books, or that their parents might talk about. The props provided encourage more in-depth play, reminding them of aspects of the work, and allowing them to imitate in their own ways. Often, all the props needed for each job are stored together in an activity box and put out for children to use in addition to the props that are regularly available. Here are just a few examples:

- Office play: office supplies, desk, typewriter, paper, briefcases
- Store: cash register, bags, pretend money, things sold in the store, such as food containers, shoes, hardware, hats, clothing
- Restaurant: tables and chairs, place settings, menus, play money, aprons, chef hats or hair nets, cooking equipment, table cloths, empty ketchup and mustard bottles and salt and pepper shakers, play foods, vase with flowers
- Construction worker: hats, shovels, tools, tool belt
- Zoo keeper: stuffed or other toy animals, things to make cages, tickets, money, uniforms, foods for animals
- Medical: gauze bandages, tape, doctor's kit, dolls, blankets, stethoscope, medicine dropper, uniforms, patients' gowns
- Farmer or gardener: gardening tools including rakes and shovels, seed packets, pumpkins, corn cobs, straw bundles, toy animals, hats
- Airplane or train: uniforms, tickets, trays, equipment for serving meals, suitcases, rows of chairs for seats, steering wheels

Themes about Fantasy

Props for fantasy allow children to act out make-believe stories in their own ways. Many children enjoy pretending to be characters they have learned about in books, movies, or TV programs. Key materials needed for this type of play are dress-ups, such as capes, hats, space helmets, or extra-fancy outfits, for example to play a queen or a king. Other dress-ups might allow children to be animals. Often, used Halloween costumes are recycled for fantasy play, as long as they are not frightening to the children. Materials might include:

- Simple, non-frightening masks or face paint
- Magic wands or other accessories
- Lots of costumes, including hats, capes, fancy dress-ups, crowns
- Things needed to act out familiar stories

Themes about Leisure

Leisure activities are those done when not working—for example during vacations, holidays, weekends, or after work. Props for leisure activities might include things needed for pretending about:

- Participating in or watching sports
- Camping
- Going on vacations to different places (beach, mountains, amusement park, zoo)
- Picnicking

Indicator

- Bird-watching
- Fishing
- Boating
- Parties (birthday party, surprise party, dance, tea party)

Note that small toys that children can pretend with, such as dolls and doll houses, small cars, trucks with a garage, or small toy animals and a barn, are also acceptable within each theme.

Older children will have their own ideas for the props they need for certain kinds of play.

Accessible means that children can reach and use the materials by themselves. This does not require that all children be able to use the dramatic play materials at the same time. Accessibility can be provided either indoors or outdoors. For materials to be considered accessible, they must be within view of younger preschoolers (2½ to 4 years). For older children (4 to 6 years), if materials are stored in closed spaces (such as prop boxes or cabinets) they can be considered accessible *only* if it is *observed* that children can freely access and use the materials.

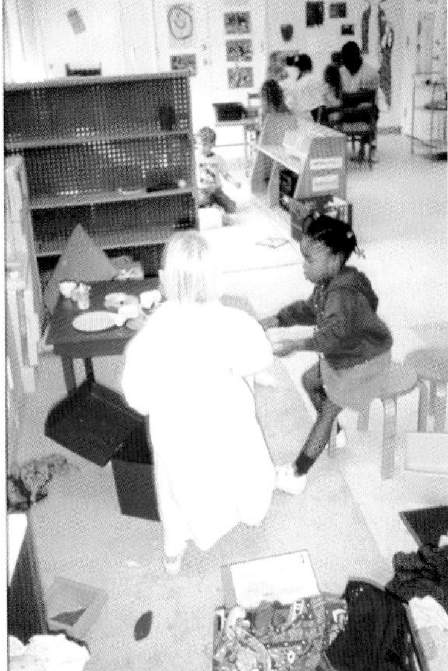

24.3.1 a Some materials are accessible—dress-up clothes, table and stools, and dishes.

Score 1.1 "Yes" if materials for dramatic play, such as those listed above, are *not* accessible. Materials should be accessible on a regular basis daily, or almost daily, to score 1.1 "No."

Indicator 1.1 should also be scored "Yes" if there are too few materials for *meaningful play* (defined in the General Information section). For example, if there are only a few spoons, but nothing else to use with them, or a toy farm building, with no small animals, people, or vehicles to use with it, meaningful play is not possible.

3.1 Accessible is defined in 1.1.

Some means enough dramatic play materials, such as those listed in 1.1, for children to be able to carry out *meaningful* pretend play. For example, if there is a pot for pretending to cook, something else for use with it would be required (such as toy stove, spoon, foods to put in it). If a doll is provided, there should be other materials to use with the doll (such as clothes, blanket, bed, chair, or baby bottle). If there is a small farm building, toys must be accessible to use with it (such as little people, animals, or vehicles). (See photos 24.3.1 a–b.)

Some requires enough materials for several children to use at one time, but choices can be limited. ***Some*** will vary with the age and ability of the children in the group, with more required for older children. Classrooms with more children will also require more materials than classrooms with fewer children.

Score 3.1 "Yes" if enough materials are accessible to the children for limited meaningful play.

24.3.1 b Some materials are accessible—food, dishes, sink and cabinet.

3.2 To score 3.2 "Yes," the materials must be ***accessible*** (see 1.1) for at least 1 hour (give or take a few minutes) per day, in a full day program. This does not mean that each child must have a full hour to use the materials. However, it is required that children have a reasonable chance to use the materials at some time if they wish.

Indicator

Less time is required for programs operating less than 8 hours a day, with the amount of time calculated proportionally, based on the ratio of 1 hour for programs of 8 hours or more. For example, if a program operates for 6 hours a day, this would be 3/4 of a full-day program, so the time required would be 3/4 of the 1 hour. If the program operates 4 hours a day, the requirement would be 1/2 hour.

The materials credited in 3.1 should be considered in scoring this indicator, although all do not have to be accessible at the same time. Materials can be accessible indoors or outdoors, as long as there are enough in either place to allow meaningful play, even if it is limited.

The 1 hour can be provided at one time or as a combination of several periods throughout the day. For example, materials might be accessible to children for 30 minutes in the morning during free play time and then again for 30 minutes in the afternoon. The materials do not have to be provided as a free choice activity but do have to be accessible for this time period. For example, children might be assigned to the center where the materials are accessible for them to use.

3.3 To give credit for 3.3 (score "Yes") dramatic play materials should be stored in an area that is designated specifically for those types of materials. The materials should not be mixed with other unrelated play materials. For example, dramatic play materials should not be stored in a toy box that also holds blocks, fine motor toys, and books. Or dramatic play materials should not be spread throughout the room, with a few in one place and others in another place. Instead, props and/or furniture should be placed so they can be used together.

It is not required that all dramatic play materials be placed together, but the majority should be. For example, all the housekeeping materials should be put together in one area, although soft animals or a pretend wood working bench with plastic tools (which also count as dramatic play materials) might be stored in other parts of the classroom.

5.1 ***Many*** means that three or more children can use the materials at one time, without undue competition, and the materials are plentiful enough to encourage more complex play. Children should be able to have choices for how they want to combine the materials, and different possibilities should exist in terms of what they can pretend. Older children and larger groups require more materials to get credit for ***many*** than do younger children or smaller groups. Photo 24.5.1 a (next page) provides an example of ***many***, contrasted with photo 24.5.1 b (next page) that shows furnishings, but no props.

Requirements for ***dress-up clothes*** are provided in the "Notes for Clarification" in the item. The dress-up clothing listed in this original note is meant to provide examples and should not be considered requirements for specific clothing. Hats, purses, and shoes count as clothing. Because children are developing gender role identity during the preschool years, they require concrete examples of dress-ups that are associated with being men or women. (See photos 24.5.1 c–e, next page.) Thus, 2-3 gender-specific examples of dress-up items are required, (such as ties or men's hats to represent men's clothes; purses, high heels, or flowery hats for women). More generic clothing, such as sweatshirts or running shoes, can also be provided, but these do not count as gender-specific dress-up clothes. "Clothing worn by men and women at work" can include work clothing typically worn at home or at a job outside the home. ***Dress-up clothes*** representing men and women are required, but only some, not many, of each is required.

Indicator

24.5.1 a There are enough materials so children do not have to compete.

24.5.1 b Only furniture is provided for dramatic play, not props.

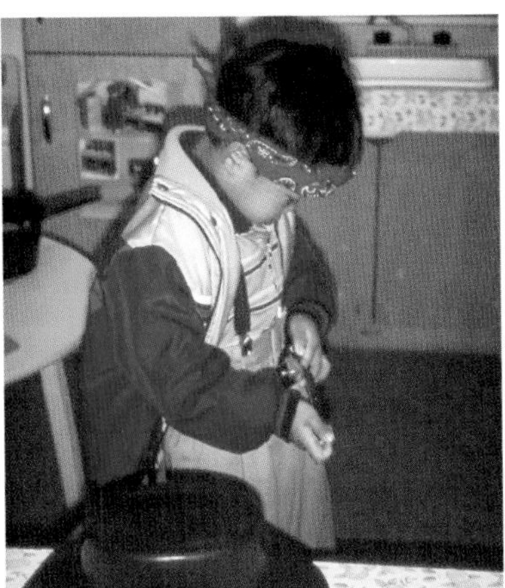

25.5.1 c Providing gender-specific dress-ups allows many choices.

24.5.1 d These girls enjoy hats and fancy tops.

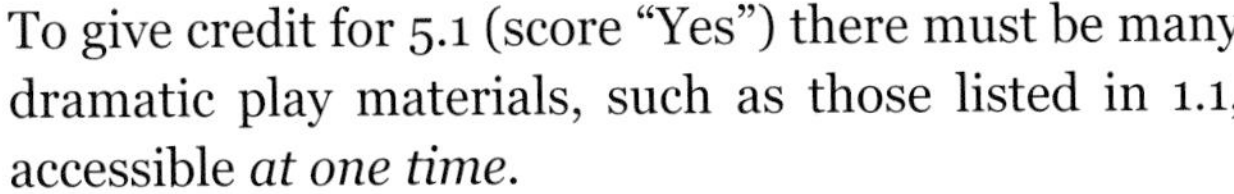

To give credit for 5.1 (score "Yes") there must be many dramatic play materials, such as those listed in 1.1, accessible *at one time.*

5.2 ***Accessible for a substantial portion of the day*** refers to the ***many*** (not just some) dramatic play materials credited in 5.1. However, all materials credited do not have to be accessible at the same time as long as there are many at any period counted towards the substantial portion of the day.

Accessible for a substantial portion of the day means that the materials are within the children's reach and can be used for 1/3 of the center's operating hours.

24.5.1 e These boys experiment with wearing fancy women's things. They think it's very funny.

See sample schedules showing calculations of whether dramatic play materials are accessible for a substantial portion of the day (on pages 250-252 at end of this section).

Consider materials both indoors and outdoors when calculating accessibility for a substantial portion of the day.

Indicator

Dress-up clothes, required in 5.1, are *not required for outdoor* dramatic play because they might cause safety hazards when children use gross motor equipment. If they are used, care should be taken to avoid long clothes, unsteady shoes, or anything that might cause strangulation if it gets caught, such as ties or a cape. However props outside must be complete enough for children to take part in meaningful dramatic play. For example:

- An outdoor house must have furniture and other props.
- Doll strollers must have dolls.
- Kitchen furniture must have things to use in the kitchen, such as utensils, pots/pans.
- Child-sized riding cars should have a gas pump or things to transport.
- Cars in the sandbox should have a garage or people.
- Toy animals should have fences, a barn.
- Rocking toys shaped like animals should have props to use with them, such as things to feed the animal or safe dress-up to wear (e.g., hats), when riding them.

5.3 The four different dramatic play ***themes*** are described in 1.1 and include *housekeeping, different kinds of work, fantasy, and leisure*. Examples of ***props*** for the four different themes are also provided in 1.1.

Score 5.3 "Yes" if there are enough props *accessible* for meaningful play for two different themes on the day of the observation. Materials in closed storage that children cannot reach and use are not counted in scoring. For example, if several closed prop boxes are stacked near the dramatic play area but only housekeeping props are accessible, do not give credit.

Props for the two themes can be accessible at the same time and place. However, they do not have to be accessible together. For example, props for housekeeping might be used for free play indoors, while props for camping might be part of the outdoor setting. (See photo 24.5.3 a–b.)

Give credit (score "Yes") if there are enough props for at least ***two different themes*** accessible for meaningful play on the same day. Enough materials are required for each theme so children can pretend with some depth. For example,

24.5.3 a

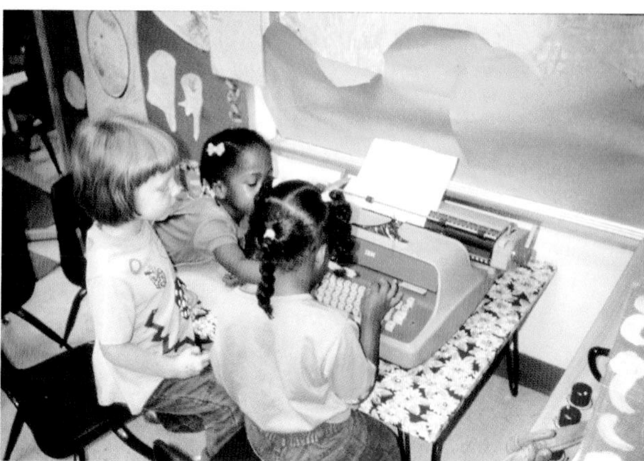

24.5.3 b

24.5.3 a–b In this class, part of the housekeeping center has been turned into an office, with typical office supplies and typewriter.

Indicator

the presence of a cash register and a few food packages would not be enough for a theme of grocery store, but with the addition of grocery bags, paper money, and shopping carts, children's play could be quite complex.

5.4 A ***dramatic play area*** is an interest center where children can participate in pretend play. As stated in Item 4, Room arrangement, an interest center is "an area where materials, organized by type, are stored so that they are accessible to children, and appropriately furnished play space is provided for children to participate in a particular kind of play."

For the dramatic play area (or interest center) to be ***clearly defined*** requires that it be in a place where the boundaries of the space to play are clear to children. Since preschool children do not understand boundaries unless they are made of real objects that they can see, concrete (not imagined) boundaries are required. For example, boundaries for the area can be created with shelves and other furniture, so that the play does not spill into other areas of the room. Simply telling children where boundaries are, without real boundary markers, is not sufficient.

Space to play in the area requires a space that allows children to actively play and use the materials without competing for space with other children, materials, or activities (See photo 24.5.4 a.) A certain square footage is not required; however, observe to make sure no problems occur because of space limitations. Children in the area should be able to play freely, without being crowded. More space is required when more children are allowed to use the area.

24.5.4 a These children can easily play in this center without competing for materials or space.

Organized storage means that the dramatic play materials are grouped by type, so that the children know where to find them and can help to put them away. Children are able to easily obtain these materials with little or no help from the staff. This might mean that it is obvious where to find things because props, and where they are stored, naturally go together (such as all dolls are stored in the doll bed, toy foods are in the refrigerator, pots/pans and dishes are stored under the sink). (See photos 24.5.4 b–c.)

Shelves or containers can also be organized with labels (e.g., pictures or pictures and words), but labels are not required if children can easily tell where things go. (See photos 24.5.4 d–e, next page.) The storage does not

24.5.4 b Dress-ups are neatly hung on a clothes rack, hats and wigs are all on a shelf, and a mirror lets the children see how they look.

24.5.4 c Dolls, phones, and other props are organized by type of material.

Indicator

24.5.4 d Children put kitchen equipment away by matching the object to its shape.

24.5.4 e It's easy to tell where things go on these shelves.

have to be perfectly neat, but things must be reasonably arranged so children do not become frustrated when they are playing in the area because it is disorganized—they cannot find things unless they empty a whole storage container, or find it impossible to open stuffed drawers.

Score 5.4 "Yes" if the primary area used for dramatic play meets the requirements for the indicator, as described above. If several areas are used, at least one must meet these requirements, and it must be the area (either indoors or outdoors) that is *most frequently* used by the children.

7.1 ***Materials rotated*** means that the accessible dramatic play props are changed so children can take on different roles, find new interests, or use props that they used before, in a new way. Rotating props keeps children from becoming bored with the choices they can make for play and adds new learning opportunities.

Materials should be rotated when children become bored with the materials because they no longer find them interesting or challenging. Then they should be put away and different materials brought out. Props should also be rotated to provide experiences to go with certain projects or themes being explored in the classroom.

Calling children's attention to a dramatic play material that is regularly accessible to children does not count as "rotating materials." Credit is given only when materials are removed from being accessible to children and replaced with materials that were formerly inaccessible.

Inaccessible materials can be made accessible as either special projects or for free play. The rotated dramatic play materials can be brought from storage, exchanged with other classrooms or newly purchased.

To give credit, some materials should be rotated at least monthly. If it is impossible to tell whether materials are rotated, ask staff the questions listed for 7.1 in the ECERS-R to find out how often this happens, if at all.

7.2 ***Diversity*** in this indicator refers to the differences in people with regard to race, culture, ability, age, or gender. ***Props provided to represent diversity*** requires that materials associated with varying groups are provided for children to use in their dramatic play. Examples include:

- Dress up clothing representing different cultures (See photo 24.7.2 a.)
- Play cooking and eating utensils from different cultures

Indicator

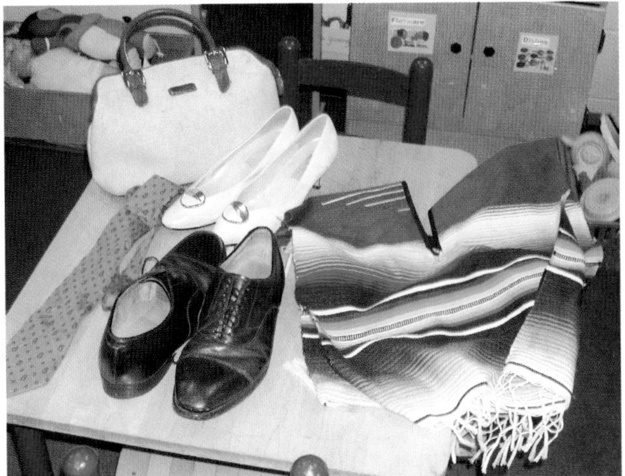

24.7.2 a Within these dress-ups, we see a poncho from Mexico and gender-specific items.

24.7.2 b Dolls with different skin tones are accessible.

- Dolls representing different races/ ages/ cultures/ abilities (See photo 24.7.2 b.)
- Play food from different cultures (See photo 24.7.2 c.)

All props must be associated with a *positive image* of the group represented. If any prop represents a group in a negative way, score 7.2 "No."

To score 7.2 "Yes," there must be at least two examples of such materials observed.

24.7.2 c Foods representing many cultures are included as dramatic play props.

7.3 See the "Notes for Clarification" that are provided for this indicator, as part of the item.

Props used outside the classroom, either outdoors or in a large indoor area, such as a multi-purpose or gross motor room, must be complete enough to permit *meaningful play* (see General Information section). For example, just having a large playhouse outdoors would not be sufficient unless the house had furniture and props that would allow the children to pretend and act out roles. (See photos 24.7.3 a–b, next page.)

Examples of props that could be provided for more active dramatic play outdoors (or in a very large space indoors) include:

- Trucks with people or things to transport
- Play houses with furniture, dolls, or other props
- Riding toys that look like cars with a gas station or gas pump
- Gardening tools with wheel barrows
- Big pieces of equipment shaped like vehicles, with things to transport, conductor hats, or other dress-ups
- Castle with props
- Toy strollers or shopping carts with dolls or stuffed animals to transport
- Water basins with baby dolls to bathe
- Prop boxes for different jobs, such as painter, fire fighter, bus driver

Score "Yes" if examples of such dramatic play materials are observed to be accessible for outdoor play or for play within a very large indoor space.

Indicator

24.7.3 a This outdoor playhouse has a small table with chairs, a grocery cart, pots and pans, a stove and play food so that children can experience meaningful play.

24.7.3 b Furniture is provided in this outdoor playhouse.

If the weather does not permit observing children as they use the outdoor space, be sure to visit the space to see what would be accessible to the children. If it is impossible to tell what children have access to outdoors, ask staff the question provided for 7.3. Such materials must be used daily, or almost daily, to give credit.

7.4 When children are provided with experiences and information about their world, they often show how they interpret this information through their dramatic play. As children are exposed to more opportunities, they broaden their pretend play to represent all that they are learning. This is especially true when they are given the dramatic play props to extend their play.

In this indicator, staff are required to do more than just provide props for meaningful play. They are also required to provide information and experiences that children can incorporate into their play with the dramatic play materials. The kinds of information provided must add to the possibilities for how children use props.

For example, if children have the props they need to play "restaurant" (such as tables/chairs, menus, play money, aprons, chef hats, cooking equipment, place settings, play foods), they will pretend about what they remember from any restaurant experiences they might have had. In addition, if a book is read or a field trip is taken to a restaurant, and certain information is pointed out to the children (such as the different things that waiters, cooks, and customers do), they will take the information they gain and incorporate it as they pretend. Thus, their pretend play becomes richer in content.

This indicator requires that ***pictures, stories, and trips*** are used to ***enrich children's dramatic play***. Any of these may be provided to the whole group, to small groups, or to individual children.

Pictures include those displayed or shown to the children. Pictures that someone has brought in to share with the class or pictures that are put into a photo album or turned into a book for the class can also be given credit.

Stories may be in books that are accessible and/or read to the children or stories told to them without a book. Flannel board stories or puppet stories can also be

Indicator

used. Audio-visual materials (such as TV, video, slides, computer software) can also be counted to meet the requirement.

Trips can be field trips away from the classroom, but they can be visits to places very close-by, even within the center. For example, a visit to the director's office gives children lots of ideas, if they are going to play "Office."

24.7.4 After a field trip to the pumpkin farm, props for farm play (pumpkins, gourds, hats, baskets) are added to the dramatic play area.

Examples of using pictures, books, and trips to enrich dramatic play include:

- Staff take children on a field trip to the fire station, then provide a cardboard fire truck, stuffed Dalmatians, fire hats, a telephone, and a pretend hose to use in dramatic play.
- The teacher reads children a story about a child who is taking a trip to the beach, and the dramatic play area has a car made from a big cardboard box, luggage, beach clothing, sunglasses, towels, and empty sunscreen bottles.
- One of the parents talks to the children about his/her job, showing pictures, and props are added to the dramatic play center that are found in that work environment, such as telephones, computers, paper, pencils, and other appropriate equipment.
- At Thanksgiving time, stories are read about the different ways that people celebrate this holiday. Many Thanksgiving props are added to the housekeeping center.
- In the fall, children visit a pumpkin farm. On the playground, or indoors, props such as bales of hay, pumpkins, tools, and toy animals are added for dramatic play. (See photo 24.7.4.)
- Children draw pictures for their parents and put them in envelopes to send through the mail, then take them to the post office and mail them. After the field trip, a post office with paper, pencils, envelopes, and stickers for stamps is set up for dramatic play.

Give credit for 7.4 if such materials are used to extend dramatic play at least once a month. All three requirements (pictures, books, and trips) do not have to be provided each month, but at least two trips must be provided in a year.

Note: To give credit, the pictures, books, and trips *must* be related to the materials children can use in their dramatic play. For example, if a field trip is taken to the post office, but no props are provided for post office dramatic play, no credit can be given.

24 Dramatic play

Indicator

Calculating "Substantial Portion of the Day"

Example 1

This schedule is based on an observation period of 4.5 hours (from 8AM – 12:30PM) and information collected during the teacher interview about how unobserved time during the day is used and what is accessible to the children.

Time	Scheduled activity	Time to use dramatic play materials
6:30 – 8:00	Breakfast in cafeteria and TV time for those who are finished with breakfast	
8:00 – 8:30	Children go to regular classrooms and play with table and rug toys (puzzles; legos; duplos with cars, people, and trucks; stringing beads and cards; pegboards)	**30 minutes**
8:30 – 8:45	Prepare for breakfast/children wash hands	
8:45 – 9:15	Breakfast	
9:15 – 9:45	Circle (teacher reading time)	
9:45 – 10:45	Centers (housekeeping, art, sand and water, nature/science, writing table, blocks, music, computer and cozy book area)	**1 hour**
10:45 – 11:15	Outdoor play (gross motor activities only)	
11:15 – 12:15	Prepare for and eat lunch	
12:15 – 12:30	Story, put out cots, prepare for nap	
12:30 – 2:45	Nap	
2:45 – 3:00	Wake up from nap; bathroom	
3:00 – 3:25	Snack and story	
3:25 – 4:25	Centers (housekeeping, nature/science, writing table, computer, fine motor area and cozy book area)	**1 hour**
4:25 – 5:30	Outdoors or indoor gross motor	
5:30 – 6:30	Table and rug toys (puzzles; legos; duplos with cars, people, and trucks; stringing beads and cards; pegboards) Prepare for departure	**1 hour**

1. Figure the total number of hours that children are allowed to attend.

   (6:30AM to 6:30 PM = 12 hours)

2. Calculate 1/3 of the operating hours to determine "Substantial Portion of the Day."

   (12 hours ÷ 3 = 4 hours)

3. Add up all times that children have access to dramatic play materials.

   (see shaded times on schedule = 3 hours and 30 minutes)

4. Compare the amount of time children may have access to dramatic play materials to the time requirement for substantial portion of the day. If the amount of time children may have access to dramatic play materials is the same or greater, then score "Yes." If the amount of time is less than the time requirement for substantial portion of the day, then score "No." For example, the schedule above indicates:

   3 hours and 30 minutes (access to dramatic play materials) **is less than 4 hours** (time requirement for substantial portion of day), and therefore the time requirement for substantial portion of the day is not met.

Indicator

Calculating "Substantial Portion of the Day"
Example 2

This schedule is based on an observation period of 4 hours (from 9AM – 1PM) and information collected during the teacher interview about how unobserved time during the day is used and what is accessible to the children.

Time	Scheduled activity	Time to use dramatic play materials
9:00 – 9:30	Arrival and centers open (cozy book area, computer, writing table, math, science, and fine motor)	
9:30 – 9:45	Snack	
9:45 – 10:00	Clean up snack/bathroom/wash hands	
10:00 – 11:00	Outside (gross motor activities and dramatic play materials)	**1 hour**
11:00 – 11:45	Free choice of centers (fine motor, art, blocks, dramatic play, nature/science, math, sensory table, computer, writing table and cozy book area)	**45 minutes**
11:45 – 12:15	Large group activity (M,W,F is music/movement and T,Th is art activity)	
12:15 – 12:45	Prepare for and eat lunch	
12:45 – 1:00	Clean up/bathroom/prepare for quiet time	
1:00 – 1:45	Quiet time/quiet centers available (cozy book area, fine motor, math, and science)	
1:45 – 2:00	Clean up all centers and prepare for departure	

1. Figure the total number of hours that children are allowed to attend.

   (9 AM to 2 PM = 5 hours)

2. Calculate 1/3 of the operating hours to determine "Substantial Portion of the Day."

   (5 hours ÷ 3 = 1 hour and 40 minutes).

3. Add up all times that children have access to dramatic play materials

   (see shaded times on schedule = 1 hour and 45 minutes)

4. Compare the amount of time children may have access to dramatic play materials to the time requirement for substantial portion of the day. If the amount of time children may have access to dramatic play materials is the same or greater, then score "Yes." If the amount of time is less than the time requirement for substantial portion of the day, then score "No." For example, the schedule above indicates:

   1 hour and 45 minutes (access to dramatic play materials) **is greater than 1 hour and 40 minutes** (time requirement for substantial portion of day), and therefore the time requirement for substantial portion of the day is met.

Indicator

Calculating "Substantial Portion of the Day"

Example 3

This schedule is based on an observation period of 3.5 hours (from 9AM –12:30 PM) and information collected during the teacher interview about whether what was observed represents the typical daily practice.

Time	Scheduled activity	Time to use dramatic play materials
9:00 – 9:20	Arrival/group time to discuss activities for the day	
9:20 – 9:45	Whole group art activity	
9:45 – 10:00	Whole group reading time (teacher directed)	
10:00 – 10:45	Outside time (gross motor activities only)	
10:45 – 11:30	Free choice of centers (fine motor, art, blocks, dramatic play, nature/science, math, sensory table, computer, writing table, blocks and books)	**45 minutes**
11:30 – 11:45	Clean up/bathroom/prepare for lunch time	
11:45 – 12:15	Prepare for and eat lunch	
12:15 – 12:30	Clean up/bathroom/prepare for departure	

1. Figure the total number of hours that children are allowed to attend.

   (9 AM to 12:30 PM = 3 hours and 30 minutes)

2. Calculate 1/3 of the operating hours to determine "Substantial Portion of the Day."

   (3 hours and 30 minutes ÷ 3 = 1 hour and 10 minutes)

3. Add up all times that children have access to dramatic play materials.

   (see shaded times on schedule = 45 minutes)

4. Compare the amount of time children may have access to dramatic play materials to the time requirement for substantial portion of the day. If the amount of time children may have access to dramatic play materials is the same, or greater, then score "Yes." If the amount of time is less than the time requirement for substantial portion of the day, then score "No." For example, the schedule above indicates:

   45 minutes (access to dramatic play materials) **is less than 1 hour and 10 minutes** (time requirement for substantial portion of day), and therefore the time requirement for substantial portion of the day is not met.

25 Nature/science

General information about this item

Most young children are curious about and fascinated by the natural world around them. To learn to understand their surroundings, they use their senses—hearing, sight, smell, taste, and touch. They need many safe hands-on opportunities to explore and experiment with the natural world. Such opportunities would be considered ***developmentally appropriate***. Developmentally appropriate is defined in the original notes for this item in the scale.

Developmentally appropriate nature/science experiences include exploring natural things, both indoors and out, learning words for natural things, and understanding natural processes. Providing nature/science materials and activities, as well as plenty of exposure to the outdoor world, gives children a wider base from which to develop vocabulary and learn to understand basic natural concepts. Most important, however, it provides opportunities to enjoy the world, beginning what can be a lifelong interest in and concern for our environment.

In scoring this item, there are four categories of materials and experiences that will need to be observed and considered. The categories are listed in the ECERS-R "Notes for Clarification" for the item, with some examples. Further definition, with additional developmentally appropriate examples, follows:

25 A These seashells are an example of a collection of natural objects.

Collections of natural objects

"Collections" require that there are groups of similar natural objects, which can be classified together. (See photo 25 A.) Sufficient numbers of the objects in each collection must be present to allow children to explore similarities and/or differences. The collections must be of natural things. Plastic collections (such as insects, dinosaurs, or zoo animals) are counted as nature /science toys. Some examples of collections of natural objects, in addition to those provided in the item, include:

- Leaves
- Seashells
- Rocks
- Different types of wood
- Pinecones
- Birds' nests

25 B These plants are examples of living things for children to care for.

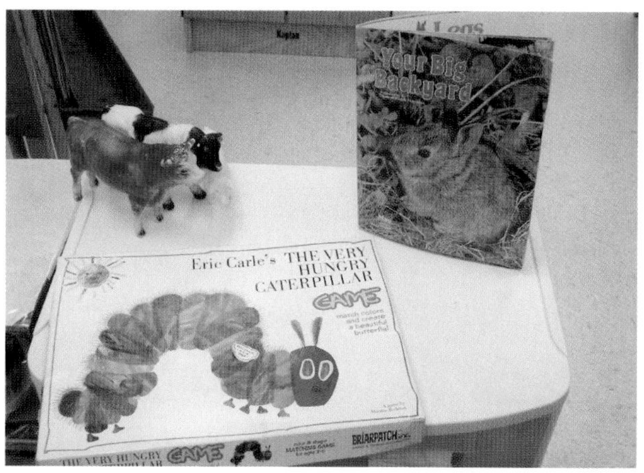

25 C Plastic animals, science board games, and books about nature are located in different areas of the room. The much-loved fantasy book about the caterpillar would not be counted as a science material because it does not show caterpillars with complete accuracy.

25 D Planting seeds and then watching the plants grow is an activity that includes staff input.

Living things

Living things include plants and various living creatures that the children actively care for and/or observe. (See photo 25 B, preceding page.). To give credit for living things, they must be observable in the children's immediate environment (in the room or the outdoor play area) or at least visited frequently as a class activity. For example, shrubbery at the entrance to the building would not be counted as a living thing for this item, unless the children are regularly taken to visit and observe the shrubs, with staff pointing out changes or characteristics, or children take part in planting and caring for them. Plants that are part of the children's immediate environment, such as grass or trees on the playground, would only be counted as examples of living things if staff encourage children to observe and care for them in some way on a regular basis. Examples of ***living things*** that would receive credit include:

- House plants, terrarium, seeds that children plant and watch as they grow to note changes
- Garden the class planted, cares for, or visits regularly
- Class pet
- Window bird feeder
- Aquarium with fish, snails, or other animals
- Ant farm (with living ants)
- Worm farm
- Butterfly hatching kit
- Eggs that hatch

Nature science books, games, or toys

Books, games and toys that can be counted for this item are likely to be scattered throughout the classroom, rather than collected in one place. Look in all areas for such materials. (See photo 25 C.)

- Books must have realistic pictures, photos, or drawings and tell facts about animals or other natural things. Fantasy stories about animals are not counted to meet the requirements of this item. Look for factual books such as those on animals, plants, birds, fish, the human body, seasons, weather, and the planets.
- Games must also be realistic and fact-based. Look for board games with a nature theme, nature picture matching cards, nature sequence cards, or body part matching games.
- Toys should realistically portray natural life. Examples include plastic sets of animals and puzzles with nature pictures or natural sequences. Stuffed animals would not be counted to meet the requirement, unless they were very natural looking rather than fantasy-based portrayals.
- If factual nature/science videos or computer games are used by children, they can be credited in this category.

Nature/science activities

Nature science activities require materials that encourage or allow children to experiment with scientific concepts or to observe scientific processes unfold. The "Notes for Clarification," therefore, list nature science activities such as cooking and simple experiments. Both of these fulfill this requirement.

Nature/science activities require more than just making materials accessible on shelves without the supplementary objects needed for experimentation or observing processes. Staff support is usually needed to encourage children to complete an experiment or cooking activity, but children can often experiment freely with materials if they have been given some initial help. (See photo 25 D, preceding page.) Nature/science activities to consider for this item include:

- Magnets with objects to experiment with, including other magnets
- Magnifying glasses with things to look at
- Sink and float activity, with objects to use in an experiment
- Racing cars down slopes that vary in length and incline
- Shaking cans filled with differing substances to match and compare sounds
- Smelling and matching cans filled with different spices
- Using plastic translucent color paddles to make colors that match objects or color cards

Some sand and water activities can also be credited under this item (e.g., sink and float activity or toy animals in the sand box).

Examples of nature/science activities that require *more* staff input (as required in Indicator 7.1) include:

- Completing a weather chart, after looking outside to see the weather
- Using a rain gauge to record how much rain fell
- Planting seeds and watching plants grow
- Planting a garden and caring for it
- Cooking foods that change when mixed, cooled, cooked, etc.
- Lifting objects with levers and pulleys
- Using different length pendulums with different weights

Indicator

- Tasting and comparing sweet, sour, bitter, salty
- Using thermometers to measure hot and cold
- Looking at objects under a simple microscope
- Making a bird feeder and keeping track of birds using it

When the materials for nature science activities are present (such as magnets, magnifying glasses, thermometers, bottles filled with oil and water to shake, plastic color mixers, and prisms), and these are not used for experimentation by children during the observation, ask staff the following question:

"How are the science materials used by the children?"

If the answer is that children rarely use them, or use them without experimenting in any way and with no support at all from staff, give credit for the materials in the "books, games or toys category" but not the "activities" category.

A closer look at each indicator

1.1 ***Accessible*** means that children can reach and use materials by themselves. For materials to be considered accessible, they must be within view of younger preschoolers (2½ to 4 years). For children 4 and 5 years of age, if materials are stored in closed spaces, they can be considered accessible only if it is observed that children can freely access and use the materials. Materials should be accessible on a regular basis daily, or almost daily, to score 1.1 "No."

No games, materials or activities for nature/science means that there are no opportunities for children to experiment with and explore using items such as those listed in the four categories described in the item and discussed more fully in the General Information section above.

If nature/science activities are present, but not developmentally appropriate (too academically focused, rather than play and exploration focused, or requiring rote memorization), do not count as representing one of the four categories. For example, if the only nature/science content is writing how many birds appear on a worksheet, do not give credit.

If the *only* experience with nature/science that the children have is playing outdoors then 1.1 should be scored "Yes." More is required to score 1.1 "No," as described in the General Information section for this item.

3.1 ***Some*** means one or more developmentally appropriate games/materials/activities are accessible to children from two of the nature/science categories listed in the General Information section for this item. At this level of quality all categories do not have to be represented; only two of the four are required. (See photo 25.3.1.)

The ***some*** must be ***accessible***, as described in 1.1.

3.2 ***Accessible daily*** requires that the materials credited in 3.1 can be reached and used by children for at least 1 hour per day in a full-day program, with very few exceptions. This does not require that all children be able to use the nature/science materials at the same

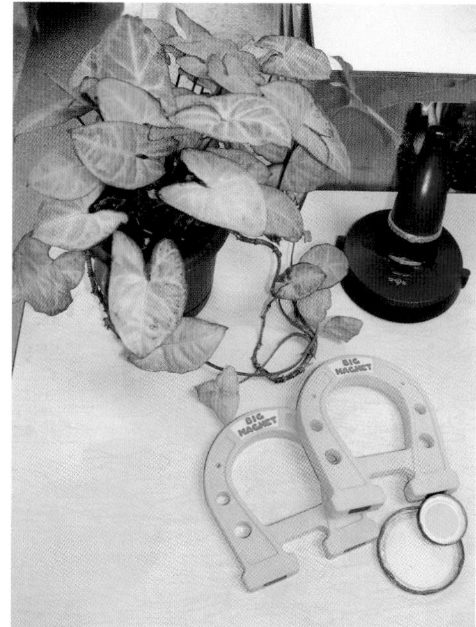

25.3.1 Two of the four categories are represented here, including living things and science activities.

Indicator

25.3.3 a Children in this classroom are gathering leaves to add to the classroom collection.

25.3.3 b Children collected leaves on the playground to add to this classroom activity.

time or that each child has a full hour to use the materials. However, it is required that children would have a reasonable chance to use materials at some time if they wished.

Less time is required for programs operating less than 8 hours a day, with the amount of time calculated proportionally, based on the ratio of 1 hour for programs of 8 hours or more. For example, if a program operates for 6 hours a day, this would be 3/4 of a full-day program, so the time required would be 3/4 of the 1 hour. If the program operates 4 hours a day, the requirement would be 1/2 hour.

25.5.1 a Materials on this science table are used in addition to many activities.

The 1 hour can be provided at one time or as a combination of several periods throughout the day. For example, some nature/science materials might be accessible to children for 30 minutes in the morning during free play time and then again for 30 minutes in the afternoon. The materials do not have to be provided as a free choice activity, but do have to be accessible for this time period, either indoors or outdoors. For example, children might be assigned to the center where the materials are accessible for them to use.

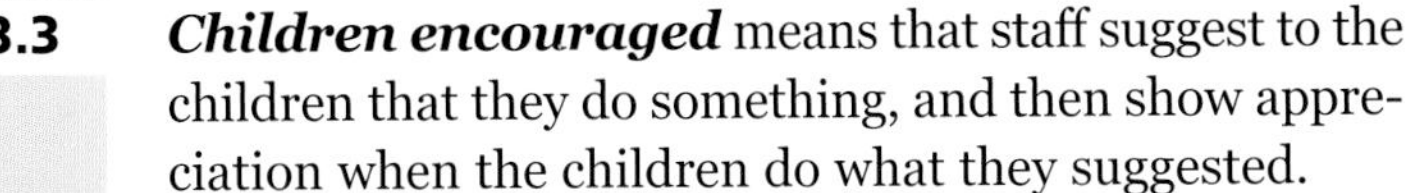

3.3 ***Children encouraged*** means that staff suggest to the children that they do something, and then show appreciation when the children do what they suggested.

The ***natural things*** are the types of items listed in the categories "collections of natural things" and "living things" in the General Information section for this item. (See photos 25.3.3 a–b.)

Examples of encouragement are listed in this item. If such encouragement on the part of staff is observed, then the indicator is true (score "Yes").

If there is not obvious evidence that this happens, ask the teacher the question listed for the indicator. If the staff report that this is done somewhat frequently, for

25.5.1 b Activities include planting and taking care of outdoor plants.

Indicator

25.5.1 c Children experiment with magnets.

25.5.1 d Children are free to use many materials throughout the room.

example monthly, or more at one time of the year than others (for example, in the fall or after summer vacation) but not monthly, then give credit for this indicator.

5.1 ***Many*** means approximately three to five examples of at least three of the four categories listed in the notes for the item and discussed in the General Information section. However, this can vary, as long as each of the three categories is represented. In some cases credit might be given for more than 3-5 of one category and less than 3-5 of another. This will also depend on the ages and the number of children in the group. (See photos 25.5.1 a–b, preceding page, and c–d.)

It helps to use a recording system to determine if this requirement is met. Below is an example of a simple chart showing the many materials found in one classroom:

Collections of natural objects:
- sea shells of different sizes and shapes
- different size pine cones
- rock collection
- large and small acorns

Nature/science books/games/toys:
- plastic dinosaur set
- plastic farm animals
- 3 puzzles with insects, vegetables and reptiles
- 10 books about animals and fish
- 2 books on how plants grow
- zoo animal matching cards

Nature/science activities:
- magnets with objects to try out
- sound matching cans

Indicator

Note that this would count as ***many***, although there are fewer than three examples for the nature/science activities category, because there are more in two other categories.

25.5.3 Materials are organized by type on the shelf.

5.2 ***Accessible for a substantial portion of the day*** means that the materials are within the children's reach and can be used by them for 1/3 of the center's operating hours. The requirements for 5.1 must be met to give credit.

"Collections" must be accessible to the children if they are to count towards meeting the requirement of this indicator.

Consider materials both indoors and outdoors when considering what can be given credit for being accessible for a substantial portion of the day. If outdoor time is included in calculating substantial portion of the day, materials from at least two categories must be accessible during the outdoor time credited.

See sample schedules on pages 263–265 demonstrating how to calculate substantial portion of the day for this item.

5.3 ***Well organized*** means that the nature/science materials are grouped by type so that the children know where to find them. Children must be able to easily obtain these materials with little or no help from the staff. (See photo 25.5.3.)

This does not mean that all nature/science materials must be placed together in one center. For example, nature/science puzzles can be accessible in the fine motor area of the room, and books on nature and science can be in the book area with other books. However, there must be a system for offering other nature/science materials that groups them into a nature/science area.

Shelves or containers should be organized and labeled with pictures and words if necessary. The organization does not have to be perfectly neat. However, children should not become frustrated when they are playing in the area because it is so disorganized that they cannot find things. During clean up time the children should understand where to return the materials.

The pieces for each game, set of toys, and activity should be stored together so they can be used as intended. For example, science puzzles should have all pieces, a set of sound cans should be complete, and magnets should have objects to experiment with. Pets and their homes should be well cared for.

5.4 There are many ***everyday events*** that children experience. Some can be used to teach nature/science, even though they are not necessarily planned. Staff take advantage of the occurrences by helping children to notice them, and learn a little about what the events are, how and when they happen, and, to a small extent, why.

Examples of such everyday events are included in the indicator. Additional examples include noticing and talking about:

- Erosion of soil after wind or rain
- How fast a ball rolls down a slope
- What happens as a result of feeding the bunny
- How rain evaporates from a puddle on a hot sidewalk, or how it drains into the ground

- Why the class plant dried out, and what happened when it did
- How the days lengthen and shorten with the seasons
- Playground grass turning green in spring
- New birds in spring
- How plants around the building change with the seasons
- The moon appearing during the day
- The phases of the moon
- How the sun makes shadows

Such everyday events can be noticed and talked about during group times, routines, or free play. Talking can be done with one child or many. Discussions can be formal or informal, teacher-directed or child-initiated, as long as they allow the child to learn about the many wonders of nature/science that are part of their everyday world.

To give credit for 5.4, one example must be observed during the observation period, or there must be clear evidence that such events are used daily to help children understand the world. For example, children's pictures of nature/science events they have experienced are displayed; a displayed weather chart is filled in for each day of the month.

25.7.1 a Staff help children prepare pretzels as one of their weekly cooking activities.

25.7.1 b Children follow recipe cards to knead, cut, and roll pretzel dough.

25.7.1 c This child rolls a pretzel into a design.

25.7.1 d The teacher helps the children by baking the pretzels.

Indicator

7.1 ***Nature/science activities requiring more input from staff*** are those that require considerable supervision and/or direction to be completed. For example, a cooking activity would need a lot of input to be successful. It is unlikely that preschool-aged children would be able to follow a recipe to completion without significant help from staff. (See photos 25.7.1 a–d.) Similarly, simple experiments require quite a bit of staff guidance if children are to carry them out as needed to see the desired result.

Examples of such activities are provided in the General Information section for this item.

Give credit for 7.1 (score "Yes") if there is reliable evidence that such activities are done with children ***at least once every two weeks.*** Evidence from an activity or curriculum planning form (lesson plan) can be given credit *only* if the form is a reliable representation of what occurs during the observation. If there is little or no relationship between what is observed and what is on the lesson plan (i.e., nothing that is on the form ever seems to happen in the class) then do not use the form as evidence. If the form is reliable evidence, then give credit if such activities are listed once every two weeks.

If no reliable lesson plan can be used to determine whether credit should be given, ask staff the question listed for the indicator. If staff indicate that they do such activities, ask for further descriptions. If possible, ask to see materials used for such activities.

7.2 ***Books, pictures, and/or audio/visual materials*** can be used to supplement ***children's hands-on experiences*** with science/nature by providing additional information in a formal way. For example, children waiting for the eggs in their classroom to hatch might see a video showing how chicks hatch from eggs and then grow up into chickens. Or a book depicting the process might be used with the children. (See photos 25.7.2 a–c.) Materials used must be fact-based and provide accurate information.

If nature/science ***books, pictures, and/or audio/visual materials*** are present, to give credit for 7.2 they *must* be related to current hands-on activities that the children are experiencing. For example, accessible books about zoo animals would be considered in scoring 5.1. But if the books were accessible when children were going on a fieldtrip to the zoo as part of learning about zoo animals, then the books would also be considered in giving credit for this indicator. No credit

25.7.2 a Children use a teacher made book to care for their rabbit.

25.7.2 b The book uses words and pictures to explain what they must do.

25.7.2 c Each child is involved in following directions for feeding the rabbit.

Indicator

would be given if the children were not getting real experiences, related to the pictorial representation.

Other examples of relating nature/science books, pictures, and/or audio/visual materials to children's hands-on experiences include:

- Storybooks and factual books about fish are used when an aquarium is added to the room.
- Video about how snowflakes are formed is used when weather forecasts snow or after a snowfall.
- CD of bird songs is used when bird feeder is busy with birds.
- Poster of how seeds sprout is displayed next to seeds children have planted.
- Video of the children planting their garden is watched after the garden is in flower.

Give credit (score "Yes") for 7.2 if such use of materials is observed with hands-on nature/science experiences. If no evidence is observed, ask staff the question provided in the indicator, and score based on the response.

Calculating "Substantial Portion of the Day"

Example 1

This schedule is based on an observation period of 4.5 hours (from 8AM – 12:30PM) and information collected during the teacher interview about how unobserved time during the day is used and what is accessible to the children.

Time	Scheduled activity	Time to use nature/science materials
6:30 – 8:00	Breakfast in cafeteria and TV time for those who are finished with breakfast	
8:00 – 8:30	Children go to regular classrooms and play with table and rug toys (puzzles; legos; duplos with cars, people, and trucks; stringing beads and cards; pegboards)	
8:30 – 8:45	Prepare for breakfast/children wash hands	
8:45 – 9:15	Breakfast	
9:15 – 9:45	Circle (teacher reading time)	
9:45 – 10:45	Centers (housekeeping, art, sand and water, nature/science, writing table, blocks, music, computer and cozy book area)	**1 hour**
10:45 – 11:15	Outdoor play (gross motor activities only)	
11:15 – 12:15	Prepare for and eat lunch	
12:15 – 12:30	Story, put out cots, prepare for nap	
12:30 – 2:45	Nap	
2:45 – 3:00	Wake up from nap; bathroom	
3:00 – 3:25	Snack and story	
3:25 – 4:25	Centers (housekeeping, nature/science, writing table, computer, fine motor area and cozy book area)	**1 hour**
4:25 – 5:30	Outdoors or indoor gross motor	
5:30 – 6:30	Table and rug toys (puzzles; legos; duplos with cars, people, and trucks; stringing beads and cards; pegboards) Prepare for departure	

1. Figure the total number of hours that children are allowed to attend.

   (6:30AM to 6:30 PM = 12 hours)

2. Calculate 1/3 of the operating hours to determine "Substantial Portion of the Day."

   (12 hours ÷ 3 = 4 hours)

3. Add up all times that children have access to nature/science materials.

   (see shaded times on schedule = 2 hours)

4. Compare the amount of time children may have access to nature/science materials to the time requirement for substantial portion of the day. If the amount of time children may have access to nature/science materials is the same or greater, then score "Yes." If the amount of time is less than the time requirement for substantial portion of the day, then score "No." For example, the schedule above indicates:

   2 hours (access to nature/science materials) **is less than 4 hours** (time requirement for substantial portion of day), and therefore the time requirement for substantial portion of the day is not met.

Indicator

Calculating "Substantial Portion of the Day"

Example 2

This schedule is based on an observation period of 4 hours (from 9AM – 1PM) and information collected during the teacher interview about how unobserved time during the day is used and what is accessible to the children.

Time	Scheduled activity	Time to use nature/science materials
9:00 – 9:30	Arrival and centers open (cozy book area, computer, writing table, math, nature/science, and fine motor)	**30 minutes**
9:30 – 9:45	Snack	
9:45 – 10:00	Clean up snack/bathroom/wash hands	
10:00 – 11:00	Outside (gross motor activities and some dramatic play materials)	
11:00 – 11:45	Free choice of centers (fine motor, art, blocks, dramatic play, nature/science, math, sensory table, computer, writing table and cozy book area)	**45 minutes**
11:45 – 12:15	Large group activity (M,W,F is music/movement and T,Th is art activity)	
12:15 – 12:45	Prepare for and eat lunch	
12:45 – 1:00	Clean up/bathroom/prepare for quiet time	
1:00 – 1:45	Quiet time/quiet centers available (cozy book area, fine motor, math, and nature/science)	**45 minutes**
1:45 – 2:00	Clean up all centers and prepare for departure	

1. Figure the total number of hours that children are allowed to attend.

   (9 AM to 2 PM = 5 hours)

2. Calculate 1/3 of the operating hours to determine "Substantial Portion of the Day."

   (5 hours ÷ 3 = 1 hour and 40 minutes)

3. Add up all times that children have access to nature/science materials.

   (see shaded times on schedule = 2 hours)

4. Compare the amount of time children may have access to nature/science materials to the time requirement for substantial portion of the day. If the amount of time children may have access to nature/science materials is the same or greater, then score "Yes." If the amount of time is less than the time requirement for substantial portion of the day, then score "No." For example, the schedule above indicates:

   2 hours (access to nature/science materials) **is greater than 1 hour and 40 minutes** (time requirement for substantial portion of day), and therefore the time requirement for substantial portion of the day is met.

Calculating "Substantial Portion of the Day"

Example 3

This schedule is based on an observation period of 3.5 hours (from 9AM –12:30 PM) and information collected during the teacher interview about whether what was observed represents the typical daily practice.

Time	Scheduled activity	Time to use nature/science materials
9:00 – 9:20	Arrival/group time to discuss activities for the day	
9:20 – 9:45	Whole group art activity	
9:45 – 10:00	Whole group reading time (teacher directed)	
10:00 – 10:45	Outside time (gross motor activities only)	
10:45 – 11:30	Free choice of centers (fine motor, art, blocks, dramatic play, nature/science, math, sensory table, computer, writing table, blocks and books)	**45 minutes**
11:30 – 11:45	Clean up/bathroom/prepare for lunch time	
11:45 – 12:15	Prepare for and eat lunch	
12:15 – 12:30	Clean up/bathroom/prepare for departure	

1. Figure the total number of hours that children are allowed to attend.

   (9 AM to 12:30 PM = 3 hours and 30 minutes)

2. Calculate 1/3 of the operating hours to determine "Substantial Portion of the Day."

   (3 hours and 30 minutes ÷ 3 = 1 hour and 10 minutes)

3. Add up all times that children have access to nature/science materials.

   (see shaded times on schedule = 45 minutes)

4. Compare the amount of time children may have access to nature/science materials to the time requirement for substantial portion of the day. If the amount of time children may have access to nature/science materials is the same or greater, then score "Yes." If the amount of time is less than the time requirement for substantial portion of the day, then score "No." For example, the schedule above indicates:

   45 minutes (access to nature/science materials) **is less than 1 hour and 10 minutes** (time requirement for substantial portion of day), and therefore the time requirement for substantial portion of the day is not met.

26 Math/number

General information about this item

Most young children become interested in numbers and mathematics, if their math experiences have a purpose and match their abilities. Since the ability to understand abstract concepts (for example that a written number stands for a quantity) develops later in the early childhood and kindergarten years, interactions with numbers and math concepts should be through experiences with the concrete. To begin to understand math, and to build the foundation for later abstract mathematical learning, preschoolers need many hands-on opportunities to explore quantity, size, and shape. Such opportunities would be considered ***developmentally appropriate.***

Developmentally appropriate for math/number is defined in the "Notes for Clarification" on page 34 of the ECERS-R for this item in the scale.

In scoring this item, there are five categories to be considered when math/number materials and activities are observed. The categories are listed in the notes for the item, with some examples. Further definition, with additional ***developmentally appropriate*** examples, follows:

The categories of math materials are counting, measuring, comparing quantities, recognizing shapes, and materials that help children become familiar with written numbers. (See photos 26 A–D, next page.)

Counting:

- Teddy bears or other small objects to count
- Money in the dramatic play center
- Pegboards with numbers printed and holes to match
- Puzzles, toys, or games where quantities of objects (pictures or real) are matched to written numbers
- Beads and bead patterns
- Pegs to fill different numbers of pegboard holes
- Raisins or other ingredients that must be counted for cooking

Measuring:

- Measuring cups and spoons for sand/water, cooking, or housekeeping center
- Balance scale with things to weigh
- Rulers and tape measures with things to measure
- Thermometers

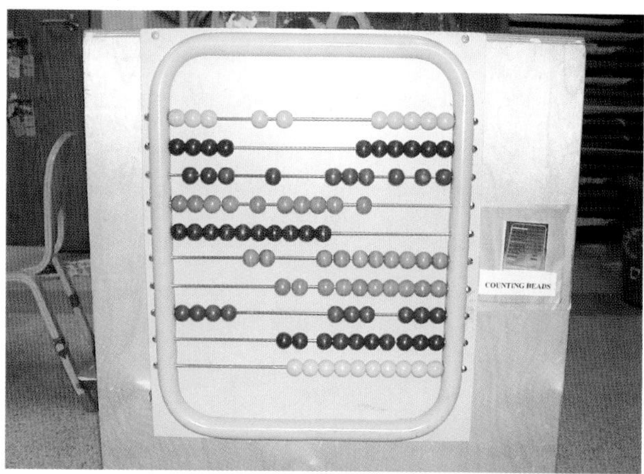

26 A Children use beads as a developmentally appropriate way to practice counting.

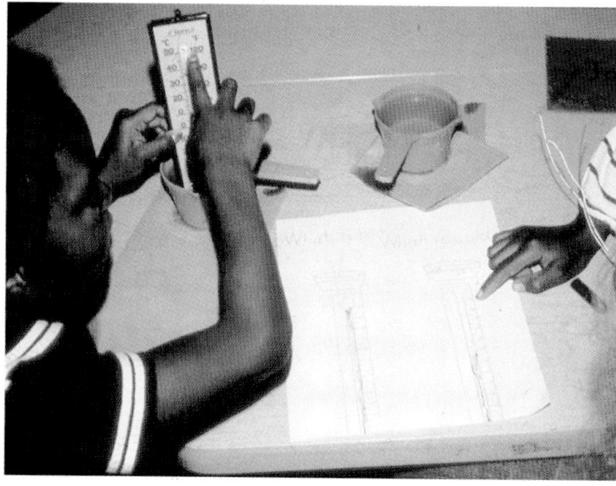

26 B Children learn how to measure temperature with a thermometer.

- Yardsticks or rulers on the woodworking bench
- Height chart
- Foot size measurer

Comparing quantities:

- Toys and games that require children to figure out "more and less"
- Cubes (interlocking or smooth) that stack up to various heights
- Nested cups
- Puzzles or three-dimensional graduated cylinders showing a sequene of different heights
- Chart and graph activities (see photos 26.7.1 a–b)
- Dominos
- Playing cards
- Abacus

26 C The child learns how to recognize different characteristics of shapes when using attribute blocks.

Recognizing shapes:

- Puzzles with different geometric shapes
- Geoboards (boards with pegs to which rubber bands are attached to make shapes)
- Unit blocks with outlines on shelves for organizing and matching shapes
- Attribute blocks (of different size, color, shape, thickness)
- Parquetry blocks
- Pattern or matching cards for any shape toys
- Magnetic shapes

26 D Children can become familiar with written numbers in their play.

Indicator

Becoming familiar with written numbers:

- Number puzzles
- Magnetic numbers
- Play telephones
- Dramatic play cash register with play money
- Number lotto
- Clocks
- Calendar
- Playing cards
- Number lacing cards
- Number books and posters

It should be noted that math worksheets are not listed here as math/number materials. Be sure to read the "Notes for Clarification" about developmentally appropriate math/number materials provided as part of the item in the ECERS-R.

Math materials, unlike materials used for block play, art, or house keeping, usually are not placed within a particular interest center. Instead, math materials appear in many interest centers throughout the room. For example, the dramatic play area may contain a cash register with play money so children have experiences counting. The nature/science interest area may contain a thermometer used for measuring and recording the indoor and outdoor temperatures each day. The fine motor area may contain puzzles with geometric shapes or numbers. The observer should look around the room carefully to find math materials because they might not be organized into a center.

Credit should be given for materials obviously designed for math learning (e.g., puzzle with graduated sizes of different shapes, pegboard with numbers printed and holes to match, balance scale with things to weigh, nested cups that require size recognition). To give credit for more generic materials (blocks, beads for stringing, sets of bears with many pieces) it must be observed that these materials are used for math learning.

A closer look at each indicator

1.1 ***Accessible*** means that children can reach and use materials by themselves. (See photos 26.1.1 a–d, next page.) For materials to be considered accessible, they must be within view of younger preschoolers (2½ to 4 years). For 4- and 5-year-old children, if materials are stored in closed spaces, they can be considered accessible only if it is observed that children can freely access and use the materials.

Score 1.1 "Yes" if no math/number materials, such as those described in the General Information section, are accessible to children at any time.

1.2 ***Rote counting*** means that children repeat the numbers in serial order without relating the words to what they actually mean. Rote counting is usually repetitive and automatic, not requiring much understanding. For example, children repeat after the teacher, "one, two, three" without understanding that each word represents a quantity. Counting, in which children are able to manipulate objects, is a more meaningful way for children to understand the relationship of numbers, counting and objects.

26 Math/number

Indicator

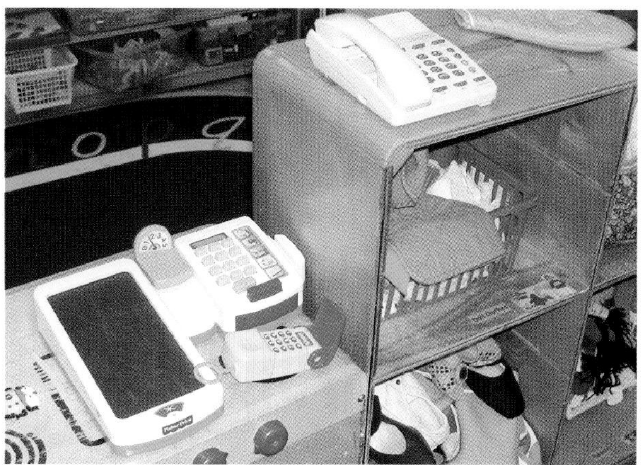

26.1.1 a Math materials that help children become familiar with written numbers in the dramatic play center are accessible—within view and easy reach of children.

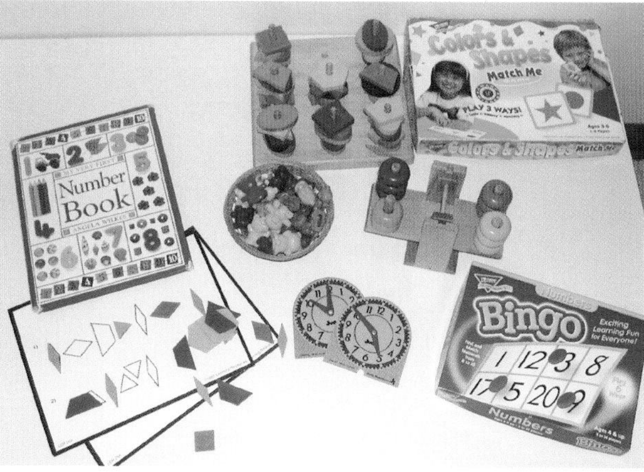

26.1.1 b. Math materials are accessible for children's use. These were collected from various areas of the room.

Math ***worksheets*** rarely provide young children with meaningful opportunities to learn about number concepts. They are usually too abstract for children to understand. They also require the ability to write or color neatly, frustrating most young children. Often children just scribble on the worksheets to be finished with an unpleasant chore.

Primarily, for this indicator, means most of the time. If rote counting and/or math worksheets make up the vast majority of the children's math/number learning experience, score 1.2 "Yes."

If rote counting and/or worksheets are used in the class, but *not* as the main experience to teach math/number to the children because there are developmentally appropriate experiences that outweigh the use of these less appropriate methods, then score 1.2 "No."

26.1.1 c A variety of math materials are stored on low shelves, which children can freely choose to use.

3.1 ***Some*** means approximately two different materials from at least three of the five categories listed in the General Information section for this item.

Be sure to see the "Notes for Clarification" listed on page 34 of the ECERS-R and the General Information section for the definition of ***developmentally appropriate*** math/number materials.

See 1.1 for the meaning of ***accessible***.

3.2 ***Accessible daily*** means that the math/number materials credited in 3.1 can be reached and used by children for at least 1 hour per day in a full-day program (give or take a few minutes), with very few exceptions. This does not require that all children are able to use these materials at the same time or that each child has a full hour to use the math/number materials. However, it is

26.1.1 d This math center has some accessible math materials to help children compare quantities and become familiar with written numbers.

Indicator

26.5.1 a Children choose to match number picture cards in this game.

26.5.1 b This game requires matching the interlocking shapes, as well as quantities to printed numbers.

required that children would have a reasonable chance to use materials at some time if they wished.

Less time is required for programs operating less than 8 hours a day, with the amount of time calculated proportionally, based on the ratio of 1 hour for programs of 8 hours or more. For example, if a program operates for 6 hours a day, this would be ¾ of a full-day program, so the time required would be ¾ of the 1 hour. If the program operates 4 hours a day, the requirement would be ½ hour.

The 1 hour can be provided all at one time or as a combination of several periods throughout the day. For example, math materials might be accessible to children for 30 minutes in the morning during free play time and then again for 30 minutes in the afternoon. The materials do not have to be provided as a free choice activity but must be accessible for this time period.

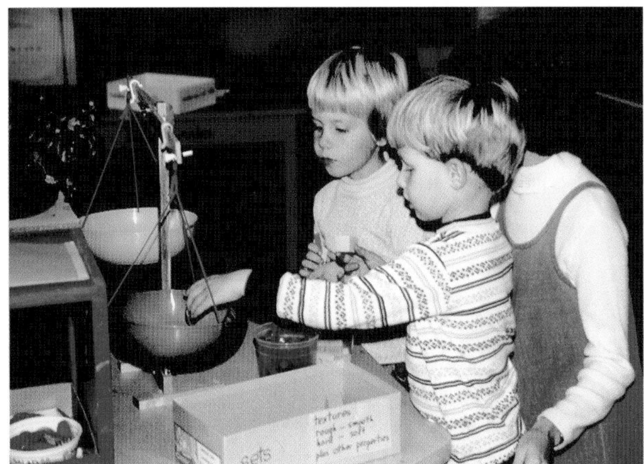

26.5.1 c Children compare the weight of two objects by using a simple balance scale.

5.1 ***Many*** means approximately three to five examples from each of the five categories described in the "Notes for Clarification" for this item, and discussed in the General Information section. However, this can vary, as long as all five categories are represented. In some cases you might give credit for more than three to five items of one type and less then three to five of another. (See photos 26.5.1 a–c.)

5.2 ***Accessible for a substantial portion of the day*** means that children can reach and use the math/number materials credited in 5.1 daily, for 1/3 of the program's operating hours. No credit can be given for 5.2 unless 5.1 is scored "Yes."

Consider materials both indoors and outdoors when deciding what can be given credit for being accessible for a substantial portion of the day. In piecing together accessibility of materials in various classrooms to give credit for substantial portion of the day (for example, including accessible materials in early AM classroom and regular classroom), the requirements for the materials in 5.1 must be met.

If outdoor time is included in calculating substantial portion of the day, materials from at least two categories must be accessible during the outdoor time credited.

See sample schedules demonstrating how to calculate substantial portion of the day for this item (on pages 276–278 at end of this item).

Indicator

5.3 ***Well-organized and in good condition*** means that the math/number materials have all pieces needed to use the materials, and that these are stored together in an orderly manner. For example, the teddy bear counters are all in the same container, and the container is stored near other containers of similar materials. The math materials do not have to be stored in an interest center designated only for "Math." Children should be able to easily reach and use these materials with little or no help from the staff. Shelves or containers should be organized and labeled with pictures and words, if necessary. (See photo 26.5.3.) The storage does not have to be perfectly neat, but children should not become frustrated when they are playing because materials are disorganized or incomplete, and they cannot find what they need. During clean up, children should be able to see where to return the materials.

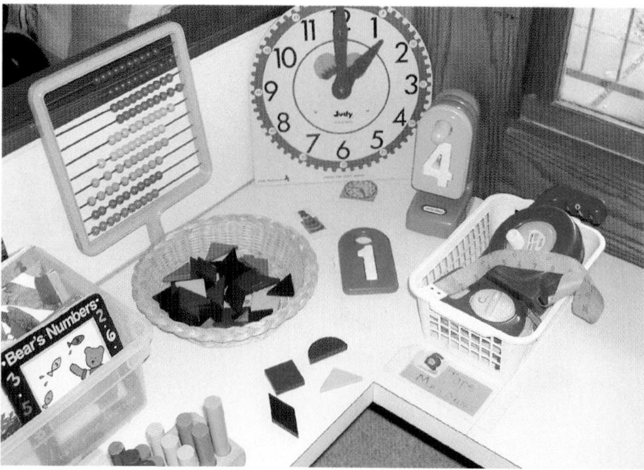

26.5.3 Children are more likely to use math materials if they are well organized and easy to locate in the room.

Most (about 3⁄4 of the materials; it is not necessary to count and be exact), but not all, materials should be well-organized as described to give credit for 5.3.

5.4 The intent of this indicator is for staff to link math and number to practical life events in the children's daily schedule. Therefore, listen for use of "number talk" (for example, using number words in conversations, talking about how much, how big, which part) or number experiences during meals or getting ready for meals (such as setting the table), time updates during transition times (5 more minutes till clean-up; 2 more minutes, etc.), using a timer to take turns, counting who is absent, etc.

Do *not* count play activities such as number games or computer games in determining the score for this indicator.

"Number talk" or number experiences as part of practical life events should be observed *more than once* during the observation to give credit for this indicator. These everyday events may take place during group time or during routines or free play. They may be teacher- or child-initiated, as long as they are part of informal daily events and allow the child to learn about math/number in some way that is developmentally appropriate

Informal opportunities to expose children to math occur as a natural part of daily activities, thus children can have many opportunities to become competent in math. These opportunities occur without any type of formal teaching. (See photos 26.5.4 a–b, next page.) More formal activities with educational materials, such as number games or computer games are not considered in this indicator. Consider the examples given in the scale as well as the examples listed below:

- While washing hands notice that the bubbles look like circles (the child learns about the different shapes).
- Have children look at the clock as staff tell them when certain events will be happening (learn about number symbols and measurement).
- While doing the calendar count how many more days until the weekend or a holiday or special occasion.
- Announce 5 minutes until clean up time, and let children know as the minutes pass.

Indicator

26.5.4 a Math is incorporated into gross motor play as the teacher and children count how many times they can dribble the ball.

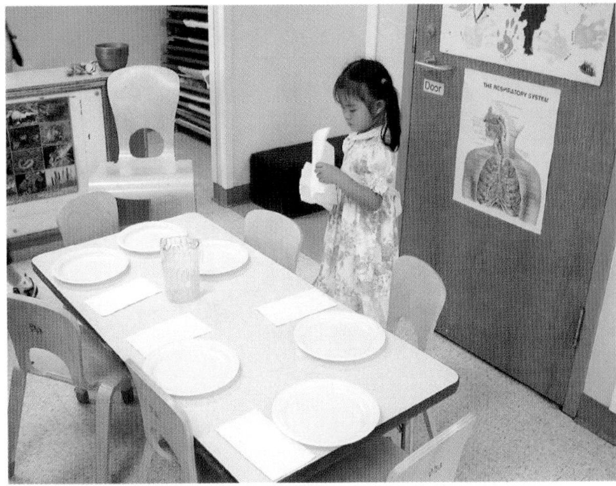

26.5.4 b This child learns about numbers as the teacher reminds her that each plate needs a napkin.

- Count how many steps it takes to get to the playground.
- Count steps as children go up or downstairs.
- Cut up snack and use the words for fractions (whole, half, third, quarter).
- Talk about what comes first, second, and so on when discussing what will be happening in the day.
- Have children count how many things are needed for the number of children who will participate.
- Talk about numbers when children are getting dressed to go outside. (How many shoes do we need to wear, how many coats?)
- Have a child help figure out how many paint brushes will be needed for the paint containers.

Give credit for 5.4 if during the observation, two or more examples of number talk or number experiences, such as those listed above, were observed.

7.1 ***Activities requiring more input from the staff*** provide children with new and challenging approaches to math concepts. Often such activities make use of accessible math materials, but staff show children how to use the materials to extend learning. At other times, the activities might go beyond accessible materials. To give credit, staff usually initiate the activities, or extend an activity that has been initiated by a child. (See photos 26.7.1 a–b, next page.) Examples of these activities are provided in the item on page 34 of the ECERS-R, and additional examples include:

- Encouraging children to sort teddy bear counters by color, and then determining which color has the most or least
- Helping children figure out how many measuring cups of water are needed to fill a quart-sized container
- Making a chart with children indicating the number of children who like riding the big or the little tricycles, and drawing conclusions about which is more popular
- Graphing the collections of objects located in the nature/science center

Indicator

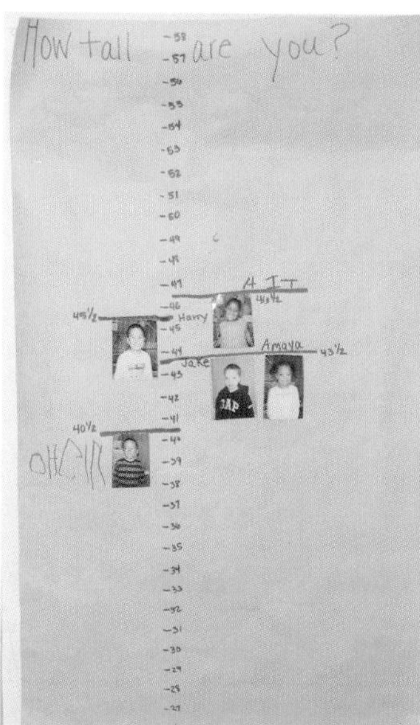

26.7.1 a Children can compare their heights with the heights of classmates by finding where they are on this chart.

26.7.1 b Kindergartners measure plants and record their height on a chart.

- Using rulers to measure all the tables in the room to determine which is the shortest and the longest
- Searching for the tallest and shortest pieces of furniture in the room
- Seeing how many big marbles it takes to fill a container; comparing with small marbles
- Determining which holes are easiest to throw bean bags into—big or small
- Following a simple recipe in cooking or making play dough, measuring the correct amounts

Simply having materials accessible for children to reach and use independently, or adding to those materials, does not meet the requirement for 7.1. To give credit, staff should set up activities to extend math/number learning, and add information to the children's experiences while allowing them to receive the benefits of learning through active involvement.

7.2 ***Materials are rotated*** means that the math/number materials that are accessible to children are changed so children can practice different skills, find new interests, and use materials that they have used before, but in a new way. Rotating materials keeps children from becoming bored with the choices they can make for play and adds new learning opportunities. (See photo 26.7.2, next page.)

Material rotation should occur when children no longer find those that are accessible interesting or challenging. The uninteresting materials should then be put away and different materials brought out. Math/number materials should also be rotated to provide new types of experiences and to relate to certain projects or themes.

Calling children's attention to a math material that is regularly accessible to children does not count as "rotating materials." For example, when staff take the

Indicator

rulers off the shelf where accessible toys are stored and place the rulers on the table with items for children to measure at free play time, credit for "rotation" is not given. Credit is given only when the math materials are removed from the accessible shelves in the classroom, and replaced with other materials that were formerly inaccessible.

Inaccessible materials can be made accessible as either special projects or for free play. The rotated math materials can be brought from storage or other classrooms or newly purchased.

To give credit, some materials should be rotated at least monthly. It is likely that to find out whether math/number materials are rotated, and how often this is done (if at all), the question provided on page 34 of the ECERS-R will need to be asked of staff.

26.7.2 When children need new challenges, this teacher replaces one set of math materials with another taken from storage.

Calculating "Substantial Portion of the Day"

Example 1

This schedule is based on an observation period of 4.5 hours (from 8AM – 12:30PM) and information collected during the teacher interview about how unobserved time during the day is used and what is accessible to the children.

Time	Scheduled activity	Time to use math materials
6:30 – 8:00	Breakfast in cafeteria and TV time for those who are finished with breakfast	
8:00 – 8:30	Children go to regular classrooms and play with table and rug toys (shape puzzles; legos; duplos with cars, people, and trucks; stringing beads with number cards; pegboards with numbers)	**30 minutes**
8:30 – 8:45	Prepare for breakfast/children wash hands	
8:45 – 9:15	Breakfast	
9:15 – 9:45	Circle (teacher reading time)	
9:45 – 10:45	Centers (housekeeping, art, sand and water, nature/science, math, writing table, blocks, music, computer and cozy book area)	**1 hour**
10:45 – 11:15	Outdoor play (gross motor activities only)	
11:15 – 12:15	Prepare for and eat lunch	
12:15 – 12:30	Story, put out cots, prepare for nap	
12:30 – 2:45	Nap	
2:45 – 3:00	Wake up from nap; bathroom	
3:00 – 3:25	Snack and story	
3:25 – 4:25	Centers (housekeeping, nature/science, writing table, computer, fine motor, math and cozy book area)	**1 hour**
4:25 – 5:30	Outdoors or indoor gross motor	
5:30 – 6:30	Table and rug toys (number puzzles; legos; duplos with cars, people, and trucks; stringing beads with number cards; pegboards with numbers) Prepare for departure	**1 hour**

1. Figure the total number of hours that children are allowed to attend.

   (6:30 AM to 6:30 PM = 12 hours)

2. Calculate 1/3 of the operating hours to determine "Substantial Portion of the Day."

   (12 hours ÷ 3 = 4 hours)

3. Add up all times that children have access to math materials.

   (see shaded times on schedule = 3 hours and 30 minutes)

4. Compare the amount of time children may have access to math materials to the time requirement for substantial portion of the day. If the amount of time children may have access to math materials is the same or greater, then score "Yes." If the amount of time is less than the time requirement for substantial portion of the day, then score "No." For example, the schedule above indicates:

   3 hours and 30 minutes (access to math materials) **is less than 4 hours** (time requirement for substantial portion of day), and therefore the time requirement for substantial portion of the day is not met.

Indicator

Calculating "Substantial Portion of the Day"

Example 2

This schedule is based on an observation period of 4 hours (from 9AM – 1PM) and information collected during the teacher interview about how unobserved time during the day is used and what is accessible to the children.

Time	Scheduled activity	Time to use math materials
9:00 – 9:30	Arrival and centers open (cozy book area, computer, writing table, math, science, and fine motor)	**30 minutes**
9:30 – 9:45	Snack	
9:45 – 10:00	Clean up snack/bathroom/wash hands	
10:00 – 11:00	Outside (gross motor activities and some dramatic play materials)	
11:00 – 11:45	Free choice of centers (fine motor, art, blocks, dramatic play, nature/science, math, sensory table, computer, writing table and cozy book area)	**45 minutes**
11:45 – 12:15	Large group activity (M,W,F is music/movement and T,Th is art activity)	
12:15 – 12:45	Prepare for and eat lunch	
12:45 – 1:00	Clean up/bathroom/prepare for quiet time	
1:00 – 1:45	Quiet time/quiet centers available (cozy book area, fine motor, math, and science)	**45 minutes**
1:45 – 2:00	Clean up all centers and prepare for departure	

1. Figure the total number of hours that children are allowed to attend.

   (9 AM to 2 PM = 5 hours)

2. Calculate 1/3 of the operating hours to determine "Substantial Portion of the Day."

   (5 hours ÷ 3 = 1 hour and 40 minutes)

3. Add up all times that children have access to math materials.

   (see shaded times on schedule = 2 hours)

4. Compare the amount of time children may have access to math materials to the time requirement for substantial portion of the day. If the amount of time children may have access to math materials is the same or greater, then score "Yes." If the amount of time is less than the time requirement for substantial portion of the day, then score "No." For example, the schedule above indicates:

   2 hours (access to math materials) **is greater than 1 hour and 40 minutes** (time requirement for substantial portion of day), and therefore the time requirement for substantial portion of the day is met.

Indicator

Calculating "Substantial Portion of the Day"

Example 3

This schedule is based on an observation period of 3.5 hours (from 9AM –12:30 PM) and information collected during the teacher interview about whether what was observed represents the typical daily practice.

Time	Scheduled activity	Time to use math materials
9:00 – 9:20	Arrival/group time to discuss activities for the day	
9:20 – 9:45	Whole group art activity	
9:45 – 10:00	Whole group reading time (teacher-directed)	
10:00 – 10:45	Outside time (gross motor activities only)	
10:45 – 11:30	Free choice of centers (fine motor, art, blocks, dramatic play, nature/science, math, sensory table, computer, writing table, blocks and books)	**45 minutes**
11:30 – 11:45	Clean up/bathroom/prepare for lunch time	
11:45 – 12:15	Prepare for and eat lunch	
12:15 – 12:30	Clean up/bathroom/prepare for departure	

1. Figure the total number of hours that children are allowed to attend.

   (9 AM to 12:30 PM = 3 hours and 30 minutes)

2. Calculate 1/3 of the operating hours to determine "Substantial Portion of the Day."

   (3 hours and 30 minutes ÷ 3 = 1 hour and 10 minutes)

3. Add up all times that children have access to math materials.

   (see shaded times on schedule = 45 minutes)

4. Compare the amount of time children may have access to math materials to the time requirement for substantial portion of the day. If the amount of time children may have access to math materials is the same or greater, then score "Yes." If the amount of time is less than the time requirement for substantial portion of the day, then score "No." For example, the schedule above indicates:

   45 minutes (access to math materials) **is less than 1 hour and 10 minutes** (time requirement for substantial portion of day), and therefore the time requirement for substantial portion of the day is not met.

27 Use of TV, video, and/or computers

General information about this item

Use of TV, video, and/or computers (called audio/visual materials or AV) are not considered absolutely necessary in preschool programs. If used in a developmentally appropriate manner, audio-visual technology can supplement children's regular hands-on experiences, adding information to what children are learning, and providing another type of experience for the children. However, the types of activities associated with audio/visual technology often require passive, rather than active, involvement, sedentary behavior, limited learning opportunities, forced participation, and few opportunities to practice important social skills. Children in our society tend to get plenty of "TV time" in their homes. Therefore, this item requires that activities of this type are restricted in preschool and kindergarten care and education settings.

Since it is not required that AV materials are used in a preschool/kindergarten environment, this item concentrates on ensuring that, if used, they are used in a developmentally appropriate manner, adding to children's experiences, rather than limiting them in any way. Therefore, as stated in the item, if no such materials are ever used with the children, the item can be scored "NA" (not applicable). However, before making assumptions about whether the item applies to a classroom, be sure to ask staff the questions provided in the ECERS-R for the item.

When scoring this item, consider *all* audio/visual materials used with children including television programs, movies, videos, and/or computer software. If you do not see a television or computer during the observation, make sure to ask the teacher if any of these materials are ever used. For example, some early childhood programs have a computer lab that children use only once a week or they may only watch movies/videos once a month, and this most probably will not be observed during an observation. This item must be scored if the classroom uses these materials *at all* regardless of frequency. If you are unable to observe children using these materials, use the questions provided in the ECERS-R to get more information to score this item.

A closer look at each indicator

1.1 ***Developmentally appropriate*** means that the materials and activities are right for the ages and interests of the children, do not encourage anti-social learning, or compromise the emotional security of any child in the group.

As noted in the examples provided in the indicator on page 35 of the ECERS-R, materials that contain graphic ***violence, frightening, or sexually explicit*** content are not considered appropriate for any preschool/kindergarten children. (See photo 27.1.1.) Children of this age often cannot

27.1.1 Videos that are frightening are not considered appropriate in the early childhood program.

Indicator

distinguish between imaginary and real occurrences, and therefore, can find violence upsetting. Young children empathize with imaginary people, animals, or other creatures that are depicted as the victims of violence and may become concerned for their own safety. Unfortunately, many children's videos or television programs contain violence and are therefore inappropriate, even though they have been created for the children's market. This may include some natural wildlife productions and cartoons. In addition, because children are not able to separate fantasy from reality, they are apt to copy violent acts depicted in audio/visual materials. This can lead to anti-social, aggressive behaviors within the classroom.

Of course, not all children respond negatively when exposed to such materials, but chances are that some might do so. It is the responsibility of the early childhood program to protect *all* children from such exposure. There are many appropriate materials that should be used in place of the inappropriate ones.

Materials that depict a biased or prejudiced attitude towards any group of people (race, culture, religion, ability, gender, profession, etc.) are not considered to be ***culturally sensitive***, and are also considered inappropriate in this indicator. These are materials that present certain groups only in a negative way. Children get definite messages from the audio/visual materials they are exposed to. They may not yet be able to put these messages into words, but they still learn them. Therefore, staff must carefully select materials to encourage children towards pro-social rather than anti-social behavior.

Audio/visual materials are also considered inappropriate when they require too much or too little of the children in terms of challenge. For example, a full-length movie is likely to be inappropriate for all children in a group because it would be too long. Or a computer game designed for toddlers might not challenge computer-knowledgeable kindergarten children. Materials used should be interesting for the children, and not frustrating.

In scoring Indicators 1.1 and also 3.1, be sure to judge the appropriateness of all audio/visual materials used with the children. This includes videos or computer games brought from children's homes, if these materials are used with the group. Ask staff if any requirements for appropriateness are considered when materials are selected or brought from home. Ask if staff are familiar with the content of all materials *before* allowing use in the program. Use the questions provided on page 35 of the ECERS-R as part of this item.

To score 1.1 "No" there should be *no* inappropriate materials used with the children. If any inappropriate materials are used, score 1.1 "Yes."

Note that some flexibility can be used in scoring with regard to appropriateness of difficulty level. If the difficulty level does not exactly match the children in the group, but this would not create problems for the children, then this would not contribute to a score of "Yes."

1.2 An ***alternative activity*** is one that children are allowed to do if they do not wish to participate in an audio/visual activity, such as watching television or using the computer. Alternative activities can include any other option that the child would prefer to the audio/visual activity. It cannot be something that the child would not prefer, such as sitting at a table with nothing to do or resting quietly on a cot. The alternative activity cannot serve as a punishment for not participating in the

Indicator

audio/visual activity. (See photo 27.1.2.) The activity may be free choice or teacher-initiated. For example, alternative activities might include:

- Quiet activities, such as looking at a book, doing a puzzle,painting at the easel, or drawing pictures
- Choices of any activity areas (active or quiet) in the classroom
- Going outside for active play (with supervision, of course)
- Participating in activities in another classroom

Children should be allowed to leave the audio/visual activity to do the alternate activity whenever they want, whether it is at the very beginning or part way through when they have become bored or restless.

27.1.2 All children must watch TV together, with "time out" in a chair as the only other option.

Sometimes children are not required to participate in the audio/visual activity, but they are not given anything of interest to do instead. They may wander around without being allowed to use any materials or they may play with a friend's hair. This type of option is *not* considered an alternative activity for this item.

If audio/visual materials are used during the observation period, base the score on what is observed. However, if this type of activity is not directly observed, scoring should be based on how staff answer the question provided for 1.2.

If at least one alternative activity is provided, score 1.2 "No." If there is no choice for an alternative activity, score 1.2 "Yes."

3.1 Materials that are violent and not culturally sensitive are discussed in 1.1.

In order to receive credit for this indicator (score "Yes") *all* of the materials considered for this item must be ***nonviolent and culturally sensitive.***

3.2 ***Accessible*** means that children can reach and use materials by themselves. For materials to be considered accessible, they must be within view of younger preschoolers (2½ to 4 years). For older children (4 to 6 years), if materials are stored in closed spaces, they can be considered accessible only if it is observed that children can freely access and use the materials.

Alternative activities are discussed in 1.2. This indicator requires that *two or more* alternative activities are accessible for children to choose while the television (including video) or computer is being used.

In order to give credit for this indicator (score "Yes"), the alternatives must be accessible as a clear choice that carries no negative message.

3.3 The intent of this indicator is to ensure that children participate in active play in which they can be creative, imaginative, move around, and have hands-on experiences with real materials rather than spending inordinate amounts of time watching TV, video, or playing computer games. In other words, the time children can spend using audio/visual materials is ***limited***.

The amount of time given in the example of this indicator is a general indication of a required time limitation, and can vary. When deciding whether adequate limits are set on the amount of time children can use the computer, consider not only how long each child's turn is, but also the number of turns each child is allowed to have, and if children spend time watching others at the computer. Computer time should be relatively short, compared to other activities. Observe to see whether time limits are enforced.

Indicator

27.5.1 a Cartoons that do not enhance children's learning and understanding are not considered good for children. All computer software should be developmentally appropriate.

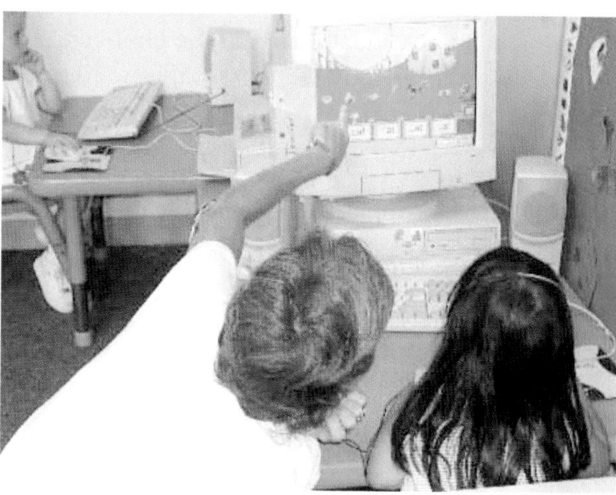

27.5.1 b Computer software that encourages children to make choices, like this pre-reading program, is considered educational.

5.1 Materials can be developmentally appropriate, in terms of meeting the requirements provided in 1.1 of this item. However, they might not be considered ***"good for children."*** For example, a children's cartoon might not be frightening, violent, sexually explicit, or show bias, and it might not be too complex or too simple for the children viewing it. Yet, it might not add much to children's development, such as to their vocabulary or understanding of the world. (See photo 27.5.1 a.)

Certain materials are developed specifically to enhance children's learning and understanding. These are considered more educational and "good for children." (See photo 27.5.1 b.)

Examples of such materials are provided in the indicator on page 35 of the ECERS-R. Other examples might include:

- Video version of a story that is considered children's literature
- Computer software that introduces preschoolers to science and math in a developmentally appropriate way
- Exercise video for children to follow
- Video showing how familiar things such as crayons or bread are made
- Video that supports a project or unit children are doing

To score 5.1 "Yes," all materials used with children must be considered "good for children."

5.2 ***Free choice*** is part of free play which, according to the ECERS-R, means that the "child is permitted to select materials and companions, and as far as possible manage play independently. Adult interaction is in response to the child's needs. Situations in which the children are assigned to centers by staff, or staff select the materials that individual children may use do not count as free play." For more information on free choice or free play, see Item 35, Free play (page 367).

Free choice activities are those that children can select and carry out. The range of activities usually includes different types of play experiences offered to children, such as those listed in the Activities section of the ECERS-R (e.g., fine motor, art,

Indicator

blocks, music, science, math, books, sand/water), or active physical play.

Many means that these activities include enough different types of play so that all children get to do things that are interesting to them, and they have the possibility of many kinds of experiences.

Computer used as one of many such activities means that there are many options for children to choose from, they make the choice themselves, and the computer is one of those possible choices. (See photo 27.5.2.) Staff should offer enough materials so children have choices other than the computer, and each can find something of interest within what is accessible. If this is true, score 5.2 "Yes."

27.5.2 Once children know how to use the computer properly, it is offered as one of many free choice activities.

Score 5.2 "No" if the computer is used only as a whole group activity, if children must use the computer as an assignment by staff, or if it is one of just a few choices, rather than many.

Score this indicator "NA" only when computers are not used at all with the children. If there is a computer in the classroom that none of the children use, ask if the computer is for the children's use and if it is working. If the computer is only for the teachers or if it is broken, score this indicator "NA."

5.3 ***Active involvement*** means that children participate in the audio/visual experience by either thinking and making decisions or by physically moving in response to the opportunities offered by the material being used. Some examples of how children can be actively involved are provided in the indicator. Others include:

- Playing musical instruments along with a music video
- Using the mouse to draw a picture on the computer
- Pausing a video at certain spots and guessing what will happen next
- Solving problems presented in computer software that go beyond simply clicking to make something happen, without much thought
- Following dance steps that a character on the television is doing
- Doing the movements to finger plays demonstrated on a video
- Acting out the story later, that was shown on a video

If children simply sit and watch without actively participating in some way, credit cannot be given. The simple act of using the equipment (for example turning on the TV, putting in a video, starting up the computer and moving the mouse), does not count as encouraging active involvement.

Most means that the *vast majority* of materials considered for this item (but not necessarily all), and those used most often with the children, encourage active involvement.

5.4 For ***staff*** to be ***actively involved*** in the use of audio/visual materials requires more than making selections of the materials for children to use and getting the hardware started. These basic actions would not be considered active involvement. Furthermore, simply watching a video with the children without adding additional information or activities to supplement the AV material does not meet the requirements.

Indicator

This indicator requires more action and thinking on the part of staff, and more interaction with the children to extend learning from the computer, television, or other AV. (See photo 27.5.4.) Some examples of active involvement by staff are provided in the indicator. Other examples include:

27.5.4 Staff show children how to use educational software before allowing independent use, and remain involved even after children learn.

- Doing exercises with children to an exercise video
- Helping child think through problems presented in computer software
- Discussing the content of the computer software with the child
- Asking the child to explain how to use software
- Helping the child teach another child how to use AV materials
- Noticing the content of computer software a child is using and showing child a related book or activity
- Stopping the video periodically to discuss what will happen
- Playing a game with a child on the computer if no other children are interested in playing

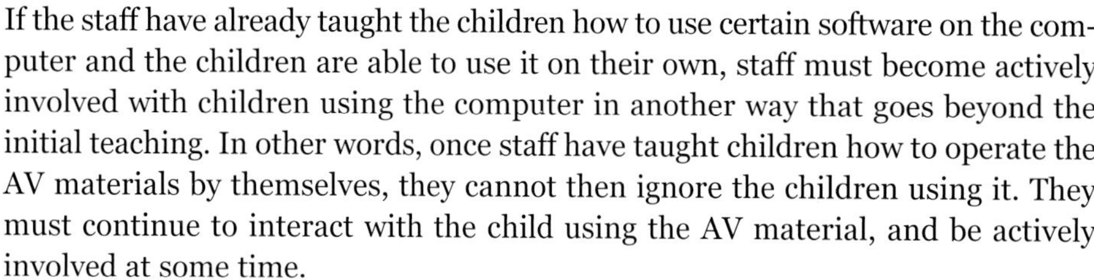

If the staff have already taught the children how to use certain software on the computer and the children are able to use it on their own, staff must become actively involved with children using the computer in another way that goes beyond the initial teaching. In other words, once staff have taught children how to operate the AV materials by themselves, they cannot then ignore the children using it. They must continue to interact with the child using the AV material, and be actively involved at some time.

If AV materials are observed being used, score 5.4 based on whether the staff are actively involved with the children at least for some time. Involvement does not have to be lengthy, but there must be some depth in terms of teaching and presenting children with learning opportunities. If no AV is observed being used, but staff have reported some use, ask what their role usually is while children use AV materials such as the computer, TV, or video.

7.1 For computer software to ***encourage creativity*** in children, it must do more than simply have children "point and click" to get a response, and it must encourage thinking, rather than rote responses. The examples provided in the indicator demonstrate the type of software that is required to give credit for 7.1.

This does not mean that this is the only type of computer software used with the children, but to score 7.1 "Yes," such software must be an option that is used regularly, for example, once a week or more frequently.

Indicator 7.1 should be scored "NA" if computer software is not used in the group being observed.

7.2 ***Classroom themes and activities*** are also known as "units" or "projects." Themes highlight special content in the curriculum through discussions and related activities. For example, in spring, the class might explore how plants begin growing at this time of year; in summer, they might pay special attention to what happens at the beach or lake. Themes, units, or projects usually take advantage of children's natural interests and help children better understand the world they live in. Typical themes include animals (zoo, farm, pets, insects, frogs, fish), community helpers, where we live, or the seasons and holidays, but there are as many possibilities as there are interests among children and staff. Classroom themes go beyond the daily learning that occurs in the classroom, such as learning numbers or colors, or practicing fine motor skills.

For AV materials to ***extend and support*** classroom themes and activities means that the materials are used specifically to provide information on the topic of interest. Examples of such use are provided in the indicator. Other examples include:

- CD or video about musical instruments when children are exploring the types of musical instruments
- Video on how bread is made when children are studying nutrition, and making their own bread
- Video about thunderstorms played as children study weather
- Videos showing what different community helpers do during community helper theme
- Computer game that helps children practice math as specific concepts are introduced
- Computer software that allows children to find pictures of different trucks when vehicles are studied

In order to get credit for this indicator, staff must use the AV materials to expand on and develop what is already being focused on in class. This is not required as part of every theme, unit, or project done with the class, but if not observed, staff must report using such materials occasionally, for example, at least four times a year.

28 Promoting acceptance of diversity

General information about this item

Diversity in the ECERS-R refers to the differences found in groups of people with regard to race, religion, culture, ability, age, or gender. For example, all races of people do not look the same, in terms of features and skin color. People of different cultures will have different kinds of interaction styles, languages, and traditions. Unfortunately, many people tend to discriminate against one group or another, leading to incorrect assumptions about members of a group, unfair treatment of people in those groups, and closed attitudes about differences. Such attitudes cause many problems in our world's societies.

Young children are not born with attitudes that cause them to discriminate against others. However, they quickly learn such attitudes as they watch and learn from what others do and say. A child who is exposed to messages saying that certain differences are bad, soon learns to believe in and act according to those messages.

Thus, in an attempt to encourage children to view others as individuals, without preconceived notions; to see a positive side to differences, rather than a negative one; and to focus on similarities rather than on differences, high quality early childhood education provides experiences to encourage ***acceptance of diversity***.

Acceptance of diversity means that instead of viewing differences as a negative, they are seen as strengths, adding more flavor to life, allowing all to contribute in unique ways. Children learn that differences among groups exist and can be respected and enjoyed, rather than feared and disliked. In addition, there is a focus on the similarities that bind us together as humans, rather than a concentration on how we differ.

In addition to this item, issues related to acceptance of diversity are found in other items of the scale. For example, aspects of accepting diversity come up in assessing the quality of dramatic play, music, and books and pictures. However, this is the primary item in the ECERS-R that looks at how well a program does in counteracting the growth of bias and encouraging constructive social attitudes.

The item focuses on the environmental messages that children receive about different people in the world's societies. It considers the images that children experience as they participate in the program and also whether overt prejudice is handled appropriately.

In some programs where there is little or no diversity represented in the children or staff, people often think that there is no need to represent diversity in materials. Staff may say that since there is only one group represented in the children in their classroom, they do not need to show anyone else in their materials. Certainly this gives the children a chance to see themselves represented, but it does not encourage learning about and accepting diversity. Therefore, *the requirements of*

Indicator

28.1.1 a All of these dolls are of one race so that children are unable to see the diversity among people represented in dolls.

28.1.1 b There is no racial diversity shown in these dolls, either.

this item apply to all programs, whether they include or do not include variation in staff and children.

A closer look at each indicator

1.1 The ***materials*** considered in this indicator include all pictorial materials, all toys, and all print and AV materials used by or with the children. Guidance for assessing the diversity in materials is provided in the "Notes for Clarification" on page 36 in the ECERS-R. Examples of the types of things to look for are included in the indicator.

For ***materials*** to ***show racial diversity*** means that more than one of the races or ethnic groups from the various continents are represented in some way. (See photos 28.1.1 a–b.) For ***materials*** to ***show cultural diversity*** means that the traditions of at least two different groups are represented in some way.

A careful assessment of all materials is required to score. For example, books must be opened and flipped through, all puzzles should be examined, and the block area should be searched for small people that might represent different races.

However, for diversity to be ***visible*** in the materials means that the observer should *not* have to search beyond what would be obvious to the children as they use the materials. For example, one picture showing diversity, found in a magazine at the bottom of a stack in the art center, would not be readily obvious to the children. An easy-to-see displayed picture, or a picture in a book easily accessible to children would be considered *visible.*

To score 1.1 "No," there must at least one example of diversity, that would be obvious to the children, found in the materials observed throughout the classroom. This can be visible within a single material (such as several races represented in a poster), or as a combination of two or more separate materials (such as two baby dolls, each representing a different race).

Note that the example observed to score "No" can show either cultural *or* racial diversity; both are not needed to score "No."

If no examples are found, score 1.1 "Yes."

Indicator

1.2 For this item, a ***stereotype*** is a standardized mental picture that is held about any group, representing an oversimplified view of the individuals within that group. Stereotypes cause people to say, "Everyone in that group is like that," without considering individual characteristics. Examples of stereotypes include:

- "Blonds" are dumb.
- Men/boys are strong; women/girls are weak.
- Old people are not competent.
- Fat people are lazy.
- Poor people steal things.
- Indians wear feathers and use bows and arrows.

28.1.2 If these puzzles were the only images children saw of people from different countries, they would get the message that the people always dress in this way. Other materials are needed to balance this.

Obviously these are not true statements, because if we look at the individuals within these groups, there would be little evidence to support such ideas. Yet, people make assumptions according to stereotypes, causing unfair treatment of many.

Stereotyped images are common in society, and can be found in the materials present in preschool classrooms. (See photo 28.1.2.) Many are seen in old materials that are not up-to-date in terms of current social beliefs and practices. For example, out-of-date pictures of people in jobs often systematically show men in certain roles (professionals, roles associated with physical strength) and women in others (stay-at-home-moms, nurses, teachers). In our current world, any of these pictures would be fine for preschoolers as long as they were balanced with the alternatives as well, for example, men as stay-at-home parents and women as doctors.

There are many stereotypes shown in children's toys, as well. For example, the traditional "Cowboys and Indians" toys depict both groups superficially, implying that members of the groups only fight with and kill the other. Certainly, this is a limited view of Cowboys and Indians, which does not represent the more positive things that group members might do, either from a historical or current point of view.

To score, look for stereotyped portrayals in all materials used by children. If groups of people are represented *only* as stereotypes, score 1.2 "Yes."

1.3 ***Prejudice*** means negative treatment of a group, or individuals within a group, because of an oversimplified view of the group's characteristics. The group or the individual is not judged by real evidence, but rather by pre-conceived notions of what they will be like. Examples of prejudiced thinking include:

- She cannot do the job because she is a woman.
- He cannot learn because he is an African-American.
- She is Jewish, so I cannot be her friend.
- Children with disabilities cannot function well in the group.
- They are stupid because they do not speak English.
- People of that culture do not care for their children well.

It is easy to observe extremely obvious prejudice, but far more difficult to know when more subtle prejudice is being shown. It is difficult to discern whether a behavior is a sign of true prejudice, shows insensitivity about some issues, or is the

Indicator

product of an over-sensitive interpretation by the observer. For example, if a child in a minority group appears to get less attention than other children, is this caused by prejudice on the part of staff, or by other reasons? It could be that the observer is very sensitive to children from minority groups being treated unfairly, and so does not notice that there are many other non-minority children in the group who also get less attention than some favorites. It might also be that the child is truly getting less attention for some reason that is not attached to being in a minority group. However, it is also possible that active prejudice is occurring in the class. It is up to the observer to look at *all* the evidence, before scoring.

Sometimes it might appear that staff are acting with prejudice, when in fact their behaviors are due to a lack of sensitivity about what is considered correct (political correctness) in our society. For example, in high-quality early childhood programs, it is not considered appropriate to ask children to sit "Indian style" because this is stereotyping the way in which Native Americans sit. It is likely to be insulting to someone who is a Native American. Many staff prefer the term "crisscross applesauce" to remind children to sit on the floor with their legs crossed because it is not potentially offensive. However, naïve use of such commonly used terms cannot be considered prejudiced behavior unless a person intends to be offensive and insulting.

If, during the observation, including the staff questioning time, staff say or do anything that is an *obvious, clear* act of prejudice against others (either children or other adults), score 1.3 "Yes."

However, the observer should be cautioned to consider all evidence. What may appear to be prejudice might actually be a lack of knowledge on the part of the staff or an overly sensitive response on the observer's part. If in doubt about an instance that might be considered prejudiced, asking a question to get clarification from staff without accusing, might help in making a scoring decision.

3.1 ***Racial and cultural diversity in materials*** is discussed in 1.1. Examples are provided in the indicator. ***Some*** means at least one example of racial diversity and one example of cultural diversity is observed. One of each must be present to score "Yes."

The examples must be easily seen by the children, and in the space that is used for a large part of the day, to give credit. For example, they must be located in the classroom where children spend most of their time, rather than in the hallway, or in another classroom used for a short period. (See photos 28.3.1 a–b, next page.)

3.2 Diversity in materials can be shown positively or negatively. Positive images give good messages about the characteristics of people; negative images give the opposite. For example, if toy soldier figures are only shown as people who use weapons to kill, and this is not balanced with other materials that show the wide range of soldiers' roles (protecting, helping others, as family members, in other job assignments), children see only one message about what soldiers do—they kill others. Similarly, if members of certain groups are shown only as being poor, in certain types of jobs, or as people who take part in illegal activities, these are also negative portrayals of diversity.

Materials show diversity in a positive way requires that the messages about people depicted are good and do not stereotype members of any group. People are shown as humans who are pleasant, capable, and to be valued. (See photo 28.3.2, next page.)

Indicator

28.3.1 a Books show both racial and cultural diversity for children in the class.

28.3.1 b Racial diversity is represented with the dolls children can play with.

Score 3.2 “No” if any examples of negative images are included in the materials used by the children. Score “Yes” if all images are positive.

28.3.2 These small people toys found in the block area show diversity in a positive way.

3.3 The meaning of ***prejudice*** is discussed in 1.3. For staff to ***intervene appropriately to counteract prejudice*** requires that:

- Staff do not ignore any prejudice that they observe.
- Staff are aware of situations involving possible prejudice (e.g., child who speaks another language, child with disability, child whose family celebrates different holidays from those of others in the group), and give those situations special attention.
- Staff take action when they observe prejudiced behavior, either by children or other adults, and make it clear that such talk and/or behavior is not acceptable. Examples are provided in the indicator.

It is more likely that staff will respond to prejudice being shown by children in the class. The most constructive response staff can have with children is to stop behavior and discuss it in simple terms, explaining why it is not acceptable. Children should be helped to see the feelings of others and the effects of their actions. Modeling the appropriate behavior is very effective as well. (See photo 28.3.3.)

28.3.3 In this program, children representing diverse groups get along very well because staff consistently help children better understand one another.

It is more difficult for staff to handle the prejudice shown by other adults. However, this must be handled if prejudice by adults comes up during the observation. For example, a parent might say to the staff, “Well,

Indicator

28.5.1 a These puzzles represent the categories of diversity positively.

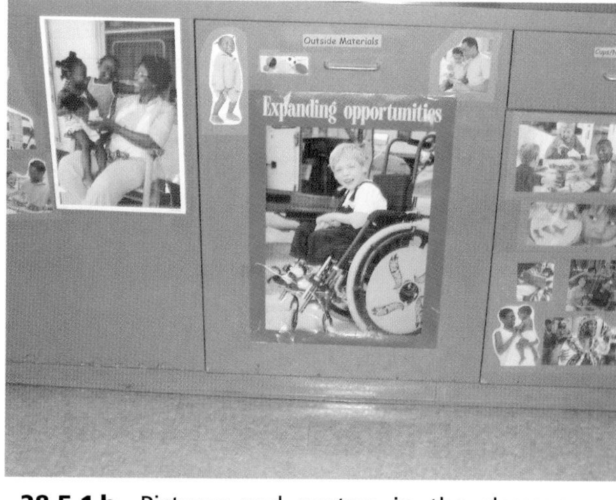

28.5.1 b Pictures and posters in the classroom show a range of diversity.

28.5.1 c Puppets represent diversity in race, gender, and ability.

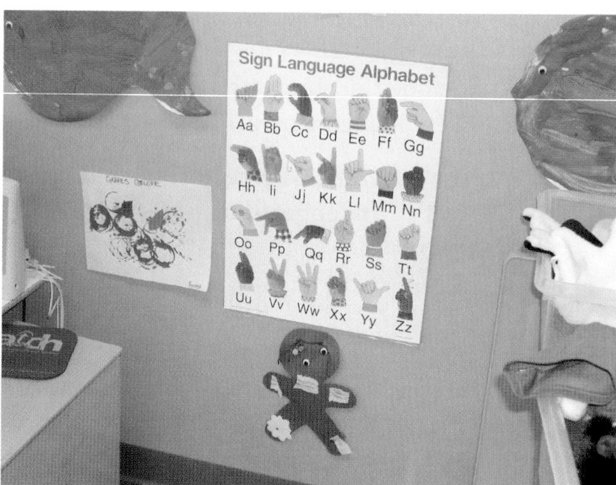

28.5.1 d This poster represents diversity in ability.

what do you expect of the child? Those people are always like that!" In this case, the teacher would be required to discuss the inappropriateness of such a statement with the offending adult, making it clear that prejudice is not shared or tolerated. This would have to be handled in a nonconfrontational, constructive, professional manner.

If ***no prejudice*** is observed, and the observer sees plenty of evidence that such behavior would be very unlikely, score 3.3 "Yes."

If prejudice is observed during the observation and staff are (or should be) aware of it, score 3.3 "No" if staff do not intervene appropriately.

5.1 Information about ***materials*** considered in this item (including books and pictures) is discussed in 1.1 and 3.1. ***Accessible*** means that children can reach and easily use the materials (books and toys) or if materials are displayed, they are easily visible to the children.

Stereotype is defined in 1.2. ***Non-stereotyping roles*** require that people are shown in their roles with no assumptions or oversimplifications made regarding individuals within any group. Examples are provided in the indicator.

Indicator

Many means that there are enough examples so that it is *easy* for the observer (and children) to experience some of them, without having to complete a difficult search. In looking at displayed materials, dolls and people figures, puzzles and other pictorial toys/games, and some of the books that children are most likely to use, the presence of diversity should be obvious. (See photos 28.5.1 a–d, preceding page.) For example, the observer should not have to search through 30 books to find one picture showing diversity. However, the observer does need to look at all the materials generally accessible to the children for their use.

For this indicator, there need to be ***many*** books, ***many*** pictures, and ***many*** materials accessible to the children, and *all* categories of diversity listed in the indicator (races, cultures, ages, abilities, gender) need to be included to some degree. However, there do *not* need to be many examples of each category.

Materials must be located in spaces children use for most of the day, such as their main classroom. If no main classroom is assigned to the group being observed, materials in all spaces used should be considered to score.

Materials located in spaces used only for relatively short periods (e.g., hallways, entry way, lunch room, early AM or late PM classroom) are not counted to meet the requirements of this indicator.

No specific required number of examples is provided, because this will vary based on the obviousness of the materials and number of children in the group.

5.2 ***Props*** are materials children use in their dramatic or pretend play. For information on props, see Item 24, Dramatic play.

This indicator requires that props for dramatic play include items that represent different cultures. Examples are given in the indicator. Additional examples include:

- Dress up clothing representing different countries and customs, such as hats, shoes, pants, shirts, and dresses
- Puppets representing people of different cultures
- Small toy people representing various ethnic groups, for use with blocks
- Play food representing different cultures
- Baby carriers from different cultures
- Play money from different countries
- Pieces of fabric or blankets typical of different cultures
- Real equipment used by people with disabilities
- Equipment for dolls representing certain disabilities

To give credit (score "Yes"), more than two examples must be observed. The examples must be accessible and obvious within the props children regularly use for dramatic play, either indoors or outdoors. (See photos 28.5.2 a–c.)

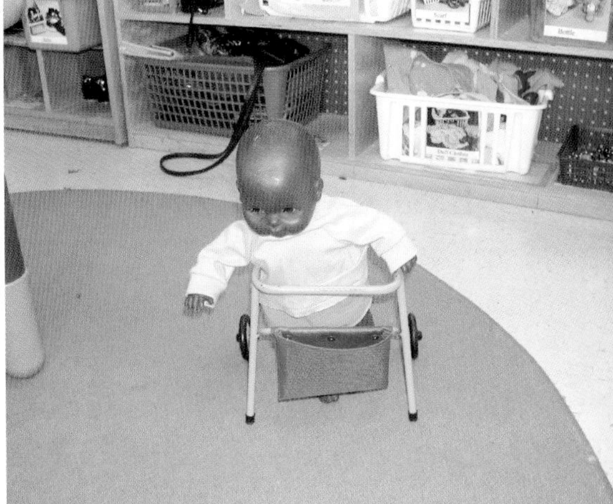

28.5.2 a Adaptive equipment for use with dolls is accessible for dramatic play.

28.5.2 b

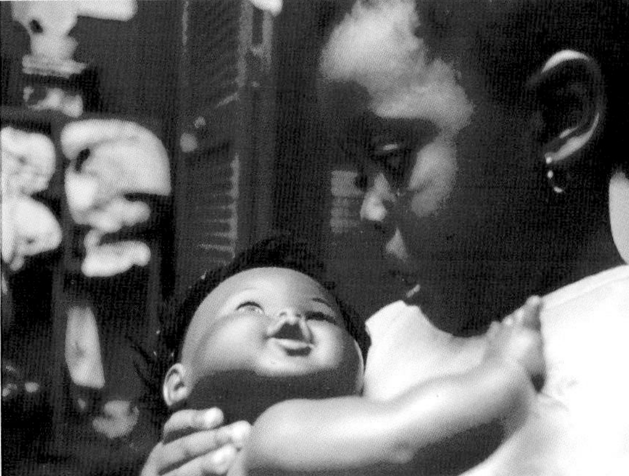

28.5.2 c

28.5.2 b–c Children can choose dolls to use that look more or less like they do.

28 Promoting acceptance of diversity

Indicator

7.1 ***Inclusion of diversity as part of daily routines and play*** goes beyond having materials showing diversity displayed or accessible for children to play with. Instead, representing diversity is a regular part of the daily experiences that children have throughout the day, each day. These experiences are the usual rather than the unusual.

Examples of ***including diversity as part of daily routines and play*** are included in the indicator. However, more specific examples include:

As part of routines:

- Ethnic foods are served often as meals or snacks.
- Staff use some words in different languages to talk about routines.
- Music from varying cultures is used at naptime.
- Staff say hello or goodbye in different languages.
- Family traditions and utensils are provided at meals and snacks, if desired.

As part of play activities:

- In cooking activities, foods representative of other cultures are prepared by children.
- "Bingo" is played in different languages.
- Children regularly dance to music from various cultures.
- Art materials associated with different cultures are used, such as colored sands for sand paintings, clay for making pottery, and origami paper for simple paper folding activities.
- Musical instruments representing varied cultures are accessible.

To give credit (score 7.1 "Yes"), at least one example should be observed during the observation, since such experiences are supposed to happen throughout the day, every day. Watch carefully to be sure such practices are noticed when observing. For example, consider foods served regularly (see menus), and remember that many foods we regularly enjoy actually represent the contributions from many cultures.

7.2 ***Activities included to promote understanding and acceptance of diversity*** can be within daily activities or special activities that do not take place on a daily basis. Therefore such activities do not have to take place during the observation.

These activities would be expected to have the specified goal of helping children to learn about diversity. It is likely that when the activities are offered to the children, staff would be quite obvious in their intentions—they would point out and talk about the characteristics of countries, cultures or the other categories associated with diversity, including differences and similarities.

Examples of these types of activities are included in the indicator. Additional examples include:

- For a cooking activity, children prepare and eat a food representative of a certain culture.
- Children celebrate winter holidays of many different cultures.
- Children do art activities associated with varied cultures.

Indicator

- People come in to teach children folk songs of different countries.
- Children learn dances from different countries.
- Children see a video of games children play in other countries.

Since it is not required that the activities for this indicator are observed, staff should be asked the question provided for 7.2 in the ECERS-R. Score the indicator based on staff report.

To give credit, staff should answer that such activities are done with children at least four times a year, and be able to give examples of what has been done or is planned.

Interaction

29 Supervision of gross motor activities

General information about this item

The requirements of this item are based on supervision provided by staff during the gross motor activity times of the day, such as outdoor physical play and indoor gross motor play, either in the classroom or in another indoor space used for gross motor activities. Obviously children may do some gross motor activity at non-gross motor times, such as running from one area to another in the classroom, climbing onto furniture, or throwing a toy. Unless these types of gross motor activities are done as part of an actual gross motor time, do not consider the supervision of such activities here. Instead, consider supervision of these types of activities under Item 30, General supervision.

To score this item, consider ALL staff observed supervising gross motor activities indoors or outdoors. In this item, ***staff*** refers to those adults who regularly work with the children during gross motor times. Adults who just drop in for a short time do not count in evaluating whether the requirements of the item are met, *unless they are observed to interact very negatively with children.*

Consider how ALL observed children of similar age/abilities as those in the group you are observing are being supervised in the gross motor area. Notice whether there are enough staff to supervise the children in the area and whether adults are supervising the most hazardous areas/activities adequately. In some cases, state-mandated staff-child ratios are met, but there still may not be enough staff to supervise adequately because of the size or configuration of the play space, or the difficulty of the equipment for the age group. (See photos 29 A–C.)

Every attempt should be made to observe staff supervision of gross motor activities, even if this requires that the observer return on another day. In some cases, observation of gross motor activities is impossible (for example, due to bad weather and no active physical play provided inside), and a return visit cannot be completed. In this case, the observer should question the teacher to find out about

29 A Consider the supervision of gross motor activities by observing all adults and children using the gross motor area, not just those that are enrolled in the group.

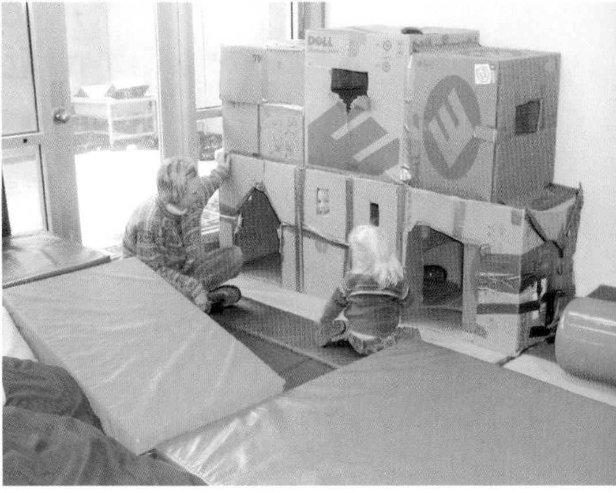

29 B Consider supervision of gross motor activities indoors as well as outdoors.

29 C [right] Supervision of non-gross motor activities is not considered in this item, even when an activity, like this gardening project, is supervised on the playground.

Indicator

29.1.1 a If teachers spend most of the time socializing with one another and not supervising the children, supervision is considered inadequate.

29.1.1 b Supervision is not sufficient when staff are usually positioned with their backs to children who are playing on the gross motor equipment.

what spaces are usually used for gross motor activities, the numbers of adults and children who use the space, positioning of staff, and the types of activities staff do when the children are in the area. An inspection of the gross motor areas should then be completed, to see how supervision might be carried out, based on the actual space and what the staff has reported, and to see whether there are obvious supervision problems in the space. All information collected should be combined with what has been observed during general supervision, and then the item should be scored.

A closer look at each indicator

1.1 ***Inadequate supervision*** means that staff severely compromise children's health or safety needs by not watching, guiding, or intervening as needed. (See photos 29.1.1 a–b.) This indicator relates only to supervision required to protect the basic health and safety needs of children, which, if missing, could be considered "neglect." The indicator should be scored "Yes" if staff leave children, and *no* adult is present to supervise them. Inadequate supervision may also be true when there are too few staff for the number of children or hazards present or inattentive staff who ignore children or attend to other interests. When children leave the area supervised by staff and are unsupervised (e.g., leave the playground to use the indoor toilet unsupervised, leave the playground unnoticed, and no adult realizes the child's absence), score this indicator "Yes."

Gross motor areas are those spaces, both inside and outside, where children use their large muscles (e.g., to run, climb, ride wheel toys, or play with balls). When scoring this item, consider supervision of all gross motor areas used by the children.

In considering whether there is enough supervision ***to protect children's health and safety***, consider only children's basic health and safety needs, which, if ignored, would constitute "neglect." Examples of failure to protect the safety of children include: children left unattended with *no* adult present to supervise children even for a short period of time; not enough adults to watch children in the gross motor area; staff busy with other activities or socializing and not paying attention to children.

Indicator

1.2 Do not score 1.2 until a wide range of interactions during gross motor activities has been observed. Sometimes the nature of interactions changes as the observation continues, with interactions usually becoming more negative as staff and children spend more time together. Consider all gross motor times observed throughout the observation to score.

Pay attention to the atmosphere on the playground and in any other gross motor space used. If staff seem punitive and overly controlling (stopping children's play without sufficient reason, constant yelling at children, unsympathetic responses to children who are hurt), score this indicator "Yes."

Most staff child interactions means the majority (over 50% of all interactions during gross motor times). It is not necessary to calculate a percentage; however, this percentage should be used as a guide. Base the score on the children's overall experience.

Staff child interactions include both the verbal (talking) and non-verbal (looks, touch) communications that occur between adults and children. For this indicator, include only those interactions that occur during gross motor times. Consider interactions among *all* staff supervising gross motor activities of the group being observed, indoors or outdoors, and *all* children in the setting at the time.

Negative staff-child interactions include those verbal or non-verbal exchanges that give children the message that they are not valuable, competent, cared for, or appreciated. Generally, negative staff-child interactions are most likely to occur as staff try to control children's behavior. It should be noted that such interactions are more appropriately handled in a positive way, when staff give good reasons for why something is not allowed, explain rules, are sympathetic to the child, and help the child solve the problem and come to a solution that is satisfactory.

Look for ***negative staff-child interactions*** that may happen at other times as well, not just when staff are trying to control children. Ignoring a child who needs attention or complaining about, teasing, or criticizing a child are examples of negative staff-child interactions.

Evidence to look for to determine whether staff-child interactions are negative includes harsh tone of voice used to give commands to children, responding with anger, and use of harsh physical contact. However, careful examination of each interaction is needed in scoring this indicator. For example, an observer's perception of a loud tone of voice does not guarantee that a child will think the same thing—that the staff member is being harsh. The most effective means of determining whether negative staff-child interactions are occurring is to observe the child's response to the adult's communication and determine the effect on the child. If the child shows a negative or hurt response, such as defiance, anger, crying, unhappiness, embarrassment, apathy or disconnecting from the adult, then the staff-child interactions should be interpreted as negative.

3.1 ***Adequate supervision*** means that there are enough staff present to watch children in the gross motor areas. They are positioned to see all areas where children may be playing, move around as needed to keep a close eye on children, and are attentive to children's needs for basic protection of health and safety. There is always an adult present, supervising, and children are never left unsupervised for any amount of time. Adequate supervision is observable and should not be based on teacher-child ratios, but rather on how effective the supervision actually is while children are involved in gross motor play. (See photos 29.3.1 a–b, next page.)

Indicator

29.3.1 a There are enough staff in the various play areas to sufficiently supervise the children during gross motor play.

29.3.1 b Adequate supervision means that staff concentrate on the more hazardous areas.

29.3.1 c

29.3.1 d

29.3.1 c–d Adequate supervision requires that staff intervene when problems occur.

Staff intervene when problems occur that could seriously compromise a child's health or safety (e.g., stop children from hurting themselves or others, ensure that all children remain within view of adults) and pay extra attention in more hazardous areas. (See photos 29.3.1 c–d.)

3.2 ***Some positive staff-child interaction*** means that most verbal or non-verbal exchanges between staff and children in the gross motor area(s) are either neutral or positive, with at least one or two instances of positive staff-child interaction observed. To give credit, most interactions cannot be negative.

Examples of positive staff-child interactions include:

- Staff comfort child who is upset or hurt. (See photo 29.3.2 a, next page.)
- Staff show appreciation of child's new skill or interest.
- Staff use pleasant tone of voice.
- Staff are affectionate with children. (See photo 29.3.2 b, next page.)

5.1 ***Act to prevent dangerous situations before they occur*** requires that supervising adults notice things that might cause accidents and correct them before an accident can occur. Staff are obviously aware of the types of things that

Indicator

29.3.2 a Positive staff-child interactions include providing comfort when a child gets hurt during gross motor play.

29.3.2 b Staff show children they are interested in them by listening and getting down low on child's eye level.

might endanger children's safety and eliminate those problems before anyone is hurt. (See photo 29.5.1.)

29.5.1 Staff warn children about walking into the trike path when children are busy riding trikes.

Examples of staff meeting the requirement of the indicator include:

- Stopping rough play before children get hurt
- Keeping the tricycle path separate from other play areas
- Removing broken toys and equipment before children's use
- Keeping the fall zones under equipment clear of obstructions
- Limiting the number of children using gross motor equipment or toys requiring close supervision (e.g., swings, merry-go-round, slide, seesaw)
- Keeping children from running in front of or behind swings or under an overhead ladder
- Sweeping slippery sand from the sidewalk
- Removing trash from the playground before children use area
- Placing mats to provide cushioning in fall zones of indoor climbing equipment—the cushioning characteristics of the mat will depend on the highest point from which a child might fall, with higher equipment needing more cushioning

5.2 ***Most staff-child interactions*** means the vast majority of verbal and non-verbal exchanges between adults and children are positive. Neutral interactions can be observed for a score of "Yes," but they must be outweighed by the positive to get credit for ***most***.

To determine whether interactions are ***pleasant and helpful***, observe closely to determine the content of the communication exchanges and the effect on the

Indicator

29.5.2 a Pulling a wagon when requested by children is an example of positive interaction.

29.5.2 b Positive interactions are reflected in the faces of those who are enjoying them.

children. Watch children's faces and other non-verbal clues and listen to what they say to see if their response to a staff interaction is positive; for example, the child is pleased, interested, reassured. (See photos 29.5.2 a–c.)

29.5.2 c Staff help to comfort children when they become upset.

Examples of ***pleasant and helpful staff-child interactions*** include:

- Speaking to children in a pleasant tone
- Responding and adding to children's interests
- Cooperating with children in tasks or play
- Helping children develop skills when needed
- Having fun with children
- Helping children solve problems
- Helping children get along with others
- Providing comfort when needed
- Providing affection when wanted by a child
- Modeling caring and positive social skills
- Supporting children when needed
- Smiling with children or showing delight in other ways

If there are mostly positive interactions and only one or two *slightly* negative (but *no* extremely negative) interactions, 5.2 may be scored "Yes."

5.3 ***Assist children to develop skills needed to use equipment*** means that staff help children learn new skills needed to use the gross motor equipment (either portable or stationary) or help them with skills that need more practice. Examples include helping a child learn to pump on swing; helping a child with a physical disability use adaptive pedals on a tricycle; or helping children bounce or catch a ball. (See photo 29.5.3, next page.)

To give credit, staff must be actively involved with children using the gross motor equipment, either verbally or through their actions. For example, staff can:

- Show children how to use equipment
- Use words to guide their movements
- Explain what needs to be done

Indicator

- Introduce new equipment and teach children how to use it
- Encourage children to practice a skill with equipment

29.5.3 This child needs help from his teacher to learn how to pedal a trike.

Often, helping the child develop skills may require that the staff modify an activity so the child can practice an easier version of the skill before moving onto the more challenging version. For example, the teacher may ask the child to jump over a lower rope first rather than a higher one, walk on a wider rather than more narrow balance beam, or throw a bigger ball instead of a smaller one.

In some instances, staff might participate with a child in the use of equipment but not actually help the child to develop the skill needed to use the equipment. For example, pushing an older child on a swing or pulling a preschooler in a wagon may not encourage skill development because the child remains passive and is not being challenged at an appropriate level. Such staff involvement with children using gross motor equipment does not count to meet the requirements of the indicator.

To give credit for this indicator, at least one creditable example must be seen during the observation, and if children obviously need help frequently, more examples should be observed.

7.1 ***Talk with children*** requires that staff have conversations with children during gross motor activities that relate to the content of their play, such as explaining or asking questions and listening to answers about what the children are trying to do.

Ideas related to their play means that the content of the talk must originate with the children, either from their actions or what they say.

Staff might add words to what children are doing, describing their actions. For example:

- "You were riding really fast. And then you stopped so quickly! Did you come to a red light?"
- "It takes a lot of strength to throw that heavy ball."
- "You jumped 20 times. Can you do it again?"

Staff might help children talk through problems. For example:

- "You both want to use this tricycle. How do you think we can solve this problem?"
- "This is quite wobbly to climb on. I am afraid you will fall and get hurt. How can we make it safe?"

Staff might extend children's play by talking about ideas. For example:

- "You're crawling through the tunnel. Have you ever been in a big tunnel—the kind of tunnel that cars go through?"
- "You're walking on the balance beam just like the tightrope dancer in the circus that we saw. Remember?"

At least one example must be observed to give a score of "Yes" to this indicator.

Indicator

7.2 ***Help with resources to enhance play*** requires that staff bring out or help children find materials that they need for successful play. For example, staff might help children get duplicate equipment when children have trouble sharing, bring out portable equipment (such as balls, jump ropes, hula hoops) to add to play opportunities, and help children set up their own play (find boards and large hollow blocks for big building projects, help set up an obstacle course for bikes and tricycles, set up basketball or soccer goals).

Sometimes materials and equipment are available, but not brought out. If there is an obvious need for additional materials/equipment during the observation, but staff do not bring them out for the children to use, score 7.2 "No." The score of "No" should be given even if staff report, during the staff interview, that they do bring things out to add to children's play, and they can show these things to the observer. If things were needed, and staff did not bring them out during the observation, it is unlikely that such materials are provided frequently enough to make a difference to the children.

7.3 ***Help children develop positive social interactions*** requires more than simply stopping problems between children. Staff should be observed doing one or more of the following:

- Modeling positive social skills, such as sharing, being friendly, cooperating, talking, or playing with others
- Encouraging an isolated child to interact with others or encouraging a social child to interact with an isolated child (See photo 29.7.3.)
- Helping children solve social problems
- Pointing out or showing appreciation for a child's pro-social behavior with others
- Providing equipment that encourages cooperation such as a two-person rocking boat, two-person tricycle, or wagon

29. 7.3 Staff can help encourage peer interactions by initiating a game of toss.

30 General supervision of children (other than gross motor)

General information about this item

The requirements of this item are based on supervision (watching and guiding of children) provided by staff during all activity times and routines, except gross motor activity times. The quality of general supervision should be evaluated in the classroom, in other indoor spaces used with the children, and outdoors. Obviously, children will do some gross motor activity at non-gross motor times, such as running from one area to another in the classroom, climbing onto furniture, or throwing a toy. Unless these types of gross motor activities are done as part of an actual gross motor time, they should be considered here. Consider supervision of all gross motor activity times under Item 29, Supervision of gross motor activities.

In this item, ***staff*** refers to those adults who are in the classroom and work with the children daily (or almost daily), for a substantial part of the day. Adults who are in the classroom for short periods of the day, or who are not a regular daily part of the classroom, do not count in evaluating whether the requirements of the item are met, unless they are observed to interact very negatively with children. For example, if a therapist, parent, or a director of a program comes into the classroom and interacts with children for short or irregular periods, these interactions do not count in scoring the item, unless they interact very negatively with the children. As an exception, in programs where the usual daily staffing pattern includes different people as teaching assistants or "floater" staff (including parent volunteers in parent co-operatives or students working in lab school settings), these assistants should be counted as staff during the observation.

To score this item, consider *all* observed staff supervising non-gross motor activities, indoors or outdoors. Concentrate primarily on the staff and children in the group being observed, but if groups mix during activity times (for example, if art or music are offered to all children outdoors), consider *all* observed children of similar age/abilities as those in the group being observed. Notice whether there are enough staff to supervise the children, and whether adults are supervising the most hazardous areas/activities adequately. In some cases, state-mandated staff-child ratios are met, but there still may not be enough staff to supervise adequately because of the size or configuration of the play space, the children's abilities, or the difficulty of the activities for the age group.

The score for this item must be based on what is seen throughout an observation. No questions should be used to gather information required to score this item. The observation must be long enough to provide a range of circumstances, including quiet and more active times, group times and free play, routine and play times, and more and less stressful periods of the day. For example, to score accurately, the observer should see supervision early in the morning, when children and staff are fresh, and continue to observe during the more stressful times of the day, such as before lunch or nap, when people are hungry or tired.

Indicator

It should be noted that a less harsh and less restrictive approach to supervision is associated with more positive child development. This does not mean that children should not be protected adequately by caring adults or not helped to learn and practice growing abilities. Yet, there are ways in which all supervisory interactions with children can be carried out in a positive way rather than in a colder, more restrictive manner.

A closer look at each indicator

1.1 ***Inadequate supervision*** means that staff severely compromise children's health or safety needs by not watching, guiding, or intervening as is required by the children's abilities or the nature of the hazards present. (See photos 30.1.1 a–d.) More diligent supervision is required for younger or less independent children or in more dangerous circumstances. For example, an older 4- or 5-year-old might be considered adequately supervised when using a toilet with the door partially closed, but easily viewed by staff in the room who are aware of the child's location.

30.1.1 a–d [below] Inadequate supervision is provided when children's health and safety needs are frequently ignored, as shown in these examples.

30.1.1 a

30.1.1 b

30.1.1 c

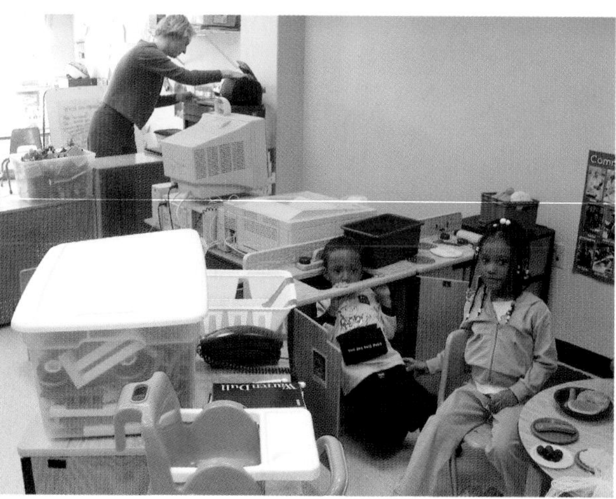

30.1.1 d

Indicator

However, a 2- or 3-year-old or an impulsive child would be considered inadequately supervised under similar circumstances.

This indicator relates only to the supervision required to protect the basic health and safety needs of children participating in non-gross motor activities, which, if not provided, could be considered "neglect." The indicator should be scored "Yes" if staff leave children, and NO adult is present to supervise them, even for short periods of time. Inadequate supervision may also be true (scored "Yes") when there are too few staff for the number of children or hazards present, or inattentive staff who ignore children or attend to other interests. When any child leaves the area supervised by staff and is completely unsupervised (for example, leaves the classroom to use a toilet located down a separate hallway, or leaves the classroom unnoticed and no adult realizes the child's absence), score this indicator "Yes."

1.2 Do not score until supervision has been observed under a wide range of circumstances. Sometimes the nature of supervision changes as the observation continues, becoming more negative as staff and children spend more time together. Consider all non-gross motor times throughout the observation to score.

Most supervision means the majority (over 50%) of all supervision, not including gross motor times. It is not necessary to calculate a percentage; however, this percentage should be used as a guide. Base the score on the children's overall experience. Pay attention to the atmosphere created by staff supervision in any spaces used by children. Watch children's responses to what staff say or do as they are supervising.

Punitive or overly controlling means that as staff watch and guide children, they punish children often or restrict what children would like to do, even when the children's requests or intentions are reasonable. Punitive or overly controlling supervision can be provided through verbal or non-verbal exchanges that give children the message that they are not valuable, competent, cared for, or appreciated.

Signs that staff provide ***punitive or overly controlling supervision*** include harsh voices, anger directed at children, much criticism, the frequent use of "No," and rough physical treatment. Careful observation of the situation is needed in scoring this indicator because observers' perceptions may be "super-sensitive" about what they perceive as being inappropriate for children. For example, a single instance of staff using a loud voice may distort a "super-sensitive" observer's picture of the nature of the supervision, even if most of the supervision observed is appropriate. The most effective means of determining whether supervision is overly controlling or punitive is to observe children's responses to the staff and determine the overall effect on the children.

3.1 ***Sufficient supervision to protect children's safety*** requires that there are enough staff present to watch children during both routines and play. The staff must be positioned to see all areas where children may be playing, move around as needed to keep a close eye on children, and remain attentive to children's basic safety needs. There must always be an adult present supervising, and children are never left unsupervised for any amount of time.

To give credit for this indicator, staff must intervene when problems occur that could seriously compromise a child's safety (for example, stop children from hurting themselves or others, ensure that all children remain within view of adults,

Indicator

or help a child with special needs climb up on the stepstool to wash hands). They must pay extra attention in more hazardous situations, such as when children are doing certain cooking activities, playing around water, or using carpentry tools or other sharp objects.

30.3.2 Minimal supervision includes staff taking action to ensure that messy activities are cleaned up so that other activities can be provided.

3.2 ***Attention given to cleanliness*** requires that staff supervision provides for keeping areas used by children, and the children themselves, reasonably clean. Messy play should be cleaned up to prevent spreading the mess, most toys should be returned to shelves after use, and children's clothes should be protected or changed as needed. However, perfection is not expected here, as long as children's and adults' basic safety or health are not endangered by a lack of cleanliness. For example, after water play, the teacher cleans up all water spills on the floor so no one will slip. The cleaning tasks can be accomplished by the staff, by the children with direction from staff, or by a combination of the two. (See photo 30.3.2.)

To prevent inappropriate use of materials requires that staff watch and guide children to minimize wasteful, destructive, or dangerous use of materials. For example, a child should be stopped from emptying an entire bottle of glue, putting too much fish food in the aquarium, breaking toys, tearing books, or throwing hard blocks. Children should also be redirected from wasting great amounts of water when using the sink or throwing food at meals or snacks. To give credit, the actions taken to prevent inappropriate use of materials must be reasonable and not harsh or overly controlling.

3.3 ***Most supervision*** means the vast majority of interactions that are used to watch and guide children.

Non-punitive requires that the supervision does not harm, threaten, or frighten children physically or emotionally (e.g., no hitting, yelling at children, making fun of, or shaming children).

Control is exercised in a reasonable way means that the classroom has a few clear, basic rules used to keep children from hurting themselves or others and to ensure the care of materials. These rules are enforced fairly and consistently, without anger, harshness, or rough handling of children. The rules are generally appropriate for the developmental level of children in the group. Control is usually positive, with very few negative examples observed (only one or two slightly negative examples, and none that is extremely negative).

5.1 ***Careful supervision of all children*** means that staff watch every child carefully, stepping in to prevent harm to the children. (See photos 30.5.1 a–b, next page.)

Supervision adjusted appropriately for different ages and abilities means that while carefully supervising all children, staff tailor their supervision to the needs of individual children. They vary their supervision, depending on the characteristics of each child. For example, younger or more impulsive children are supervised more closely and kept closer to the staff. (See photo 30.5.1 c, next page.) Older, more responsible children are supervised less closely and given more free-

Indicator

30.5.1 a Careful supervision is easier when children are grouped together for an activity.

30.5.1 b Careful supervision is also possible when children play in different areas of a room, but different tactics must be used by staff.

30.5.1 c Staff provide closer supervision for younger preschoolers doing a messy activity. Older children might not need to be supervised as closely for this activity.

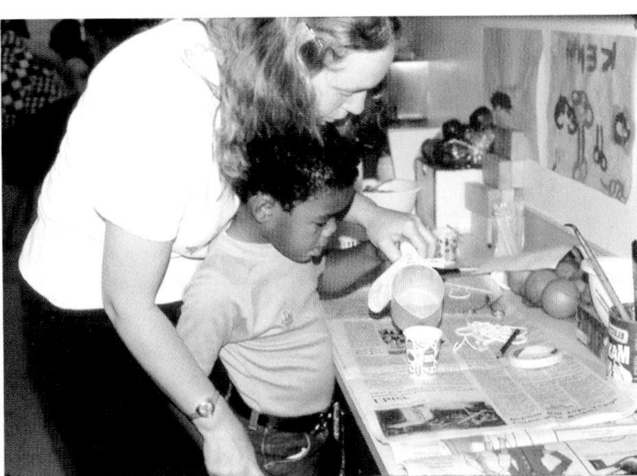

30.5.1 d During this candle-making activity, staff provide very close supervision to keep children safe when pouring the hot wax.

dom to act independently, but they are never left unsupervised. Children in more hazardous situations are always supervised more closely than are others, for example, during carpentry or cooking activities. (See photo 30.5.1 d.) Similarly, children on a fieldtrip need closer supervision by more adults than when in the classroom. Children may differ in their supervision needs from day to day. For example, a child who is not feeling well might need closer supervision than usual.

5.2 To ***give children help when needed*** requires that staff set up toys and activities to make it possible for children to play as independently as possible, then watch children to see when they need help and provide help as needed. To give credit, there should be evidence that adults step in and offer help when children seem to be having trouble or are frustrated, for example, in using equipment/materials, in getting along with others, or in getting involved in play. (See photos 30.5.2 a–c, next page.) Credit can be given if children never seem to require actual "help" from staff during the observation because the challenges match children's abilities and the setting allows children to play independently, in a satisfying way. However,

30.5.2 a Staff help children wash hands properly as they supervise getting ready for lunch. When preschool children's handwashing is not well supervised, it is often incompletely done.

30.5.2 b Often help can be given as staff participate with children in their play.

30.5.2 c In this situation, the teacher provides the child with additional encouragement so that she can successfully complete the puzzle.

some positive adult-child interaction must be observed during the children's play to give credit, even if it is not "helping." Credit should not be given if the staff help is usually intrusive and interferes with children's play, or it is not needed by the children.

The extent to which children need help will vary by child and the activity in which he or she is involved. Some children simply need more help than others, and they should not be forced to do things on their own before they are ready. Younger children, children with certain disabilities, or those who do not feel secure in their competence, will need more help in most activities than others. Staff can help by providing simpler tasks or materials or by adapting tasks and activities to allow the child to have success. Some examples of giving help when needed include:

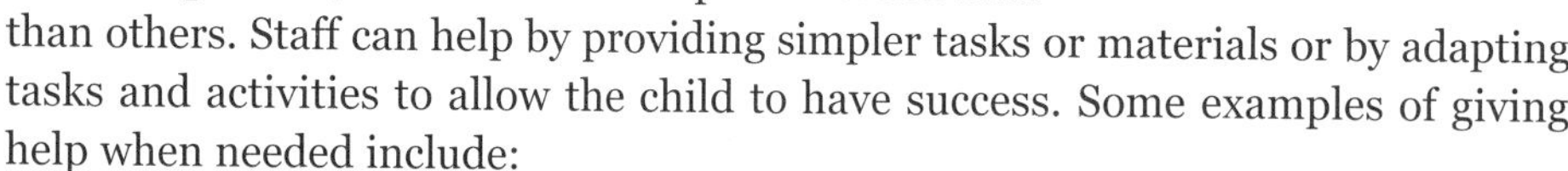

- Making sure the children have the things they need to be successful in activities (e.g., making sure all the puzzle pieces are together, getting additional materials to enhance children's play, or providing a child-sized chair so the child can reach the snack comfortably)

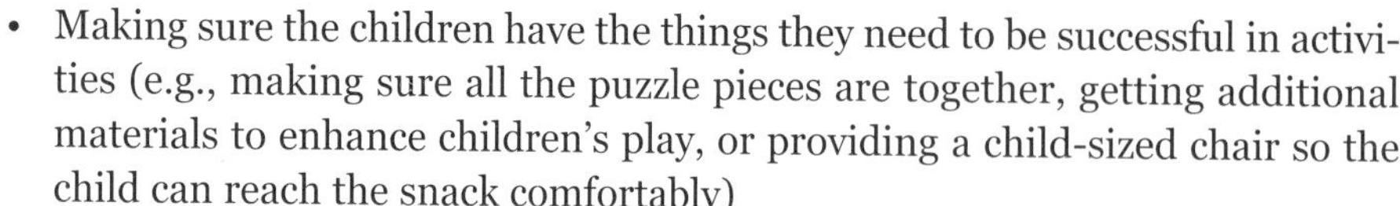

- Providing more simple materials to work with when more complex ones are too difficult (e.g., putting paint cups into a sturdy container at the art table to help a child who tends to spill things or giving children a small pitcher to use to pour beverages rather than a larger one)
- Showing children how to do a task or use materials (e.g., how to wipe the paint brush while using water color paints, how to hold the nail for safe hammering, or how to wash hands correctly)
- Guiding children by talking them through the steps needed for success (e.g., helping children figure out how to clean up an activity area by breaking the

Indicator

task into many smaller steps and talking them through each, talking a child through balancing a block structure or figuring out a puzzle, or guiding a child through the steps needed for toileting)

- Helping children work out problems with others (e.g., guiding children to come to satisfying solutions, redirecting children away from continuing problems, or comforting children who are hurt or upset)

To ***give children encouragement when needed*** requires that staff observe children at play or during routines, show interest in what children do or try to do, and let them know that success is possible. The success does not have to happen immediately after encouragement is given. Instead, encouragement can help a child know that, at some time in the future, success can come if one keeps trying. For example, staff respond by saying "You want to do it so much. Keep trying and someday you will." Children that may have low self-confidence in their ability need special encouragement. The message given is that children are competent and that they will be able to master skills.

To give credit for this indicator, no specific number of examples must be observed. However, it must be evident that the requirements of the indicator are a general practice used by staff throughout the day.

5.3 First, this indicator requires that staff respond to things that happen in the total area or classroom used by the ***whole group*** of children. Second, the indicator requires that this "whole area supervision" be done even when staff are ***working with one child or a small group***. It must be obvious during the observation that staff watch, listen to, and remain aware of what is happening in the entire area used by children. Evidence of meeting the requirement includes:

- Staff frequently scan the room, even when working with one child or a small group.
- Staff coordinate their supervision, so that no area being used by children is unsupervised.
- Staff generally notice where children are located and what they are doing.
- Staff interrupt work with a small group or an individual child to respond when needed to prevent problems or to give help.

The indicator is not met (score "No") when staff often miss obvious problems that occur or rarely take action to solve problems. For example, staff may focus on supervising only a small group or an individual child rather than scanning the whole group.

5.4 This indicator requires that staff are aware of what all the children are doing, recognize when they try to do things in both routines and play, and respond to whatever children have done in some way. This recognition can come in many forms and may not always be delivered to the child verbally. It should be provided regularly, even when children's efforts are not successful, but they are trying.

Some examples of staff behaviors that meet the requirement for this ***showing appreciation of children's efforts and accomplishments*** include:

- Showing positive interest in what a child is trying to do or has done, either by looking at the child's work/play or by talking to the child about it
- Showing non-verbal delight in what a child has done or is doing (e.g., smiling at the child, clapping, patting on the back, or hugging)

Indicator

- Praising a child verbally for what he or she has done or for the effort shown ("Thank you for throwing away your napkin." "I like the way you moved over so she could join us in circle.")
- Labeling what the child has done or is trying to do ("I see you carried the paints without spilling them." "You have built a very tall tower with these rectangular blocks.")

To give credit for this indicator, no specific number of examples must be observed. However, it must be evident that the requirements of the indicator are a usual practice of the staff.

7.1 This indicator requires that staff find out, by watching and listening, what children are interested in as they play, and then talk with them (not at them) about those interests. The voices of the children should be well represented in the discussion. The conversations should not be dominated by adults.

The indicator also requires that while ***talking with the children*** about their interests, staff use ***questions*** to encourage children to explain and think. (See photo 30.7.1 a.) Questions that ask *how, what happens if,* and *why* should be used more than questions requiring single word answers because they encourage children to think more deeply and explain their thoughts. For example, "Why did you cover the baby with a blanket?," "How did you make this play dough?," and "What happened when you fed grapes to the hamster?" are more challenging than, "What did you feed the hamster?"

Adding information to extend children's thinking about their play is also part of the requirement for the indicator. This means that when children talk about something, staff add more information, through words or by providing resources to the children. (See photo 30.7.1 b.) For example:

- If children are playing "bus," staff might talk about checking the bus schedule, buying tickets, or deciding where the bus is going. To add resources, staff might provide paper to make tickets and hole punches to use to cancel tickets. Knowing that children are interested in bus travel, books on the topic might be brought out either during play to answer an immediate question or later to bring in new ideas.

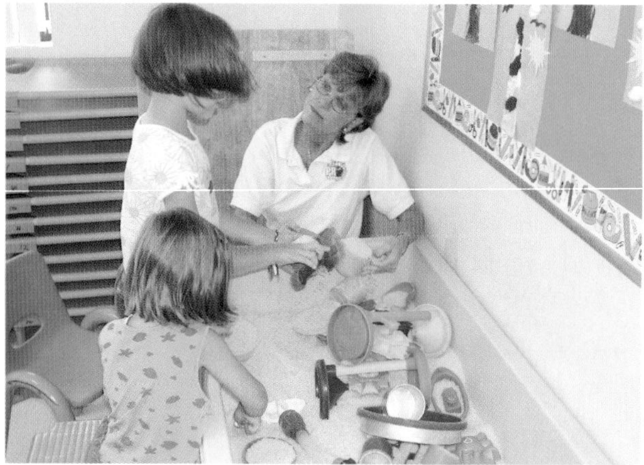

30.7.1 a The teacher extends this activity by asking children how many scoops of sand it takes to fill the various cups and containers.

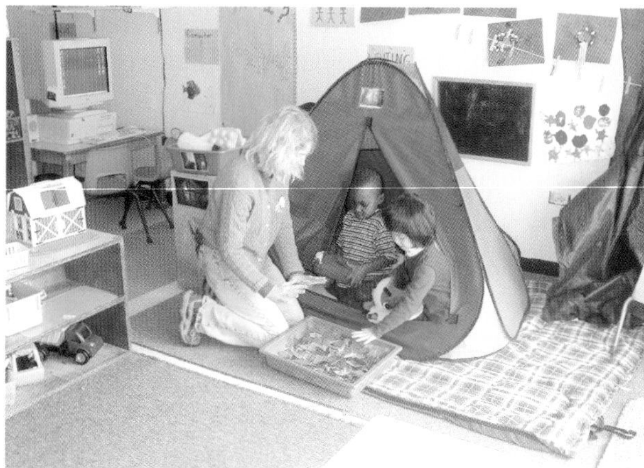

30.7.1 b This camping activity is set up so that children can use it independently, while staff introduce new ideas about a camp fire.

Indicator

- If children are playing with toy dinosaurs, staff can talk about the different kinds of dinosaurs or share books, magazines, or videos to extend children's knowledge. Staff can add activities in other areas of the classroom about dinosaurs. For example, in the art area, children can make drawings or papier maché dinosaurs so that they can explore the shapes, colors, and sizes of different dinosaurs.

To give credit for this indicator, no specific number of examples must be observed. However, it must be evident that the requirements of the indicator are a usual practice of the staff.

7.2 This indicator requires that staff are sensitive to children's need to play ***independently*** and in their own way, while recognizing that adult interactions with children during play are beneficial to extending children's knowledge and understanding. The ***balance*** required will not be the same for each child; some will benefit from being allowed to continue their ongoing activities with no interruptions, while others will want staff to participate more. The intent of this indicator is that the child takes the lead in playing with materials, and the teacher supervises so that she can add language, help children think more deeply about what they experience, and provide materials at the appropriate times.

To give credit for the indicator, it should be obvious that staff input into children's play is usually not an intrusion, but that rather, the staff enters play as a welcome guest. The observer should watch children's responses to staff input to score the indicator. If children generally enjoy staff participation in their play, and the staff are adding to children's knowledge or understanding by participating, then credit should be given (score "Yes").

Obviously, when children's independent explorations are dangerous in some way (for example, a child is rough with class pet, uses a stick as a dagger, or builds a high block tower that could fall and hurt a nearby child) or disruptive, and the teacher intervenes, the child's response might not be positive. In this case, if the intrusion is handled positively, to help the child learn a better way to manage his play, credit should also be given.

31 Discipline

General information about this item

Discipline carries many meanings in our society. Some interpret the word to mean "punishment." (See photo 31 A.) To others, it carries the meaning of "guidance." (See photo 31 B.) In all cases the intention of discipline is to help children learn how to behave according to the established rules of conduct. In this item, ***discipline*** means the methods used by staff to manage children's behavior.

At the lowest level of quality of this item, discipline is either too strict or too permissive, so that children have few opportunities to receive the kinds of guidance that allow them to learn to manage their own behavior—to develop "self-discipline." For a child to develop self-discipline takes time, learning, and maturation on the part of the child, as well as a lot of patience and effort on the part of the adults who care for the child. But all of this is well worth it, because once self-discipline is a part of the child, less external guidance is needed to enforce rules. Children who have achieved self-discipline can follow rules on their own, making their own choices about how they will act, based on their understanding of how their actions affect themselves and others.

31 A Discipline may mean punishment, which children receive negatively.

Discipline that is too strict allows adults to manage the behavior of most children through fear. This works well in the short term, but at some point in the lives of most children, fear is no longer something that controls them. They learn that they can behave inappropriately when there is no one watching or no one stronger around to control them. They do not develop self-discipline.

Discipline that is too lax does not help children learn that they are responsible for their actions. Often, adults who do not exert reasonable control fail to make clear to children what the rules and expectations for behavior are. Without proper guidance, children do not learn self-discipline.

31 B Discipline may also mean guidance, which allows a more positive relationship between staff and children.

There is a middle ground between the extremes of strict and lax discipline that has been shown to work best in helping children develop the skills required for self-discipline. In this middle ground, rules are clear, expectations for behavior are age and developmentally appropriate, and guidance is non-punitive and educationally sound. Children need to learn about rules, limits, and being responsible. But these behaviors cannot be forced upon them with long-term success.

At the higher levels of quality in this item, the emphasis is on teaching self-discipline to children in a realistic way—without demanding what children are not yet able to do.

31 Discipline

Indicator

In this item, ***staff*** refers to those adults who are in the classroom and work with the children daily (or almost daily). This can include volunteers, if they are in the classroom for a substantial amount of time.

Adults who are in the classroom for short periods of the day, and who are not a regular daily part of the classroom, do not count in evaluating whether the requirements of the item are met, unless they are observed to interact very negatively with children. For example, if a therapist, parent, or a director of a program comes into the classroom and interacts with children, for short or irregular periods, these interactions do not count in scoring the item, unless they are negative with the children. As an exception, in programs where the usual daily staffing pattern includes different people as teaching assistants or "floater" staff (including parent volunteers in parent co-operatives or students working in lab school settings), these assistants should be counted as staff during the observation.

Information required for scoring all indicators (except 7.2 and 7.3) in this item must be observed in order to score. Questions should be used only to supplement or confirm uncertainties, and to gather information needed to score 7.2 and 7.3, if not observed.

An observation period of at least 2 ½ to 3 hours should be completed before scoring. This is to ensure that a range of conditions, requiring varying types of staff responses, is observed. For example, the observer should see the discipline methods used during both relaxed and more stressful periods of the day. Keeping notes throughout the observation is helpful when deciding on a score.

A closer look at each indicator

1.1 ***Severe methods*** used to ***control children*** are those that are considered very strict or punitive and are associated with harming children either physically or emotionally. Such methods are considered harsh, and if frequently used, have been shown to be both harmful and ineffective in helping children develop self-discipline. (See photo 31.1.1.) Usually harsh methods of controlling children are used when staff lose their own control and become angry, causing them to handle children in a way that they would never want to be handled themselves. If children acted similarly, they would certainly be punished.

31.1.1 Using long periods of time out and yelling at children are considered severe methods of discipline.

Examples of severe methods are provided in the indicator, but other examples include:

Physical punishment:

- Hitting, pinching, yanking, or pushing
- Burning with hot water, hot stove, or cigarette
- Exposing to cold or other discomforts
- Tying up or holding very tightly
- Having another child hit or physically punish a child
- Washing a child's mouth out with soap or putting "hot sauce" on tongue

Other severe methods:

- Embarrassing, teasing, or taunting
- Yelling or shouting at a child

Indicator

- Withholding food, drink, or sleep
- Restricting a child from an activity, such as keeping a child in at outside time
- Isolating a child for longer than just a few minutes, such as with prolonged "time out," standing in the corner or hallway, confining in a closet, or having to stay on a cot or mat
- Forcing a child to eat or drink something he or she does not like
- Forcing a child to repeat any disagreeable task numerous times, such as walking across the classroom over and over to make the child remember not to run.

There are certainly other harsh methods that are used to discipline young children. The observer should watch carefully to be sure to understand how discipline is handled.

If no harsh discipline methods are observed, and it is obvious that such methods would *never* be used, score 1.1 "No." If it is difficult to tell whether or not such methods are ever used, ask staff the question provided as part of the item. However, what has been observed will carry most of the weight in scoring.

1.2 When ***discipline is so lax that there is little order or control,*** staff generally pay little or no attention to children's behavior, or the methods that they use to maintain order are not effective. Examples of ***little order or control*** include constantly allowing children to endanger themselves or others or destroy materials and equipment. Children are often allowed to hurt/hit other children and/or the staff, destroy others' projects, or engage in unsafe activities, all with little or no effective intervention on the part of the staff.

Naturally, there will be times when control is less successful, but staff should be able to regain control without having to use harsh methods of discipline.

If much of the observation is characterized by chaos and children are often allowed to hurt or endanger themselves or others or to be destructive, score 1.2 "Yes."

1.3 ***Expectations for behavior*** are what staff think children should be capable of doing successfully. These expectations determine what they try to get children to do. There are many kinds of expectations—for what children should know, understand, and be able to do intellectually, physically and socially. Different adults may have different expectations for the same child—some will expect more and some will expect less. It is important to relate expectations to where children are in their actual abilities. Thus, staff should try to challenge children, but not to frustrate them.

Children learn and grow gradually. Adults cannot expect children to be "instant" adults, or to act like children who are older and more mature than they really are. Expectations are ***inappropriate for age and developmental level*** when staff think that children *should* be able to do what they *cannot* yet actually do. ***Inappropriate expectations*** can also come from staff thinking children are *unable* to do what they actually *can do.*

Inappropriate expectations, or when children are expected to do what older children or adults can do, have been shown to be the reason for many adults' mishandling of children. Adults who misinterpret children's misbehavior as defiance often discipline them harshly or too strictly, sometimes leading to child abuse. If an adult thinks that a child should be able to do something, and they do not do it, the conclusion too often is that the child is just being "bad." Thus children are punished with the expectation that they will obey next time, but since they will not be able to do so,

Indicator

31.1.3 a Discipline issues often occur when children are expected to stand in line for long periods of time. Note the last child in line who is starting to annoy the child in front of him.

31.1.3 b It is difficult for the children to wait in this long line to play with the one basketball. Adding more balls would help prevent irritation on the part of both staff and children.

stronger punishment is used. In fact, most often the children are not doing what is being required because they have not yet developed the ability to do so.

Examples of inappropriate expectations are included in the indicator. Some other examples include expecting preschool-aged children to:

- Sit quietly in a large group for long periods or wait in line as a large group for long periods (See photos 31.1.3 a–b.)
- Learn school skills through rote memorization or drill, such as being able to read, write, add, and subtract
- Understand and avoid dangers, such as busy streets, high unprotected places where falls could happen, sharp objects, and poisons
- Understand the effects of their actions, such as understanding that if they climb up on chairs they might fall or if they grab another child they will cause the child to be angry or hurt
- Have mature social skills, such as sharing, taking turns, and cooperating
- Always understand what adults tell them
- Obey immediately when asked to do something
- Have perfect self-help skills, such as using the toilet with no accidents, help, or reminders, managing eating with no mess, or cooperating at naptime

Inappropriate expectations that underestimate what children should be able to do are also harmful to children's development. If expectations do not challenge children, the children are less likely to progress well. Children who are bored can exhibit behavior problems. Examples of such expectations would be *not* expecting or allowing preschool-aged children to:

- Be able to talk, ask questions, and have opinions
- Be able to play well with others for short times
- Listen to a short story, under the right conditions (children can see the book, book has good pictures, story not too long, and children not crowded)
- Manage some self-help routines without too much help from an adult, such as feeding themselves, putting on "easy clothes," and washing hands
- Understand a few safety rules, but not necessarily always follow them

Indicator

Of course, even within the preschool years there will be differences in what to expect of a child. Younger children will not have developed the same skills as older preschoolers. Children with disabilities may not have developed all the same abilities as their typically developing peers. Even within the same age group, each child will have individual differences, with some more advanced, and some less so. Expectations should take all these differences into consideration.

Indicator 1.3 is true (score "Yes") when the expectations are ***largely inappropriate*** for the children in the group. This means that many examples are observed, that often cause problems for the group—either by staff being too strict or too lax.

Do not score "Yes" if there are a few examples of inappropriate expectations observed, especially if these do not cause significant problems for the children. For example, children may be asked to sit for longer than is optimal at circle time, but this does not cause big problems, resulting in adults mistreating children or children suffering. Or children may be asked to complete a work sheet on an academic subject, but it is not handled with coercion or force, and children are not harmed or upset in any way.

3.1 ***Physical punishment and severe methods*** are described in Indicator 1.1. This indicator should be scored "Yes" if no such methods are observed being used. If unsure about whether such methods are ever used, ask staff the question provided in the ECERS-R for 1.1 of this item.

If *any* physical punishment or severe methods are *ever* used, (reported or observed) score "No."

3.2 To ***maintain enough control to keep children from hurting one another*** requires staff to watch carefully and intervene to stop aggressive behavior before any child is hurt.

Hurting means to cause more than just a small amount of discomfort, either emotionally or physically. For example, if children hit, the hitting must be hard enough to really cause pain, not just irritate or offend. If cruel words are used, the impact must be strong and not fleeting in its effect. This major hurting does not allow the recipient to recover quickly, and usually he or she will not want to play with a child who hurts in this way. Hurting that carries major emotional or physical pain should rarely, if ever, happen in a classroom. Staff should prevent this kind of behavior most, if not all, of the time.

Children often slap at one another without really causing pain or say "mean" things that are bothersome, but not really painful in their impact. The children recover quickly and often continue playing or socializing together. A certain amount of this kind of irritating behavior is to be expected in almost any group of preschoolers who are still learning social skills. However, this type of behavior should not happen frequently because staff should stop such interactions. If such minor instances of hurting happen frequently, this is also counted as ***hurting***.

Usually means that staff maintain the control required to keep children from hurting one another most of the time, with only a few exceptions during the observation. (See photo 31.3.2.) This means that staff supervise the children and do not become involved in activities that prevent them from protecting the children.

31.3.2 This teacher noticed a disagreement over the tricycles and quickly intervened before children got angry with one another.

Indicator

Often observers are tempted to accept more hurting during an observation when children who have less self-control are in the group. For example, if younger preschoolers or children with behavioral disabilities are present, the observer is tempted to allow for more hurting. However, this is not acceptable in scoring this indicator because no children should be expected to accept being hurt, rather than being protected by the staff. Children must know that they are in a safe place and will not be hurt by others.

Programs in which children who are aggressive are allowed to hurt the other children are not meeting the requirements of this indicator, which are that staff protect children. If children who tend to hurt others are in a group, accommodations must be made to ensure the safety of all children. There are many strategies for doing this, without having to exclude any child from the group, such as reducing the number of children per adult, assigning a special staff member to maintain supervision of an aggressive child while actively teaching positive social skills, or eliminating situations from the class that encourage aggressive behaviors. To get credit for this indicator, such steps should be taken, and control to prevent hurting should be maintained.

3.3 ***Expectations for children's behavior*** is discussed in Indicator 1.3. ***Appropriate*** expectations are well matched to children's interests and abilities—they challenge, but do not frustrate the children.

Indicator 3.3 is true (score "Yes") when the expectations are ***largely appropriate*** for the children in the group. This means that *most* of what each child is required to do or understand during the observation matches the child's abilities. No children are under a great deal of stress to perform what is too difficult, nor are any children unchallenged to the extent that they become disruptive.

To score "Yes," there can be a few examples of inappropriate expectations observed, especially if these do not cause significant problems for the children. For example, children may be asked to sit for longer than is optimal at circle time, but this does not seem to cause big problems. Or children may be asked to complete a work sheet on an academic subject, but it is not handled with coercion or force, and children are not harmed or upset in any way.

5.1 ***Non-punitive discipline methods*** are those that allow staff to control children without harming them, either emotionally or physically. These methods are more effective in helping children learn self-discipline (how to behave positively) and cause less anger and hurt. Two examples of non-punitive discipline methods that can be used very effectively are provided as part of the indicator on page 39 of the ECERS-R. More information about each follows:

31.5.1 a In this classroom, children frequently receive positive personal attention from adults; thus, they are less likely to seek attention through inappropriate behavior.

Giving attention for good behavior

Children enjoy getting positive personal attention from adults. (See photo 31.5.1 a.) It is best if this attention does not always come as verbal praise ("I like how Ben is sitting," "What a nice picture," "Good boy"). Verbal praise is often empty of meaning if given too often, making children devalue it, or on the other hand, perform only for the praise. Instead, giving attention for good behavior must genuinely show the children that they are appreciated as individuals. This type of attention is powerful in guiding children's behavior. For example, when staff show interest in what children are doing, show them affection or sympathy, listen to them express ideas, have fun or relax with them, or help them, a bond is created so that children trust, listen to, and want to please that adult.

When most of the personal attention children get is for undesirable behavior, then children may do more of such behavior because it gets attention, even if the attention is not pleasant. However, when they know that they will get plenty of personal attention for doing acceptable things, then they are far more likely to use the positive behaviors that get attention.

Redirection

Redirection means that when a child is acting inappropriately, staff help the child focus on something to do instead, that is appropriate to achieve his or her goal. For example, if a child grabs a block from another child, staff point out that there are plenty of the same type of blocks to use on the shelf and help the child get those instead. Or if a child is throwing toys, and staff recognize that the child really wants to practice throwing, they encourage her to throw bean bags into a box. If a child is wandering aimlessly (and heading for trouble), staff help him to become involved in an activity he enjoys. If a child climbs on furniture, staff redirect her to another acceptable activity, such as climbing on an acceptable piece of equipment. Giving alternatives to aggression that are peaceful, such as helping children use words instead of fists, is also an example of redirection.

There are other non-punitive methods used for discipline besides the two described above. Sometimes staff can solve problems that come up between children by suggesting a solution, for example, by telling them who will ride a tricycle first and starting a "waiting list" for turns. The children then go along with the "judge's" decision and a conflict is avoided. (See photo 31.5.1 b.)

31.5.1 b Staff can effectively stop an argument between children by providing a solution. However, children learn more when the staff help them find their own solution.

Non-punitive methods must be used ***effectively*** if they are to ensure that children are cooperative in the group, not dangerous to themselves or others, or destructive in any way. ***Effectively*** means that the non-punitive methods work reasonably well to maintain the control of children's behavior that is necessary for order and safety in a classroom.

For any method to be effective, staff may need to follow up with extra attention, help, and guidance. For example, if staff ask children to "use their words" to tell another child to stop annoying them, the staff must observe to be sure the children's words have the desired effect. If the child pays no attention to the children's words, the adult must step in to call the child's attention to the verbal request, and to help the child engage in constructive activity.

The observer should be careful to objectively judge the effect of the non-punitive methods used by staff. In many cases, staff may choose a method that the observer would not have chosen. If the method used by staff is non-punitive and effective in managing the children's behavior, credit should be given, even though the observer might have handled the problem in a different way.

If there are no discipline problems observed, and punitive methods are not ever used, obviously the discipline methods being practiced are working well, so score 5.1 "Yes."

If there are many disruptions, and staff are too often not able to control children to maintain order and safety, score 5.1 "No."

Indicator

5.2 Certainly, the best discipline strategies prevent problems from even coming up, or at least minimize problems that are likely in groups of preschoolers. Staff in a program that is ***set up to avoid conflict and promote age-appropriate interaction*** understand what children are able to do well and what causes problems among them. They then arrange the children's environment to allow children to get along well with one another, without unnecessary restriction or "booby-traps" that cause difficulties. Some discipline strategies that are preventative in nature include:

- *Maintaining a dependable routine*

More problems are likely, and more discipline is needed, when children are grumpy. Therefore, if reliable classroom routines that meet the children's needs are in place, then children do not become stressed and irritable. For example, a reliable schedule means that the schedule is relaxed, but dependable. Children eat at regular times; they get rest when needed; and routines are not handled in a regimented way. All of these practices help keep young children from becoming irritable or stressed, so discipline problems are less frequent.

- *Keeping children busy, challenged, and interested*

Many strategies focus on avoiding problems by keeping children interested and busy. For example, having many interesting materials and activities for children to choose from each day, with new things added regularly, helps keep children engaged so there are fewer problems. Also, there are efforts to make sure children have lots of time for active play so they can use their energy in a positive way.

- *Avoiding competition and crowding*

Preschoolers do not do well with competition. They become aggressive or hurt, and they do not have the social skills needed to solve the problems that come with having to compete. Therefore, if staff provide plenty of materials and duplicates of popular toys, then children do not have to compete over things. Staff also ensure that children are not crowded and do not have to line up or be regimented in other ways. This helps minimize fights over territory and position.

Score 5.2 "Yes" if the program is set up to avoid problems and thus runs smoothly.

5.3 For staff to ***react consistently to children's behavior*** means that there is a similarity in the way they respond to and handle situations and the children. The basic rules for positive behavior in a group (e.g., not hurting self or others, staying safe, and not being destructive) are enforced equally by all staff. The same rules are used for all children and by all staff. For example, one staff member cannot ignore hitting while the other responds to stop such behavior. Consistency also means that things are handled similarly at different times.

This does not mean that there can be no flexibility in the way staff handle the children. But the flexibility cannot affect or change the important basic rules. Beyond the basic rules, there may be *some* different expectations for each child, based on the child's abilities. For example, a very active child might not be expected to sit in a large group for as long as others. He would be allowed to leave, while others would be expected to stay. However, this child would still need to be held to the basic rules—no hurting or disruptive behavior.

Staff may also differ in personality. One might be a more calm, quiet person, while another might be more enthusiastic. They might talk to children in somewhat

Indicator

different ways, using different kinds of words. These differences are acceptable as long as they use similar methods for the same reasons. For example, redirection should be used by all staff when there are problems over toys, but the staff might differ in the specifics of how they handle the redirection, based on the child's characteristics or their own personalities.

To score, watch carefully to see how *all* staff handle children's behavior throughout the observation. If differences in the handling of specific children or among different staff members are minor and do not seem to cause unfairness or give mixed messages to children, score 5.3 "Yes." If problems are observed due to a lack of consistency between staff score "No." For example, if one staff member has the difficult task of handling all the problems because the other is not involved, or one child is, for some reason, allowed to hurt others, while the rest of the children cannot, or if one staff member is punitive while the other uses positive methods, score "No."

31.7.1 In this argument over a toy (hidden behind the boy's back), the teacher patiently talks about the problem until the children come to a satisfying solution.

7.1 To ***actively involve children in solving their problems and conflicts*** requires that staff are not the ones who give solutions to children. Instead, when problems come up with children, the staff intervene and stop any behavior that goes against the basic rules (e.g., not hurting others or not being destructive). They then help the child find a solution to the problem in some way, often through talking about why the problem came up, asking questions to clarify things, helping children to recognize the effect they have on others, and then helping them to find a solution to the problem that is satisfying for them. (See photo 31.7.1.)

For example, if two children are fighting over a tricycle, staff might involve children in solving the problem as follows:

STAFF "What's going on here? I can see that you are pretty angry with each other."

CHILD 1 "I want to ride this trike, and he has it."

CHILD 2 "I had it first, and she pulled me off." [*crying*]

STAFF "What can we do about this? How can we solve this problem?"

CHILD 2 "Make her go away. Send her inside."

CHILD 1 "No! I want to ride!"

STAFF "It sounds like both of you want to ride the trike. But you cannot pull him off the trike. See his face? How did that make him feel?"

CHILD 1 "Bad."

STAFF "And did that get you what you wanted? Do you have the trike now?"

CHILD 1 "No, but I want it."

STAFF "Can we figure out how both of you can ride trikes? Are there any other trikes around? Look and see if there is one."

CHILD 2 "You can ride the trike by the tree."

STAFF "Would that work?"

Neither child answers, but Child 1 runs to ride the other trike.

Indicator

It takes longer and more staff effort to help children figure out solutions. But the effort becomes worth it when staff see children using such problem solving methods on their own. It takes time for children to develop problem-solving skills, but the skills are less likely to develop if children are not taught how to use them by staff.

The amount of help required in teaching children to solve their problems will vary, depending on the age and abilities of the children. Younger children will need more help than older children. However, this method should be used with all children in groups being evaluated with the ECERS-R.

To give credit for 7.1 (score "Yes"), staff must help children to solve their conflicts and problems, not by giving the solution, but by having children put some effort of their own into the process. At a minimum, staff should help children understand the effects of what they do, in terms of feelings or outcome. For older children, more involved methods should be used where children are led to coming up with their own solution to a problem.

This kind of problem-solving strategy does not have to be used each time a problem comes up during the observation, but it must be obvious that it is regularly used if there are problems.

In some cases, no problems are observed during an observation. In this case, staff may be asked what they do in case conflicts arise, and the indicator should be scored based on the response. However, if any problems are observed, the score must be based on how the problems are usually solved.

7.2 The major way in which children learn how to get along with one another is through playing together, with positive adult guidance when problems come up. However, certain activities can also be used to supplement children's understanding of social skills.

Examples of ***activities to help children understand social skills*** are provided in the indicator. Others include:

- Reading stories about common conflicts and problems
- Using group discussions to develop class rules
- Using puppets or role play to act out common conflicts and problems and different ways to solve them
- Having children identify the feelings that a variety of faces are showing

Examples of less formal activities include singing songs about how to be nice to friends, drawing pictures of special friends, asking questions of children in the housekeeping center about how dolls might feel. There are curriculum materials and kits that focus on helping children learn positive social skills. The use of such curriculum materials also counts as an example of this type of activity.

To give credit for 7.2 (score "Yes"), the activities must be done regularly enough to make an impact on the children's understanding. Therefore, such activities should be used at least once a week, especially the activities that can be integrated into children's usual play.

7.3 In some cases, it helps to get assistance from an outside expert when children cannot be handled well by staff. Teachers sometimes need another point of view that is not found within the classroom or the center. For example, something in the program might be causing great challenges for a child who has difficulties getting along with others. The staff might not be able to tell that the issue could be resolved with some environmental changes. Another professional is likely to look at the child and the environment more objectively, and help the staff see the child from another point of view.

Since staff do not always have the answers, this indicator requires that they ***seek advice from other professionals concerning behavior problems***. This is most necessary when the behavior problems are serious, endangering the child or others.

In most cases, ***other professionals*** means someone from outside the program that specializes in the area of concern. Examples of such professionals include mental health specialists, psychologists, social workers, special educators or therapists with special training, and pediatricians. In some cases, however, a program staff member can count as the "other professional" if the person has a specialization in the area of concern and can give an unbiased perspective.

Score "Yes" to 7.3 if the staff has ever used outside professionals to help with behavior problems. If no other professionals have ever been used, score "Yes" if staff can provide the name of an agency or practitioner they would use if needed. If staff say that outside help is never used or would never be needed, do not give credit (score "No").

32 Staff-child interactions

General information about this item

Young children must often depend on adults to meet the many needs they have for protection, learning, and positive relationships. In early childhood programs, much of what children need must be provided through the interactions staff have with them.

Information required for scoring the indicators in this item must be observed in order to score. No questions should be used to gather information required to score this item.

An observation period of at least 2½ to 3 hours should be completed before scoring, to ensure that a range of conditions, requiring varying types of staff responses, is observed. For example, the observer would want to see what interactions are like during both relaxed and more stressful periods of the day.

For this item, ***interactions*** refers to the ways in which staff relate to the children. These interactions can be shown through physical contact and other non-verbal communication, such as gestures, the focus of attention, or facial expressions. They can also be shown in the verbal communication that occurs between staff and children.

Interactions are usually classified as being negative, neutral, or positive. Negative interactions often carry messages of anger, coldness, disrespect, impatience, or unhappiness. When received by others, they make the recipients feel less valuable, competent, appreciated, or loved. Positive interactions are the opposite, carrying messages of being happy, content, relaxed, patient, respectful, and interested, helping the recipient to feel more valuable, competent, appreciated, and loved. Neutral interactions do not give strong messages of any type—they are neither harmful nor supportive.

The impact of negative interactions on the recipient is considered to be stronger than the impact of either positive or neutral interactions. In other words, negative interactions tend to be given more weight when scoring because it takes many positive interactions to balance the effect of one negative interaction.

When observing a group, it is likely that all three types of interactions will be observed, in differing amounts. It is up to the observer to see the average effect of all interactions on all children in the group. When there are different staff members, with different interaction styles, or if one staff member uses different types of interactions throughout the observation, the observer must see if the overall interaction climate sufficiently meets the needs of the children.

Interactions can also be characterized as warm or cold. Warm interactions may be shown in appropriate physical contact, such as hugging or putting an arm around a

Indicator

child. Warmth can also be shown by smiling, looking pleased, making eye contact, or using a pleasant tone of voice. Cold interactions can be shown through impersonal or distant behavior, disinterest, or by using physical contact only to control children's behavior.

It helps to consider the classroom interaction climate in terms of the warmth (or coldness) that the children feel, and then consider whether the setting is warm enough for each child to be comfortable. For example, think of each staff member as a heater, whose job it is to keep the classroom at a comfortable temperature. One might be extremely warm, putting out enough heat to keep the classroom warm enough, even though another staff member tends to be neutral or slightly cold in interactions. However, if one staff member is like an air conditioner in the room, often blasting out cold air, then it is unlikely that the warmer teacher would be able to counteract this effect on the classroom temperature.

In addition, be sure to observe the effects of adult interactions on all children. Remember that even when a negative interaction is directed at only one of the children, the others experience the interaction second hand. The other children can become fearful or anxious, thinking that such negative interactions might be directed at them, or they might take such negative behavior as an example of how to act towards others.

In all items involving any type of interaction, ***staff*** refer to those adults who are in the classroom and work with the children daily (or almost daily), for a substantial portion of the day. This can include volunteers, if they are in the classroom for the required amount of time.

Adults who are in the classroom for short periods of the day, or who are not a regular daily part of the classroom, do not count in evaluating whether the requirements of the item are met, *unless they are observed to interact very negatively with children*. For example, if a therapist, parent, or a director of a program comes into the classroom and interacts with children for short or irregular periods, these interactions do not count in scoring the item, unless the visitors are negative with the children. As an exception, in programs where the usual daily staffing pattern includes different people as teaching assistants or "floater" staff (including parent volunteers in parent co-operatives or students working in lab school settings), these assistants should be counted as staff during the observation.

A closer look at each indicator

1.1 Being ***responsive to and involved with children*** means that staff pay attention to the children's interests, activities, needs, concerns, or requests and provide them with what is needed. Children need adults to interact with them for many reasons—for example, they may need someone to help them, to share in what they are doing, or to provide affection, comfort, or information. Staff can meet the children's needs for interaction either verbally or non-verbally.

Staff who are ***not responsive and involved with children*** might be observed to have their minds on other things and not on the children. (See photo 32.1.1, next page.) They might show that they do not share the children's interests or consider what children want to be important or necessary. They will not respond to what children need. They might also ignore the children or seem preoccupied.

Indicator

Additional examples (besides those in the indicator in the ECERS-R) of staff *not* being responsive to or involved with children include:

- Ignoring or not answering a child's question
- Telling a child to be quiet when she wants to say something
- Reprimanding a child who is hurt because he is crying
- Paying no attention when a child shows what he has created
- Not checking a child who says she feels sick
- Continuing a group activity when it is clear that children are not interested
- Ignoring children when they fight or are cruel to one another
- Not reacting to children's signs of being tired, hungry, or needing to use the toilet
- Belittling children's fears
- Teasing a child who is upset or embarrassed
- Ignoring a child who shows a need for physical affection
- Spending much time on tasks not involving the children

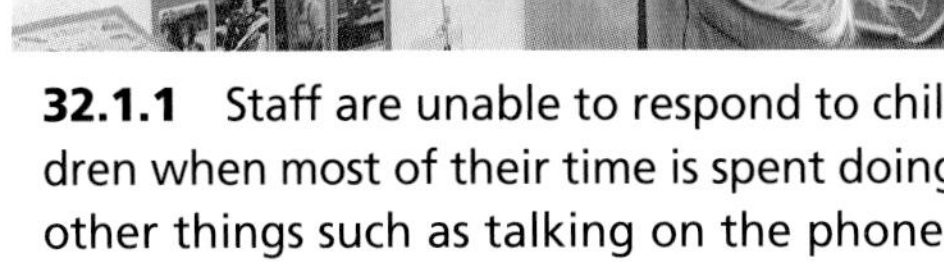

32.1.1 Staff are unable to respond to children when most of their time is spent doing other things such as talking on the phone.

Of course, there will always be some lack of response when staff are working with groups of children. However, such examples should not be observed regularly throughout an observation. They should be the exception, rather than the general behavior of the staff.

Score 1.1 "Yes" if staff, on average, show a lack of response to or involvement with the children. This means that there is much ignoring of children, with many examples observed such as those listed above and in the indicator itself.

1.2 At times, an observer may have a preference for certain types of staff interactions with children. For example, one observer may think that if an interaction is not enthusiastic, then it is not pleasant. Another observer may think that if staff are not very physically affectionate, then their interactions are unpleasant. Yet another may think that soothing, calm interactions are preferred to enthusiastic, lively ones.

For this indicator, ***unpleasant interactions*** are those that make children have bad feelings about themselves, e.g., that they are incompetent, of little value, not loveable, not capable, or wrong. Unpleasant interactions give a message that is opposite to the message given by pleasant interactions, which support the children's good feelings about themselves.

To determine whether staff ***interactions with children are unpleasant***, it is best to observe not only what staff say or do, but the children's responses as well. An interaction that might sound unpleasant to one observer might sound fine to another. It is the child's reaction or expression that will give the answer about his response. When children respond to unpleasant interactions, they may look anxious, hurt, frightened, unhappy, or "turned off" in another way. They will not look relaxed, interested, happy, engaged, or secure.

Indicator

In addition to those listed in the indicator, other examples of unpleasant interactions include staff:

- Yelling at children
- Ordering children to do things
- Being sarcastic or critical
- Being rude to the children
- Handling children roughly
- Belittling, teasing, or embarrassing children
- Constantly telling children "No"
- Discounting children's feelings

Score 1.2 "Yes" if *many* unpleasant interactions are observed either throughout the observation or during any period of the observation. More than just one or two brief examples must be observed to score this indicator "Yes."

1.3 ***Physical contact*** includes any instance of staff touching children. Staff can use such contact to either control children or to show affection, interest, or support. Young children will need both kinds of touch.

When physical contact is used ***principally for control***, staff *usually* touch children to move, stop, or guide them but do not touch children to show support or affection. The contact is not carried out with any warmth. Certainly some physical contact may need to be used to control preschool-aged children, but this should not be the primary use and should be balanced by contact to show support or affection. Note that physical contact can be used to control children *and* to show support and affection at the same time. If this is true, then the physical contact is not being used principally to control the children—there is a balance.

When physical contact is used ***inappropriately***, the contact is intrusive to the child. Such contact can often be identified by watching the child's response—if the contact is perceived as being negative, the child may pull away or show a facial expression that suggests dislike or discomfort. In addition to the examples given in the indicator, hitting, yanking, or other physical punishment are inappropriate uses of physical contact, as well as continuing any physical affection a child does not want or enjoy, such as forcing a child to accept kisses.

To score this indicator, pay attention to the kind of physical contact (touching) used by staff throughout the full observation and especially to the children's responses to that contact. Keep track of when physical contact is used, the intention, and the children's responses to determine the usual practice.

Score 1.3 "Yes" when most of the physical contact is used to control the children (without showing support or affection) or when it is not received well by the children. (See photo 32.1.3.) Remember that this negative use would need to be the usual practice, rather than the exception to score "Yes."

32.1.3 This is a rare example of staff in this classroom using physical contact for control. If most of the physical contact is used to control, children do not experience the affection they need from their caring adults.

Indicator

32.3.1a The teacher responds to this child by listening attentively to his questions.

32.3.1b This teacher shows great interest in what this child has to say.

32.3.1 c

32.3.1 d

32.3.1 c–d These children know that caring adults will always help them when they are upset.

3.1 Staff who ***respond to children*** are doing so in answer to a child's need for attention. The child might show a need for the attention either verbally or non-verbally. Responding in a ***warm, supportive manner*** means that the staff answer the child's needs in a way that is satisfying to the child. Such a response helps children to have good feelings about themselves—they feel safe, competent, and valuable. (See photos 32.3.1 a–d.) A warm, supportive response shows that staff share the children's interests, consider the children's needs to be important, and act to meet them. They will not ignore the children. Additional examples (besides those in the indicator) of staff responding in a warm supportive manner include:

- Answering a child's question
- Listening attentively to a child when she wants to say something
- Comforting and reassuring a child who is hurt or crying
- Paying attention when a child shows what he has created
- Showing concern and following through when a child says she feels sick
- Ending a group activity when it is clear that children are not interested
- Intervening when children fight and cooperating with them to solve the problem

Indicator

32.3.1 e

32.3.1 f

32.3.1 e–f A teacher will participate in neutral interaction at times, while being positive at others.

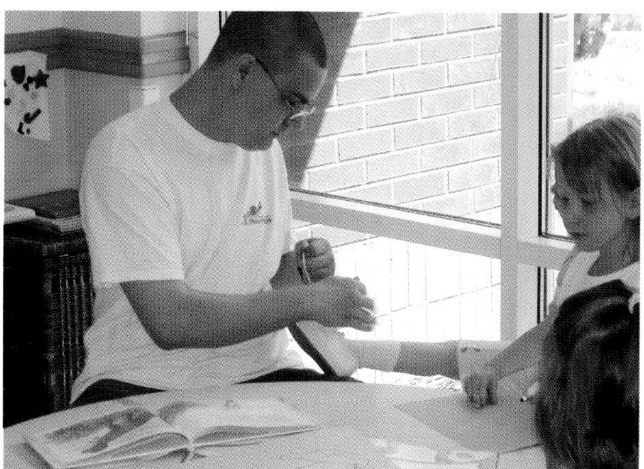

32. 3.1 g Neutral interactions (neither positive nor negative) often occur during routine tasks, such as this shoe-tying.

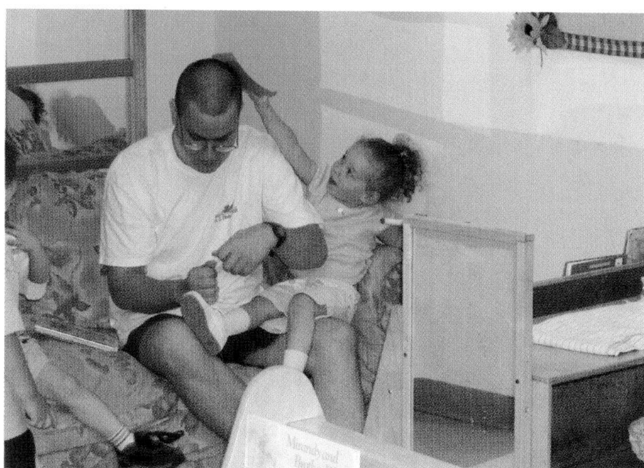

32.3.1 h However, tying a shoe can become a positive interaction when the child sits on her teacher's lap.

- Providing what children need when they are tired, hungry, or need to use the toilet
- Helping a child deal with fears, anger, or disappointment
- Comforting a child who is upset or embarrassed
- Giving a child physical affection when needed

Of course, there will always be missed opportunities for providing warm and supportive responses when working with groups of children. However, missed opportunities should be the exception, and warm, supportive responses the general rule.

A mix of positive and neutral interactions usually occurs in any classroom. Watch the children's responses to see what message they are getting from how the staff respond. (See photos 32.3.1 e–i.)

32.3.1 i Look at the faces of the children to see how they receive the interaction. Is it negative, neutral or positive?

Indicator

Score 3.1 "Yes" if staff, on average, show warm and supportive responses to the children. This means that there is very little ignoring of children or responding to them in a neutral or negative way. Many positive interactions should be noted throughout the observation, such as those listed above and in the indicator itself.

Even with children whose behavior is more difficult for staff to manage, the vast majority of responses to the children should be warm and supportive, since such responses are more likely to help any child develop positive social skills and a positive sense of self.

3.2 See 1.2 for the meaning of ***unpleasant interactions***.

Few, if any, means that unpleasant interactions are observed rarely, if at all, during an observation. If a few unpleasant interactions are observed, they should be mild enough in their impact, to cause no lasting unhappiness, anger, or frustration in children.

Inevitably, some unpleasant reactions by children (crying, complaining, or an unhappy facial expression) may be observed, for example, when staff prohibit children's behaviors that are potentially dangerous or destructive. Even when done in a supportive, warm way, stopping a child from doing something that cannot be allowed may make a child unhappy. Yet, few such interactions should be necessary. These types of interactions can be minimized by setting up an environment where few restrictions for children are necessary—for example, because staff have developmentally appropriate expectations for children's behavior, lots of safe, interesting activities, safe spaces, and equipment for children to use, and maintain a calm atmosphere.

Score 3.2 "No" if more than just a few unpleasant interactions are observed, either with the group or with any child. Unpleasant interactions cannot be excused for any reason (e.g., "But that child's behavior was so provocative" or "She was doing the best she could under those circumstances"). If there are more than just a few observed during an observation, for any reason, then this indicator cannot be scored "Yes."

5.1 As stated in 1.3, ***physical contact*** includes any staff touching of children. This indicator requires staff to use this contact to show ***warmth***, which gives a positive message of affection, encouragement, appreciation, interest, or support to the child.

When physical contact is used ***appropriately***, the contact is pleasant and not intrusive to the child. Such contact can often be identified by watching the child's response—if the contact is perceived as being positive, the child will not pull away or show a facial expression of dislike or discomfort.

For physical contact to be ***warm and appropriate***, it does *not* always have to be extremely obvious. An example of obvious warm, appropriate contact is when a teacher enthusiastically hugs or cuddles with a child, and the contact lasts for more than just a second or two. (See photo 32.5.1 a, next page.) Warm, appropriate contact is also seen in the *more subtle*, less obvious actions such as the quick, unnecessary touches of children (smoothing hair, touching a hand or shoulder, sitting close enough to touch, holding hands, or gently touching while guiding or controlling a child). Such touches let children know the teacher is present and supportive. (See photos 32.5.1 b–c, next page.)

Indicator

32.5.1 a

32.5.1 b

32.5.1 a–b Staff can sit on the floor to encourage physical contact with children.

In some cases, what staff think of as affectionate physical contact can be inappropriately used, because it is unwanted by the child. Some children, for example, will not want to be hugged tightly, kissed, tickled, or cuddled. In addition, overly enthusiastic physical contact often causes things to get out of control, and staff are unable to calm children without having to resort to negative interaction. Thus, for example, staff allowing children to "climb all over them" would not be considered appropriate. And of course, any physical contact considered sexual in nature would not be appropriate.

32.5.1 c During free play the teacher talks with all children, and adds to the warmth of classroom through touch.

There is a range of what is acceptable to meet the requirements of this indicator, as long as it is positive from a child's point of view—not intrusive or distasteful to a child and does not lead to over-stimulation or misinterpretation.

When scoring this indicator, all children do not need to be observed receiving the same amount of appropriate physical contact, but warm physical contact with children should be generally true. Score "Yes" if many of the children, at some point during the observation, receive some appropriate physical contact that carries a message of warmth. Many instances, including the more subtle signs of affection, must be observed.

5.2 ***Show respect for children*** means that staff interact with all children in a way that lets them know they are valuable human beings. Often, this means that staff treat children with no less politeness and concern than they would give to their own friends. It also means that staff treat children as they themselves would prefer to be treated by others. (See photos 32.5.2 a–c, next page.) In addition to examples listed in the indicator, staff might:

- Respond to children's feelings in a way that shows acceptance
- Consider children's ideas
- Use polite words and actions with children

Indicator

32.5.2 a This teacher takes the child's feelings seriously as he listens to what she says.

32.5.2 b

32.5.2 c

32.5.2 b-c Children feel valued when staff are interested in what they are doing.

- Guide, rather than "boss" children
- Share with the children
- Show patience and support
- Appreciate each child for who he or she is, without comparing to others or emphasizing the negative

To score 5.2 "Yes," staff must show throughout the observation that they accept children for who they are and treat them politely and kindly, showing that each child is important. This must be consistently observed across all children, with only minor lapses, if any.

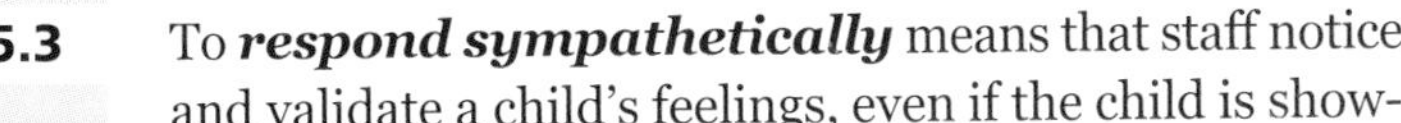

5.3 To ***respond sympathetically*** means that staff notice and validate a child's feelings, even if the child is showing emotions that are often considered unacceptable, such as anger or whining. The feelings should be accepted, although inappropriate behaviors, such as hitting or throwing things, should not be allowed. (See photos 32.5.3 a–b.) Often, when a child's feelings are validated through a sympathetic response by staff, the problem a child is having is vastly reduced, and the problem can be solved more easily than if the staff had responded with anger or impatience. A negative response by staff only lets the child know that he or she is not understood and that no one cares.

32.5.3 a Staff respond sympathetically even though a little bump may not be a big problem.

32.5.3 b Staff take the time to help children when they are feeling upset.

Indicator

32.7.1 a

32.7.1 b

32.7.1 c

32.7.1 d

32.7.1 a-d Staff can show enjoyment of being with children in many ways.

A sympathetic response should be provided in most, but not necessarily all, cases. If children are able to solve minor issues for themselves, then staff response is not needed. For example, if a child falls down and makes a very small complaint ("Oh!"), but quickly gets up and moves on happily, no staff response is needed. Very strong sympathetic responses, when not perceived as needed by a child, can be unsettling and give the child a message that does not reassure him that he can handle things independently.

Indicator 5.3 is not true (score "No") when staff discount children's feelings as being unnecessary, inappropriate, or incorrect. This is usually shown by ignoring the child, reprimanding, or punishing the child for unacceptable feelings.

The observer needs to get an overall impression of the responses of the staff. If minor problems persist and are ignored or if staff respond in an unsympathetic manner, do not give credit for this indicator.

7.1 Whether staff truly enjoy being with the children cannot actually be observed. Instead, the observer can only tell if staff ***seem to enjoy being with the children.*** Obvious signs that staff seem to enjoy being with the children include:

- Showing interest in what the children are doing
- Being pleasant with the children

Indicator

- Showing some enthusiasm about what children do
- Showing affection or appreciation for the children
- Paying attention to their work with the children, not to unrelated things
- Initiating social conversations
- Facilitating or joining in play without taking over.

The extent to which staff demonstrate their enjoyment of being with children will vary from person to person. Some individuals are obviously more overt in their enjoyment of children, while others are more quiet or restrained. (See photos 32.7.1 a–d, previous page.) Either is acceptable, as long as there is no obvious detachment, neutrality, or negativity shown.

Give credit for 7.1 (score "Yes") when all staff show enjoyment in being with the children. Variation among staff and the amount that any staff member enjoys being with each child is acceptable, as long as the enjoyment is clearly present.

7.2 Indicator 5.2 requires that staff show respect for children, meaning that staff interact with all children in a way that lets them know they are valuable as individuals. This indicator requires more—that staff encourage the development of mutual respect between children and adults. ***Mutual respect*** means that one individual respects the other equally. In this case, staff not only respect the children, but the children are also encouraged to respect the staff. (See photo 32.7.2.)

32.7.2 By working together as partners to complete routine tasks, children and staff develop mutual respect.

This does not mean that children must consistently treat the staff with respect—that they are polite to them and accept them for who they are. Young children have not yet learned the social skills adults have that allow them to show respect for others. It is up to the adults in the children's lives to help them learn through modeling and gentle guidance.

Staff model respect for the children by treating all people, both adults and children, as if they were good friends. They are polite and acceptant, solve disagreements without anger, do not discriminate or show prejudice in any way, and always make an attempt to give attention and consideration to the point of view of others.

Staff guide children to learn the skills needed to show respect to staff. For example, they discuss their own feelings, remind children of the rules for how people should be treated, and then gently explain that they would not treat others in such a way. They do not usually ignore children's inappropriate behavior. For example, if a child yells at a staff member, she would respond, not with anger, but by briefly letting the child know that the yelling hurt her feelings and that staff would never yell at a child. The fairness of the situation would be emphasized.

Score 7.2 "Yes" if, throughout the observation, mutual respect is shown between children and adults. It is not necessary to see "teaching" of mutual respect, although if this is observed, it must be handled positively (explaining), rather than negatively (disciplining or forcing).

Of course, demanding or actively teaching children to be respectful of staff, without staff showing equal respect to the children, is not acceptable. It is not sufficient for giving credit for 7.2.

33 Interactions among children

General information about this item

Helping children develop the social skills needed to get along well with other children is a major task faced by the staff in early childhood programs. Young children in group care are not old enough to understand how to best get along with one another. It takes a long time and lots of patience to help children learn the necessary social skills, such as cooperation, sharing, and understanding the feelings of others. In addition, children require the time to grow and develop before they gain the skills to interact well with others. ***Interactions among children (peer interaction)*** refers to the relationships children form with one another—how well they play together and whether they fight or get along well.

The methods staff use to encourage positive social behavior among children is of great importance. Forcing good behavior usually does not help create the abilities needed by children to get along well, independently, without having a "police officer" supervising—an adult who ensures that the rules are followed. Restricting children, so they can rarely interact naturally, might keep children from being troublesome with their peers (the other children in the group), but it does little to help them learn to get along well. When children have to depend on an adult to ensure that they follow the rules for getting along well, without actually learning to get along well by themselves, they miss the chance to learn *self-discipline*, because the discipline must always come from supervising adults.

Children generally want to play with others and to have friends. This comes more easily to some children than to others, but all children will need guidance from staff if they are to learn how to get along well with others. There are specific methods that have proven to be effective in helping children develop social skills. These include having staff:

- Give children many chances to interact—to play together, to do routines together, to communicate. But avoid putting children into impossible situations with others that they do not have the ability to handle. For example, young children have problems sharing (as do adults, quite often). Therefore, minimize the need to share, and when sharing is required, actively and positively help the children to work together.
- Supervise children's interactions closely so that when problems come up (as is natural), staff can step in to help children work things out.
- Model the way to interact with others—do not expect children to act nicely with one another if staff do not show them how to do this by demonstrating positive interaction in their own behavior towards one another, other adults, and towards the children.
- Emphasize cooperation, and facilitate it, but never force it.

Indicator

- Accept the feelings of the child and of others, even if the behavior cannot be accepted. For example, if one child is angry with another child and hits that child, staff need to make it clear that they understand the anger, but will not allow the hitting.

These are the ideas represented in the indicators of this item. At the lower levels of quality, it is required that children have the many chances needed to interact with one another, and that when problems come up, the staff intervene. In addition, there must be some positive interaction among the children.

At the higher levels of quality, staff play a stronger teaching role, modeling what is needed and providing children with the learning opportunities that will eventually allow them to get along well with others all by themselves, without an adult needing to be "right there."

Information required for scoring the indicators in this item must be observed. No questions should be used to gather information required to score the item, except if the information needed to score 7.2 is not observed. In that case, ask the question provided in the scale.

In this item, ***staff*** refers to those adults who are in the classroom and work with the children daily (or almost daily), for a substantial portion of the day. This can include volunteers, if they are in the classroom for the required amount of time.

Adults who are in the classroom for short periods of the day, or who are not a regular daily part of the classroom, do not count in evaluating whether the requirements of the item are met, *unless they are observed to interact very negatively with children.* For example, if a therapist, parent, or a director of a program comes into the classroom and interacts with children for short or irregular periods, these interactions do not count in scoring the item, unless they are negative with the children. As an exception, in programs where the usual daily staffing pattern includes different people as teaching assistants or "floater" staff (including parent volunteers in parent co-operatives or students working in lab school settings), these assistants should be counted as staff during the observation.

An observation period of at least 2½ to 3 hours should be completed before scoring to ensure that a range of conditions, requiring varying types of staff responses, is observed. For example, the observer would want to see what interactions are like during both relaxed and more stressful times of the day and in routines in and play.

A closer look at each indicator

1.1 ***Interaction among children (peer interaction)***, as stated above, refers to the relationships children form with one another, not with adults—how they play together, their communication, and whether they fight or get along well.

Interaction among children ***not encouraged*** means that there is little support provided, either by staff, schedule, or the environment itself, to help children play and communicate with one another. In some cases this is because staff actively discourage interactions, for example, by:

- Requiring children to do their work or play alone, with no interruptions from others

Indicator

- Requiring children to do the same thing at the same time, but with little communicating or playing together
- Maintaining very strict control, or a punitive atmosphere, that makes children too uncomfortable to interact with one another

Score 1.1 "Yes" when interaction among children is actively discouraged.

1.2 ***Positive peer interaction*** means that children get along well, with relatively few major disagreements, fights, or hurt feelings. The interaction is pleasant among children, they enjoy it and seek it out. In other words, the children are friendly and respectful towards one another.

As noted earlier, it takes time and staff support for young children to develop the abilities required for positive peer interaction.

Little or no staff guidance means that staff are not taking the steps required to help children succeed as they attempt to interact positively with one another. They can either not take action at all or their action can create negative social situations. For example, indicator 1.2 is true when staff:

- Are detached and pay little attention to the children
- Encourage negative interactions among children, such as allowing children to punish others, favoring certain children and not handling issues fairly, or encouraging children to "fight back"
- Demonstrate or use biased or prejudiced treatment of a child (as described in Item 28, Promoting acceptance of diversity)

Score 1.2 "Yes" if most of the action taken by staff does not provide guidance for positive peer interaction among the children.

1.3 See Indicator 1.2 for the meaning of ***positive peer interaction***.

Little or no means that positive peer interaction is rarely observed during the observation. Either children do not interact much at all, or there is an overwhelming amount of negative interaction among the children. (See photo 33.1.3.)

It is to be expected that since young children rarely have the skill or understanding required for constant positive relationships, there will always be some negative or neutral interactions observed in any group. This does not mean that there is little or no positive peer interaction. To score, pay attention not only to the negative, but to all peer interactions across the observation. Notice when children are getting along well, even though the negative interactions might be more compelling. Be sure to score based on the whole picture, not just on any negative interactions observed.

33.1.3 Arguments result when there are too few materials for children to play with.

Indicator 1.3 is true (score "Yes") when it is very difficult to find instances of positive, or even neutral, interactions among children. The vast majority of interactions among the children are negative (e.g., hurtful or unpleasant). These negative interactions may be verbal such as teasing and bickering as well as physical, such as hitting, kicking, and biting. There are few times during the observation when things are pleasant and peaceful among the children.

33 Interactions among children

Indicator

3.1 ***Peer interaction encouraged*** means that there is some support provided by staff to help children play, communicate, and get along with one another. In some cases staff actively encourage peer interactions, for example, by:

- Allowing interaction and helping children to listen to and understand others as they communicate
- Providing considerable time in the schedule when children are allowed to choose their own companions
- Maintaining a relaxed, rather than strict, atmosphere that makes children comfortable enough to interact with one another
- Helping children become involved with one another in play or routines
- Allowing children to do their work or play in small groups rather than all together or alone. Small groups, especially those that the children form themselves, are most likely to encourage children to get along well.

Interaction is also ***encouraged*** when the program is set up so that the environment actually helps children get along with one another, rather than hindering them. For example, staff ensure that:

- the room arrangement never requires children to be crowded together.
- the schedule is dependable but flexible, so that children are relaxed.
- activities are set up to minimize competition over space and materials, for example, by providing enough materials and choices, and by controlling the number of children in an area at one time if needed.

Score 3.1 "Yes" when interaction among children is usually encouraged (supported, helped along) in some way during the observation. There can be periods or instances when interaction is not encouraged, but these must not represent the usual practice observed to give credit for this indicator.

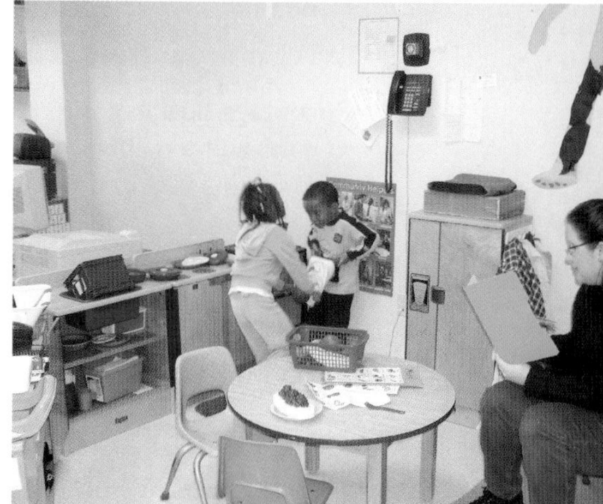

33.3.2 a This staff member is busy with another task and ignores children fighting over the toy.

3.2 ***Negative and hurtful peer interactions*** are those that make children unhappy. Examples include children picking on one another, being "mean," physically harming, teasing, grabbing things away, pushing, interrupting or destroying what someone is working on, making faces, saying "bad" words, or showing prejudice. Any of these interactions can happen in an early childhood program, and it is up to staff to minimize their occurrence.

Score 3.2 "Yes" when it is observed that staff stop most of the negative interactions between children. It is possible that staff will miss some of the negative interactions that the observer notices. If negative interactions are major and recurring (causing a lot of hurt to a child) and frequently ignored or missed, then credit cannot be given. However, if only a few minor negative interactions are missed, or if they are resolved with no intervention from staff, credit can still be given. (See photos 33.3.2 a–b.)

33.3.2 b In contrast, this staff member stays close to an activity that requires children to cooperate, guiding to avoid negative interactions.

Indicator

At this minimal level of quality, the expectation is only for staff to stop the negative behavior being shown. For example, the staff may stop hitting by saying "no" and "stop." At the higher levels of quality, in addition to stopping the negative behavior, staff are required to also work through the conflict with further discussion.

There may be times when the children being observed get along very well with one another, and the observer does not witness children fighting and arguing at all. In this situation, the indicator may be scored "Yes," and the assumption is made that staff manage children's behavior so there are few occurrences of negative behavior.

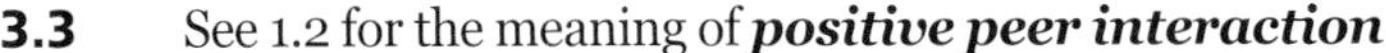

3.3 See 1.2 for the meaning of ***positive peer interaction***.

Some means that positive peer interaction is observed occasionally during the observation. (See photo 33.3.3.) The rest of the interaction tends to be more neutral than negative. *Neutral* means that the children's interaction is not negative (giving an unpleasant message) but yet not actively pleasant or positive (giving a pleasant message). There is not an overwhelming amount of negative interaction observed among the children, nor is positive interaction the regular practice.

To score, pay attention not only to the negative, but to all interactions across the observation. Notice when children are getting along well or neutrally, even though the negative interactions might be more compelling. Be sure to score based on the whole picture, not just on any negative interactions observed.

Indicator 3.3 is true (score "Yes") when it is not difficult to find instances of positive interactions among children. The vast majority of interactions among the children are *not* negative (hurtful, unpleasant). There are times during the observation when children communicate well with one another and play side-by-side or together with no problems, and things are pleasant and peaceful among the children.

5.1 To ***model good social skills*** means that staff are responsive, polite, interested, and cooperative with every person the children see them interacting with. This includes all children, other staff, parents, and others who become part of the children's environment. (See photos 33.5.1 a–b.)

Children copy what they see adults doing. If adults are physically and verbally aggressive with others, then it is likely that the children who see this will also act out the same behavior. When adults are kind, gentle, and respectful of others, children will be more likely to copy this type of behavior also. It is often said that "Children do what we *do*, not what we *tell* them to do." This emphasizes the power of using modeling as a teaching tool.

Usually, ***staff model good social skills*** when interacting with other adults. However, they are less likely to show children the same kind of respect. When staff ignore children, yell at them,

33.3.3 Children play side-by-side and communicate with one another.

33.5.1 a Children watch staff interact well with other adults and learn about how to get along with others.

33.5.1 b Children have seen teachers helping their friends so often that they want to do it too.

Indicator

33.5.2 a The teacher reminds a child to slow down so that her passenger will be safe.

33.5.2 b Staff encourage the children to cooperate with one another to make this telephone work.

boss them around, shout demands, spank or punish, show impatience, are cynical, tease to belittle, or do other things that the children find unpleasant, they are *not* modeling good social skills.

Of course, it is necessary for staff to maintain control in a group—to be the adult. But this can be done with respect, sincere interest, politeness, and gentle guidance. When such positive methods are used consistently, then credit can be given for 5.1 (score "Yes").

5.2 The intent of this indicator goes far beyond what is required in 3.2. Here staff must not simply stop negative interactions; rather, they are required to help children develop positive interaction with peers. Some of their teaching can be proactive, such as making children aware of the effect of their actions on others, or suggesting ways to cooperate (see photos 33.5.2 a–b). At other times staff can guide children who are involved in a conflict to use discussion and negotiation, so that useful learning comes out of the negative interactions.

Social behavior with peers means the ways in which children act with one another—how they get along. ***Appropriate social behavior*** is that which allows children to get along *well* with one another. Some of the behaviors include cooperating, being friendly, taking turns, being able to tell what another child wants, being able to see the effects of one's own actions on others, being able to solve problems through discussion and not aggression, talking and listening, showing interest in what others do, and helping. Adults need to remember that these behaviors are goals for children to work towards and that it takes a long time and much learning for children to establish them.

Appropriate social behavior also means that the behavior is developmentally appropriate for the children—they are able to do it without facing impossible odds. Thus, expectations for behavior should be matched to different ages and abilities, and children should not be expected to do what is too difficult for them. For example:

- Children are not expected to share when this means that it would be difficult to do an activity in a satisfying way. However, sharing and its benefits would be taught through cooperative activities where sharing was enjoyable, such as using a walkie-talkie or rocking in a rocking boat.

Indicator

33.7.1 a Children in this mixed-age group cooperate to have fun on this rocker that needs two children.

33.7.1 b While children play together with the sand and trucks they learn about taking turns and working collaboratively.

- Children are not expected to be perfectly polite, always having to use words such as "please, thank you, or excuse me," although gradually learning to use such words should be encouraged. Adults should be careful to model polite behavior towards the children and praise them for using it.
- Children are not expected to have absolute self-control, but rather a "good heart" or good intentions towards others. However, gradual learning and understanding of self-control should be supported.
- Children are not expected to work out difficult problems with one another independently, but staff work with them to help them find a satisfying solution to the problem.
- Shy or isolated children are not expected to find friends to play with on their own, but with plenty of help from the staff.

33.7.1 c Children get along well and enjoy being with their classmates.

Score 5.2 "Yes" if examples of such teaching are seen during the observation.

Indicator 5.2 is not true (score "No") if the staff *usually* force children to interact positively with peers, provide solutions to all problems between children, ignore children's feelings, do nothing to help shy or less popular children to find people to play with, and do not intervene to help when needed.

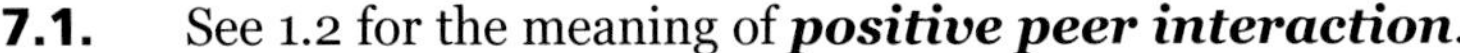

7.1. See 1.2 for the meaning of ***positive peer interaction***.

Usually positive means that *most* of the peer interaction that takes place during the observation is pleasant, cooperative, and rarely negative. Children are relaxed with one another and generally happy. If there are some less pleasant interactions, they are not major, and they are resolved in a way that does not continue bad feelings. (See photos 33.7.1 a–d.)

33.7.1 d Children enjoy playing together with gross motor equipment.

To score, pay attention to all peer interactions across the observation. Notice when children are getting along well or neutrally, even though negative interactions might be more compelling because they are often more dramatic. Be sure to score based

Indicator

on the whole picture, not just on any negative interactions observed.

Indicator 7.1 is true (score "Yes") when it is easy to find instances of positive interactions among children because they happen so frequently. These positive interactions are never overwhelmed by negative interactions between children. If one child tends to have more difficulty in participating in positive interactions, this is supervised and consistently handled well by the staff, even if extra staff or special training is required to make this possible.

7.2. ***Working together to complete a task*** means that more than one child must do the activity (work or play) in order to finish it. (See photos 33.7.2 a–f, next page.) When staff encourage children to work together to complete a task, it facilitates the development of appropriate skills such as cooperation, taking turns, and problem solving.

Examples of working together to complete a task are provided in the indicator in the ECERS-R. Other examples include children working together to:

- Get out cots for nap
- Make vegetable soup for lunch
- Clean up after play
- Push or pull a heavy cart
- Play with a big parachute
- Turn the rope for others to jump
- Decorate the room for a special occasion
- Set the table

If examples of working together are not observed during the observation, or no evidence is seen in the classroom (such as a group mural displayed), ask staff the question provided in the scale for this indicator. Give credit if staff can give examples of such activities that happen at least once a week.

Indicator

33.7.2 a To use the drill in carpentry, kindergartners cooperate—one holds the drill steady while the other turns the drill.

33.7.2 b Children work together to complete a group work of art.

33.7.2 c Together, children work cooperatively to clean up the floor puzzle.

33.7.2 d Partners help to prepare the table for snacks.

33.7.2 e

33.7.2 f

33.7.2 e–f Anyone interested can take part in making a big pot of vegetable soup for the whole class.

Program Structure

Indicator

34 Schedule

General information about this item

For this item, ***schedule*** means what children actually experience (or live) each day, in terms of how time is used. The score is based primarily on how the children spend the time in the classroom, rather than on what appears on a written schedule. The only indicator that considers the existence of a written schedule is Indicator 3.2.

To score this item, focus on the sequence of events and the use of time in the classroom. The observer will have to document what happens at different times of the day, by taking notes on what happens during the observation. This is called the "observed schedule." The amount of time spent on each activity should be noted, as well as what the children are doing and the types of materials they can use. See the sample observed schedule shown in this section (next page).

If there is a ***written schedule*** (see photo 34 A), this can only be used as evidence for the children's experiences when it reflects reasonably well what is actually occurring during the observation. Small variations from the written schedule are acceptable but not great differences.

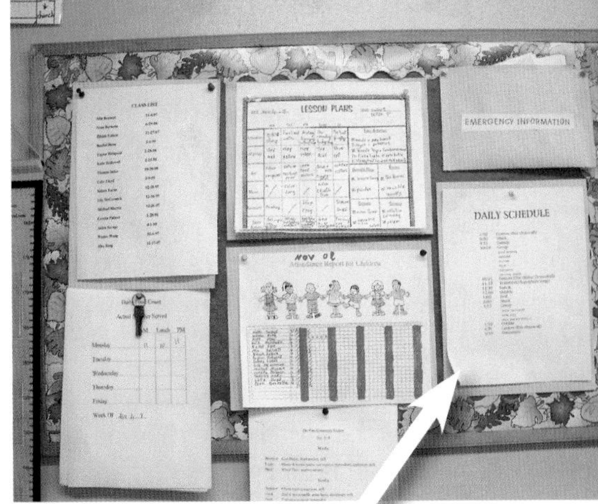

34 A The written schedule should be posted where it can be easily seen by staff, substitutes and parents.

Information from the "observed schedule" always takes precedence over the "written schedule" in determining the score for the item. For example, if a written schedule shows that the children participate in free play for 1½ hours in the morning, but it is observed that children do group activities all day, then score the item based on what is observed.

If the written schedule matches what has been observed, it can be used to gather reliable information about the rest of the day that is not included in the observation.

If the written schedule cannot be used to figure out the amount of time usually spent on the different activities during the whole day (because it does not reasonably match what was observed), then questions must be asked to get the needed information from the staff.

A closer look at each indicator

1.1 A schedule that is too ***rigid*** ignores the flexibility in time that is needed during the day to meet the individual needs of children. A rigid schedule may rarely allow children to satisfactorily complete activities at their own pace. For example, all children may be required to complete play activities in the same amount of time,

Indicator

making some wait for the others to finish, while some do not get to finish at all; or perhaps the playground is only available to the class for a short, specified time, so the children must go out whether they are ready or not.

A rigid schedule may also not allow for any individual differences in completing routines. For example, all may have to use the toilet at the same time, either causing accidents or requiring children to sit on the toilet when not needed; or a child who arrives late may not receive breakfast, even though he or she is hungry. Children who are forced to live on an overly rigid schedule, which does not allow for individual needs, will often appear to be either frustrated or apathetic.

At the other extreme, a schedule that is too ***flexible*** provides too little dependability or structure to the day. Children will have no idea what is supposed to happen or what they are supposed to do next. Staff will also appear to be uncertain, and the atmosphere in the classroom will usually be chaotic. For example, the staff may direct children to go outside and then change plans and have snack instead. Meals might be very late, too early, or unexpected, so that pre-meal preparation cannot be completed. Children may have to wait long periods with nothing to do.

To score "Yes" for 1.1, the schedule must be either very rigid or much too flexible. If there is a reasonable balance of flexibility with dependability, score 1.1 "No."

Sample of Observed Schedule

Observer in classroom 8:15 AM

8:15 – 9:00	Children involved in free play (block, house-keeping and book areas only) Children go into restroom as needed Teachers float around classroom and engage in conversations about activities
9:00 – 9:08	Teacher announces clean up Children wash hands for snack in large group (line up 4 minutes)
9:08 – 9:15	Children sit at snack tables (4 children at each table); when finished allowed to leave snack and go to book area
9:15 – 9:30	Large group story time – all children Teacher reads book and has discussion using calendar
9:30 – 9:38	Children line up, put on coats to go outside
9:38 – 10:30	All children go outside Free play using portable balls, trikes and stationary climbing equipment and slide Children use sand box with toys Children use paint at easel Children play in pretend play house with pots, pans and plastic foods
10:30 – 10:35	Children line up, wait for others to finish playing
10:35 – 10:38	Children take off coats, hats and place in cubbies
10:38 – 11:30	Children go to free play areas (nature/science, books, art and manipulative areas only)
11:30	Teacher asks for three children to help set lunch table, wash hands
11:34 – 12:00	Teacher reads story, children wash hands in small groups and go to table, some children washing hands while others remain at story time First child sits at 12:03 and waits for others to come to table
12:15	Lunch is served.
12:15 – 12:35	Children eat lunch During lunch teacher places sleeping mats on floor When finished with lunch children individually wash hands and go to sleeping mats

3.1 A ***basic daily schedule*** is a sequence of daily events that children are familiar with and expect will happen. For example, children know that every day after lunch they will wash up, brush teeth, and then have time to rest. They know that every morning the class will gather together to sing before playing with materials in centers. The staff may have to guide them in the various tasks required, but there will not be confusion about what is supposed to happen.

To score 3.1, determine if the children are familiar with the basic daily schedule. Watch to see if children proceed from one activity to another without many problems. Observe to see if they are confused or if they seem to understand what is going to happen next.

Indicator

3.2 The ***written schedule*** is a timetable of events that shows what is *supposed* to happen throughout the day. It is not to be confused with the actual schedule that the children experience (the "observed schedule"), because written schedules do not always represent the real use of time and sequence of events in a classroom. In other words, the written schedule may be there, but not followed. In order to see if that is true, the observed schedule should be recorded and compared to the written schedule.

The ***written schedule*** is to be distinguished from "activity plans" or "curriculum plans" that are also frequently displayed in a room, but that do not represent *when* specific activities and routines will happen, or how time is used during the day. Instead, these plans contain a list of the activities intended to develop certain skills for children. For example, they may show what is planned for the different areas used by children, such as the art center, outdoors, or the gathering or circle time. The plan may also outline what will be covered in a curriculum unit or show how specific goals for children will be addressed. These plans are helpful in gathering information about what children do, such as the types of activities and the materials used. However, for this indicator, they do not count as a written schedule.

The written schedule must ***generally relate to what occurs***—in other words, it must represent, reasonably well, what is seen happening during the observation, and what staff report happens at the other times of the day. The written schedule should be up-to-date and followed for the particular group being observed.

Some differences between the written schedule and what is observed are acceptable, because flexibility to meet the special needs of any day is to be expected. For example, on a rainy day, outdoor time may not happen, even though it is listed on the written schedule. Or if children are particularly interested in an activity, the next activity on the written schedule might be delayed to meet the children's needs that day. As long as the sequence of events is generally the same as that shown on the schedule, relatively small differences in time are acceptable.

Schedules may change seasonally. For example, a summer schedule for very hot days might require that outdoor times be in the early morning when it is cooler, while during the rest of the year, outdoor times might be later in the day, when it is warmer. For such anticipated long-term changes, the posted written schedule must match what is observed. If different schedules are used seasonally, then the posted schedule must represent what happens during the current season.

The written schedule must be ***posted in the room*** (displayed in an easy-to-see place, either on the wall or in some other easily viewed place), so that staff (especially new staff or substitutes) can regularly and easily refer to this timetable. This allows staff to maintain the flow of events that children expect and helps to avoid confusion that causes problems. The schedule must be posted where it is easily viewed by staff working in the room, not in any other area, such as outside the classroom in the hallway, on the inside of a closed cabinet door, in a closed notebook, on a parent bulletin board in the entry area of the building, or in the office. If the group uses several spaces, then the schedule should be posted in the room where the group spends most of the day. If desired, additional copies of the schedule may be posted in other areas, but only the schedule posted in the room used most of the day is required.

If a program uses a generic written schedule that loosely applies to many or all classrooms, a more specific written schedule is required for the group being

Indicator

34.3.3 a Dramatic play is child-initiated because children can choose what to play and with whom.

34.3.3 b This teacher-directed fine motor activity allows the child to practice cutting.

observed unless the generic schedule accurately reflects, in some detail, what happens in the classroom being observed.

To give credit for 3.2, look for a written schedule posted in the room. If it is present, and relates reasonably to what has been observed as described above, give credit (score "Yes").

3.3 Children do much of their learning through the experiences they have in playing with materials or toys, doing activities, and playing with one another. It is during play that children develop knowledge and the cognitive, language, and social skills needed for later success.

An ***indoor play period*** is a time (or a combination of several times) that equals no less than 1 hour for a full-day program. During this hour children are able to use toys or participate in play activities inside, such as those listed in the Activities subscale of the ECERS-R (such as fine motor, art, blocks, music, or dramatic play). Less time is required for programs operating less than 8 hours a day, with the amount of time required calculated proportionally, based on the ratio of 1 hour for programs of 8 hours or more. For example, if a program operates for 6 hours a day, this would be 3/4 of a full-day program, so the time required would be 3/4 of the 1 hour. If the program operates 4 hours a day, the requirement would be 1/2 hour.

During the ***indoor play period***, children must be actively involved, allowed to use toys and other materials, and able to interact with others if they wish. A play period can be a free play time, in which the play is child-initiated and self-selected (see photo 34.3.3 a), or it may be more structured, with teacher-initiated activities (see photo 34.3.3 b). Indoor play periods should not be confused with more passive whole group times, such as circle times, when children mostly listen to a staff member, routine times, time spent passively watching TV or videos, or when children are required to work on specific non-play tasks, such as work sheets.

An ***outdoor play period*** is a time (or combination of times) of no less than 1 hour (for a full-day program), during which children are able to actively use toys or participate in other play activities outside, such as those listed in the Activities subscale of the ECERS-R. Outdoor play time usually includes active physical play and sand/water, but also other activities such as art, nature/science, blocks, and dramatic play. Less time is required for programs operating less than 8 hours a

Indicator

day, with the amount of time required calculated proportionally, based on the ratio of 1 hour for programs of 8 hours or more. For example, if a program operates for 6 hours a day, this would be 3⁄4 of a full-day program, so the time required would be 3⁄4 of the 1 hour. If the program operates 4 hours a day, the requirement would be 1⁄2 hour.

Outdoor activities in which the children are required to be passive, rather than actively involved in play, or involved in routine care activities, are not considered an outdoor play period. Playing on a playground in free play activities is preferred, but doing group games or taking a walk are all activities that count as play for this indicator. The outdoor play period cannot be routinely done indoors, such as in a gymnasium or gross motor room, although these are good options to use on the unusual days when outdoor play is impossible due to inclement weather.

Weather permitting means that the outdoor play period must be carried out if the weather allows children to play outdoors. There will be relatively few days in most areas where children will not be able to play outdoors at all. Even in climates with more severe weather, children should be dressed properly and allowed to play outdoors unless there is a danger associated with outdoor exposure. To an extent, whether children should be allowed to play outdoors is a location-related consideration. For example, people who live in very rainy climates will be more likely to take children outdoors on wet days than people who live in drier climates. Similarly, people who live in cold climates are more likely to take children outside on snowy days than are those for whom snow is less usual. In some areas, pollution levels can become dangerous to the health of children on certain days. On those unusual days, children should not play outdoors.

In most cases, however, children can be taken outdoors every day to get fresh air, and to be more active and noisy than they can be when indoors. On days of poor weather, the 1 hour requirement can be relaxed with less, or even no, time being spent outdoors. More often, children may not be able to go out at the usual time, but this can be made up earlier or later in the day. When the weather is bad at the regularly scheduled outdoor time, staff should try to schedule another time during the day to go outside instead. Options for getting the children outdoors should be explored rather than simply not going out at all. If the playground is too wet, use of a covered area or taking a walk around the neighborhood should be considered in place of playground time.

To give credit for 3.3, at a minimum, one indoor and one outdoor play period as described above, of at least 1 hour per day each in a program of 8 or more hours, must be used with the children. The time requirement can be proportionally reduced for part-day programs.

If outdoor play is not possible for more than a week or two, for any reason, (such as construction on the playground, long periods of very bad weather, or dangerous outdoor environment) and no substitute arrangement is made where children can be as active and noisy as they would be outdoors, then credit cannot be given (score "No").

3.4 Preschool-aged children are continuing to develop and coordinate their large muscles. Plenty of ***gross motor play*** helps children develop the physical skills they need to stay in good physical condition (e.g., maintain healthful weight, have strong and well-coordinated bodies). ***Gross motor play*** includes more active types of movement such as running, jumping, climbing, throwing, catching, pedaling wheel

Indicator

34.3.4 a Gross motor play includes active physical play such as riding trikes.

34.3.4 b Children have opportunities for active play outdoors.

34.3.4 c

34.3.4 d

34.3.4 e

34.3.4 f

34.3.4 c–f Less active play may include activities such as sand and water play, art activities, and reading.

toys, or dancing. It also includes slower movement involving the large muscles, such as lifting or pushing heavy objects (such as large wooden hollow blocks), using a balance beam, or standing on one foot. Gross motor play may be provided either indoors or outdoors, as long as children have room to move freely and be active. (See photos 34.3.4 a–b.)

Indicator

Less active play, in contrast to gross motor play, includes more quiet activities, such as using manipulative toys, art and writing materials, sand/water, unit blocks, many pretend play materials, or books. Less active play may be provided either indoors or outdoors. (See photos 34.3.4 c–f.)

Both gross motor and less active play must not be confused with routine care activities or passive non-play activities such as sitting in a big group with little active involvement or watching TV.

To give credit for 3.4 (score "Yes"), both types of play must be provided each day.

5.1 ***Structure*** in a schedule provides dependability, so that everyone in the classroom knows what to expect. Routine care activities take place when children need them, and there is a regular sequence of play activities. Structure reduces confusion.

Flexibility in a schedule allows time to meet the needs of the group and also allow for special circumstances. (See photo 34.5.1.) Flexibility helps to make things in a classroom more relaxed, but if too much flexibility exists, things can become confusing and chaotic.

A ***balance of structure and flexibility*** means that the basic schedule is set, and everyone can depend on it. Yet the schedule can be changed or modified, depending on the day—the weather, moods and interests of the children, and special activities or events that come up and should be utilized.

34.5.1 Variations are made in the schedule so that on rainy days children can play in the indoor gross motor room.

Examples of this type of balance in the schedule are:

- There are several regular toileting times on the schedule for all who wish to participate, and individual toileting is added on an as-needed basis.
- Indoor play is scheduled for a certain time, but if children are very engaged in their play, the indoor time might be extended, and outdoor play shortened.
- Outdoor time is scheduled, but on days with bad weather, indoor active play experiences are substituted.
- Outdoor times can be extended on days with very nice weather.
- Regularly scheduled activities can be replaced with a special activity or fieldtrip.
- If children seem especially tired, nap can be earlier, or if children do not seem tired, nap can be delayed.
- If circle time is not going well, it can be shortened and another more interesting activity substituted.
- If children are especially hungry, lunch can be earlier or an extra snack offered.
- Extra water play times can be added on very hot days.

Score 5.1 "Yes" if the balance of structure and flexibility meets the needs of most children in the group. Notice if the schedule provides the dependability that avoids confusion, while also providing the flexibility that prevents much frustration caused by rigidity, and allows for making needed changes.

5.2 A ***variety of play activities*** means that children are offered different types of play experiences, such as those listed in the Activities subscale of the ECERS-R (fine motor, art, blocks, music, science, math, books, or sand/water). The variety should

Indicator

include enough different types of play so that all children get to do things that are interesting to them, and have the possibility of many kinds of experiences. The play activities should offer enough materials and time so children have choices, and each can find something of interest. Such variety should be offered ***each day***.

The variety of activities must include those that are both teacher-directed and child-initiated. ***Teacher-directed activities*** are those that are planned and started by the staff, and children are invited to participate. (See photo 34.5.2 a.) Staff direct the activity, guiding children in what they do. Often these are whole group or small group activities, but staff can also offer teacher-directed activities during free play as well. If used during free play, children get to choose whether or not to participate, and alternative activities are available. However, the activities still count as teacher-directed because a lot of staff input and help is needed.

34.5.2 a Teacher-directed activities are initiated and guided by staff.

Examples of teacher-directed activities include:

- Reading a story to children at circle time
- Initiating a group circle game outdoors, such as "Farmer in the Dell" or "Ring around the Rosy"
- Helping a small group play a picture matching game, such as Lotto
- Setting up and helping children do a cooking activity
- Setting up and guiding children through a craft activity
- Inviting children to help clean the hamster's cage

34.5.2 b

Child-initiated activities are started by the children themselves, using materials that are accessible to them. (See photos 34.5.2 b–c.) Children select the materials and type of play, and the play goes as they want it to. Staff can join in to help with materials and resources, show interest and talk with children about their play, help children work out problems with one another, or play with the children without taking over.

Examples of child-initiated activities include:

- Taking art materials from the art shelf and drawing their own creative design
- Choosing to use paints at an easel
- Climbing on the outdoor climber
- Playing house in the pretend play area
- Choosing to read books and relax in the book corner
- Digging in sand with a friend
- Choosing to put on and listen to a music tape or asking staff to help with putting the tape on
- Choosing to play with a magnet game in the science area
- Deciding to build a road and buildings in the block area

34.5.2 c

34.5.2 b–c Child-initiated activities are started by the children using accessible materials.

Indicator

In scoring 5.2, consider the range of activities that were observed, and ask questions of the staff to find out what children do during non-observed times. If a schedule and/or activity plan provide reliable evidence (because they represent what children actually experience during the observation), use these as sources of information also. Score "Yes" if children get to experience a variety of activities each day, and the activities include both teacher-directed and child-initiated activities.

If the variety is insufficient (not enough materials and toys to choose from for many different types of experiences), and/or if both teacher-directed and child-initiated activities are not used every day, score 5.2 "No."

5.3 A ***substantial portion of the day*** means 1/3 of the center's operating hours. The substantial portion of the day can be calculated by dividing the "total number of hours the program is open" by "3." For example, if a program is open for 12 hours a day, the substantial portion of the day would be 1/3 of the 12 hours, or 4 hours. If a program is open for 10 hours, the substantial portion of the day would be 10 hours divided by 3, or 3 hours and 20 minutes. Children should spend at least 1/3 of the center's operating hours doing play activities. The play activities can take place in whole groups, small groups, or individually. Play can include both teacher-directed and child-initiated activities. Play can be either indoors or outdoors. However, ***play activities*** in which children are actively involved and not passively engaged must occur. Routine care times and times when children are passively involved do not count as play activities.

34.5.4 a When children spend long periods of time waiting in line there is less time available for educational activities.

The ***substantial portion of the day*** does not all have to occur at one time. In fact it is preferable that play activities be spread throughout the day.

The requirement of the ***substantial portion of the day for play*** leaves 2/3 of the time the program is open to be used for other non-play activities, such as routines, circle times, times when children are not actively involved in play, or transitions.

To score 5.3, calculate whether the required amount of time is used for play, keep track of times when children play during the observation, ask about or use reliable schedules to see when children get to play during non-observed times, and add up all the play time. If the sum of the time children can participate in play activities equals 1/3 of the hours the program is open, give credit (score "Yes") for 5.3. (See sample schedules on pages 364–366.)

5.4 To give credit for this indicator, the schedule must be organized so that there are no long periods of waiting between daily events. A ***long period of waiting*** means waiting without any activity for 3 minutes or more. During long periods of waiting, when children have nothing positive to do, learning time is wasted, and problems with discipline may come up, often forcing staff to control children unnecessarily. (See photos 34.5.4 a–b.)

34.5.4 b Hand washing for meals is handled in small groups so that less waiting is required.

Transitions are times when children change from one activity period to another. Usually a number of steps are needed to end one activity and prepare to move to another. For example, a transition from indoors to outdoors might require that children clean up indoors after activities, put on coats and hats and then walk to the outdoor area. A transition

Indicator

to naptime might require that children use the toilet, wash their hands, get a book, take off their shoes, and then get onto their cots.

This indicator refers only to periods of waiting that occur ***during transitions between daily events***. This means waiting between one activity period and another, rather than waiting within any activity period. For example, if a child wants to paint at the easel but has to wait for another child to finish, and the child chooses to wait rather than to do something else, this is considered waiting within an activity period and is not considered here. However, if children clean up toys, wash hands for lunch, go to the table, and then wait for more than 3 minutes with nothing to do before the food arrives, this is a ***long period of waiting between daily events.*** During this time children are waiting for the next activity with nothing to do.

Staff can usually provide something for children to do while they have to wait. They can sing songs with the children, read books to them, or play other games. In this case, children are not considered to be waiting with nothing to do, unless the waiting time is so long that the activity no longer interests the children.

To give credit for 5.4 (score "Yes") there can be *no* long periods (3 minutes or more) of waiting between daily events observed. If it seems that children have to wait a long time during a transition, keep track of the amount of time they wait to see how long it actually is.

7.1 ***Transitions*** are times when children change from one activity period to another, and need to do whatever is required to move onto the next activity. (See 5.4 for some examples of transitions.)

When children must change from one activity to another, adults are often occupied with managing the tasks that are required to move along. For example, staff might be helping children with their coats before going outside to play. Because the staff are often involved with specific children at such times or taking care of their own transitional tasks (getting their own coat on), children are less well supervised than usual. Often they have nothing of interest to do. Troublesome behaviors can happen, such as children getting into fights, wandering away, or running around uncontrolled. Transitions are difficult times to handle, unless staff have thought through how to make these times go well.

Smooth transitions between daily events means that children flow smoothly from one activity period to the next, without long waits or troublesome behavior. Transitions work best when staff have planned ahead, avoid having children wait, and keep them actively involved as much as possible. (See photo 34.7.1.) Examples of smooth transitions include:

- Doing an activity with children if they have to wait
- Having a few children transition at a time, rather than having the whole group wait for everyone else
- Using staff in a coordinated way, so that one helps children through transition tasks, while the other moves those who are finished on to the next activity
- Doing toileting or handwashing individually or in small groups rather than as a whole group to avoid waiting
- Making clear to children what the transition tasks are and guiding them

34.7.1 During transition to story time, some children clean up the art materials while others select books.

Indicator

34.7.2 a Children can individually use the restroom.

34.7.2 b Flexibility in the schedule allows children the opportunity to finish snack at their own pace.

- Allowing children to stay actively involved until the next activity is ready
- Having children participate in getting things ready for the next activity

Score 7.1 "Yes" if transitions are usually smooth and relatively trouble-free. Perfect transitions are not required, but children should not have to wait for long periods with nothing to do, and changes should *never* be chaotic, with children fighting, or getting into other kinds of trouble. Also, transitions should *never* require harsh treatment of children to avoid trouble and force compliance. If either of these is observed during any transition, score 7.1 "No."

7.2 ***Variations in a schedule*** are part of the flexibility required in Indicator 5.1 of this item. ***Variation*** means that the schedule can be changed to meet the current needs of the whole group in indicator 5.1. However, for this indicator, variation in the schedule is required ***to meet individual needs***. (See photo 34.7.2 a–b.) This means that not only are the needs of the group considered, but also the needs of each child.

Some examples of such variation in the schedule to meet individual needs, in addition to those shown in the indicator, include:

- Children can individually use the restroom when needed, not all at once.
- A child who comes in after breakfast can still have breakfast if she is hungry.
- A child who is not tired at naptime can do quiet activities instead of having to stay on his cot or mat.
- A child who is especially involved in an activity can continue working, even though everyone else is moving on to something else.
- A child who is not feeling well can do quiet activities instead of going outdoors for active play.
- A child who does not want to participate in whole group time can do an alternate activity.

Score 7.2 "Yes" if variation in the schedule, to meet the needs of one or more children, is observed.

Indicator

Calculating "Substantial Portion of the Day"

Example 1

This schedule is based on an observation period of 4.5 hours (from 8AM – 12:30PM) and information collected during the teacher interview about how unobserved time during the day is used and what is accessible to the children.

Time	Scheduled activity	Time for play
6:30 – 8:00	Breakfast in cafeteria and TV time for those who are finished with breakfast	
8:00 – 8:30	Children go to regular classrooms and play with table and rug toys (puzzles; legos; duplos with cars, people, and trucks; stringing beads and cards; pegboards)	**30 minutes**
8:30 – 8:45	Prepare for breakfast/children wash hands	
8:45 – 9:15	Breakfast	
9:15 – 9:45	Circle (teacher reading time)	
9:45 – 10:45	Centers (housekeeping, art, sand and water, nature/science, writing table, blocks, music, computer and cozy book area)	**1 hour**
10:45 – 11:15	Outdoor play (gross motor activities only)	**30 minutes**
11:15 – 12:15	Prepare for and eat lunch	
12:15 – 12:30	Story, put out cots, prepare for nap	
12:30 – 2:45	Nap	
2:45 – 3:00	Wake up from nap; bathroom	
3:00 – 3:25	Snack and teacher directed story	
3:25 – 4:25	Centers (housekeeping, nature/science, writing table, computer, fine motor area and cozy book area)	**1 hour**
4:25 – 5:30	Outdoors or indoor gross motor	**1 hour and 5 minutes**
5:30 – 6:30	Table and rug toys (puzzles; legos; duplos with cars, people, and trucks; stringing beads and cards; pegboards) Prepare for departure	**1 hour**

1. Figure the total number of hours that children are allowed to attend.

   (6:30AM to 6:30 PM = 12 hours)

2. Calculate 1/3 of the operating hours to determine "Substantial Portion of the Day."

   (12 hours ÷ 3 = 4 hours)

3. Add up all times that are scheduled for play activities.

   (see shaded times on schedule = 5 hours and 5 minutes)

4. Compare the amount of time children may have play activities to the time requirement for substantial portion of the day. If the amount of time children may have time for play is the same or greater, then score "Yes." If the amount of time is less than the time requirement for substantial portion of the day, then score "No." For example, the schedule above indicates:

   5 hours and 5 minutes (time to play) **is greater than 4 hours** (time requirement for substantial portion of day), and therefore the time requirement for substantial portion of the day is met.

Indicator

Calculating "Substantial Portion of the Day"

Example 2

This schedule is based on an observation period of 4 hours (from 9AM – 1PM) and information collected during the teacher interview about how unobserved time during the day is used and what is accessible to the children.

Time	Scheduled activity	Time for plays
9:00 – 9:30	Arrival and centers open (cozy book area, computer, writing table, math, science, and fine motor)	**30 minutes**
9:30 – 9:45	Snack	
9:45 – 10:00	Clean up snack/bathroom/wash hands	
10:00 – 11:00	Outside (gross motor activities)	**1 hour**
11:00 – 11:45	Free choice of centers (fine motor, art, blocks, dramatic play, nature/science, math, sensory table, computer, writing table and cozy book area)	**45 minutes**
11:45 – 12:15	Large group activity (M,W,F is music/movement and T,Th is art activity)	**30 minutes**
12:15 – 12:45	Prepare for and eat lunch	
12:45 – 1:00	Clean up/bathroom/prepare for quiet time	
1:00 – 1:45	Quiet time/quiet centers available (cozy book area, fine motor, math, and science)	**45 minutes**
1:45 – 2:00	Clean up all centers and prepare for departure	

1. Figure the total number of hours that children are allowed to attend.

   (9 AM to 2 PM = 5 hours)

2. Calculate 1/3 of the operating hours to determine "Substantial Portion of the Day."

   (5 hours ÷ 3 = 1 hour and 40 minutes)

3. Add up all times that children have for play.

   (see shaded times on schedule = 3 hours and 30 minutes)

4. Compare the amount of time children may have play activities to the time requirement for substantial portion of the day. If the amount of time children may have time for play is the same or greater, then score "Yes." If the amount of time is less than the time requirement for substantial portion of the day, then score "No." For example, the schedule above indicates:

   3 hours and 30 minutes (time for play) **is greater than 1 hour and 40 minutes** (time requirement for substantial portion of day), and therefore the time requirement for substantial portion of the day is met.

Indicator

Calculating "Substantial Portion of the Day"
Example 3

This schedule is based on an observation period of 3.5 hours (from 9AM –12:30 PM) and information collected during the teacher interview about whether what was observed represents the typical daily practice.

Time	Scheduled activity	Time for play
9:00 – 9:20	Arrival/group time to discuss activities for the day	
9:20 – 9:45	Whole group art activity	**25 minutes**
9:45 – 10:00	Whole group reading time (teacher directed)	
10:00 – 10:45	Outside time (gross motor activities only)	**45 minutes**
10:45 – 11:30	Free choice of centers (fine motor, art, blocks, dramatic play, nature/science, math, sensory table, computer, writing table, blocks and books)	**45 minutes**
11:30 – 11:45	Clean up/bathroom/prepare for lunch time	
11:45 – 12:15	Prepare for and eat lunch	
12:15 – 12:30	Clean up/bathroom/prepare for departure	

1. Figure the total number of hours that children are allowed to attend.

   (9 AM to 12:30 PM = 3 hours and 30 minutes)

2. Calculate 1/3 of the operating hours to determine "Substantial Portion of the Day."

   (3 hours and 30 minutes ÷ 3 = 1 hour and 10 minutes)

3. Add up all times that are scheduled for play activities.

   (see shaded times on schedule = 1 hour and 55 minutes)

4. Compare the amount of time children may have play activities to the time requirement for substantial portion of the day. If the amount of time children may have time for play is the same or greater, then score "Yes." If the amount of time is less than the time requirement for substantial portion of the day, then score "No." For example, the schedule above indicates:

   1 hour and 55 minutes (time for play) **is greater than 1 hour and 10 minutes** (time requirement for substantial portion of day), and therefore the time requirement for substantial portion of the day is met.

35 Free play

General information about this item

Free play, according to the definition in the ECERS-R, means that the "child is permitted to select materials and companions, and as far as possible manage play independently. Adult interaction is in response to the child's needs. Situations in which the children are assigned to centers by staff, or staff select the materials that individual children may use do not count as free play."

Having sufficient free play is important in early childhood programs because it is during this type of activity that children learn to make their own choices, interact with others socially, and use their imagination. It is also during free play that children can choose to play and learn in the way that is most effective for their own personality, following their interests and working on the skills that they really need to develop.

35 A In this classroom children are free to use various interest areas, including art, dramatic play, blocks, and fine motor materials.

Free play does not mean a "free for all" with no rules and "anything goes." Instead, free play requires an organized structure, where the choices are clear to children, safe options are plentiful, and staff supervise carefully to ensure productive and engaged behavior. These provisions ensure that a wide range of learning opportunities can take place.

Free play does not mean that all areas of the classroom must be open at one time, with all materials accessible. A more limited number of choices may be available, since free play takes place if children are allowed to choose where they will play, and with whom, from the choices allowed.

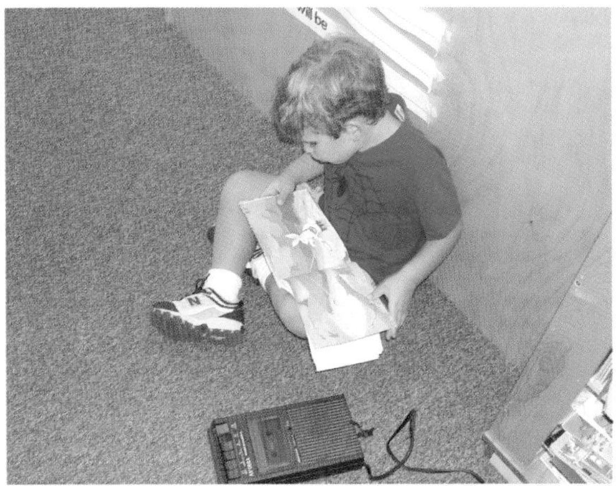

35 B During free play children can choose to play with others or alone.

When observing a classroom, characteristics of free play to look for are:

- Children are playing in various activity areas or centers of the room or outdoor play space, with access to all, or almost all, areas. (See photo 35 A.)
- Children are playing in self-selected small groups or individually. (See photo 35 B.) They can move from one social group to another when they wish.
- Children can choose toys, other materials, or equipment to use, either indoors or outdoors.
- Children can move from one area to another when they wish to. (See photo 35 C, next page.)

Indicator

35 C Children can move to other play areas during free play.

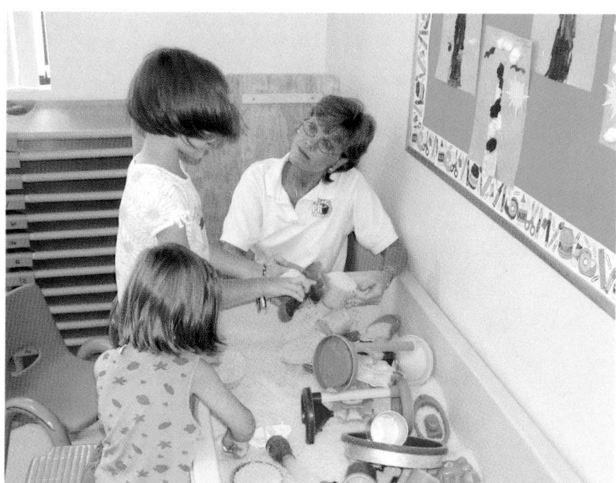

35 D Staff remind children to keep sand and toys in the sand table.

Staff may impose some restrictions on children during free play, for example to:

- Ensure the children's health and safety
- Ensure proper, non-destructive use of materials (See photo 35 D.)
- Encourage cooperative, positive interactions among children
- Help children take turns with popular materials
- Guide children in clean-up

However, when staff tell children what they must play with, for how long, and with whom, free play is not being provided to the children.

A closer look at each indicator

1.1 ***Little opportunity for free play*** means that children can participate in free play for less than 1 hour daily in full-day programs. Less time is required for programs operating less than 8 hours a day (see Indicator 3.1). Thus the vast majority of time each day is spent in routine care activities and whole group or small group times, where children can make few choices about what to play with, for how long, and with whom.

Much of day spent in ***unsupervised free play*** means that children choose activities and playmates and spend time with the different types of play, but staff are relatively uninvolved in supervising the children. Staff may be absent at times during the free play, or they may not pay attention to the children, especially to the extent that children's major health and safety needs are not ensured.

Score 1.1 "Yes" if either of the situations described above occurs during the observation, or if, during the questioning time, the staff report such a situation.

1.2 ***Inadequate toys, games, and equipment*** means that there are not enough play materials for children to use without undue competition. In addition, there are too few play materials to interest the children, challenge them, and encourage extended play. Materials may simply be lacking, there may be too few for the number of children in the group, or they may be in such poor repair that they cannot be used constructively by the children.

Indicator

35.3.1 a **35.3.1 b**

35.3.1 a–b Free play takes place indoors or outdoors.

When scoring this indicator, be sure to consider the materials that are ***accessible for children's use*** during any observed free play periods, indoors and outdoors. Sometimes materials are present in the children's play areas, but the children are not allowed to use them during free play times.

If the materials that children can use during free play are inadequate, as described above, score 1.2 "Yes."

3.1 ***Some free play***, at the minimal (3) level, means that children can participate in free play for approximately 1 hour daily in full-day programs. The 1 hour may take place at one time, or be a combination of times throughout the day. Less time is required for programs operating less than 8 hours a day, with the amount of time calculated proportionally, based on the ratio of 1 hour for programs of 8 hours or more. For example, if a program operates for 6 hours a day, this would be 3/4 of a full-day program, so the time required would be 3/4 of the 1 hour. If the program operates 4 hours a day, the requirement would be 1/2 hour.

To give credit, a portion of the free play must happen ***indoors*** and a portion must happen ***outdoors***. (See photos 35.3.1 a–b.) The indoor and outdoor times can be combined for the total amount of time required. Outdoor play is required, ***weather permitting***, which means that the outdoor free play must be carried out if the weather allows children to play outdoors. There will be relatively few days in most areas where children will not be able to play outdoors at all. Even in climates with more severe weather, children should be dressed properly and allowed to play outdoors unless there is a danger associated with outdoor exposure. To an extent, whether children should be allowed to play outdoors is a location-related consideration. For example, people who live in very rainy climates will be more likely to take children outdoors on wet days than people who live in drier climates. Or people who live in cold climates are more likely to take children outside on snowy days than are those for whom snow is less usual. In some areas, pollution levels can become dangerous to the health of children on certain days. On those unusual days, children should not play outdoors.

If the required amount of time for free play is not provided to the children, or if free play is provided either indoors *or* outdoors, but not in both locations, score 3.1 "No."

35 Free play

Indicator

35.3.2 a At this moment, staff are watching children during free play but do not talk or interact with them. This type of supervision is minimal.

35.3.2 b At this moment, staff are busily involved in organizing their supply cabinets, and therefore are not minimally supervising the children during this part of free play.

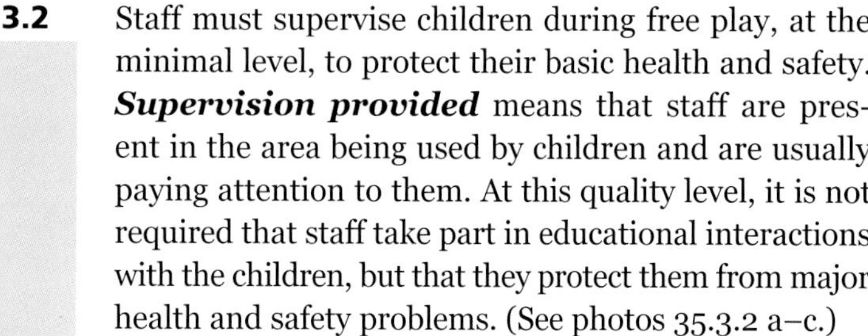

3.2 Staff must supervise children during free play, at the minimal level, to protect their basic health and safety. ***Supervision provided*** means that staff are present in the area being used by children and are usually paying attention to them. At this quality level, it is not required that staff take part in educational interactions with the children, but that they protect them from major health and safety problems. (See photos 35.3.2 a–c.)

This indicator, as part of the "Free play" item, is to ensure that children are supervised to minimize *major* hazards to their health and safety (e.g., children are supervised so that they do not play with matches or swallow poisons, etc.). Do not score Indicator 3.2 "No" unless supervision during free play is extremely lax. If staff are present during free play and paying attention to prevent major problems, score this indicator "Yes."

35.3.2 c Because staff are not able to see the children playing on equipment, they are not able to provide the minimal supervision needed to protect the children from harm.

3.3 ***Some toys, games and equipment*** means enough for children to use in free play without undue competition. In addition, there must be enough materials so that children can make some choices about what to play with.

Materials/equipment must be ***accessible*** to the children—children can reach and use them. There can be no barriers to using the materials. Materials that are present, but that cannot be used for any reason, are not counted among the accessible materials.

The materials must be in usable shape to be counted for this indicator, so that children can actually do what is required for an activity. For example, there is paper to use with crayons, the puzzles generally are complete, some balls are inflated, there are enough things in the housekeeping area so children can pretend, there are some books with pages, and wheel toys have wheels. If free play is provided in a space that is not used during the observation (another classroom, for example), the observer must be sure to look at and evaluate the materials children can access during free play.

Indicator

35.5.2 a

35.5.2 b

35.5.2 a–b In addition to protecting children's health and safety during free play, staff help children succeed with what they want to do.

To score this indicator, observe to see the range and quantity of materials children can use during free play, both indoors and outdoors. If free play is not observed, ask the staff about whether free play is provided, and if so, what materials children can use during that time, indoors and out. If the materials meet the requirements described above, score 3.3 "Yes."

5.1 A ***substantial portion of the day*** means 1/3 of the center's operating hours. The substantial portion of the day can be calculated by dividing the "total number of hours the program is open" by "3". For example, if a program is open for 12 hours a day, the substantial portion of the day would be 1/3 of the 12 hours, or 4 hours. If a program is open for 10 hours, the substantial portion of the day would be 10 hours divided by 3, or 3 hours and 20 minutes.

Free play for a substantial portion of the day can be provided all at one time, but preferably it will be provided during several periods that happen throughout the day. To calculate whether free play is provided for a substantial portion of the day, note all the times in which free play is provided in a typical day and add them up to get a total. Observed free play periods should be added to what the staff report is provided during unobserved times (or use the written schedule *if it is followed* to determine how much free play is provided during unobserved times).

To give credit for 5.5, children should spend at least 1/3 of the center's operating hours in free play activities. Free play must occur both indoors and outdoors (required in 3.1), so add up both indoor and outdoor free play times to get the total free play provided per day.

For an example of calculating whether free play is provided for the required amount of time, see the sample schedules provided on pages 375–377.

5.2 ***Supervision that facilitates children's play*** means supervision in which staff *help* children during free play, but without intruding. (See photos 35.5.2 a–b.) Examples of staff facilitating children's play are:

- Helping children get the materials they need for play
- Showing children how to use new materials
- Adding new materials that children can choose to use

Indicator

- Reading to children or playing or pretending with them
- Encouraging children to finish an activity
- Talking with children socially during their play
- Stopping negative interactions among children

Facilitation of children's play is in addition to supervision of children's health and safety, as required in 3.2.

Score 5.2 "Yes" if staff generally facilitate children's play during periods of free play. If free play is not observed, but it is provided during an unobserved time of the day, ask staff to describe their role during that time. Base the score for 5.2 on how staff have supervised children during the observed periods of non-free play and on their response to the question. If staff do not tend to interact with children in a helpful manner during the observed time, it is unlikely that they will interact helpfully during unobserved free play times.

35.5.3 Children can choose from many interesting materials, toys, and games during free play.

5.3 ***Ample and varied toys, games and equipment*** means that children have *many* choices of materials/equipment to use during free play. (See photo 35.5.3.)

Varied materials/equipment are required so that each child can find a satisfying challenge within the free play environment, and when finished with one experience, can move onto another interesting thing to do. Since children have different learning styles, work on different skills at different times, and have special interests, ideally free play should be a time when all children can take advantage of the opportunities offered and learn in the way best suited to their individual personalities. Therefore, a *variety* of activities must be provided.

Free play areas must offer many different types of play choices, including materials for both quiet and more active play. Most, but not all, types of ECERS-R activities should be represented in what the children can choose to do (gross motor, books, writing, fine motor, art, music/movement, blocks, sand/water, dramatic play, nature/ science, math/number, and computer). There should usually be at least three to five choices of *different* things to use within each of the types of materials/ equipment provided, however some types of activities may have fewer choices.

Score 5.3 "Yes" if there is evidence that the requirements described above are met during free play times. Note that all types of play do not have to be accessible to children at the same time during free play. For example, gross motor equipment might not be provided during indoor free play. Or one center might be closed for one of the several free play periods offered. However, many types of activities for children to choose from are required during any free play period, and variation (many different types of choices) must be provided throughout the day.

7.1 ***Supervision that is used as an educational interaction*** means supervision in which staff encourage extra learning to come from the children's free play activities, but they do so without intruding. (See photos 35.7.1 a–b, next page.) Examples of using supervision as an educational interaction are when staff:

- Help children think through problems encountered with materials, not just by showing, but by cooperatively finding the solution
- Help children work out conflicts with one another, talking through the problem and coming to a satisfying solution

Indicator

35.7.1 a During dramatic play, the teacher encourages children to use the phone book to find phone numbers that they can pretend to call.

35.7.1 b During outdoor free play, staff discuss a gardening activity that children enjoy.

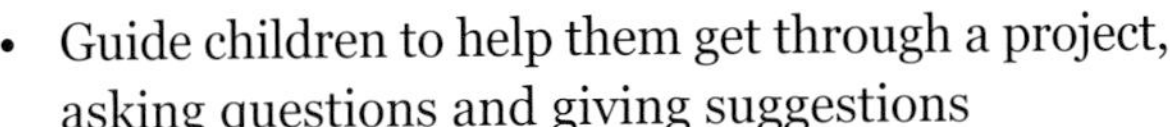

- Guide children to help them get through a project, asking questions and giving suggestions
- Ask questions that will help expand play by encouraging children to remember and apply past experiences
- Have children explain what they are doing or thinking about in their play
- Add new words and ideas to what the children are doing
- Add reading, writing, and math opportunities when they fit well with the play

Score 7.1 "Yes" if staff demonstrate educational interactions during free play times. Remember that these interactions must occur during free play and not during group "teaching" times. If free play is not observed, but it is provided during an unobserved time of the day, ask staff to describe their role during that time. Base the score for 7.1 on how staff interact with children during the observed periods of non-free play and on their response to the question. If staff do not tend to interact educationally with children during the observed time, it is unlikely that they will interact in a different way during unobserved free play times.

7.2 ***New materials and experiences*** go beyond what is normally accessible for play and learning. They add to children's learning opportunities, widening their knowledge and encouraging new interests. Examples of new materials/equipment being added for free play are:

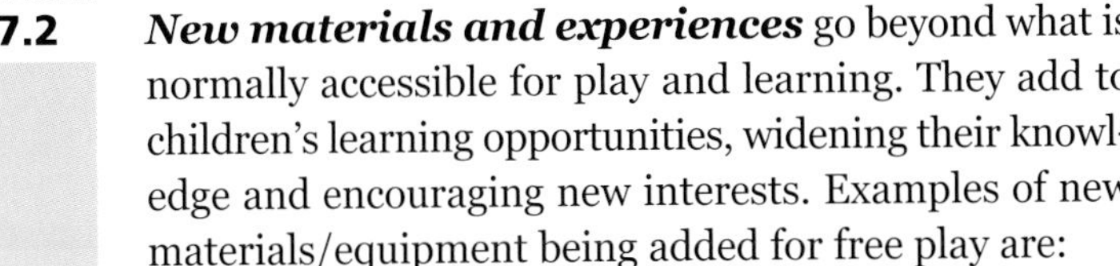

- New books are added to the book area to represent topics being covered in the class or the current season of the year. (See photos 35.7.2 a–b.)

35.7.2 a

35.7.2 b

35.7.2 a–b Staff add books to the book shelf to reflect current classroom topics.

Indicator

35.7.2 c

35.7.2 d

35.7.2 c–d So that children have new experiences with materials, staff frequently take old toys off the shelf and rotate them with other materials.

- Different cooking activities are done every week.
- New props are added to the dramatic play area so children can pretend about a variety of roles.
- Different art materials are featured weekly, in addition to the art materials that are always accessible.
- Fine motor materials are changed to create new interest and allow the practice of new skills.
- A new pet is added to the science area, with books that tell about the pet.
- Different types of toys are used with sand/water play.
- Different portable gross motor equipment is added outdoors regularly.
- Indoor materials, such as art materials, fine motor toys, or books are added to the outdoor play area.

In order to give credit for this indicator (score "Yes"), new materials/ experiences must be added to the free play opportunities *at least once a month* and preferably more often. (See photos 35.7.2 c–d.) To determine whether new materials are added, observe to see if obviously new activities are being offered (the children's response should be a good clue). Also, check curriculum or activity plans, but only if the plans are followed during the observation. In addition, ask staff whether there are other materials or activities that are done during free play times, and if so, to describe some examples and how often they are used.

Indicator

Calculating "Substantial Portion of the Day"

Example 1

This schedule is based on an observation period of 4.5 hours (from 8AM – 12:30PM) and information collected during the teacher interview about how unobserved time during the day is used and what is accessible to the children.

Time	Scheduled activity	Time for free play
6:30 – 8:00	Breakfast in cafeteria and TV time for those who are finished with breakfast	
8:00 – 8:30	Children go to regular classrooms and can choose to play with table and rug toys (puzzles; legos; duplos with cars, people, and trucks; stringing beads and cards; pegboards)	**30 minutes**
8:30 – 8:45	Prepare for breakfast/children wash hands	
8:45 – 9:15	Breakfast	
9:15 – 9:45	Circle (teacher reading time)	
9:45 – 10:45	Centers (children can choose housekeeping, art, sand and water, nature/science, writing table, blocks, music, computer and cozy book area)	**1 hour**
10:45 – 11:15	Outdoor play (gross motor activities only)	**30 minutes**
11:15 – 12:15	Prepare for and eat lunch	
12:15 – 12:30	Story, put out cots, prepare for nap	
12:30 – 2:45	Nap	
2:45 – 3:00	Wake up from nap; bathroom	
3:00 – 3:25	Snack and story	
3:25 – 4:25	Centers (children can choose housekeeping, nature/science, writing table, computer, fine motor area and cozy book area)	**1 hour**
4:25 – 5:30	Outdoor or indoor gross motor free play	**1 hour and 5 minutes**
5:30 – 6:30	Table and rug toys (children can choose puzzles; legos; duplos with cars, people, and trucks; stringing beads and cards; pegboards) Prepare for departure	**1 hour**

1. Figure the total number of hours that children are allowed to attend.

   (6:30AM to 6:30 PM = 12 hours)

2. Calculate 1/3 of the operating hours to determine "Substantial Portion of the Day."

   (12 hours ÷ 3 = 4 hours)

3. Add up all times that are scheduled for free play activities.

   (see shaded times on schedule = 5 hours and 5 minutes)

4. Compare the amount of time children may have free play activities to the time requirement for substantial portion of the day. If the amount of time children may have free play is the same or greater, then score "Yes." If the amount of time is less than the time requirement for substantial portion of the day, then score "No." For example, the schedule above indicates:

   5 hours and 5 minutes (time for free play) **is greater than 4 hours** (time requirement for substantial portion of day), and therefore the time requirement for substantial portion of the day is met.

Calculating "Substantial Portion of the Day"

Example 2

This schedule is based on an observation period of 4 hours (from 9AM – 1PM) and information collected during the teacher interview about how unobserved time during the day is used and what is accessible to the children.

Time	Scheduled activity	Time for free play
9:00 – 9:30	Arrival and centers open (children can choose cozy book area, computer, writing table, math, science, and fine motor)	**30 minutes**
9:30 – 9:45	Snack	
9:45 – 10:00	Clean up snack/bathroom/wash hands	
10:00 – 11:00	Outside (gross motor activities)	**1 hour**
11:00 – 11:45	Free choice of centers (fine motor, art, blocks, dramatic play, nature/science, math, sensory table, computer, writing table and cozy book area)	**45 minutes**
11:45 – 12:15	Large group activity (M,W,F is music/movement and T,Th is art activity)	
12:15 – 12:45	Prepare for and eat lunch	
12:45 – 1:00	Clean up/bathroom/prepare for quiet time	
1:00 – 1:45	Quiet time/quiet centers available (children can choose cozy book area, fine motor, math, and science)	**45 minutes**
1:45 – 2:00	Clean up all centers and prepare for departure	

1. Figure the total number of hours that children are allowed to attend.

   (9 AM to 2 PM = 5 hours)

2. Calculate 1/3 of the operating hours to determine "Substantial Portion of the Day."

   (5 hours ÷ 3 = 1 hour and 40 minutes)

3. Add up all times that children have free play.

   (see shaded times on schedule = 3 hours)

4. Compare the amount of time children may have free play activities to the time requirement for substantial portion of the day. If the amount of time children may have free play is the same or greater, then score "Yes." If the amount of time is less than the time requirement for substantial portion of the day, then score "No." For example, the schedule above indicates:

   3 hours (time for free play) **is greater than 1 hour and 40 minutes** (time requirement for substantial portion of day), and therefore the time requirement for substantial portion of the day is met.

Indicator

Calculating "Substantial Portion of the Day"

Example 3

This schedule is based on an observation period of 3.5 hours (from 9AM –12:30 PM) and information collected during the teacher interview about whether what was observed represents the typical daily practice.

Time	Scheduled activity	Time for free play
9:00 – 9:20	Arrival/group time to discuss activities for the day	
9:20 – 9:45	Whole group art activity	
9:45 – 10:00	Whole group reading time (teacher directed)	
10:00 – 10:45	Outside time (gross motor activities only)	**45 minutes**
10:45 – 11:30	Free choice of centers (fine motor, art, blocks, dramatic play, nature/science, math, sensory table, computer, writing table, blocks and books)	**45 minutes**
11:30 – 11:45	Clean up/bathroom/prepare for lunch time	
11:45 – 12:15	Prepare for and eat lunch	
12:15 – 12:30	Clean up/bathroom/prepare for departure	

1. Figure the total number of hours that children are allowed to attend.

   (9 AM to 12:30 PM = 3 hours and 30 minutes)

2. Calculate 1/3 of the operating hours to determine "Substantial Portion of the Day."

   (3 hours and 30 minutes ÷ 3 = 1 hour and 10 minutes)

3. Add up all times that children are scheduled for free play activities.

   (see shaded times on schedule = 1 hour and 30 minutes)

4. Compare the amount of time children may have free play activities to the time requirement for substantial portion of the day. If the amount of time children may have free play is the same or greater, then score "Yes." If the amount of time is less than the time requirement for substantial portion of the day, then score "No." For example, the schedule above indicates:

   1 hour and 30 minutes (time for free play) **is greater than 1 hour and 10 minutes** (time requirement for substantial portion of day), and therefore the time requirement for substantial portion of the day is met.

36 Group time

General information about this item

This item considers how different types of groups are used in a classroom throughout the day. Typically, preschool children are involved in a variety of different groupings with their peers, during both routines and times for play and activities. Sometimes they may be permitted to play alone, with a friend, or with a small self-selected group. At other times, they may be asked to join a medium-sized group whose members and activities are selected by staff, or expected to join a large group composed of all the children in the class. The amount of time children spend in each different type of group is an aspect of program structure that influences the learning opportunities offered to children.

Children learn most naturally and effortlessly if they are allowed to follow their own preferences, abilities, and interests with the attention of a teacher who adds to and facilitates learning. The type of group best suited to this approach to learning is relatively small (one child alone, with a friend, or a small group), and the members are self-selected. The activity is also child-initiated or self-selected from among a number of possibilities.

Generally, large group activities do not promote the type of learning from which young children benefit most because they are not individualized, hands-on, flexible, and self-directed. Having preschool-aged children participate in large group activities, where all do the same thing at the same time, requires them to set aside their own needs and participate in a setting where individual needs are not emphasized. Although some young children may be able to do this, many children are at a disadvantage in such groups. Large group meetings can be successful if they are relatively short, include experiences children enjoy doing together, focus on topics of current interest, and children are not forced to remain in the group.

A closer look at each indicator

1.1 ***Whole group*** generally means *all* the children in the class or in any combinations of classes. It does not mean a *small group*, which includes only a part of the total group of children enrolled in a classroom. However, if one classroom has a very large enrollment (for example, 30 or more preschoolers), the whole group might be divided into two smaller groups that would still be considered "large," based on the ages of the children (for example, 15 or more of the 30 preschoolers). In this case, the concept of "whole group" should be considered true (score 1.1 "Yes") if all children within the group must do the same things at the same time. This is true, even though the group being observed may not actually consist of all children enrolled in the class.

36 Group time

Indicator

36.1.1 a During whole-group gatherings, there is little accommodation to individual interests or learning needs.

36.1.1 b Children are expected to participate in the same activities during whole-group gatherings.

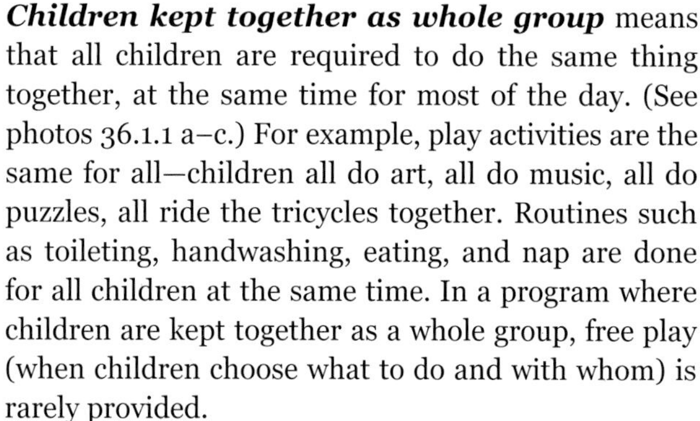

Children kept together as whole group means that all children are required to do the same thing together, at the same time for most of the day. (See photos 36.1.1 a–c.) For example, play activities are the same for all—children all do art, all do music, all do puzzles, all ride the tricycles together. Routines such as toileting, handwashing, eating, and nap are done for all children at the same time. In a program where children are kept together as a whole group, free play (when children choose what to do and with whom) is rarely provided.

36.1.1 c All children in this class of seven children are expected to participate in this art activity.

To decide whether children are taking part in a "whole-group" activity, it helps to observe whether the children can make choices about what to do within the activity.

Here are some examples of whole group activities:

During Play:

- All go outside and must play circle games together.
- All watch a video together.
- All listen to a story at circle.
- All march to music or sing songs.
- All go to computer class.
- All paint at tables.
- All cook together, each taking turns doing a small part.

During Routines:

- All are expected to be on their cots at the same time for nap.
- All go to use the toilet together (some wait while others use the facilities).
- All eat together, either at several smaller tables or one large one.
- All put on jackets to go outside; all wait for the last person before they can go out.

Indicator

36.1.1 d Young children often get bored and lose interest during whole-group activities. Note the children who are not engaged in the activity, indicating a loss of learning.

36.1.2 In this large group story time, most children receive little personal interaction. Such group activities should therefore be limited to short periods.

Whole group times can certainly be of some benefit to preschool-aged children. During these times they gain experience with cooperating and conforming to meet the needs of the group, while keeping their own needs under control. But young children do not profit from being in whole groups for long periods of time, and children who have not developed the skill to participate should not be forced to do so, because coercion often results in greater resistance.

Under whole group conditions, young children lack the opportunities to make their own choices, follow their own interests, and face their own personal challenges. (See photo 36.1.1 d.) They also miss out on the opportunity to make friends under natural conditions or work out their own problems with others. Finally, when the children's personal interests are not considered, they get the message that their own needs or feelings are unimportant. Then, frustration or anger can grow within the children, or they learn to see themselves as not being valued or respected. Such feelings have a negative impact on maturation and self-image, making readiness for formal schooling more difficult.

Most of the day means for the vast majority (75% or more) of the time children are in the program. If there is some time when children are not required to do things with the whole group, (for example, during outdoor time children have free play), but these times are rare, then "most of the day" is still true.

1.2 Young children require close, focused staff-child interactions to get the most from relationships and learning opportunities. Thus, each young child's needs are best met during small group or individual times when the staff can personalize what they say and do with each child.

When adults interact with children who are in whole groups, they have two interaction choices:

- They can address all children at once, in a very impersonal way.
- They can address one child at a time, ignoring (or giving little attention to) all the others. (See photo 36.1.2.)

Thus, there are few opportunities for the close, focused interactions that benefit young children so much.

Indicator

36.3.1 a These children work on specific skills as they participate in a teacher-assigned small group.

36.3.1 b Two friends have chosen to sit together and look at books, creating a self-selected small group.

Indicator 1.2 is scored "Yes" when teachers *usually* (for more than half of the observation) interact with children under "whole group" conditions. They have little chance to interact with one child or a few children who are involved in individual or small group activities. This is true, even when staff interact with one or two children in the whole group, because under whole group conditions, most of the other children are left with no meaningful activity in which they can participate and are not getting the type of interaction they need for positive development.

36.3.1 c Two children have chosen to work with art materials in this self-selected small group.

3.1 This indicator considers the grouping of children during ***play activities*** (such as books, fine motor, art, music/movement, blocks, sand/water, dramatic play, nature/science, math/number, TV/video/computer, or gross motor play). The indicator does *not* consider grouping during routines (such as toileting/diapering, meals/snacks, or nap).

The ***play activities*** to consider for this indicator can be indoors or outdoors, active or quiet, and teacher-initiated or child-initiated. Pay attention to all play activities during the observation.

To play in ***small groups or individually*** means that the play is not done all together in a large or whole group. Thus, some variety in the types of activities and materials is provided.

Children can be assigned to the ***small groups*** by staff (see photo 36.3.1.a), or children can choose with whom they want to play to create self-selected small groups (see photos 36.3.1 b–c). For example, when a teacher assigns a few children to play in each center, this is considered a "small group" play activity. Or when a teacher plays a game at a table with a selected small group of children, this is also a small group play activity.

Children play ***individually*** means that they are not a part of any group, either

Indicator

36.3.1 d

36.3.1 e

36.3.1 d–e Children often choose to play alone during free play.

through their own preference or by teacher suggestion. (See photos 36.3.1 d–e.) Some examples where children decide to play individually are:

- A child reads books by himself while other children play in different areas of the room.
- A child uses the computer by herself.
- A child chooses to play in the sand box while others do more active play outdoors.
- A child might decide to ride a tricycle on her own, rather than playing with anyone else.

Sometimes a teacher might suggest that a child do a play activity on his or her own. For example:

- Space might be available at the easel, and the teacher might invite a child to paint.
- The teacher might suggest that an unoccupied child play at the computer or listening center.
- The teacher might suggest that a child use the jump rope she has been waiting for.

"Playing individually" should not be confused with "time-out" or punishment by isolating a child.

To give credit for ***some play activities*** requires that children are *not* kept together as a whole group most of the day (described in 1.1). The actual amount of time children are allowed to play in small groups or individually can vary from classroom to classroom to give credit for 3.1.

3.2 Allowing children to be part of ***self-selected small groups*** requires that the children be permitted to choose with whom they will play. The staff cannot make this decision for children if small groups are to be considered "self-selected."

Self-selected small groups are usually found during indoor and outdoor free play times. However, self-selected small groups are also possible during some routines. For example, self-selected small groups are created when snack time is flex-

Indicator

ible for a few children at a time, and children can choose with whom they will eat their snack and when they will eat it.

The observer will notice that the self-selected groups of children might often change—children enter and leave groups depending on their interests and how they are getting along with one another. The groups can be contained in specific play areas, such as a dramatic play center or a book area, or interact over large areas, such as when children use wheel toys together. Usually, there will be some children who choose to play alone as well.

Some opportunity requires that children have the chance to participate in one or more self-selected groups, as described above, at least one time during the day. It is *not* required that this provision is available during most of the day or for a substantial portion of the day, but there must be some meaningful opportunity for this type of grouping.

Credit cannot be given for 3.2 if membership in the small groups is determined by the staff.

5.1 See 1.1 for the definition of ***whole group***. ***Whole-group gatherings*** refers to when whole group times take place.

To determine whether "whole-group gatherings" are ***limited to short periods, suited to age and individual needs of children***, the observer must watch the children to see how they respond to whatever is being required of them when they are kept together. The original "Note for Clarification" in the ECERS-R provides information to help score this indicator. In addition, the observer should consider whether any of the children appear to be bored, are "tuned out," have trouble remaining in the group, or require frequent correction by staff. In this case, it will be unlikely that the amount of time the children are required to remain in a whole group is appropriate.

The requirement that the group time is limited to meet ***individual needs*** requires that the group time be acceptable for *all* children required to participate, not just some or most of them. (See photo 36.5.1.) If any child has significant problems with the time required for whole group, and this is not handled positively by staff (for example, by allowing the child to leave the group and do another activity or shortening the whole group time), then credit cannot be given for 5.1.

5.2 For definition of ***play activities***, see 3.1.

To give credit for ***many***, at least half of all play activities observed should be completed with children in small self-selected groups, small groups, or as individual play activities. All children must have the opportunity to participate in such small group or individual play activities. (See 36.5.2 a–b.) If many such opportunities are *not* seen during the observation, then it is unlikely that the program has many opportunities for small group play activities, and this indicator should be scored "No."

36.5.1 Large group gatherings can be used for a short period of time and only when children remain interested.

36.5.2 a

36.5.2 b

36.5.2 a–b Classrooms often look like these two settings when many play activities are done as small groups or individually.

Indicator

It is not necessary to "time" the minutes children spend in small group or individual play activities. If it is difficult to tell whether half of the time is spent in such play, ask staff how the grouping of children is handled during the times of the day that are not observed. If small groups and individual play activities are reported to be a daily, and frequent, part of the children's day, give credit for 5.2.

5.3 ***Routines*** include meals/snacks, nap/rest, and toileting/ diapering, as well as other personal care activities such as handwashing or dressing to go outdoors.

36.5.3 a Children waste too much learning time while waiting in line when routines are handled as a large group.

36.5.3 b The best way to handle basic routines is independently or in small groups.

Indicator 5.3 is scored "Yes" when some of these activities are done in small groups or individually, rather than in a large or whole group. This practice eliminates the need for children to wait for long periods of time, with nothing to do, as well as allowing for a more flexible schedule that better meets each child's personal needs. (See photos 36.5.3 a–b.) In addition, children do better socially when in smaller groups or by themselves. They can interact more easily and can be more relaxed.

Here are some examples of small group routine activities:

- Staff take children to the toilet in a small group, rather than all together.
- Several children go to wash hands rather than lining up with the whole group.
- A few children start to put on coats to go outside, while others continue to play.
- Several children are brushing teeth while others continue eating, and some are already on cots for nap.

Here are some examples of individual routine activities:

- Children use the toilet as needed, not at a scheduled time for everyone.
- Children can choose when to have snack during a longer snack period; they do not have to all sit down together.
- A child who is very tired can rest on her cot in a quiet place while others play.
- Children wash hands as needed, rather than all at one time.

7.1 The ***different groupings*** that are possible include whole or large group, small group, small self-selected group, or individual play. Each has been defined in earlier indicators for this item. (See photos 36.7.1 a–b.)

36.7.1 a

36.7.1 b

36.7.1 a–b In this classroom, children have opportunities to be involved in many different groupings throughout the day.

36 Group time

Indicator

36.7.2 a

36.7.2 b

36.7.2 a–b Staff interact educationally with children during small-group and large-group activities.

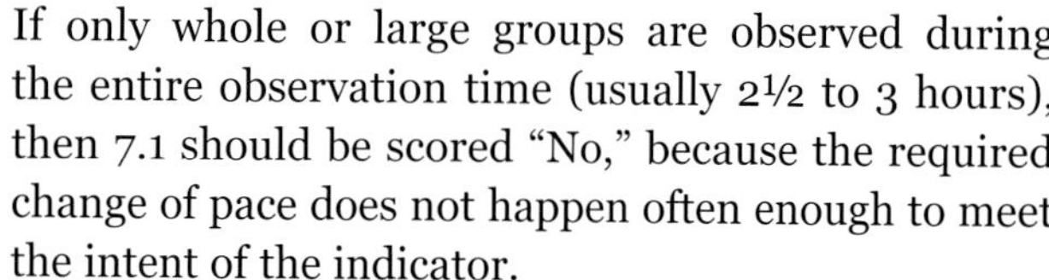

If only whole or large groups are observed during the entire observation time (usually 2½ to 3 hours), then 7.1 should be scored "No," because the required change of pace does not happen often enough to meet the intent of the indicator.

36.7.3 During several long periods of the day children can choose from many self-selected small group activities.

If several different groupings are observed during the observation time, it will still be necessary to determine what groupings are used during the remainder of the day before this indicator can be scored. During the observation one may see that in the morning there is a large grouping for the teacher to discuss the schedule for the day, and then children move on to free play including a small group art activity, followed by individual choice on the playground. Under these circumstances, this indicator can be scored "Yes."

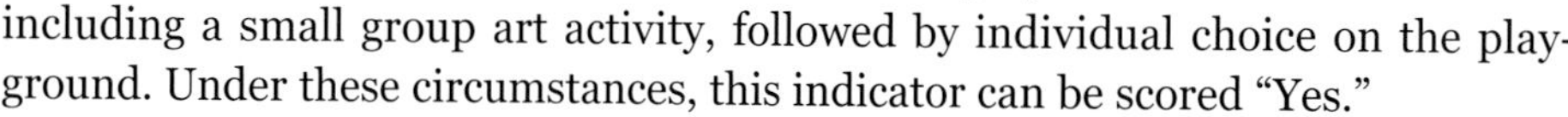

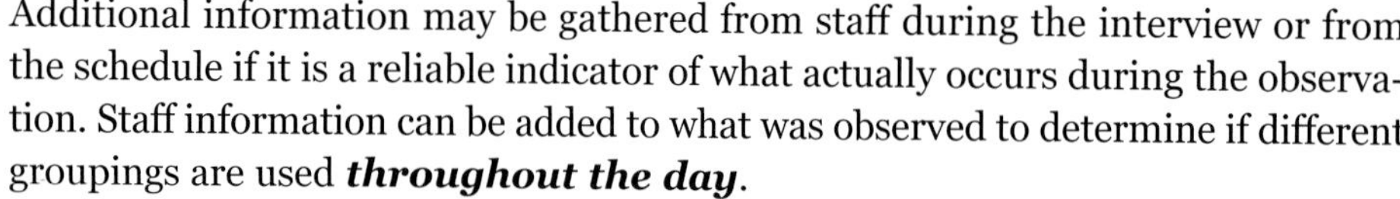

Additional information may be gathered from staff during the interview or from the schedule if it is a reliable indicator of what actually occurs during the observation. Staff information can be added to what was observed to determine if different groupings are used ***throughout the day***.

Credit can be given for 7.1 (score "Yes") when it is observed that some different groupings take place during the observation and are also used at other times in the day.

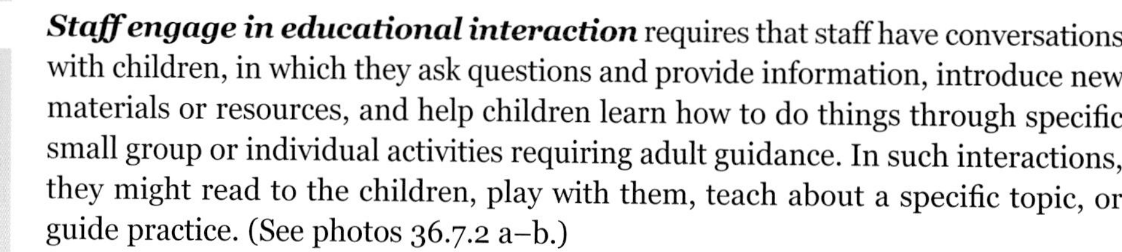

7.2 ***Staff engage in educational interaction*** requires that staff have conversations with children, in which they ask questions and provide information, introduce new materials or resources, and help children learn how to do things through specific small group or individual activities requiring adult guidance. In such interactions, they might read to the children, play with them, teach about a specific topic, or guide practice. (See photos 36.7.2 a–b.)

To give credit for 7.2 (score "Yes"), these types of interactions must happen, not just in large or whole groups (such as circle time or table work time), but during the more flexible activity times that often occur while children are doing small group or individual activities, usually during free play times, indoors or outdoors.

Indicator

7.3 ***Self-selected small groups*** are defined in Indicator 3.2. To give credit for this indicator (score "Yes"), the observer must see *several* examples of such groupings, lasting for a reasonable period of time during the observation. (See photo 36.7.3.) In addition, there must be evidence that such groupings are a usual part of the remaining unobserved day (either through teacher report or an accurate schedule that provides the needed information).

37 Provisions for children with disabilities

General information about this item

In the ECERS-R "Notes for Clarification" for this item, it is stated that this item is to be used only if a child with a diagnosed disability is included in the program.

A child with a diagnosed disability is one who has completed a formal assessment procedure and is receiving (or is eligible for) early intervention services. If no assessment has been completed on any child who is thought to possibly have disabilities, score this item "NA."

The assessment procedure must have been completed by professionals who specialize in psychology, pediatrics, physical therapy, early childhood special education, or other appropriate areas, and who have formally assessed the abilities and needs of a child who does not appear to be developing typically. Upon assessment, the child then has been classified as having a disability, usually categorized by either a specific condition, (such as Down Syndrome, Cerebral Palsy, Hearing Impairment, or Autism), or by the type of disability, such as physical/sensory, cognitive/language, social/emotional, or a combination of these.

Younger preschoolers might be diagnosed and classified as being "at risk" for a disability, without being classified with a specific condition. If a child, who has been diagnosed in this way, is enrolled in the group being observed, and is *receiving early intervention services*, then the item should be scored.

If a child is diagnosed with a disability (or is diagnosed as being at risk for a disability), then intervention services (such as physical therapy, occupational therapy, or speech and language therapy) will usually be provided, or the child might be waiting for services to start. In either case, this item is to be completed, for the one or more children enrolled in the group being assessed. Usually, a plan, with goals made up by a team of people interested in the child's progress (such as parents, special educators, classroom staff, and doctors), will be developed to guide the services to be provided to the child. In the United States, these plans are called an Individual Family Services Plan (IFSP) or an Individual Education Plan (IEP). Neither is required to begin scoring the item, but a plan with goals must be used if requirements of the higher quality levels are to be reached.

To find out whether a child who meets the requirements, is enrolled in the group being assessed, question program staff (usually the director or classroom staff) *before* the observation begins. Fill in the information collected in the space provided on the first page of the score sheet. However, do not score the item until questioning of classroom staff has been completed, since the scoring of this item will have to be based partly on teacher report.

Observers are cautioned to make sure that the child in question has *already* been evaluated and diagnosed, and that staff are not simply reporting their own informal

Indicator

37 A The use of language and books with this child, and all others, would be considered in the Language-Reasoning subscale of the ECERS-R.

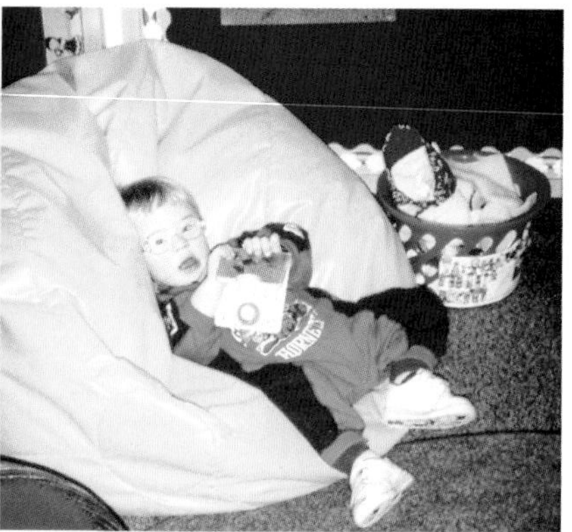

37 B The softness accessible to this child, and all others, would be considered in ECERS-R item 3, Furnishings for relaxation and comfort.

concerns about the development of a child. Although program staff are often among the first people to express concern when a child does not seem to be developing typically and are often proven correct in their informal assessments, an official diagnosis is required to score the item. This is because many of the requirements in the indicators are based on the premise that the diagnosis and services are in place.

Whether the classroom meets the needs of any child in the group being observed, including those with disabilities, is examined in all items in the ECERS-R. (See photos 37 A-B.) This item, however, focuses primarily on issues relating to how information from the assessment is used and the extent to which the child is included in, as opposed to excluded from, regular classroom activities.

To score the item, a combination of observation and questioning of staff is needed. If the enrolled child with special needs is easy to identify in the group, the observer should evaluate whether the child is handled in a way that would promote development. For example, the child is not segregated from peers but included with the other children to the extent possible, and any necessary adaptations are provided so the child can participate in classroom activities as fully and positively as possible.

Do not ask the program staff to give any information that a child's parents might consider private. The staff do not need to point out the child in question or tell about the particulars of the disability being considered, in order to adhere to confidentiality requirements. If the child is not easy to identify, always assume that parents want their privacy protected, and simply ask questions needed to score this item.

1.1 This indicator is scored "Yes" when program staff report that a child meeting the requirements discussed above is enrolled in the class being observed, and staff report that they do *not* try to find out assessment information and know nothing about the child's special needs or the results of the formal assessment. No one (such as parents) has communicated the necessary information to the staff, nor has staff attempted to find out about the assessment.

If staff report that they are aware of the diagnosis, but have not had the opportunity to talk with parents or to find out about the assessment, then score 1.1 "Yes." Also,

Indicator

if program administrative staff report the enrollment of a child with a diagnosed disability in the group being observed, but classroom staff report not being aware of the child's special needs or condition, 1.1 is scored "Yes."

1.2 ***Attempts to meet children's special needs*** may take many forms, depending on the nature of the needs. In some cases, for example, when a child is at risk for a disability due to premature birth or lack of appropriate early stimulation, a child's special needs might be met by providing a good, stimulating early childhood program alone. For children with more specific disabilities, special action by staff or early interventionists will be required. For example, staff might need to handle the learning needs of the child in a special way, specific accommodations might be needed in the furnishings or classroom, the schedule might need to be adapted, or therapy activities might need to be implemented. Being able to meet a child's special needs requires that the staff know what the need is and what it requires from them.

Indicator 1.2 is true (score "Yes") if classroom staff report that a child in the group has special needs (the child has been evaluated and diagnosed and is eligible for special services), but they do nothing to meet the needs within the program. However, remember that the provision of a *good* quality program, in itself, may meet the special needs of some children with disabilities, and that no accommodations beyond that provision are required. In case no special accommodations are needed, score the indicator "No."

1.3 For this indicator, ***involvement of parents*** means that parents (or other responsible adults who have the parenting responsibility) share information with staff about their child's special requirements (***needs***) and/or ***goals*** set for the child. The goals (usually the steps or milestones parents want their child to work towards) for the child can be in the form of an IFSP or IEP (see introductory information for this item) or less formally set. If no communication takes place between parents and staff, about what the child's disability requires, and how to best meet the special needs of the child, score 1.3 "Yes."

Sometimes parents may not choose to share information about how to best meet the needs of their child. Some reasons for this lack of communication might be that the parents do not communicate well with anyone, they cannot find the time for such communication, they are uncomfortable talking with staff, or they do not speak the language the staff speak. If this is the case, 1.3 is still true (score "Yes") if no involvement or communication between parents and staff takes place. This is considered inadequate because the child's development is compromised when parents and staff do not work together to meet a child's needs. Even if staff have put significant effort into encouraging parental involvement, if such efforts are unsuccessful, 1.3 is still scored "Yes."

1.4 When children with disabilities are segregated from other children, learning opportunities are missed, by the child who is segregated and by the other children as well. Therefore, it is desirable to have children with disabilities included with their peers as much as possible during the play/learning activities and routines. This is what is meant by ***involvement*** with other children, ***or the rest of the group.***

Sometimes it is easy to involve a child with disabilities in all the children's activities. In other instances, it takes more thought and effort on the part of the staff to figure out how a child can be included. For example, a child with reduced physical abilities may need a ramp to take part in active physical play on a climber or slide. Or

Indicator

37.3.2 a Giving a child a little extra help at snack time is a minor modification that meets this child's needs.

37.3.2 b Providing a special chair for the child (with glasses) is a minor modification that facilitates her participation with others in circle time.

a child, whose social skills are developing less quickly than those of her peers, may require an adult's help to participate in play with others.

Very little involvement means a child with disabilities does not usually participate with others in the class and is segregated from the other children most of the day.

Indicator 1.4 is true (score "Yes") when a child with disabilities is usually separated from peers in the group, for example, eats separately, is not included in circle time, naps in a different place or at a different time, or does not go outside with the others. Staff do not ensure that the child is included with others as much as possible, or the child is needlessly segregated.

37.3.2 c A ramp has been installed so that children with physical disabilities can easily access this area of the playground.

3.1 See the General Information section of this item for the definition of ***assessments***.

This indicator is scored "Yes" when program staff report that a child meeting the requirements discussed above is enrolled in the class being observed, and staff report that they know about the child's special needs and the results of the formal assessment. Someone (such as parent, special educator, or therapist) has communicated the assessment information to the staff. Staff should be able to describe, in general terms, the child's disability. The staff do not have to have the written report—verbal communication is sufficient to score 3.1 "Yes."

3.2 ***Minor modifications made to meet the needs of children with disabilities*** include small changes that take place in the regular classroom operations and staff behaviors. Minor modifications should not require intense, regular, specialized help from professionals or extra staff members. They may require small changes in a classroom, such as in the furnishings, room arrangement, how people interact with a child, the amount of attention given to a child, what is taught, or the schedule. (See photos 37.3.2 a-c.)

Indicator

Here are some examples of minor modifications:

- Special foods are served to a child who may have problems eating due to a disability.
- Staff provide more help to a child who has difficulty playing.
- A more flexible schedule is used to accommodate a child's need for less rigid time periods.
- Staff stay closer to a child who has more difficulty getting along with others.
- Diapering facilities are provided for a child who is taking longer to become toilet trained.
- Pathways in the room are widened to allow a child using a walker or wheelchair to access the various play areas.

To score this indicator, the observer can depend on two sources of information. First, if the observer can identify the child in the group and knows something about the child's disability, modifications might be observed during the observation. Second, staff can tell about any special modifications that are carried out to meet the needs of the child during the staff interview.

3.3 See 1.3 for definitions of ***parent involvement*** and ***goals***.

To score "Yes" for this indicator, the parent(s) of the child with disabilities and the classroom staff must communicate in some way to decide on the goals for the child. Involvement of center staff who are *not* a regular, daily part of the child's classroom, (such as the director, assistant director, or therapist) are not considered to meet the requirement of this indicator, even though such staff can provide helpful, positive input into goal-setting for a child.

Some involvement by classroom staff can take place through formal meetings, informal conversations, or phone or written communications. At this quality level (minimal), the involvement does not have to be extensive, but it does have to take place, and goals for the child must come from the communication.

3.4 See 1.4 for a definition of ***involvement in ongoing activities with other children.***

Some involvement means a child with disabilities sometimes participates with others in the class, and at other times does not. The child may be segregated from the other children at some times, but not at all times of the day. (See photos 37.3.4 a–c.)

Indicator 3.4 is true (score "Yes") when the child with disabilities sometimes (but not necessarily always) participates in play or routine care activities with peers in the group. For example, the child may eat separately but is included in circle time and naps in the same place, or she goes outside with the others but does not play on the same equipment.

5.1 All classroom staff, and other professionals who work with children, can profit from sharing ideas that come from others. This allows new perspectives to influence the work done with children. In the case of

37.3.4 a If this photo represented the usual experiences for the child, during an observation there would be little involvement in ongoing activities with other children.

37.3.4 b With staff help and guidance, this child can successfully play with materials.

37.3.4 c Other children are encouraged to join in the child's play.

Indicator

teaching children with disabilities, the recommendations from others who specialize in treating disabilities can make a big difference in the ability of classroom staff to better meet the special needs of a child. A cooperative, collaborative approach works best. (See photo 37.5.1.)

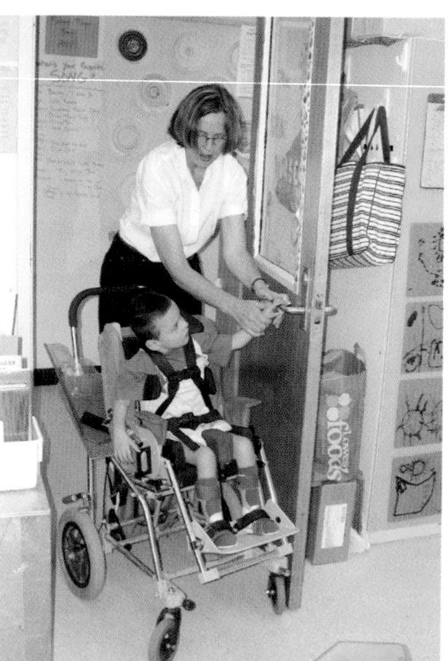

37.5.1 Parents, professionals, and staff all work together to ensure that children learn the skills they need for maximizing independence.

There are specialized ***professionals*** who have the experience and knowledge required to make recommendations for the care of children with disabilities. For example, a psychologist can help a child with a social/emotional challenge; a speech and language therapist can define what a child with communication difficulties needs; or a physical therapist can determine the experiences that will best help a child improve motor skills. ***Classroom staff*** can gain knowledge by finding out what specialists recommend for a child and by ***following through*** with their suggestions.

Recommendations are usually suggestions for activities or interactions that will help the child meet the challenges caused by a disability. For example, an occupational therapist might suggest that a child who has difficulty coordinating his hands be given a special spoon at meals/snacks so he can feed himself. Or a speech and language therapist might recommend that staff consistently make eye contact with a child who has hearing difficulties and speak more clearly and simply than with other children. Special activities and interactions are often recommended for both routines and play.

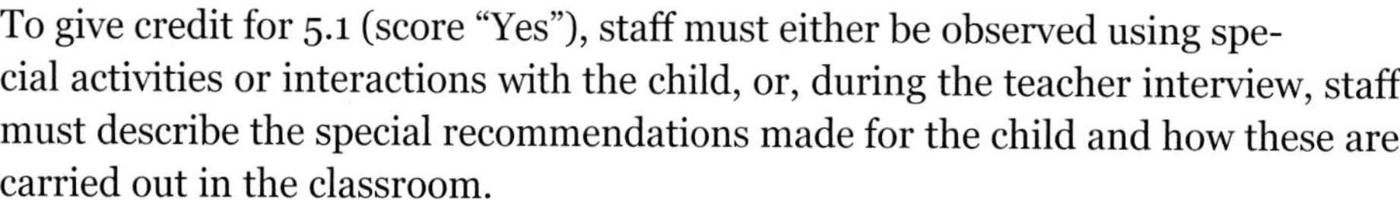

To give credit for 5.1 (score "Yes"), staff must either be observed using special activities or interactions with the child, or, during the teacher interview, staff must describe the special recommendations made for the child and how these are carried out in the classroom.

If staff are not observed doing special activities or using special interactions with the child or obviously do not know about recommendations made by specialists, score 5.1 "No."

5.2 ***Modifications*** in this indicator, at the "good" level of quality, include *any* changes needed to allow the child with disabilities to participate in many of the classroom activities with others. In some cases these modifications may not be particularly demanding, but in others, they may require a lot of creativity, new arrangements, additional staff, and resources. (See photos 37.5.2 a-e, next page.)

Modifications in the environment include changes in the facility (the building or classroom), furnishings and equipment, or arrangement of spaces used. Examples of such modifications are:

- Installing a toilet that is accessible to those with disabilities
- Providing a ramp or elevator to access the building
- Providing special lighting
- Rearranging classrooms to provide wider pathways
- Installing special accessible play equipment on playgrounds
- Providing specialized furnishings, such as chairs or prone boards, to allow a child to access materials and play with them

Modifications in the program include changes in staff-child ratio and/or group size; the provision of special activities, toys and materials; using different teaching or behavior management practices; including therapists as part of classroom staff;

Indicator

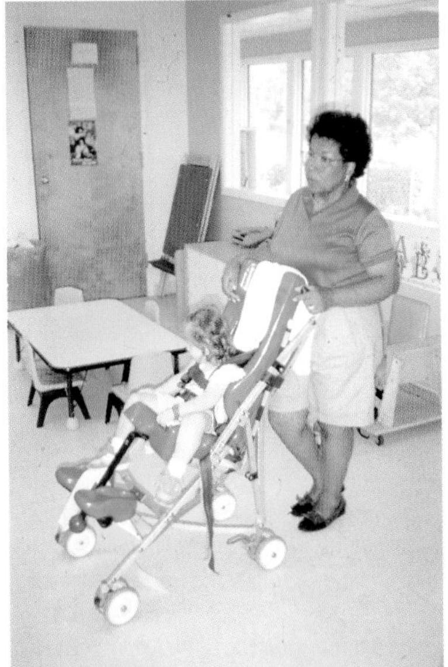

37.5.2 a Extra staff are available to help meet the needs of children who require more assistance.

37.5.2 b Addition of special equipment to the outdoor play space enables children with physical disabilities to swing.

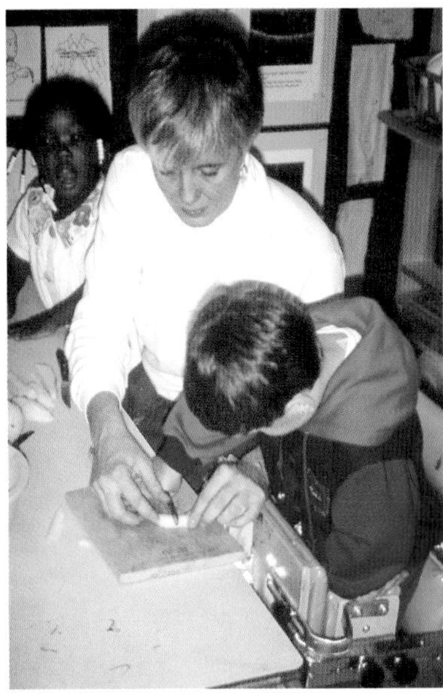

37.5.2 c Special adaptive furnishings and extra help allow this child to participate with others in making vegetable soup.

37.5.2 d A special chair enables this child to be included at meal times.

37.5.2 e Staff ensure that all children can choose to participate in any classroom activity.

and more intensive parent/staff cooperation and communication. There are a great number of modifications that might be needed to allow a child with a disability to participate in activities with others. A limited list of examples includes:

- Reducing class size to better meet the needs of all children enrolled
- Adding an additional staff member to provide extra attention to the child with a severe disability who requires more intense help
- Providing either more structured or less structured activities, depending on the special needs of the child
- Providing a greater range in difficulty levels of play activities
- Targeting activities to help a child practice very specific skills

Indicator

- Using special modes of communication, such as signing, word boards, switches, or photographs
- Handling special equipment, such as hearing devises, glasses, or medical equipment
- Giving special medications

Modifications in schedule include changes in the sequence of events experienced by the children, but also in the schedule for attendance at the center. Examples of such modifications are:

- Providing a more flexible, individualized rest time for a child who tires easily
- Shortening some large group activities
- Allowing a child with a disability to attend half-days in a normally full-day program
- Freeing staff from classroom responsibilities so they can attend meetings with parents, therapists, and other professionals involved in the care of the child

The modifications required to allow a child to participate in many (but not most or all) activities in the regular classroom will depend on the needs of the child. If little or nothing is required for the child to participate in many activities, score 5.2 "Yes."

If the possibilities for participation in many activities are not met reasonably well because obvious, needed changes are not being made in the environment, program, or schedule, do not give credit for 5.2 (score "No").

5.3 To score "Yes" for this indicator, the communication described in 3.3 must take place frequently. Daily (or almost daily) informal communication is required, and formal meetings, in which issues can be handled in more depth, should take place at least twice a year.

7.1 ***Professional intervention*** consists of activities designed specifically to optimize the development of a child with disabilities. The activities can be carried out during routine care or play times and will help a child reach the goals set by those who are most interested in the child's well-being, such as parents and classroom staff. For example, activities might be designed to help a child with physical disabilities learn to feed himself with a spoon or to walk. Or activities might be developed to help a child who has unusual difficulties getting along with others to form friendships and to play with others.

The special activities have been shown to be most effective when they are carried out as a usual part of a child's home or classroom experiences. When ***most*** of the intervention is incorporated into regular classroom practices, a child gets more chances to develop the skills being targeted.

To give credit for 7.1 (score "Yes"), a specialist must usually carry out most of the intervention activities ***within the classroom setting*** (indoors or outdoors). Only under unusual circumstances should the activities be carried out in a segregated setting.

Credit can also be given for 7.1 when classroom staff carry out the intervention activities. To be sure the activities are being implemented properly, it is preferred that professionals, such as therapists, explain and demonstrate the activities to regular classroom staff before the staff take over.

Indicator

7.2 In many cases, children with moderate disabilities can be so well integrated into most classroom activities that the observer has to search hard to identify the child. This is a sign that the requirements for 7.2 are being met.

To score this indicator, consider the nature and severity of a child's disability. Look to see how well the child with disabilities blends into the group and determine whether the child is being excluded when he or she could be included.

A child with disabilities should be included in most play activities and routines, just as every other child is, with special modifications or interventions being carried out as smoothly and inconspicuously as possible. Remember that most therapies or interventions should be carried out as part of the regular classroom activities that include both the children with disabilities and their typically developing peers. Only in relatively unusual cases, when a child has extremely severe disabilities, should the child be segregated in any way, and no child should often be segregated from the group.

7.3 Like parents, classroom staff have significant knowledge about how a child is progressing as well as ideas for activities that will help encourage the child's development. Classroom staff see the child in a different environment, where he may not behave in the same way as at home or during a formal assessment in a strange place. Having *all* the responsible adults in the child's life give input about the child to determine his developmental level and make plans for the future, gives the child a better chance for success.

To score this indicator, ask staff if they participate in the assessments of the child's developmental status and help in creating the intervention plans. If staff can describe participating in these activities, score 7.3 "Yes."

Parents and Staff

38 Provisions for parents

General information about this item

Parents and staff are partners in the care and education of children. Things go more smoothly for a child when these key adults get along well and act as a team. As the professional partner in the team, it is the responsibility of the staff to reach out to parents with information about the program and to provide a warm welcome to participate actively. Staff need to remember that the parent comes into an unfamiliar program and may be uneasy at first or concerned about leaving the child. It is the staff's responsibility to help the parent feel at ease.

Parents will vary in the amount of time they have to be involved in the program and in the ways they express their interest. This item looks at what is offered to the parents by the program, not how the parents respond to the provisions made for them by the program.

At a minimum, parents must have key administrative information about the program, such as fees, hours of operation, rules for exclusion for health reasons, etc. They must also be treated with respect by the staff and administration. If staff set a high standard of behavior, parents may follow suit and behave with respect towards the staff in return. A free exchange of information about the child forms a good basis for teamwork between parents and staff. Although programs vary in their involvement of parents, all programs must have an "open door" policy, so that parents are free to visit at any time.

It is sometimes a challenge to find meaningful ways to get busy parents involved in their children's preschool-kindergarten program, but we know that children, parents, and staff all benefit if there is an easy, friendly relationship between these key adults in a young child's life.

Parental involvement in their child's school experience is valuable to parents, staff, and children. Parents become better informed and start to feel ownership of the program. Staff can offer a more varied program if they use the additional help from parents wisely. Children benefit from seeing that the key adults from the separate worlds of home and school are closely connected.

Much of the information needed to score this item must be collected by asking questions of program staff. Ask the classroom staff the necessary questions first, and if they are not able to give the answers, then the director or other program administrators may be asked. There are sample questions printed in the ECERS-R to guide the interview. Whenever possible, look for concrete evidence to determine whether an indicator is true. For example, ask to see the written materials provided to parents, if staff report they are used.

Additional information relating to the interaction between parents and staff is assessed in Item 9, Greeting/departing.

Indicator

A closer look at each indicator

1.1 This indicator is scored "Yes" if no information about the program is ***given to the parents in writing***. Verbal information can be misunderstood and there is no proof about what was actually told to parents; therefore, only giving information verbally is considered inadequate.

1.2 ***Parents discouraged from observing or being involved*** in the program means that parents are kept out of the program. Programs that discourage parents from observing or do not allow them to observe, cause anxiety and alienation in families. Not being allowed to observe also causes parents to be misinformed about their child's experience.

Parents receive reassurance and a better understanding from visiting to see how their child and others are being treated. Such visits can form a basis for trusting the staff and administration. Excuses for excluding parents, such as telling parents that their child will adjust more quickly if they do not visit, often prolong a child's adjustment period. Putting excessive demands on parents to make appointments to visit only at certain times or on certain days makes it difficult for parents to visit and should be considered examples of discouraging parents from visiting. If the program has parents drive up and drop off their children at the curb, watch to see if parents and children are greeted. If parents are allowed to bring their children in but some prefer to use the curb drop-off, do not score 1.2 "Yes."

3.1 At a minimum, parents must be given ***administrative information in writing*** before they enroll their child. The administrative details, such as fees and when they are due, hours of service, absence policy, and health rules for attendance, should spell out clearly the responsibilities of the program and the responsibilities of the parent. Prototypes of forms are sometimes available from Resource and Referral Agencies and child care provider organizations.

38.3.1 The director reviews the administrative information in the center's parent handbook with each parent.

If staff report that such materials are provided to parents in writing, ask to see a copy to assure that the basic administrative information is covered.

Parents, whose primary language is not the language used in the written materials or who cannot read, may need help with accessing the information. It is essential that all parents receive the information about the program and are clear about the content.

Thus, to give credit for this indicator, the observer also needs to find out whether all parents of children in the group being observed are able to read the materials. (Are there any parents who do not speak the language used in the materials? Are there any parents who are unable to read?) If any of the parents fit the criteria, the staff must take responsibility for ensuring that parents have the information they need, for example by being sure arrangements have been made to have someone read or translate the materials for those parents. A question should be asked to find out whether staff have ensured that parents can access the information. Acceptable help might be provided by another parent, an older child who is bilingual or can read well, or a staff member who speaks the required language.

Score 3.1 "Yes" if written materials for parents meet these requirements, and staff have ensured that all parents can access the information. (See photo 38.3.1.)

Indicator

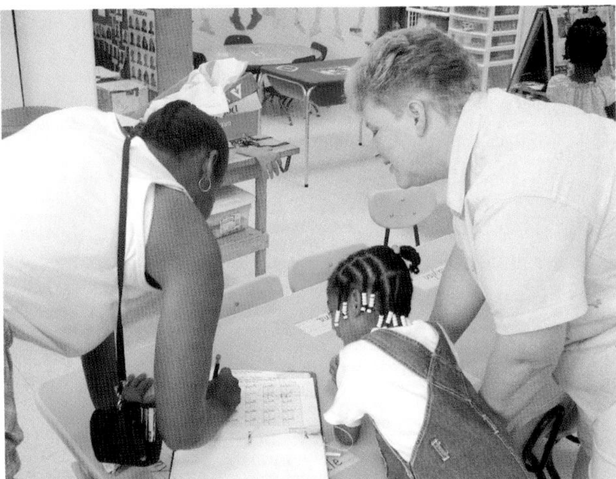

38.3.2 a Drop-off and pick-up times are good opportunities for informally sharing information with parents about their child.

38.3.2 b At pick-up time, parents appreciate hearing about activities their children participated in.

3.2 ***Some sharing of child related information*** must occur between parents and staff to be given credit for this indicator at the minimal level. This can consist of informal communication between parents and staff at arrival and departure times, through written notes to parents who do not bring their children, or conferences at the parents' request. Information can be shared by parents, such as a situation at home that is upsetting the child, or by the staff, such as an activity the child enjoyed that day or a new friendship the child has made.

Check to see if such sharing of information occurs when parents and staff interact during the observation, for example at greeting and/or departing time. If neither greeting nor departing is observed, ask the staff the questions provided in the scale for this indicator, and base the score on their answers. (See photos 38.3.2 a–b.)

3.3 ***Some possibilities to be involved in the children's program*** means at least two different types of possibilities are offered to parents and family members to contribute to the children's program. Examples include:

- Inviting parents to attend a potluck dinner
- Having the parents bring the birthday treat on their child's birthday
- Donating some scrap materials for art projects
- Assisting the teacher in the classroom
- Sharing an interest or skill with the class
- Serving on a committee or an advisory board

Parent involvement in the children's program requires active participation, not only sharing information, as in 3.2. To score 3.3 "Yes," at least two possibilities for parent involvement must be present.

3.4 ***Interactions between family members and staff*** must be ***generally respectful and positive*** in order to meet this indicator. (See photo 38.3.4, next page.) If the assessor has the opportunity to observe greeting and/or departing, a judgment can be made based on how the staff and parents interact. Do the staff greet the parent in a pleasant tone; does the parent respond in kind; have there been any complaints or serious conflicts?

Indicator

If the scale is being used as a self-assessment by the staff, it is important for staff to be as honest and objective as possible in order to achieve a baseline for planning improvement. It helps to have an observer who watches the staff's interactions with parents, especially those who arrive later when the staff are busy.

In scoring this indicator, note the word ***generally***. This means that an occasional lapse in respectful and positive interaction between parents and staff should not cause a score of "No." Score Indicator 3.4 "Yes" if the staff and parents deal positively or neutrally with one another with only an occasional lapse. However, *no* strongly negative interaction can be observed or reported.

38.3.4 Respectful, positive interactions between staff and family members form a basis for good communication.

5.1 A good program invites parents to ***observe the group*** that their child will be attending ***prior to enrollment***. Parents need to be able to make an informed decision before they place their child in a program. This can only be done if the parent is not only invited to observe, but the program strongly advises or requires it.

Ask whether the program has a policy that actively encourages parents to observe before enrollment, and if most parents do so. Score "Yes" if the policy is in place and practiced regularly. (See photo 38.5.1.)

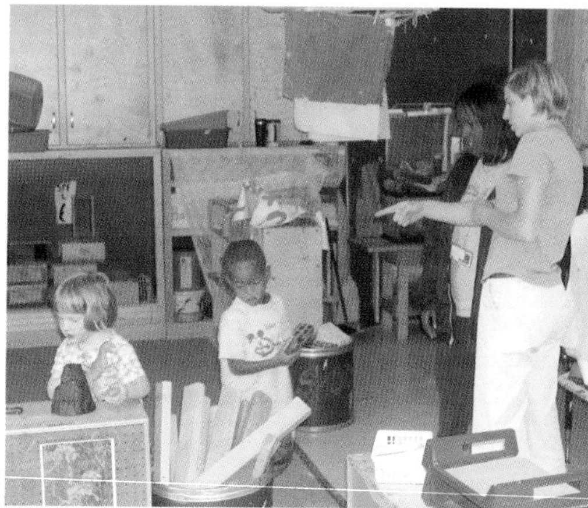

38.5.1 Prior to enrollment, this program requires all parents to observe during operating hours, so that they can see the program in action.

5.2 Making parents aware of the ***philosophy*** and child development ***approaches*** used in the program *in writing* is important because it adds information that parents need in order to decide whether the program is the right one for their family. Parents will want to know the discipline policy and the general educational philosophy as well as the types of activities in which their child will be involved.

Major discrepancies in child rearing approaches can cause serious conflicts between parents and staff. Discussion of these issues during the initial contacts and coverage of them in a clearly written handbook that is given to parents might avoid later problems. (See photo 38.5.2.)

To score this indicator, look at documents provided to parents such as the parent handbook, to decide whether the required information is provided. If any parents cannot read the information, arrangements must be in place to provide help as described in Indicator 3.1.

38.5.2 This Parent Handbook includes administrative information as well as a description of the educational philosophy and activities used at the center.

5.3 ***Much sharing of child-related information*** means that in addition to frequent informal conversations at drop-off and pick-up times, a planned conference is regularly offered to the parents of each and every child. Parent conferences provide time for staff and parents to discuss the child's progress and strengths as well as any difficulties the child or family may be having. Conferences deepen the relationship between parents and staff and help in joint planning for the child's development.

A good program also provides additional communication opportunities, such as:

- Group meetings for parents
- A parent library with parenting information to check out

Indicator

- A parent bulletin board
- Weekly or daily notes sent home to parents
- A newsletter containing information about the other children and their families as well as current activities

At least one ongoing print communication material, in addition to a parent handbook, and two face-to-face communication opportunities, such as a planned individual conference and a parent meeting, are required in addition to daily informal communication to give credit for this indicator. (See photos 38.5.3 a–c.) If any parents cannot understand the information, arrangements must be in place to provide help as described in Indicator 3.1.

5.4 In order to increase the possibility that parents can become involved in their child's program, the center offers a ***variety of alternatives for involvement***. (See photos 38.5.4 a–f, page 406.) For example, working parents might find it easier to attend an evening pot luck dinner, while a parent who attends school part-time may want to volunteer in the classroom during the program's operating hours. Because different parents will have preferences for how they would like to be involved, varying options must be provided. Some options are provided as examples in the indicator, but others might include:

- Assisting staff when the group takes a field trip
- Sharing a family cultural custom with the class
- Helping with a special activity, such as a science project
- Collecting materials needed for crafts and other projects
- Bringing a special visitor, such as a family pet or a new baby
- Playing a musical instrument so children can sing or dance to it
- Having parents talk to the class about their jobs
- Donating objects to a yard sale
- Helping with fund-raising events
- Participating in a clean-up day
- Helping to provide a "teacher appreciation" event

The score for this indicator is based on the variety of possibilities offered, not the degree to which the parents take advantage of them. At least three alternatives are required to give 5.4 a score of "Yes."

7.1 An ***annual evaluation*** by parents is requested by the program in order to make sure that parents have a way to express their opinions about the program. Parent evaluations should be treated as a source of new ideas as well as a forum to allow parents to express concerns.

It is difficult to get honest evaluations from parents because they might feel threatened by the staff or guilty about leaving their child in a program they are not happy with. Despite the difficulties involved, excellent programs conduct evaluations by parents in

38.5.3 a A parent bulletin board that is frequently updated catches parents' attention.

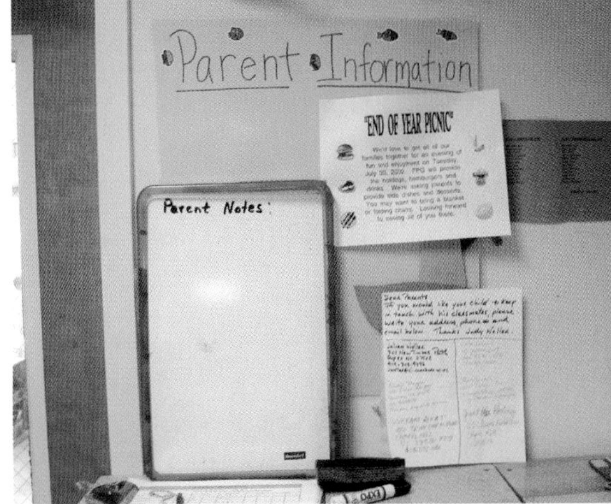

38.5.3 b Parents have their own place to add notes on this bulletin board.

38.5.3 c A regularly planned parent conference provides time to review the child's work and discuss other issues related to his or her progress.

Indicator

A variety of alternatives is offered for parent involvement.

38.5.4 a Having parents help in the classroom makes additional activities possible.

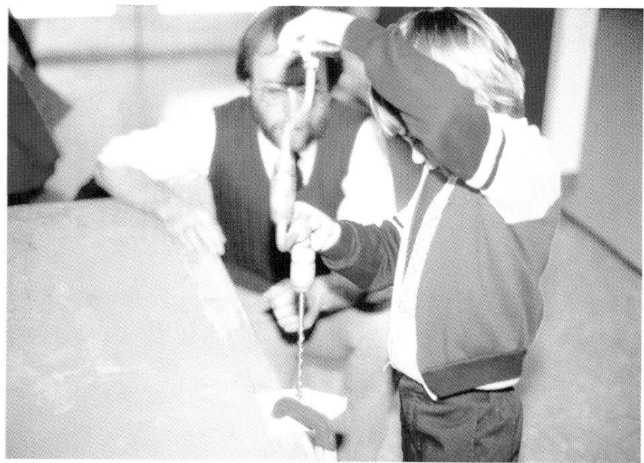

38.5.4 b Fathers are welcome to supervise activities.

38.5.4 c Parents enjoy bringing their child's birthday treat and joining in the celebration.

38.5.4 d Older siblings, as well as parents, can contribute special activities to enrich the children's program.

38.5.4 e Parent volunteers share their enthusiasm for outdoor activities such as this soccer game.

38.5.4 f Parents help provide the extra supervision needed on fieldtrips.

Indicator

an effort to find out if changes are needed. Making parents' evaluations anonymous might help. This can be done if all evaluations are gathered by one or two parent representatives and presented as ideas from the parent group. (See photo 38.7.1.)

38.7.1 An annual parent evaluation gives parents a chance to express their opinions about the program anonymously, if they wish.

To give credit for 7.1 evidence must be present that a formal parent evaluation is requested from parents at least once a year. Staff should be able to show the evaluation form and describe the process.

7.2 During the early years, timely ***referrals*** to specialists may avoid later, more serious problems. This indicator requires that ***parents are referred to other professionals*** by the staff when they feel it is needed for the well being of the child.

The program staff have the opportunity to see a child among his peers in many different situations that offer varying perspectives. Because of their wide experiences with children and their early childhood education background, staff can often see problems that are missed by the parents or by the child's physician, who is usually the only other professional with whom the child comes into contact. Providing referrals and assisting in the diagnosis and treatment of child development-related difficulties are important roles that staff sometimes must take on. (See photo 38.7.2.)

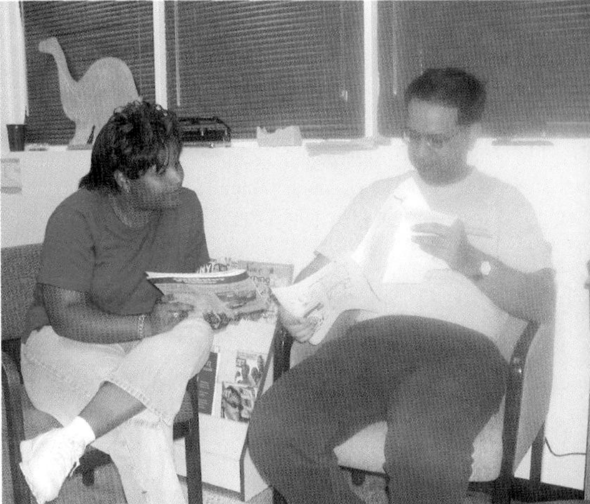

38.7.2 Staff and parents discuss the child's progress before referrals to other professionals are made.

It is essential that a staff representative (often, but not always, the director) talks to parents if the classroom staff feel a referral may be needed. The staff representative should come prepared to such a parent conference with specific information about the issue that is causing the concern and some suggestions for how the parents and/or staff can access the right services for help.

As parents develop trust in the staff and administrators, they may also seek advice about broader family matters such as concerns about their other children, harmonizing work and family responsibilities, or financial problems. It is important to remember that early childhood program staff should not be expected to provide advice outside their professional area of expertise, but rather to provide referrals to qualified agencies or individuals.

Since each state organizes its services differently, the state licensing consultant for the center is a good initial contact for information about available services for different types of concerns. A brief description of the various local agencies available, the services each one offers, and some contact information is helpful for center administrators to have on hand, in case it is needed. The most important thing in making a referral is to be supportive, helpful, and non-judgmental.

Credit for 7.2 should be based on the answers of the staff and/or administrators to questions such as those included in the ECERS-R. If referrals are made when needed, credit should be given (score "Yes"). Credit can also be given if no referrals have ever been required or made, but staff show that they are willing and well informed to provide this service.

7.3 Parents can be actively involved in ***decision-making roles*** by serving on the program's advisory board or on various committees that have an advisory role. (See photo 38.7.3, next page.) For example, Head Start mandates the involvement of parents at all levels, from participation in the classroom to serving on advisory

Indicator

boards. Many other programs also involve parents at all levels including parent cooperatives, some demonstration programs, laboratory schools, and exemplary programs recognized by various state or local agencies.

This indicator, at the highest level of quality, addresses the need for parent input into decisions that affect all the children in the program, not only the decisions that affect their own children or the group being observed. Parents have a unique perspective that can contribute to the general quality of the program.

Score 7.3 "Yes" if it is reported that any parents are currently involved on advisory boards or in other decision-making roles. To give credit, the parents do not have to have a child in the classroom being observed, but they must have a child currently enrolled in the program.

There is a suggested question in the scale to ask for this information.

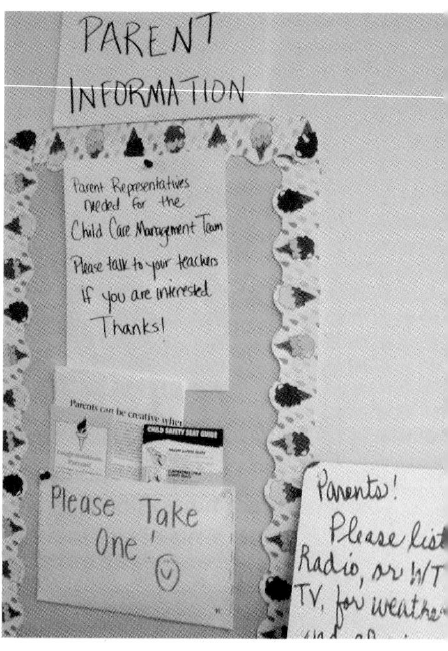

38.7.3 Parent representatives help make decisions that affect their children's program.

39 Provisions for personal needs of staff

General information about this item

Working with children is a demanding job that requires intense concentration while the staff are responsible for the care of the children. Therefore, staff need breaks to maintain their focus and good humor. It is necessary to plan for appropriate coverage for those times when staff need to be out of the room for personal reasons. Personal reasons for staff to leave children include times for morning, midday, and/or afternoon breaks for refreshments, meals, or bathroom breaks, and time to handle other personal matters requiring a short period, such as answering an emergency telephone call.

The number of breaks and the length of break times should be suited to the number of hours the staff member works daily, the number of staff present, the required staff-child ratio, and the children's schedule. Break times should be planned so that they do not interfere with the children's program. Although most breaks should be planned in advance so that competent staff who know the children can be scheduled in the classroom as substitutes, someone who knows the program must always be available on-site for short, unscheduled emergency breaks, if these are needed.

Some flexibility should be possible in break times so that staff who prefer to leave early in lieu of breaks or who need one longer break instead of several shorter ones, should be able to have such needs met, if this is arranged in advance and does not adversely affect the children's program. At a minimum, a 15-minute break for every 3 hours worked in the classroom should be provided to staff. In addition, staff should have a meal break if they work a full day.

In addition to time away from children, classroom staff need an "adults only" restroom, and a safe, convenient place to store their personal belongings, such as their coat or purse.

Staff who have their personal needs met are more likely to feel respected as "people" by the administration of the program. They can also do a better job with the children because they are under less stress when their personal needs are being considered and met.

When scoring this item, ask the classroom staff (not administrative staff) for information needed to score.

A closer look at each indicator

1.1 ***No special areas for staff*** means no space, separate from that used by the children, is available for staff to use when meeting their personal needs. This includes not having a separate restroom from the children, a place to sit down and take a break, or storage for personal belongings, such as a coat or purse.

Indicator

39.1.1 a In this center, staff have no separate restroom, only a closed stall with an adult-sized toilet in the children's restroom.

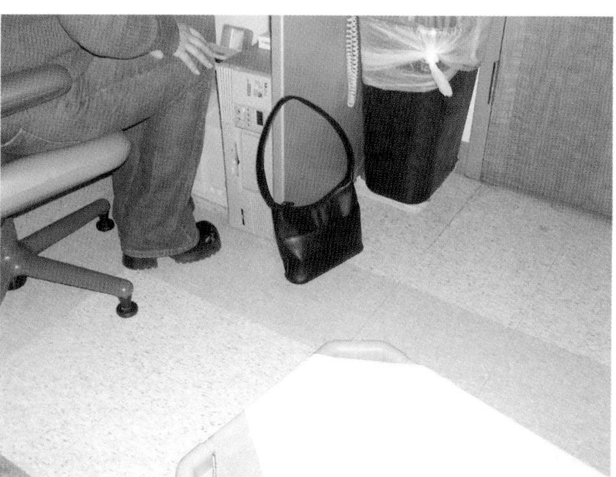

39.1.1 b Since the staff have no storage space for personal belongings, they are left out in the room where they may cause safety problems for curious children.

Score 1.1 "Yes" if *no* such accommodations are made for the staff who work in the classroom being observed. (See photos 39.1.1.a–b.)

39.3.1 At a minimum, a separate restroom that is not shared with the children is available to the staff.

1.2 ***No time provided away from the children*** means that the staff do not have breaks from being responsible for the children, nor time when another person takes over this responsibility. This can cause staff to be tired, irritable, or non-attentive to children.

If classroom staff report having *no* breaks at all, including no break for a meal for full-time staff, then score 1.2 "Yes."

3.1 ***Separate adult restroom*** means that no children use this restroom area and that the toilet and handwashing fixtures are adult-sized. This restroom may be shared with other adults who work in or visit the facility. (See photo 39.3.1.)

3.2 ***Some adult furniture available outside of the children's play space*** means that staff have access to some adult-sized seating separate from the children's play area but reasonably close to it, so that staff can use it within the allowed break time.

To score 3.2 "Yes," the adult-sized furniture for staff may be in the program office or in the entry lobby if there is no teacher lounge, but it cannot be located in the children's classroom. (See photos 39.3.2.a–b, next page.)

3.3 ***Some storage for personal belongings*** means that staff have some place to hang coats and store purses and other personal items. At this minimal level, only

Indicator

39.3.2 a

39.3.2 b

39.3.2 a–b When it does not conflict with other uses, staff can use the adult-sized chairs and table in the office during breaks.

the space is required, but no specifications are included as to the adequacy of the provision. Thus, using a hook in the classroom or a drawer in the director's office, even though it is not convenient or private, meets this indicator. (See photo 39.3.3.)

3.4 This indicator requires that ***staff have at least one break daily***. A break is time when a staff member is relieved from the responsibility of caring for the children. The break should allow enough time to visit the restroom, have a little quiet time, or make a short phone call. A minimum of 15 minutes should be provided for a break.

To score, ask classroom staff if they have any breaks, and base the score on their response. To score "Yes" on 3.4, full-time staff who work at least 8 hours a day, must each have at least one break of 15 minutes.

3.5 If any staff member in the program has disabilities of any kind, ***accommodations*** need to be made to meet the individual's needs. The accommodations needed to make a facility accessible to individuals with disabilities are handled under Item 1, Indoor space. Other accommodations that might be needed are books with large print for staff with visual impairment, a fire alarm system with flashing lights for staff with hearing impairment, or handrails in the restroom. "NA" is permitted if no staff member has a disability that requires accommodations. (See photo 39.3.5.)

5.1 A ***lounge*** means an area, separate from the space used by the children, with ***adult-sized*** furniture, where the staff may sit and relax when not responsible for the children. The lounge does not have to be used only for

39.3.3 Although the space is crowded, it meets the minimal requirement for storage of personal belongings.

39.3.5 A handicapped accessible toilet with handrails is required if any staff member needs such accommodations. "NA" is permitted if no accommodations are needed by staff.

Indicator

this purpose, but can have another use as well. The ***dual use***, or other use, can be as an office, conference room, or other area that adults use. It must be clear that staff may use this area as a lounge in order to score 5.1 "Yes." (See photo 39.5.1.)

39.5.1 Staff use the couch and chairs in the director's office as their lounge area.

5.2 ***Convenient storage*** means a place that is within easy reach for staff to keep their personal belongings, such as a coat, purse, extra shoes, books, or briefcase. A place is considered ***convenient*** if it does not require the staff to leave the classroom or neglect the care of the children to get to their belongings.

Security provisions when necessary means that staff can lock belongings away so that they are safe from tampering by others. Security provisions are required only if there is any danger that tampering or theft may occur.

Ask classroom staff where they can store their personal belongings, and whether this causes any problems. If needed, ask staff to show the place(s) used for storage. If the storage for their personal possessions is convenient and safe, give credit for 5.2 (score "Yes"). (See photos 39.5.2 a–b.)

5.3 Sufficient time away from the children must be ***provided daily*** so that staff can take short breaks to meet personal needs. Breaks of 15 minutes in the morning and afternoon and a ½-hour midday lunch break are required to meet this indicator for any staff who work at least 8 hours per day.

Sometimes state regulations specify the length of breaks based on hours of service. If the state regulations are less than the requirements given for this indicator, and the program only provides that amount of time away from the children, score this indicator "No."

If the classroom staff say they receive the required amount of time, or more, credit should be given for 5.3.

39.5.2 a

39.5.2 b

39.5.2 a–b There is a convenient, safe, locked cabinet in the classroom to store the staff's personal belongings.

Indicator

39.5.4 a

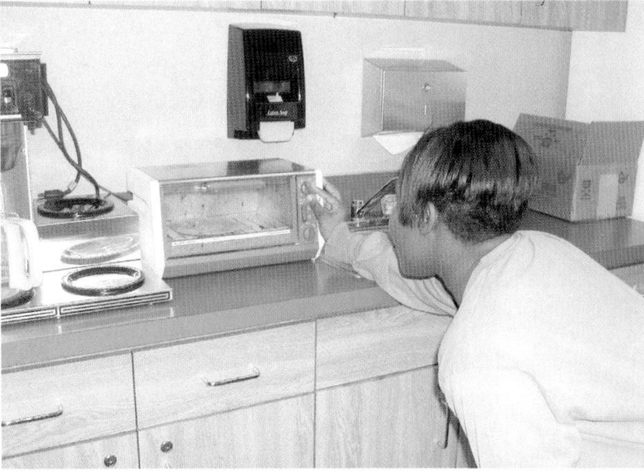

39.5.4 b

39.5.4 a–c Provisions are available for staff to store, heat, and eat meals during lunch breaks.

39.5.4 c

Some flexibility in timing is allowed in this indicator, so that staff can arrange with the administration to leave early or take a longer break at midday, in lieu of three shorter breaks, if that is mutually acceptable. If the combined breaks equal the time requirements in this indicator, score 5.3 "Yes."

5.4 ***Facilities provided for staff meals/snacks*** means that basic provisions, such as refrigerator space, a stove or microwave for cooking or heating meals, and a place to eat meals with adult-sized furniture, are accessible for staff use. If classroom staff report that such provisions are available and can be used, give credit for 5.4. (See photos 39.5.4 a–c.)

7.1 ***Separate adult lounge*** area means that the space is used only as a staff lounge area. To give credit for 7.1, the staff lounge must be separate not only from the children's program, but also from dual use by other adults (such as for an office) during the time the staff may use the space. (See photo 39.7.1.)

7.2 ***Comfortable*** adult furniture means that the furniture is not only of the appropriate size, but also suits the various intended purposes well. Thus, chairs and tables for meals and snacks or reading and record keeping should be sturdy and properly proportioned (elbows fit above tables, knees underneath tables, feet on floor). There should be soft chairs or couches for resting or reading in the lounge area. The requirement in this indicator is for functionality and comfort, not for aesthetic appeal. The furniture should, however, be serviceable, clean, and generally in good enough repair to cause no major

39.7.1 This room is set aside as a staff lounge area. There is comfortable adult-sized furniture of various types for relaxing, reading, and meals. The professional library is kept in the lounge.

Indicator

problems, in order to give credit for this indicator. (See photo 39.7.2.)

Before scoring, be sure to observe the furniture in the staff lounge.

7.3 ***Some flexibility*** in deciding when to take breaks means that there is some leeway so that the staff can decide when to take breaks, within reason. This usually requires that there is enough staff in the center to cover break times during the day. Substitutes to take over groups may include the director, other administrators, or a floater who serves as a relief person for breaks as well as an "extra hand" for special projects or during busy times, such as the children's lunch time.

Base the score on the answer given by classroom staff about whether there is any flexibility possible in break times.

39.7.2 Comfortable adult-sized furniture is available in the staff lounge, where staff can read the professional periodicals set out on the table.

40 Provisions for professional needs of staff

General information about this item

In order to do a professional job as a preschool-kindergarten staff member, space, furnishings, and some equipment are required to meet professional needs as well as personal needs. This includes space to prepare and store the materials used with the group and to keep information on file for each child. When individual conferences are conducted with parents or with other staff, suitable space is needed, separate from that being used by the children, with some provision for privacy. Group meeting space, for staff and/or parent meetings, with suitable adult-sized furniture is also needed. Group meeting space should not interfere with the ongoing program for the children.

Relatively few early childhood programs are conducted in purpose-built facilities. Even those that have good space to conduct the children's program often lack suitable space for the staff and parents to use. As plans are developed for custom-built facilities, the planners need to be sure to include the space needed to meet the professional needs of staff. Space to make materials, store materials, and hold individual conferences and large group meetings are all necessary to support staff as they implement a high quality program for children.

A closer look at each indicator

1.1 ***No access to phone*** means that there is no telephone within reasonable access for staff to use. For example, if the telephone is on a different floor or in another building, access may be so difficult that it prevents the use of the telephone. Also, if the phone is located in an office, and staff sometimes cannot access it because the office is locked or being used by someone else who cannot be interrupted, then there is no access to the phone.

Necessary professional use of the phone includes incoming and outgoing communication with parents, reporting the need for urgent services for the classroom, as well as handling emergencies that might arise with staff or children.

At this level of quality, the phone does not have to be located in the classroom, but it must be readily accessible. Score 1.1 "Yes" only if there is no telephone, or the telephone is difficult for classroom staff to access.

1.2 ***No file or storage space for staff materials*** means that the staff does not have any file or storage space anywhere in the facility to store information or materials needed for preparing or conducting classroom activities. Staff materials that require storage might include:

- Books, toys, and games for use in the classroom
- Supplies to make or repair materials

40 Provisions for professional needs of staff

Indicator

- Files containing information about the children
- Parent education materials for the families included in the group

Storage space in the room, such as high open shelves or closed cabinets not accessible to the children, count as storage for staff professional needs, if appropriate materials are stored there. Also, any other storage space in other parts of the facility, for example, file cabinets in an office or in a reasonably accessible closet, may count as storage for professional needs of staff, if such materials are stored there. Storage space for routine care supplies such as juice, paper cups, and paper towels, does not count to meet this indicator.

40.1.2 Staff resource books are kept on the children's toy shelves because there is no file or storage space for staff professional materials.

Even if no file or storage space is seen in the classroom, the observer should ask the staff whether they have access to any file or storage space, to describe where it is, what is kept there, and whether the space is "fairly limited" (information needed to score Indicator 3.2) or "ample" (information needed to score Indicator 5.1).

If storage space is reported to be available, ask to see the space and what is stored there, in order to give appropriate credit. Score 1.2 "Yes" only if there is *no* file or storage space for staff materials. (See photo 40.1.2.)

1.3 This indicator addresses the need for ***individual conference space*** when children are in attendance. If there is any space that has some privacy that can be used by staff for a confidential conference with parents or other staff members during school hours, this indicator is scored "No."

The space does not have to be used solely for conferences, but dual use should not interfere with the privacy or concentration required for an individual conference. For example, if the only space available during program hours is in an empty classroom, but the conference will not be interrupted, this indicator should be scored "No" because *some* space is available, even though it is not completely satisfactory. Score 1.3 "Yes," only if *no* space is available while children are in attendance.

3.1 ***Convenient access to a telephone*** means that staff have a phone in the room for emergency calls or for brief conversations with parents. A portable or cell phone is acceptable if it is easily accessible to all staff in the classroom. (See photo 40.3.1.)

If a staff member is observed talking for a long time on the telephone, with serious negative consequences to the supervision of children, consider this under the Supervision Items, 29 and/or 30.

3.2 ***Some file and storage space*** means access to even a little space to store professional materials. Note that *both* some file space and some storage for other materials is required to score 3.2 "Yes." See 1.2 for examples of such space. (See photos 40.3.2 a–b, next page.)

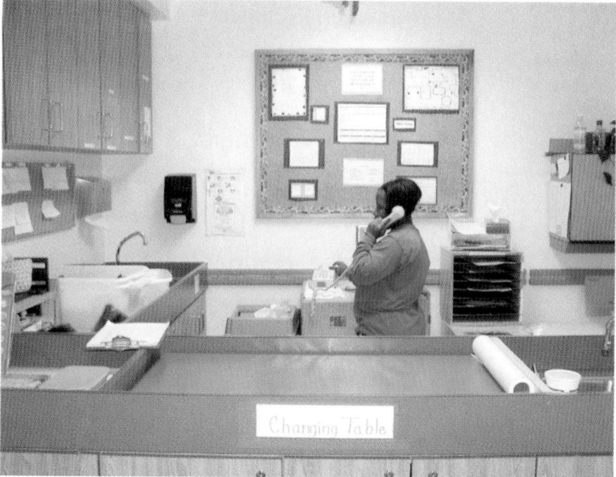

40.3.1 A telephone in the classroom is convenient for emergency calls or brief, but necessary, communication with parents.

Indicator

40.3.2 a This staff member has some file and storage space in the classroom.

40.3.2 b A closet in the classroom provides some storage space for professional materials, including extra toys to use with the children. Unless this staff also has some file storage space, credit cannot be given for 3.2.

3.3 ***Some space available for individual conferences*** means that there is a place where staff can sit down with parents or other staff for a confidential, private conference without fear of being overheard or interrupted. Any space that can be arranged during the children's program to provide the privacy required is acceptable to score 3.3 "Yes." (See photo 40.3.3.)

40.3.3 While the children are using another space in the center, a staff member can have a conference with parents in the empty classroom.

5.1 ***Access to ample file and storage space*** means there is a large enough space to comfortably store professional materials of classroom staff without the crowding or disorganization caused by insufficient space. See 1.2 for examples of such space. (See photos 40.5.1 a–d, next page.)

5.2 In order to give credit for this indicator, there must be a ***separate office space***, *on site*, used for the administration of the program. The director's office in a child care center or the office in a public school where a preschool-kindergarten is housed, is considered separate office space for the program, as long as the classroom is housed at the same site as the office. Credit can be given if the office is located in a different building on site, as long as it is reasonably accessible to classroom staff. (See photo 40.5.2, next page.)

5.3 At the good level, satisfactory space for both individual conferences *and* adult group meetings is required. ***Satisfactory space for individual conferences*** means that the space:

- Provides both visual and auditory privacy
- Is protected from interruptions
- Contains adult-sized furniture
- Is relatively easy to schedule for conferences, even if the space is used for other purposes at other times.

40.5.1 a In this center's office, ample file space is assigned to each classroom to keep information needed by the administration and staff about the children and their families.

40.5.1 b Ample, well organized storage space makes it easy for staff to access materials for use with children.

40.5.1 c Ample space for staff resource books and articles helps keep the materials organized and accessible.

40.5.1 d Space, equipment, and supplies to make or repair educational materials supports a staff's professional performance.

Satisfactory space for adult group meetings means:

- There is enough space for the number of adults in the group
- There are enough adult-sized chairs, tables, and other furniture needed for the meeting
- It is relatively easy to schedule group meetings, even if the space is used for other purposes at other times.

Thus, an evening meeting for parents and staff might be held in space used by children earlier in the day, if the space can be sufficiently cleared of the children's furniture to accommodate enough adult-sized furniture. This accommodation would be considered satisfactory

40.5.2 A separate, well equipped office is used for the administration of the program.

Indicator

40.7.2 a This meeting room, located at the same site as the children's program, can be scheduled for either individual conferences or adult group meetings.

40.7.2 b Having a comfortable room, separate from the space used by the children, makes it easier to conduct adult meetings, such as those for parents and/or staff.

space for adult meetings and 5.4 would be scored "Yes," even though a lot of work is required for set-up and clean-up.

7.1 ***Well-equipped office space*** means that the office has the necessary equipment to conduct the administrative functions of the program efficiently. Examples of such equipment include a telephone, an answering machine that takes messages 24 hours a day, 7 days a week, the furniture needed for office work, a photocopier, sufficient computer capacity, and a fax machine. The intent of this item is that the office has the capacity to serve the needs of the staff for communication, clerical tasks, record keeping, and reproducing materials.

To score this indicator "Yes," all examples listed are not required. However, the basic necessities for efficient program operation are required, including a telephone with answering machine, office furniture, and basic office supplies.

7.2 At the excellent level, the space used for individual conferences *and* group meetings must be ***conveniently located***, which means easy for staff and parents to get to, ***comfortable***, which means furnished to be comfortable for adults, and ***separate from the space used for children***, which means space used only for adults. (See photos 40.7.2 a–b.)

Having space that is ready to be used for individual conferences and group meetings avoids the problems of scheduling and rearranging space caused by dual use. Separate space for conferences and group meetings makes it easier for a program to conduct these important support functions for parents and staff.

If the space that staff describe and show the observer meets all of these requirements, score 7.2 "Yes."

41 Staff interaction and cooperation

General information about this item

Staff members working with the same group of children need to work closely as a team in order to best meet the needs of the children for whom they jointly provide care. Teamwork requires developing a shared context for care and education based on information about the children, their families, the curriculum, program policies, and daily procedures. In the ECERS-R, the word ***staff*** means all the people who work directly with the children in a particular group for a substantial portion of the day, most days of the week. Additional adults who work in the classroom, such as practicum students, volunteers, and/or therapists, may be counted as staff only if they work with the children daily or almost daily for a *substantial portion of the day* (at least 1/3 of the time the center is open). One exception to this definition of staff occurs in parent cooperatives or lab schools, where different people are present every day to serve as assistants to the permanent staff. Since the regular staffing pattern in such classrooms includes different people daily for a substantial portion of the day, they are counted as regular staff during the observation.

In all other cases, adults who come into the classroom and interact with the children for shorter periods of time or for fewer days of the week are not counted as staff unless the observed effect is *extremely negative*. This includes student teachers, volunteers, or therapists/ specialists who come into the classroom for short periods and/or to work with specific children.

Since we want our sample of how staff interact with one another to be typical of what the children experience on a daily basis, it is not wise to count the positive or neutral interactions with temporary helpers that might be observed, because it does not contribute information about the nature of the ongoing interaction among the staff. However, any negative interactions among adults should be counted since it adversely affects the general atmosphere of the classroom. Negative interactions include angry voices or actions, or demeaning remarks.

The word "staff" in this scale is always plural because few classrooms have only one staff member. If there is only one staff member with a group all day (no one else regularly cares for the children at any time during the day), this item may be scored "NA." However, if two or more staff members work with a group at different times, or at the same time, this item must be scored. For example, if one staff member has responsibility for the early arrivals in a class until the regular teacher arrives and takes over the responsibility for the group, then the item must be scored. This is also true if the regular teacher leaves before the end of the day and another staff member takes over the group for the end of the day.

Communication among staff members about the children, as well as the curriculum and environment, is essential in order to provide consistency in the program.

41 Staff interaction and cooperation

Indicator

Daily informal communication of specific information is needed about practical matters, such as:

- A change in the drop-off or pick-up times for any of the children
- A different adult who will be picking up one of the children that day
- Unusual behavior on the part of a child that might signal possible illness or emotional stress
- Information shared by a parent about family problems or other events that might affect the child's behavior
- Additional tasks that staff must remember to complete before they leave
- Last minute changes in the schedule or in a planned activity

However, such informal communication is no substitute for regular planning, which is also essential in order for staff to conduct a high quality program.

The interpersonal relationship among staff members affects their work as a professional team. If staff members are too friendly with one another, they might spend a lot of time relating to one another rather than to the children. On the other hand, staff members need to be helpful, respectful, and pleasant to one another to create a wholesome and efficient working situation. As with many other aspects of program quality, achieving a balance between one's personal interest and professional responsibilities is necessary.

In addition to observing how staff communicate and get along with one another, questions must be asked of classroom staff to get the information needed to decide on a score for this item.

A closer look at each indicator

1.1 ***No communication of necessary information*** among staff means that even essential information of immediate practical importance is not clearly communicated to each staff member. For example, if a parent has told a morning staff member that she will be picking her child up before nap, and this has not been communicated to the afternoon staff member, the child may be put down for his nap and not be ready for departure. Communication of other information concerning children's health, safety, social/emotional, and learning needs must also not be neglected. If the observer is present to see whether information is communicated when necessary, then the score can be based on what is observed. If the evidence is not observed, classroom staff should be asked whether any information is exchanged among staff responsible for the group, and if so, how this is this done. The suggested questions in the ECERS-R may be used to elicit information.

Score this indicator "Yes" only if *no* child-related information is communicated in any way, verbally or in writing, among staff.

1.2 This indicator describes a negative condition where the staff's ***interpersonal relationships interfere with*** or hinder the staff in carrying out their caregiving duties. This may be caused by the staff being overly friendly so that they are distracted by personal conversations much of the time and neglect the children during either indoor or outdoor activities. (See photo 41.1.2, next page.) The other extreme, namely staff who behave in a hostile or curt manner with one another, may also cause lapses in caregiving.

The information needed to score this indicator must be based on observation. If no problems are obvious, score 1.2 "No."

Indicator

1.3 ***Staff duties*** need to be ***shared fairly*** in order to maintain good relationships among staff as well as to fulfill all the staff responsibilities of conducting the program. ***Sharing work fairly*** means that a similar amount of effort or work is put into meeting the various needs of the children by the various staff members. In any team effort (and staff members make a team), the skills, interests, and abilities of the various team members, as well as the organization of the team (the job descriptions), will play a part in how work is divided. The important thing to observe is whether the work is shared in such a way that all staff members are busily involved and the work gets done.

41.1.2 The interpersonal relationships among staff members can interfere with caregiving responsibilities. If staff either socialize instead of supervising children, or do not get along well enough to work cooperatively, the program suffers.

There are many different kinds of tasks involved in providing group care and education for children. Some are associated with routine care such as meals/snacks, nap, and toileting. Others are associated with conducting activities, such as reading to the children, interacting with them as they use various materials, and managing transitions. Both types of tasks require preparation and clean-up as well as interacting with children to help them enjoy and learn from their experiences.

Staff that communicate and work well together as a team have various ways of sharing duties fairly including:

- Staff rotate routine tasks, such as preparing for and cleaning up after lunch or putting out the mats for nap.
- To avoid contamination and cut down on illness, one staff member handles toileting tasks while another handles tasks associated with food.
- Preparation of materials, such as paint, play dough, and special activities, is rotated among staff members and assigned during the staff planning time.
- Each staff member takes primary responsibility for particular interest centers for a specified amount of time, including rotating materials for interest, removing materials that are incomplete or in poor repair, and ordering new materials when needed.
- One staff member takes responsibility for ensuring routine care activities are done properly, while the other takes responsibility for organizing the play and learning activities.
- Each staff member contributes her own particular interests and areas of expertise, including new ideas from early childhood education courses, for example on math or early literacy.

41.3.1 Important health information, such as children's allergies, needs to be communicated to all staff, as well as substitutes. Posting such information in the classroom makes it readily available to all.

Observe to see if there is a sensible balance of work, with each staff member contributing towards meeting the needs of the group. This indicator should be scored "Yes" only if problems are observed.

3.1 ***Some basic information is communicated*** means that, at a minimum, staff share information to meet children's health needs or other information of immediate concern. (See photo 41.3.1.) If such communication is not observed, ask classroom

41 Staff interaction and cooperation

Indicator

staff the sample questions in the ECERS-R to elicit this information and score the indicator based on their answers.

Health-related information, such as about allergies or medications, must be written and communicated to all staff and substitutes. Other information of immediate concern, such as a child needing to leave early, can be communicated verbally or in writing.

3.2 Observe to see whether the ***interpersonal interaction among staff*** is pleasant or at least neutral so that it ***does not interfere*** with the caregiving responsibilities of the staff.

To score "Yes," this indicator requires only that the interactions are neutral and do not interfere by being too friendly and social or hostile.

3.3 ***Staff duties shared fairly*** means that there seems to be a balance of effort on the part of the staff members so that the needs of the children are met. The skills and job description of each staff member should also be considered here. Score 3.3 "Yes" if staff seem to be similarly involved, not necessarily both doing the same tasks, but putting out a similar amount of effort to meet the needs of the group being observed. (See photo 41.3.3.)

41.3.3 Although it is not required for this indicator, this classroom found that posting a schedule for specific tasks helped in sharing tasks fairly among staff.

5.1 At this level, communication is required among staff of ***child-related information*** that is of educational and developmental significance. During the observation, look to see whether staff talk informally about specific interests of various children or suggest activities related to a child's interest. Supplement the observed information by asking classroom staff the questions suggested in the ECERS-R. Note that this indicator requires ***daily*** communication of child-related information and that all children need to be considered, but not each child each day. This may be done verbally or in writing, depending on whether staff schedules overlap and verbal communication is possible. (See photo 41.5.1.)

41.5.1 Staff who work with the same group need to communicate daily about planned activities, the needs of individual children, and urgent practical matters.

5.2 This indicator must be based on observation of ***staff interaction***. Look for a warm, supportive, positive feeling and an easy relationship among staff members while they are concentrating on caring for the children's needs. Although some interactions may be neutral, no negative interactions among staff may be observed to score 5.2 "Yes."

5.3 The result of sharing duties fairly should be that ***both care and play activities*** are handled smoothly, with no long delays or problems, even during transitions. When staff members communicate effectively and work together to meet commonly held goals, the program usually runs smoothly for the children.

The score for this indicator should be based on what is observed. Score 5.3 "No" only if it is obvious that care and play activities suffer because work is not properly shared by staff.

Indicator

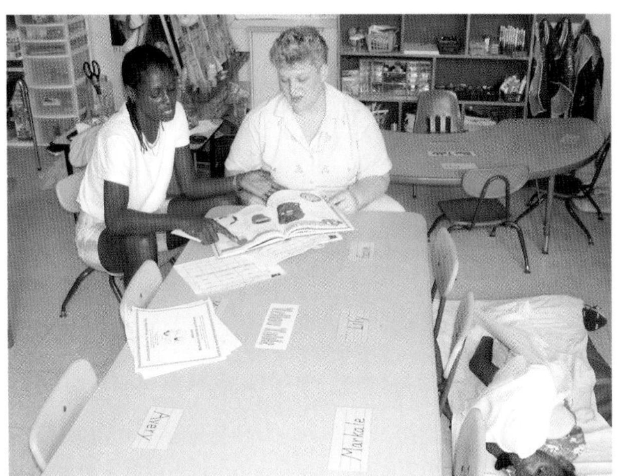

41.7.1 a Staff are trying to plan while they are supervising nap time. Since they are likely to be interrupted, credit cannot be given for 7.1, planning time.

41.7.1 b During planning time staff need to be free of caregiving responsibilities, so that they can concentrate on planning.

7.1 ***Planning time*** is required for the staff working with the same group or in the same room. The staff should be able to meet together to organize curriculum and materials for their group or to discuss approaches needed for specific children. During their planning time, the staff members should be free of caregiving responsibilities so that they can concentrate on planning. Therefore, if staff are responsible for supervising children during naptime and might be interrupted, this cannot be considered planning time.

It is helpful for as many as possible of the staff members who work with a group to plan together. For example, if there are two staff members working with the same group during the major part of the day, and one comes early and the other stays later when fewer children are present, their planning time should take place when both are there and can be free of caregiving responsibilities. (See photos 41.7.1 a–b.)

In cases where a number of part-time assistants, student teachers, or volunteers assist the lead teacher in a classroom, the staff member or members who are there most of the time should be involved in making plans, but all the adults working with the group should be informed about the plans, so that their interactions with the children can be helpful and relevant. Although it is not required for this indicator, a weekly written activity plan that is posted in the classroom can help inform part-time assistants about planned activities.

Some programs gather children together from various classrooms in a combined early morning or late afternoon group. Often, this fact is ignored when planning occurs for the individual classrooms. This omission is counter-productive because the children's experiences throughout the entire day are valuable play and learning opportunities.

In the ECERS-R, the *substantial portion of the day* required for many of the activities is based on the total time the program is open daily, not only on the time spent in the group's main classroom. Therefore, all time should be planned with children's developmental needs in mind. The staff that take major responsibility for a particular group should know what is accessible to their children during the time spent in other classrooms. Some sharing of program content, across the vari-

Indicator

41.7.2 a The difficult transitions associated with lunch and nap are handled smoothly, with little waiting or disruption, because staff responsibilities are clearly defined for each staff member.

41.7.2 b The children enjoy a story read by one staff member, while the other staff member puts out the cots before nap time.

ous staff members that are responsible for the same group of children at various times of the day, is essential if the program is going to provide consistency. The staff members from various classrooms need not plan together, but they should know something about one another's plans if they share children at any time.

When classroom staff have time to plan together they can make decisions on key matters including:

- Themes or major focal points for the next few weeks
- Various materials and activities needed to carry out new themes
- Dividing the work to implement the activities for the upcoming week or two.
- Evaluating how each of the various interest centers are functioning and making plans for improvements
- How routines might be handled more efficiently
- How to better meet the needs of children who are having a difficult time

Planning time is required at least ***every other week*** to meet this indicator.

Base the score on the answer given by the classroom staff to the question about planning time in the ECERS-R. The perceptions of the classroom staff and administrative staff may differ on the availability of planning time.

Score this indicator "Yes" if classroom staff report that they have planning time together at least every two weeks.

7.2 In order to assure that the program runs smoothly, staff duties and ***responsibilities should be clearly defined***. This does not mean that the same staff member must always handle the same tasks, but it does help to have some level of continuity. For example, specific tasks might be assumed by a staff member for a month at a time, then rotated, if desired, in order to prevent boredom. During the planning time, specific responsibilities can be selected by each staff member.

Having staff members take responsibility for daily routines is particularly important to keep the schedule running smoothly. Thus, one staff member might be the assigned "greeter" while another either sets out materials or prepares breakfast. The

Indicator

"greeter" will continue to watch the entryway and greet late comers, even after the program is underway. Similarly, the person in charge of preparing the room for nap might involve a few children as helpers while the others are having a story read to them by another staff member. (See photos 41.7.2 a–b.)

Since there are many different activities going on in a classroom every day, each staff member will need to assume and follow through on a number of responsibilities to keep the program running smoothly. For example, although daily clean-up of materials is the responsibility of the staff member who is conducting a particular activity, it helps to divide the activity centers among all the staff members for major weekly clean-up duties. At the end of every week each staff member then has certain centers to get ready for the coming week. Materials may need to be changed for next week's theme, depleted materials replenished, or additional materials ordered. When staff members work together to keep the facility functioning smoothly, they assume joint ownership of the program.

Staff responsibilities need to be clearly defined for the upkeep of the facility, planning of the curriculum, and conducting the daily program. Base the score for this indicator on observation and the answers given to the questions in the ECERS-R.

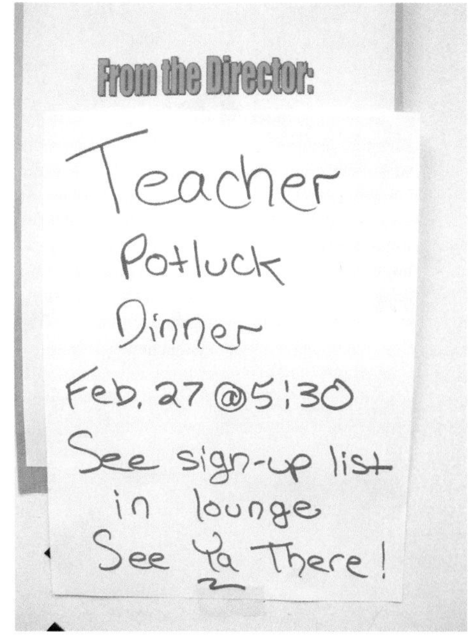

41.7.3 Social events help to promote positive interactions among staff.

7.3 Staff members are people as well as professionals, and early childhood is an emotionally and physically demanding field in which to work. Therefore, it is necessary for programs to ***promote positive interactions*** among staff members if they want a high level of performance from them.

Social events, such as recognizing and celebrating staff birthdays, organizing occasional social events such as luncheons during a training, or facilitating group attendance at professional meetings, create the social ties that promote positive interaction.

The information for this indicator can be obtained by asking the classroom staff the questions suggested in the ECERS-R. Credit can be given if classroom staff report that the administration encourages some social event at least two times a year. (See photo 41.7.3.)

Indicator

42 Supervision and evaluation of staff

General information about this item

A high quality program for children requires competent staff. Regular supervision, observation, and evaluation of all classroom staff, timely and complete feedback, and planning for and implementation of corrective action, are needed for staff to continue to grow as professionals. When staff feel valued by the administration and their strengths as well as their weaknesses are identified during the evaluation, some of the tension involved in the evaluation process may be lessened.

If the program is conducted by one person alone with no other staff, then this item must be scored "NA."

It is best to obtain the information to score this item from the classroom staff member who is being supervised rather than from the supervisor. However, if the classroom staff member states that she does not know whether staff are supervised, for example, because she is new to the facility, then ask the director of the program. The reason it is preferable to ask the person who is being supervised is because only that person knows how the supervisor is being perceived. The supervisor might think that her feedback is being given in a helpful and supportive way, but the recipient of the feedback may not perceive it that way. The perception of the person being supervised is very important in the feedback process.

Both formal, planned evaluations with written feedback and shorter, more informal, ongoing observations with feedback are valuable, and considered in this item. It is important to engage staff in active participation in the evaluation process by working cooperatively to find solutions to problems they perceive as well as those perceived by the supervisor. Feedback that is given in a helpful, calm, supportive manner, where both supervisor and supervisee cooperate to find a solution, is a more positive experience for both parties. It is important to stress that the purpose of supervision is to improve the program for children.

A closer look at each indicator

1.1 ***Supervision*** means that a member of the administrative staff, or a representative chosen by them, observes a classroom staff member in action with the children, in order to see how well the staff member is performing her duties. The supervision may be quite informal, for example, through a daily visit to see if everything is all right. In order to score this indicator, ask classroom staff the suggested questions in the ECERS-R, and base the score on their answers.

Score 1.1 "Yes" only if *no* supervision is provided.

1.2 ***Feedback or evaluation*** means giving the person being supervised information about his or her performance, based on the observation done by the supervisor. If no feedback is given, either about strengths or weaknesses, score this indicator "Yes."

42 Supervision and evaluation of staff

Indicator

42.3.1 The director is visiting this classroom for a short, informal observation during group time.

42.3.2 Later in the day, the director stops in to give the lead teacher some feedback about what she observed during circle time.

3.1 ***Some supervision*** means that classroom staff are observed by administrative staff at some time while staff are working with children to see how well they are performing their duties. This indicator is at the minimal level, so supervision for any reason is acceptable. This might be a short observation in the classroom as part of a director's daily routine, or an informal observation of a new staff member. Ask classroom staff the questions in the ECERS-R, and base the score on their answers. (See photo 42.3.1.)

3.2 ***Some feedback*** means that the supervisor reports back to the person being supervised about what was observed. This feedback may be done verbally or in writing, and may be fairly general to meet the minimal requirements of this indicator. Comments such as, "You've reorganized the book center—it's much better to have a bigger area," or "Let me get my camera to take a picture of your new bulletin board. It's so colorful," can be considered favorable feedback. "You've got to get in at least half an hour earlier to get things set up before the children arrive," or "Mary needs to be getting set up for breakfast, not you, because you need to be free to talk to parents," can be considered suggestions for improvement. Base the score on the answers of the classroom staff to the questions printed in the ECERS-R for this indicator. If any feedback or suggestions are given at all based on observation by the supervisor, score 3.2 "Yes." (See photo 42.3.2.)

5.1 The ***annual supervisory observation*** required in this indicator is intended as a safeguard to assure that all staff members continue to perform at a high level of quality. This observation should be of sufficient length (at least 1-3 hours) and done at a time when the children are awake and active. Short, informal observations such as a director's daily walk-through, cannot be used to satisfy this indicator, which requires a more formal, sustained observation of considerable length. (See photo 42.5.1, next page.)

Each staff member should receive an ***annual*** (once a year) ***supervisory observation.***

If two or more staff members have joint responsibility for a group and work together most of the day, credit can be given if the supervisor observes them both during one longer observation or each during separate observations. However, the

Indicator

42.5.1 A supervisory observation is done on each staff member once a year. The director observes the teacher for 1-3 hours, focusing on many aspects of the teacher's performance and the environment she is providing for the children.

42.5.2 A written evaluation of the annual supervisory visit is reviewed with the teacher, identifying both strengths and areas needing improvement.

supervisor will have to be careful to note in detail each staff member's strengths and weaknesses, in order to give personalized feedback to each one.

During the annual observation, the supervisor should focus on the important aspects of the particular staff member's performance, such as whether:

- Both verbal and non-verbal interactions with children, parents, and other staff members are generally upbeat and positive
- Action is taken to protect children's health and safety both indoors and outdoors
- The arrangement of interest centers and most materials in them are functional and inviting
- Hands-on activities to encourage children's learning and promote positive self-esteem and independence are plentiful
- Appropriate language stimulation for children through reading, conversing, and explaining occurs throughout the observation

Although, in this indicator, it is not required that the supervisor use a recognized process quality assessment instrument to conduct the annual supervisory observation, many administrators find it very helpful to do so. There are a number of commonly used assessment instruments that the supervisor could consider in order to select the best one for his or her particular early childhood program. It is also acceptable if the program wishes to develop its own guidelines for the supervisory observation.

Score this indicator "No" if some, but not all, classroom staff members are observed, if the observation is less than 1 hour in length, or if it is completed less than yearly.

5.2 This indicator requires that a ***written evaluation of performance is shared with each staff member at least yearly.*** To give credit, staff performance must be observed while staff are working with the children (as described for Indicator 5.1), and a written evaluation must be based on the observation. (See photo 42.5.2.)

Indicator

If two or more staff members, who have joint responsibility for a group and work together most of the day, are observed at the same time, a separate written evaluation is required for each. The supervisor must give personalized feedback to each. Any suggestions for improvements needed in the classroom environment, such as for adding new materials to the interest centers, updating the display, or rearranging the daily schedule, should be given to both staff members since they will need to work together to make these changes. The suggestions for improving teaching performance, including interactions, language, discipline methods, staff cooperation, supervision of children, and facilitation of play, will need to be handled separately. It is probably best to arrange to provide feedback on teaching performance personally to each staff member, although the classroom suggestions may be handled together.

A copy of the evaluation must be given to the staff member, and a copy must be kept by the administrator in the staff member's file. Having an evaluation in writing leaves less room for misunderstanding and also preserves what has been observed that particular year, so that it can be compared with earlier or later observations.

Base the score for this indicator on the answers given by the classroom staff to the questions in the ECERS-R. However, if classroom staff have been employed a relatively short time and have not had a supervisory observation, the administrative staff should be asked to explain their procedures and to show an example of a written evaluation done recently for another staff member in the facility.

42.5.4 a During the supervisory observation, the director noticed that the library center needed improvement. Here the director and staff work together to review the books, removing those that need repair or are unsuitable, and planning for new additions.

5.3 Identifying ***strengths of staff as well as areas needing improvement*** gives support as well as constructive criticism. Staff may feel discouraged if they only hear criticism in an evaluation. On the other hand, if only praise for strengths is given, change may not occur because areas of weakness are not acknowledged. To give credit for 5.3, a balanced report is required because it has the best chance of resulting in a willingness to work to improve practice.

Give credit for 5.3 if classroom staff indicate that both aspects of performance are presented in the evaluation.

5.4 This indicator addresses how evaluation gets translated into change. It requires that ***action be taken to implement the recommendations of the evaluation***. (See photos 42.5.4 a–b.) The sample questions printed in the ECERS-R may be used to gather information to score this indicator. In order to give credit, look for concrete examples of implementations, such as descriptions of training sessions that were given to correct some shortcoming or materials that were purchased so improvements could be made.

42.5.4 b The teacher has many ideas for implementing the recommendations of the annual evaluation.

Additional examples of possible corrective action that might be taken after an evaluation are:

- Additional children's books showing cultural diversity and inclusion are purchased or borrowed from the library, to round out the classroom collection.

Indicator

- Lunch is scheduled earlier because the children become hungry.
- A floater is assigned to the classroom to ease the transition between lunch and nap.
- Staff members who work together rearrange their break times to avoid the disruption that seems to be causing unruly behavior.
- Various in-service workshops are organized to correct similar weaknesses in a number of classrooms (e.g., on discipline, art).
- Policies that seem to be misunderstood by classroom staff are spelled out more clearly, and some new policies are articulated.
- Several staff members who show unusually strong skills are asked to share these with the whole group through presentations at staff meetings and other on-site training sessions.

If needed, use additional questions to ask about specific examples of actions that have been taken to implement changes in the program. However, if staff have been employed a relatively short period of time and have not had an annual supervisory observation, ask the administrative staff to explain how implementation of evaluations are carried out.

"NA" is permitted only if no problems have been identified, and therefore no changes are needed.

7.1 Being evaluated is difficult for everyone, because it forces individuals to see themselves from another's point of view. The shock of an impersonal, objective view of oneself can be softened if the ***staff member participates in self-evaluation*** and gains some experience in looking more objectively at his or her own performance.

Self-evaluation has become an accepted part of many program improvement efforts, including NAEYC accreditation. Often the staff member uses the same instrument for self-evaluation that the supervisor uses to evaluate staff. In this case, the two evaluations can be compared and discussed before recommendations for improvement are made based on a joint decision.

Score 7.1 "Yes" if self-evaluation is part of the annual (or more frequent) supervisory evaluation. (See photo 42.7.1.)

7.2 ***Frequent observations and feedback*** make it possible to make improvements in small steps. This approach also has the advantage of getting staff accustomed to being observed, so that they start to feel more comfortable. Frequent observations can be less formal and shorter. Give credit for this indicator, if observations and feedback are provided about every other month. Some variation in the number of observations is permitted, based on the needs of individual staff members. More frequent observations may be needed for new staff, less frequent ones for more experienced staff.

42.7.1 When classroom staff conduct a self evaluation following the same guidelines used during the annual supervisory observation, they can be more actively involved in planning for program improvement.

7.3 This indicator emphasizes the importance of the manner in which the feedback is given. If feedback is given in a ***helpful, supportive manner***, much of the threat of disapproval and failure is neutralized. Then the staff member can feel that the supervisor is going to be part of the solution. Score "Yes," if classroom staff report that the tone used in giving feedback meets this requirement.

43 Opportunities for professional growth

General information about this item

In order to deliver consistently high quality care and education to children, programs require well trained, professional classroom staff. This item addresses the various steps a program can take to stimulate and support the professional development of their classroom staff.

Staff at all levels of expertise, from the novice to the highly trained professional, benefit from ongoing opportunities for professional growth. When a new staff member is hired, he or she must be oriented to the philosophy, policies, and procedures of the center. Over time, through regular staff meetings that include staff development activities and cover administrative issues, a cohesive team can be built with commonly held beliefs and consistent practices. By encouraging and supporting staff to utilize both on-site and community educational resources, each classroom staff member can be helped to continue to learn and grow professionally as an early childhood educator.

In order to score the indicators in this item, the observer will need to ask the classroom staff to answer the questions in the ECERS-R. If the classroom staff has been employed for less than three months and state that they do not know some of the answers about the indicators on the 5 and 7 levels of quality, the administrative staff need to be asked these questions. It is preferable to get the information about opportunities for professional growth from the classroom staff because in order to improve, the classroom staff must know about and make use of these opportunities.

A closer look at each indicator

1.1 An ***orientation*** to the program means that all new staff are given a systematic introduction that covers their basic responsibilities and requirements for carrying out the program with the children. Basic orientation includes, at a minimum, the emergency, safety, and health procedures required. More thorough orientation includes guidelines for interaction with children and parents, discipline methods, and instruction about appropriate activities for the children.

In-service training means training provided *while* the staff is working in the program. In contrast, pre-service training is training that is required *before* an individual can work in the program. The person might be employed by the program, but cannot take responsibility for the tasks assigned to his or her position before the pre-service training is completed.

Score 1.1 "Yes" only if classroom staff who have been employed for six weeks or longer report that they have not received any basic information about the program including emergency, health, and safety procedures.

43 Opportunities for professional growth

Indicator

43.3.1 During orientation, the director meets with a new teacher to explain the center's procedures for food preparation and other health issues.

1.2 ***Staff meetings*** are meetings conducted by the director or other administrative staff to discuss center concerns, which are attended by classroom staff and any other employees invited by the administrative staff. Staff meetings can cover a variety of issues including:

- Administrative concerns, such as changes in days and hours of operation, variation in daily or weekly schedule, purchasing of materials and equipment, assignment of staff and part-time assistants, or changes in children's grouping patterns
- State licensing and other regulatory issues, such as changes in state regulations, status of center license, or upcoming regulatory visits
- News items, such as introducing a new employee, new children enrolled, an honor the center has received, or inclusion of the center in a newspaper article
- On-site in-service education including a guest speaker, presentations by staff members who have attended a course or a conference, or meeting time for staff members working with the same age group in different classrooms
- Announcements about training opportunities in the community, such as courses offered by community colleges or resource and referral agencies or local, state, and national conferences
- Display of and discussion about new books or other teaching resources and educational materials added to the on-site professional library for all staff to use

To decide on a score for this indicator, use the classroom staff's answers to the questions in the ECERS-R for Indicators 1.2, 3.5, and 5.3. If staff, who have been employed less than six weeks, state that they do not know whether staff meetings are held, ask the administrative staff. Score "Yes" on 1.2 only if no staff meetings are held by the center for classroom staff.

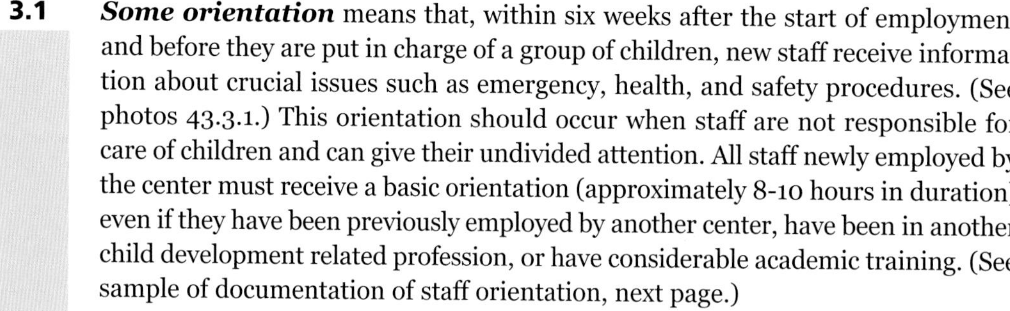

3.1 ***Some orientation*** means that, within six weeks after the start of employment and before they are put in charge of a group of children, new staff receive information about crucial issues such as emergency, health, and safety procedures. (See photos 43.3.1.) This orientation should occur when staff are not responsible for care of children and can give their undivided attention. All staff newly employed by the center must receive a basic orientation (approximately 8-10 hours in duration) even if they have been previously employed by another center, have been in another child development related profession, or have considerable academic training. (See sample of documentation of staff orientation, next page.)

Score 3.1 "Yes" if all new staff are required, within six weeks of employment, to attend orientation that covers, at a minimum, the emergency, health, and safety procedures of the center. Base scores on the answers given by classroom staff, using the questions in the ECERS-R.

3.2 ***Some in-service training*** means that, *at least once a year*, training is provided by the center, and the classroom staff are expected to attend. This training may be conducted on-site, for example by inviting guest trainers or by using video training, or off-site, if the center administration arranges for classroom staff to participate in a community training workshop.

Indicator

Documentation of Staff Orientation

Employee____________________________ Date Hired_______________

In the first six weeks of employment, each new employee shall receive a minimum of 10 clock hours of on-site orientation. Employee will attend training on topics below. The trainer will sign and indicate the hours of orientation training provided on each topic.

TOPIC	TRAINING PROVIDER	HOURS	DATE
Review of Personnel Policies			
Review of individual's job-specific duties and responsibilities/job description			
Review of child day care licensing/NAEYC accreditation standards			
Review of Center's history/purposes/goals			
Review of Center's operational policies/ parents handbook, including discipline policy			
Health and safety standards/emergency procedures			
Child Abuse reporting procedure			
Special services component and reporting requirements			
Observation of Center operations			

I have received training in the topics listed above.

____

Employee Signature

____

Date

Adapted from FPG Family & Child Care Program, "Documentation of Staff Orientation."

43 Opportunities for professional growth

Indicator

To give a score of "Yes" for Indicator 3.2, classroom staff must describe examples of in-service training they have attended, or administrative staff must show documentation of in-service training that occurs at least yearly.

43.3.3 Staff meetings are held at least two times a year to discuss administrative concerns and other issues.

3.3 ***Some staff meetings*** means that, *at least two times a year*, staff meetings are held by the director and/or administrative staff, and the classroom staff are expected to attend.

Administrative concerns, such as those listed for Indicator 1.2, are required to be included in the staff meetings, although additional matters may also be discussed.

Score 3.3 "Yes" if classroom staff describes the staff meetings held at the center at least two times a year, or if administrative staff documents a sufficient number of staff meetings that cover, at a minimum, administrative issues. (See photo 43.3.3.)

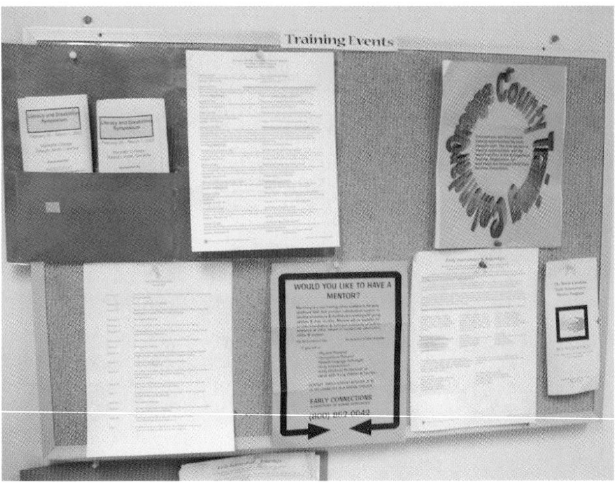

43.5.2 In-service training is provided on a regular basis by the program for its staff, at least twice a year, either on-site or off-site. Course offerings at local colleges, as well as on-site training sessions, are posted.

5.1 ***Thorough orientation*** means that new staff are provided a longer basic training (at least 16 hours) to introduce *sound social/emotional practices*, such as supportive interaction with children and parents, and effective discipline methods, as well as *programmatic issues*, such as ways to conduct appropriate activities.

Base the score for this indicator on answers given by classroom staff to questions in the ECERS-R for Indicators 1.1, 3.1, 3.2, 5.1, and 5.2. Ask specific questions if needed to get further information about the nature of the orientation provided for new staff. If staff have been employed at the center for less than 6 weeks and state that they do not know, ask the administrative staff about the length and content of the orientation and to provide documentation for their answers.

5.2 For the definition of ***in-service training***, see Indicator 1.1. ***Provided regularly by program*** means that training is provided for all classroom staff *at least two times a year*, either on site or in community workshops. (See photo 43.5.2.)

To give credit for this indicator, attendance by classroom staff must be required at the twice yearly in-service training sessions.

In-service training might be conducted for all the classroom staff together, such as training on reporting child abuse and neglect, or for subgroups of staff members on age-appropriate topics, such as effective discipline methods for younger preschoolers.

The score for 5.2 should be based on classroom staff's answers to the questions in the ECERS-R for this indicator. If staff have been employed for less than 6 months and state that they do not know about any in-service training, ask administrative staff to describe the center's in-service training program and document that it is

Indicator

being carried out. Documentation can include a dated training agenda, a description of a recent community workshop attended by staff, or a record of attendance at various in-service sessions by staff at the center.

43.5.3 Monthly staff meetings include staff development activities.

43.5.4 Some resource materials are located in the director's office, and staff are encouraged to use these materials.

5.3 ***Monthly staff meetings*** means at least one staff meeting a month, for the portion of the year the program is in session. In order to get credit for including ***staff development activities*** as part of the staff meetings, each staff meeting must include at least one activity (e.g., short presentation and discussion) that adds to the competence of the staff, such as:

- A staff member gives a book report on a new professional book that has been added to the center's library, and other staff ask questions and discuss.
- A staff member shares some practical ideas she has tried from a course she is taking on a curriculum topic such as art, music, language stimulation, or relating to parents.
- A center-wide monthly parent newsletter that each group contributes something to is discussed, and new features are added.
- Some new materials or games that are being added to the on-site resource library are introduced, and staff discuss how to use them.
- A short educational video is shown and discussed.
- Staff visit a classroom in the center that is doing a particularly successful theme, to see the display and talk with the staff member whose class it is.

To give credit for 5.3, use the answers classroom staff give to the questions printed in the ECERS-R for Indicators 1.2, 3.3, and 5.3. Further questions may need to be asked about whether staff development activities are included in the monthly meetings. Ask for examples of such activities to score 5.3 "Yes." (See photo 43.5.3.)

5.4 ***Some professional resource materials*** means *at least 25 books, pamphlets, or AV materials* in good condition that staff can use as resources for their own professional development, and several issues of at least one early childhood focused magazine or journal (for example, *Young Children*, NAEYC's journal).

The resources must be ***on site***, which means at the center(for example, in the director's office or in the staff lounge), and ***available*** for staff to use. (See photo 43.5.4.) These resources can include materials that have been borrowed from another library, but when they are returned, other materials must be made available.

Ask to see the professional resources, if the classroom staff (or administrative staff) respond that there are such resources (use the questions in the scale for 5.4 and 7.2). Look through the resources to see whether the topics are appropriate for the staff. Professional resources might include:

- Curriculum activity books for use with various ages from infancy through school-age, suited to the age range served at the center
- Books or pamphlets on child development topics such as language development, discipline, literacy, health, inclusion of children with disabilities,

Indicator

encouraging acceptance of diversity, working with parents.

- Videos on various curriculum areas and child development topics (If staff may not borrow the AV resources from the library, there must be suitable equipment for them to use at the center.)
- Copies of professional journals such as *Young Children* and magazines such as *Parent's Magazine* or those designed for preschool teachers
- Labeled file folders with articles clipped or copied from professional magazines and journals

43.7.2 a This professional library is located in the teachers' lounge and contains many current books, magazines, journals, and AV materials.

7.1 In order to encourage staff to participate in courses, conferences, or workshops provided in the community, ***support*** or help should be made available by the program to enable staff to participate. Various types of help may be given credit to meet this indicator including:

- Staff are given released time to attend a program during work hours, and substitutes are hired to take over their childcare responsibilities.
- Travel costs are reimbursed, or the program provides transportation in their school van, so that staff may attend a workshop or conference.
- Scholarships covering course or conference fees are available for classroom staff.

To score 7.1 "Yes" at least two ongoing provisions yearly for support should be described by classroom staff (or administrative staff) in response to the question in the ECERS-R for this indicator.

43.7.2 b A good on-site professional library for use by staff contains materials on curriculum and child development for various age groups.

7.2. A ***good professional library*** is one that contains ***current materials***, meaning that most of the books in the library have been published within the last 10 years, and the journals and magazines are issues from the past 2 years. Books, such as the work of Piaget and Erikson are exceptions, since they are classics on which many of our current ideas are based.

The library should contain at least 60 books and 3 series of periodicals (magazines and journals) that belong to the center. (See photos 43.7.2 a–b.) The library should have a balanced collection of books on a ***variety*** of early childhood subjects including:

- Curriculum and activity books containing practical classroom ideas for children of the ages enrolled in the center
- Books and articles on child development theory and practice (e.g., ages and stages, discipline, language development)
- Materials on working with families, diversity, or inclusion

Ask to see the library to decide on a score for this indicator.

Indicator

7.3 ***Formal education*** means education that is awarded credit and can be applied to a degree, credential, or other recognized certificate of completion. Although attendance at workshops and conferences is important in developing professional competence, working towards a particular certificate of completion such as the GED (General Education Diploma), a credential such as the CDA (Child Development Associate) or a Birth through Kindergarten teaching credential, or a degree such as an AA (Associate of Arts) or BA (Bachelor of Arts), requires a longer period of study and a more comprehensive, systematic set of courses. Although more sustained work is involved, the rewards are also greater. As the early childhood field grows in professionalism, staff members will be required to have degrees and credentials to serve as lead teachers. Requiring staff with less than an AA degree to continue their formal education will benefit both the staff members and the center.

"NA" is permitted for this indicator if all staff have an AA degree or higher.

Give credit for 7.3 (score "Yes") if the center has a policy requiring staff with less than an AA degree to continue their formal education. Base scores on the answer given by classroom staff (or administrative staff) and documentation of implementation of the policy.

Other Materials By the Authors:

Each book includes reproducible scoring pages.

Environment Rating Scales
By Thelma Harms, Richard M. Clifford, Debby Cryer. From the Frank Porter Graham Child Development Institute of the University of North Carolina. Evaluates physical environment, basic care, curriculum, interaction, schedule, program structure, and parent and staff education.

17-11841	**ECERS-R** (spiral bound)	***$17.95***
17-46798	**ECERS-R** (Spanish)	***16.95***
17-42149	**Video Observations for the ECERS-R, VHS**	***58.95***
17-42150	**ECERS-R Video Guide & Workbook** (for VHS)	***4.95***
17-13600	*NEW!* **Video Observations for the ECERS-R, DVD** (with instructor's guide)	***58.95***
17-10308	**ITERS-R** (spiral bound)	***17.95***
17-11218	**ITERS-R** (Spanish)	***16.95***
17-50943	**Video Observations for the ITERS-R, VHS**	***58.95***
17-31436	**ITERS-R Video Guide & Workbook** (for VHS)	***4.95***
17-13599	*NEW!* **Video Observations for the ITERS-R, DVD** (with instructor's guide)	***58.95***
17-33503	**SACERS School Age Care**	***16.95***
17-33504	**SACERS Scoring Sheets** (30)	***8.95***
17-13598	*NEW!* **Family Child Care Environmental Rating Scale: FCCERS-R** (spiral bound)	***17.95***

Environment Rating Scales Activity Series

Active Learning Series
Based upon ITERS-R and ECERS-R, each book has over 300 easy-to-read, age appropriate activities. Includes planning guides, activities for listening and talking, activities for social growth, and suggestions for physical development, and creative learning.

YOUR CHOICE! $29.50 each

17-33210	**Fives** (450 pgs.)	*17-15676*	**Twos** (330 pgs.)
17-33211	**Fours** (450 pgs.)	*17-15675*	**Ones** (218 pgs.)
17-15677	**Threes** (354 pgs.)	*17-15678*	**Infants** (193 pgs.)

17-33995 **Active Learning for Children with Disabilities** ***$23.50***
17-33588 **Nutrition Activities for Preschoolers** (255 pgs.) ***32.95***

Convenient Order Options

Order Toll Free 1-800-334-2014
Monday–Friday 8 am–6 pm EST
Fax Orders: 1-800-452-7526
Order Online: www.Kaplanco.com
Customer Service: 1-800-334-2014
Monday–Friday 8 am–6 pm EST

Shipping Charges

Order Size	UPS Items	2nd Day Air	Next Day Air	Truck Items
Orders OVER $1500.00	FREE Shipping*	25% of order value. $14.56 minimum.	30% of order value. $36.40 minimum.	15% of order value. $62.50 minimum.
Orders UNDER $1500.00	15% of order value. $5.00 minimum.	25% of order value. $14.56 minimum.	30% of order value. $36.40 minimum.	15% of order value. $62.50 minimum.
All Orders Shipping to AK, HI, PR, VI, & Canada	UPS not available. USPS+ 25% of order value.	30% of order value. $26.80 minimum.	35% of order value. $44.40 minimum.	Contact Total Customer Care for a freight quote.

Note: International orders, call Total Customer Care for shipping quotes: 1-800-334-2014

Ship To:

Name ____________________
Street Address ____________________
City __________ State ______ Zip ______
Phone (___) ____________________
Email ____________________

Bill To: (if different from Ship To)

Name ____________________
Address ____________________
City __________ State ______ Zip ______
Phone (____) ____________________
Email ____________________

Method of Payment: (Sorry No COD's or Cash)

Account Number (if known) ____________________
Purchase Order No. ____________________
Check or Money Order (enclosed) to Kaplan Early Learning Company
Visa MasterCard American Express Discover
Card No. ____________________ Exp. Date ______
Signature ____________________
Cardholder Name ____________________
Address ____________________
City __________ State ______ Zip ______

*Orders over $1,500.00 will receive free shipping on UPS items, but will incur regular shipping charges on truck items.
+USPS is United States Postal Service.
No free shipping to Alaska, Hawaii, Puerto Rico, Virgin Islands and Canada.
Orders shipped complete Alaska, Hawaii, Puerto Rico, Virgin Islands and Canada..

Prices: Prices subject to change without notice. Terms: net 30 days. 1 1/2% late fee for past due invoices.

Qty.	Item #	Description	Price Each	Total Price

Subtotal	
Sales Tax: For delivery in AL, AR, AZ, CA, CO, CT, FL, GA, ID, IL, IN, KY, LA, MA, MD, MN, MO, NC, NJ, NY, OH, OK, PA, SC, SD, TN, TX, VA, and WA, please add applicable tax or submit tax exempt certificate.	
Delivery Charges	
Total	

P.O. Box 609 • 1310 Lewisville-Clemmons Road
Lewisville, NC 27023-0609
Corporate Headquarters: 336-766-7374
email: Info@Kaplanco.com